ROGERS' THERAPEUTIC CONDITIONS:
EVOLUTION, THEORY AND PRACTICE

Volume 4

Contact and Perception

edited by
Gill Wyatt and Pete Sanders

PCCS BOOKS
Ross-on-Wye

First published in 2002

PCCS BOOKS
Llangarron
Ross-on-Wye
Herefordshire
HR9 6PT
United Kingdom
Tel (01989) 77 07 07
website   www.pccs-books.co.uk
email   contact@pccs-books.co.uk

This collection © Gill Wyatt and Pete Sanders.
Individual chapters © the authors 2001 unless otherwise stated:
for details, see first page of each chapter.
All rights reserved.
No part of this publication may be reproduced,
stored in a retrieval system, transmitted or utilised
in any form by any means, electronic, mechanical,
photocopying or recording or otherwise without
permission in writing from the publishers.

**Rogers' Therapeutic Conditions:
Evolution, Theory and Practice
Volume 4: Contact and Perception**

ISBN 1 898059 32 2

Cover design by Old Dog Graphics
Printed by Bookcraft, Midsomer Norton, Somerset, United Kingdom

Contents

Gill Wyatt	Introduction to the Series	i
Pete Sanders and Gill Wyatt	Introduction to Volume 4: Contact and Perception	vii

PART ONE: Historical Perspectives

1. *Pete Sanders and Gill Wyatt*	The History of Conditions One and Six	1
2. *Godfrey T. Barrett-Lennard*	Perceptual Variables of the Helping Relationship: A measuring system and its fruits	25

PART TWO: Theory and Practice

3a. *Garry Prouty*	Pre-Therapy: An essay in philosophical psychology	51
3b. *Garry Prouty*	Pre-Therapy as a Theoretical System	54
3c. *Garry Prouty*	The Practice of Pre-Therapy	63
4. *Margaret S. Warner*	Psychological Contact, Meaningful Process and Human Nature. A Reformulation of Person-centered Theory	76
5. *William J. Whelton Leslie S. Greenberg*	Psychological Contact as Dialectical Construction	96
6. *Shaké G. Toukmanian*	Perception: The core element in person-centered and experiental psychotherapies	115
7. *Elisabeth Zinschitz*	'You really understand what I'm talking about, don't you?' Basic Requirements for Contact and Perception in Person-centred Therapy and the Implications for Clients with Learning Disabilities	133

| 8. Ton Coffeng | Contact in the Therapy of Trauma and Dissociation | 153 |
| 9. Dion Van Werde | Prouty's Pre-Therapy and Contact-work with a Broad Range of Persons' Pre-expressive Functioning | 168 |

PART THREE: The Wider Context and Links to the Other Conditions

10. Peter F. Schmid	Presence: Im-media-te co-experiencing and co-responding. Phenomenological, dialogical and ethical perspectives on contact and perception in person-centred therapy and beyond	182
11. Shellee Davis	Psychological Contact Through Person-Centered Expressive Arts	204
12. Dominic Davies and Maggie Aykroyd	Sexual Orientation andPsychological Contact	221
13. Ivan Ellingham	Madness and Mysticism in Perceiving the Other: Towards a radical organismic, person-centred interpretation	234
14. Rose Cameron	In the Space Beween	259
15. Regina Stamatiadis	Sharing Life Therapy: A personal and extended way of being with clients	274
16. Pete Sanders and Gill Wyatt	Contact and Perception: A beginning	288

Index of Authors 294

Contributors to this Volume 298

Dedication

To John Shlien

Introduction to the Series
Gill Wyatt

The concept for this series grew out of my idea to publish a book of edited papers on congruence and Pete Sanders (of PCCS Books) vision of extending this to Rogers' six conditions. We felt it crucial that all six conditions would need to be addressed in order to avoid repeating a recent pattern of emphasising the significance of what has become 'the three core conditions' i.e. congruence, empathy and unconditional positive regard. The four volumes of *Rogers' Therapeutic Conditions: Evolution, Theory and Practice*, are then,
> Vol 1 Congruence (condition three)
> Vol 2 Empathy (condition five)
> Vol 3 Unconditional Positive Regard (condition four)
> Vol 4 Contact and Perception (conditions one and six)

The editors of each of these volumes, where appropriate, have included:
- both previously published papers and newly commissioned work;
- client incongruence as it affected the theme of that volume;
- international contributors;
- the full diversity of person-centred therapy would be represented — client-centred, experiential and process-directed
- an historical review of the conceptualisation and development of the condition;
- research projects and findings;
- at least one contribution in each volume which focuses on the (re)integration of the volume condition with Rogers' other conditions.

The more experience I gain as a psychotherapist and counsellor and the more examination of theory I make, the more I realise the complex and subtle interplay of the six conditions. I used to see congruence, empathy and unconditional positive regard as the therapist conditions; client incongruence as the client's condition; and contact and the client's perception as the conditions of the relationship. It made sense on many levels. Now, however, I see all these conditions as more relational in their nature and more entwined in practice. Others have hypothesised that there may be only one therapeutic condition and that Rogers' conditions are facets of this meta-condition (Bozarth, 1998; Wyatt, 2000; Schmid, 2001, [this series Chapter 14, Vol. 1]). So although this series is in some respect separating the conditions from one another, I want the reader to understand that the spirit of this separation is in the hope that the examination of the separate parts will facilitate a deeper exploration of the inter-relationship of the conditions and how they create a whole.

ROGERS' SIX CONDITIONS

It has been suggested by many writers that Rogers' theoretical statement of 1957

CONTACT AND PERCEPTION

The Necessary and Sufficient Conditions of Therapeutic Personality Change was the most critical event in the development of client-centred therapy — and perhaps even for psychotherapy as a whole (Barrett-Lennard 1998). In writing this paper he had set himself the task '... to state, in terms which are clearly definable and measurable, the psychological conditions which are both necessary and sufficient to bring about constructive personality change' (Rogers, 1957, p. 95). He hypothesised that no other conditions were necessary, if these six conditions existed and continued over time '... this is sufficient. The process of constructive personality change would follow' (ibid.). 'Constructive personality change' meant a change in the personality structure of the individual which would lead to 'greater integration, less internal conflict,' (ibid.) an increase in energy for living and a shift in behaviour away from what is regarded as 'immature' to behaviours regarded as 'mature'. Rogers had successfully delivered to the psychotherapy world a crucial statement that described the basic attitudes and conditions necessary for an effective therapeutic relationship for all theoretical orientation.

In 1959 Rogers published his major theoretical conceptualisation of Client-centred Therapy *'A Theory of Therapy, Personality, and Interpersonal Relationships, as Developed in the Client-Centered Framework'*. Here he writes his theory of therapy and personality change as an 'if-then' statement. If the conditions of the therapeutic process exist then a process is set in motion by these conditions and the result of this process will be 'certain' outcomes in personality and behaviour (Rogers, 1959, p. 212). In an interview with R. T. Hart (1970) Rogers explained that this theory formulation in Koch (1959) was actually written in 1953–54 and so although his 1959 paper was published after his 1957 statement it has to be seen as an antecedent for his 1957 statement. Other sources of this pivotal theoretical exposition can be found in earlier writings (1939, 1942, 1946 and 1951). In the little known 1946 paper Rogers described '... six "conditions" of therapist attitude and behaviour which ... led predictably to a pattern of described qualities of therapy process and outcome.' (Barrett-Lennard, 1998, p. 66). These conditions included creating a warm, safe non-judgmental environment, to 'respond with deep understanding' of the client's emotional experience, 'to set limits on behaviour but not attitudes and feelings', and for the therapist to withhold from '... probing, blaming, interpreting, reassuring or persuading.' (Rogers, 1946, quoted in Barrett-Lennard, 1998, p. 66).

Then, in *Client-Centered Therapy* (1951), Rogers developed these precursors of his conditions referring to the importance of warmth (p. 41), therapist attitudes, deep understanding, and respect and acceptance; that these attitudes needed to be deeply and genuinely held by the therapist to be effective; and that the therapist should relate to the client 'in a deeply personal way' (p. 171). Within his personality theory he first coined the term 'congruence' and finally, the forerunner of condition six can be identified by Rogers giving attention to how the client perceives the counsellor (p. 42).

A wealth of research was also being carried out at the Chicago Counseling Center during the 1950s. This included The Parallel Studies Project and the research findings published by Rogers and Dymond (1954). This research revealed a surprisingly regular process during client-centred therapy, raising questions about the requirements for the occurrence of this process. (Barrett-Lennard 2001, personal communication). Looking for an answer to this brought Rogers a step closer to his 'conditions statement'.

Two other factors were part of this evolution. In 1954 Standal published his PhD thesis on *The Need for Positive Regard* in which he developed the idea of unconditional positive regard (UPR). The warmth, acceptance and respect that Rogers had referred to earlier came to fruition in Standal's concept. UPR was the term that Rogers used in his future writings. There was also an elaboration on the idea of the therapist needing to be genuine in his ability to step into the client's frame of reference and to relate 'in a deeply personal way'. Streich and Bown both accentuated the significance of the therapist being a whole person, with Bown advocated therapists allowing their (strong) emotions into the therapeutic relationship (Raskin, 1996), and Seeman wrote about the importance of the 'integration' of the therapist (1951). The therapist's congruence as one of Rogers' conditions was taking form.

Rogers 1957 conditions statement was integrative in the sense that it applied equally to all theoretical applications whereas his 1959 theoretical statement was specifically addressing client-centred therapy. There are some minor differences between Rogers' two theoretical statements of his six conditions. In 1959 he expressed them as follows and I have shown the (later) 1957 wording when different in italics. Before researching this chapter I believed the changes occurred between the 1957 paper and the 1959 paper and that the dates represented the chronological order of writing. Now we need to understand any significance of these changes in reverse. I have been unable to find any discussion of the importance of the changes, whether they were connected to the shift from a client-centred statement to an integrative statement or reflected other developments in Rogers' thinking.

1) That two persons are in *(psychological)* contact
2) That the first person, whom we shall term the client, is in a state of incongruence, being vulnerable, or anxious.
3) That the second person, whom we shall term the therapist, is congruent *(or integrated)* in the relationship.
4) That the therapist is experiencing unconditional positive regard toward the client.
5) That the therapist is experiencing an empathic understanding of the client's internal frame of reference *(and endeavours to communicate this to the client)*.
6) That the client perceives, at least to a minimal degree, conditions 4 and 5, the unconditional positive regard of the therapist for him, and the empathic understanding of the therapist. *(The communication to the client of the therapist's empathic understanding and unconditional positive regard is to a minimal degree achieved)*.

In the late 1950s and 1960s there was a profusion of research studies based on Rogers' Necessary and Sufficient Conditions. Barrett-Lennard developed his Relationship Inventory (BLRI) to measure the presence of the conditions in the therapeutic relationship to facilitate quantitative research. His research in 1962, although criticised later, did imply that the perceived therapist's conditions were 'involved in the generation of the associated change' of the client (Barrett-

CONTACT AND PERCEPTION

Lennard, 1962 p. 31). Rogers, with colleagues, undertook the Wisconsin Project with hospitalised clients who were diagnosed 'schizophrenic '(Rogers, Gendlin, Kiesler and Truax 1967). This was an ambitious research project that failed to produce the hoped for results that unequivocally supported the conditions. Despite this disappointing conclusion, much more work was carried out that continued to explore the link between the therapeutic conditions and personality change for the client. The BLRI continued to be used, as were the rating scales of therapist congruence, empathy and UPR generated by Truax (Truax and Carkhuff, 1967). The results of this research, and later reviews of these studies, produced conflicting conclusions. Truax and Carkhuff (1967), Truax and Mitchell (1971), Patterson (1984), Gurman (1977) Stubbs and Bozarth (1994) reported evidence ranging from 'significant' to 'overwhelming' in support of the relationship between client-perceived therapist conditions and client outcome. On the other hand Mitchell, Bozarth and Krauft (1977), Parloff, Waskow and Wolfe (1978), Lambert, DeJulio and Stein (1978), Watson (1984) Beutler, Crago and Arizmendi (1986) and Cramer (1990) concluded that none of the studies had been designed, (a) to deal with the complexity of all of the therapeutic conditions in determining outcome; (b) to deal with the relational nature of these conditions; (c) to address sampling difficulties or (d) to utilise accurate enough measures. These findings suggested that Rogers' therapeutic conditions had not been tested rigorously enough. Whether this is true or not, there does seem to be overwhelming evidence from this time (1950s and 1960s), and more recent reviews, which support the hypothesis that the client-counsellor relationship and client variables (factors unique to each client and their environment) are the major determinants in client outcome rather than therapist-employed techniques or the particular theoretical orientation of the therapist (Duncan and Moynihan 1994, Bozarth, Zimring, and Tausch in press).

Rogers moved to La Jolla in 1963 and established the Center for Studies of the Person in 1968. His focus during these 'California years' moved strongly away from clinical work, as he became fascinated with groups in general and the encounter movement in particular. He increasingly turned to the application of the client-centred philosophy beyond the therapeutic relationship — including education, facilitation of client-centred therapists, large groups and international cultural conflicts. He was not to return to his earlier clinical focus and so he made no further major theoretical additions to his 1957 and 1959 conditions statements

The one notable exception was a paper written by Rogers and Sanford published in 1984. In this paper the first condition concerning 'psychological' contact is dropped. The condition related to the therapist's congruence is expanded to include the therapist's communication and the last condition is extended from the therapist's empathy and UPR, to now include the therapist's 'realness' needing to be perceived minimally by the client (Rogers and Sanford 1984, p. 1382–83). Again I have been unable to trace the significance of what would appear to be a major shift from his 1957/1959 conditions statement.

There have been three developments arising from Rogers clinical research and theoretical writings: (a) Gendlin, drawing from European existential philosophy, emphasised the significance of the experiential process of the client and developed 'focusing' (and subsequent evolution into experiential psychotherapy); (b) Wexler and Rice, using cognitive learning psychology, concentrated on the client's style of information processing (developing into process-directed therapy); and (c) Truax and Carkhuff's elaboration of a skills based eclectic model of the helping relationship.

The impact of Rogers' therapeutic conditions on psychotherapy, counselling and the helping professions has been immense. Even though the mainstream psychotherapy world challenged his findings, they also publicly awarded him honours and validation during the 1950s and early 1960s. Since then there has been a decline in the appreciation of his work, particularly in the United States. This is despite the fact that most, if not all, theoretical orientations acknowledge the significance of the therapeutic relationship and the importance, particularly of empathy. Psychotherapy research over the last 10 years has been specificity-based — defining specific treatments for specific psychological problems. This, along with the ill-informed criticism that client-centred and experiential psychotherapies lack depth of theory and cannot be applied to 'disturbed' clients, has meant that Rogers and his conditions are seldom acknowledged. Furthermore, client-centred and experiential psychotherapies are often misrepresented and dismissed as valid theoretical orientations.

Over the last ten years there has been renewed interest in person-centred therapy, particularly in Britain and Europe where numerous successful training programmes for person-centred counselling and psychotherapy have been developed. There has been renewed interest in research by, among others, Tausch et al., Greenberg, Lietaer, McLeod and there has been the theoretical contributions of Prouty, (Pre-therapy), Warner (Fragile Process) and Mearns (Working at Relational Depth and Configurations of Self). These contributions may help to elevate the standing of person-centred therapy. This series is another endeavour to extend the theoretical and clinical standing of person-centred therapy so that it can take its rightful place within psychotherapy, counselling and related mental health professions.

REFERENCES

Barrett-Lennard, G.T. (1998). *Carl Rogers' Helping System: Journey and substance*. London: Sage.

Barrett-Lennard, G. T. (1962). Dimensions of therapist response as casual factors in therapeutic change. *Psychological Monographs*, 76(43), whole 562.

Beutler, L. E., Crago, M. and Arizmendi, T. G. (1986). Research on therapist variables in psychotherapy. In S. L. Garfield and A. E. Bergin (Eds.), *Handbook of Psychotherapy and Behavior Change*. New York: Wiley, 3rd ed. pp. 257–310.

Bozarth, J.D. (1998). *The Person-Centered Approach: A revolutionary paradigm*. Ross-on-Wye: PCCS Books.

Bozarth, J.D., Zimring, F.M. and Tausch, R. (in press). Client-centered therapy: Evolution of a revolution. In D. Cain and J. Seeman (eds) *Handbook of Research and Practice in Humanistic Psychotherapies*. Washington D.C.: American Psychological Association

Cramer, D. (1990). Towards assessing the therapeutic value of Rogers' core conditions. *Counselling Psychology Quarterly*, 3, pp. 57–66.

Duncan, B. L. and Moynihan, D. (1994). Applying outcome research: Intentional utilization of the client's frame of reference. *Psychotherapy*, 31, pp. 294–301.

Gurman, A. S. (1977). The patient's perception of the therapeutic relationship. In A. S. Gurman and A. M. Razin (Eds.), *Effective Psychotherapy: A handbook of research*. New York: Pergamon, pp. 503–43.

CONTACT AND PERCEPTION

Hart, J.T. and Tomlinson, T.M. (1970). *New directions in client-centered therapy.* Boston: Houghton Mifflin.

Lambert, M. J., DeJulio, S. J. and Stein, D. M. (1978). Therapist interpersonal skills: Process, outcome, methodological considerations, and recommendations for future research. *Psychological Bulletin,* 85, pp. 467–89.

Mitchell, K. M., Bozarth, J. D. and Krauft, C. C. (1977). A reappraisal of the therapeutic effectiveness of accurate empathy, non-possessive warmth, and genuineness. In A. S. Gurman and A. M. Razin (Eds.), *Effective Psychotherapy: A handbook of research..* New York : Pergamon , pp. 482–502.

Parloff, M. B., Waskow, I. E. and Wolfe, B. E. (1978). Research on therapist variables in relation to process and outcome. In S. L. Garfield and A. E. Bergin (Eds.), *Handbook of Psychotherapy and Behavior Change: An empirical analysis.* New York: John Wiley and Sons, 2nd ed. pp. 233–82.

Patterson, C. H. (1984). Empathy, warmth, and genuineness in psychotherapy: A review of reviews. *Psychotherapy* , 21(4), pp. 431–38.

Schmid, P. F. (2001). Authenticity: The person as his or her own author. Dialogical and ethical perspectives on therapy as an encounter relationship. And beyond. In G. Wyatt (Ed.), *Rogers' Therapeutic Conditions. Volume 1: Congruence.* Ross-on-Wye: PCCS Books, pp. 213–22.

Standal, S. (1954). The need for positive regard. A contribution to client-centered therapy. Unpublished doctoral dissertation, University of Chicago.

Raskin, N.J. (1996). Person-centred psychotherapy. In W. Dryden *Twenty Historical Steps in Developments in Psychotherapy,* London: Sage, pp. 1–28.

Rogers, C.R. (1939). *The clinical treatment of the problem child.* Boston: Houghton Mifflin.

Rogers, C.R. (1946). Significant aspects of Client-Centered Therapy. *American Psychologist,* 1, pp. 415–22.

Rogers, C.R. (1951). *Client-Centered Therapy.* Boston: Houghton-Mifflin.

Rogers, C.R. (1957). The necessary and sufficient conditions of therapeutic change. *Journal of Consulting Psychology,* 21, pp. 95–103.

Rogers, C.R. (1959). A theory of therapy, personality, and interpersonal relationships, as developed in the client-centered framework in Koch S. (Ed.), *A Theory of Therapy, Personality and Interpersonal Psychotherapy.* New York: McGraw Hill, pp. 184–256.

Rogers, C. R. and Dymond, R. F. (1954). *Psychotherapy and Personality Change.* Chicago: University of Chicago Press .

Rogers, C. R., Gendlin, G. T., Kiesler, D. V. and Truax, C. B. (1967). *The Therapeutic Relationship and its Impact: A study of psychotherapy with schizophrenics.* Madison: University of Wisconsin Press.

Rogers, C.R. and Sanford, R.C. (1984). Client-centered psychotherapy. In Kaplan, H.I. and Sadock, B.J. (Eds.) *Comprehensive Textbook of Psychiatry, IV.* Baltimore: Williams and Wilkins Co, pp. 1374–88.

Stubbs, J. P. and Bozarth, J. D. (1994). The dodo bird revisited: A qualitative study of psychotherapy efficacy research. *Journal of Applied and Preventive Psychology* , 3(2), pp. 109–20.

Truax, C. B. and Carkhuff, R. R. (1967). *Toward Effective Counseling and Psychotherapy: Training and practice.* Chicago: Aldine .

Truax, C. B. and Mitchell, K. M. (1971). Research on certain therapist interpersonal skills in relation to process and outcome. In A. E. Bergin and S. L. Garfield (Eds.), *Handbook of Psychotherapy and Behavior Change.* New York: Wiley, pp. 299–344.

Watson, N. (1984). The empirical status of Rogers' hypothesis of the necessary and sufficient conditions for effective psychotherapy. In R. F. Levant, and J. M. Shlien (Eds.), *Client-Centered Therapy and the Person-Centered Approach: New directions in theory, research, and practice* . New York: Praeger, pp. 17–40.

Wyatt, G. (2000). *Presence: Bringing together the core conditions.* Paper presented at ICCCEP Conference in Chicago, USA.

Introduction to Volume 4: Contact and Perception

Contact and Perception
Pete Sanders and Gill Wyatt

In the 1950s my father worked as a carpenter for a firm of high-class cabinet-makers and shop-fitters making jointed cabinets and drawers to fit each shop — a bespoke service. They would make most of the furniture and fittings at the workshop and some would be made on-site. Everyone had great pride in their work, there was great camaraderie and the men would have private jokes and catch-phrases they would shout to each other as they worked. As a young boy of six or seven, I was taken on jobs with my dad during the school holidays. I remember one catch-phrase vividly. When taking an awkwardly-shaped fixture or cabinet into the shop or site they would carefully manoeuvre it through doorways and between working men, tools and debris. This process would often be supervised by the carpenter who had made the cabinet — they would see their work through to being fitted. At some point someone would jokingly call out 'Does it fit?' And almost immediately — from the craftsman who had made the cabinet — the reply would come 'Is it in the building?'. The joke was that if it fitted through the door then such was their skill as craftsmen, that a perfect fit in the designated space was assured.

Pete Sanders

We fear that for many years, therapists (and we include ourselves in this) had the same attitude with regard to psychological contact and the client's perception as these craftsmen had in regard to the fit of a cabinet. We therapists assumed that if the client was in the room and looking roughly in our direction then, hey presto, there was *automatic* psychological contact and the client *was* perceiving our empathy, unconditional positive regard and congruence! The craftsmen based their assumptions on an understanding of their skill. What, we wonder, did we base *our* assumption on and can we assure ourselves that our practice really has changed that much?

CONDITIONS ONE AND SIX

The six conditions that Carl Rogers identified as being necessary and sufficient for therapeutic personality change (Rogers, 1957) may be divided into (a) the 'therapist-provided', or 'attitudinal' conditions (empathy UPR and congruence); (b) the 'relationship' conditions (psychological contact and the client's perception of the attitudinal conditions), and (c) the 'client condition' Condition Two, client incongruence. In parenthesis we would stress that in saying this we do not mean to deny the essential relational nature of the 'therapist provided' conditions of empathy, UPR and congruence.

The concept of 'relationship' has mutuality and reciprocity at its core. Condition One, 'psychological contact' embraces the perception of the client and assumes that the client is receiving *something* or *somebody*. Condition Six requires that the client receives sufficient of the therapist-provided conditions to make a minimal impact.

When psychological contact is made, many things become possible.[1] Increasingly we hear people talk of 'making a connection' and the humanising potential of opening up to the other rather than disconnecting and closing down. The latter signal de-humanisation, ill-health and death, for both the relationship and, eventually, the individual. When the client experiences the therapist as empathic, unconditionally accepting and real, then therapeutic change becomes possible. The opposite features — misunderstanding, judgement and façade signify a very different, non-therapeutic relationship.

Over the years Conditions One and Six have had scant attention paid to them by theorists and practitioners. As the main figures in the development of client/person-centred theory and practice (including Carl Rogers) each pursued their own preferred speciality within the approach, two notable contributors ploughed lonely furrows: Garry Prouty drew attention to psychological contact and Godfrey Barrett-Lennard attempted to put the client's experience of the therapist at the centre of research endeavours.

Chapter 1 of this book charts the patchy history of these 'lost' conditions (Tudor, 2000) and attempts to put these 'relationship' conditions where they belong — at the heart of the therapeutic process. If Conditions One and Six are absent, there is no relationship. The other therapeutic conditions are then redundant, impossible to implement in a void, unreceiveable regardless of transmission; in short, useless.

The context of Conditions One and Six in theory is delineated as Godfrey Barrett-Lennard (Chapter 2) and Garry Prouty (Chapters 3a, b and c) revisit their seminal contributions to our appreciation of these under-studied conditions, and Peter Schmid completes his philosophical exploration of Rogers' conditions with a detailed examination of these fundamentals of human relationships in Chapter 10. William Whelton and Leslie Greenberg take this theoretical appreciation in another direction in Chapter 5 by considering the relationship conditions in terms of dialectical constructivism (e.g. Greenberg and Pascual-Leone, 1995). Integrating ideas from many sources they build up a picture of the complex elements which contribute to the lived experience that we call 'psychological contact'. In Chapter 4, Margaret Warner presents a theoretical reformulation of psychological contact drawing on Rogers, Prouty and evolutionary psychology. In this chapter she also challenges the assumptions

---

1. When writing about psychological contact, we are *not* assuming that it is an on-off event, but rather that it is a continuum, with many degrees of contact being possible. However, we accept Rogers' basic hypothesis that a *minimum* degree of contact must be present, before it is possible to say that therapeutically facilitative contact is made.

implicit in the language of psychology.

In this book, we have at least counterbalanced, and possibly rectified, the idea that contact and perception can be *assumed* or taken-for-granted, and the idea that they are binary events, on or off, present or not present. Following the work of both Prouty and Barrett-Lennard, both conditions are clearly multiplex continua, each capable of existing in many domains and on many levels. The *breadth* of the conditions and how this can affect practice is explored by Regina Stamatiadis (Chapter 15), Shellee Davis (Chapter 11), Rose Cameron (Chapter 14) and Dominic Davies and Maggie Aykroyd (Chapter 12). Personal and professional prejudices and expectations, culture and our world-view, all affect the ability of the therapist and client to make good enough psychological contact and also have the potential to affect the client's perception of the therapist. Each author challenges us to look at ways of extending contact and the client's perception of the therapist through personal development, exploring extended therapeutic boundaries and creatively expanding our modes of communication.

The *depth* of the provision of the conditions and how psychological contact and the clients perception of the therapist play central roles in our practice with different client groups is surveyed by a group of authors whose contributions also break new theoretical ground. Margaret Warner (Chapter 4) relates her work on fragile and dissociated process to psychological contact and the development of self; Ton Coffeng (Chapter 8) develops theory and practice in work with clients who have experienced trauma, Elisabeth Zinschitz (Chapter 7) considers the links between development of self and the ability to establish and maintain psychological contact. Dion Van Werde (Chapter 9) presents a detailed account of different levels of experiencing in clients and links these to different levels of therapist-provided psychological contact. Shaké Toukmanian reviews the literature and presents a new view of communication and perception of the therapeutic conditions in Chapter 6. In different ways, Ivan Ellingham and Rose Cameron present strong critiques and propose alternatives to psychological orthodoxy in Chapters 13 and 14 respectively. Substantial and exciting new theory and associated practice is presented in all of these chapters

CONDITIONS ONE AND SIX AND CLIENT INCONGRUENCE

The ability of an individual to make psychological contact and their ability to experience the communications of others in an undistorted fashion are central to the concept of client incongruence.

Prouty (Chapters 3a, b and c) explains that psychological contact has three facets, contact with self, contact with the world and contact with others. Impairment of these contact-functions becomes manifest as various forms of psychological disturbance such as dissociation, hallucinations, and 'fragile process' or can be the result of organic dysfunction such as dementia, injury or congenital learning disability. Authors in this volume explore in detail how these contact functions come to be impaired in these cases, and how, through appropriate therapist contact, may be *repaired*. The chapters mentioned above by Coffeng, Van Werde, Zinschitz and Warner all look at the way therapists may make contact with people whose contact-function may be impaired in these ways. They directly engage with, and put flesh on the bones of, the rather minimalist notion of client incongruence as delineated by Rogers (Rogers, 1951, 1959). In Chapter 13, Ivan Ellingham develops a detailed analysis of one aspect of client incongruence as he explores traditional explanations of the nature of distorted perception before proposing a view taken from an organismic perspective. William Whelton and Leslie Greenberg's Chapter 5 also builds a detailed picture of the relationship between the client's perception and client incongruence as does Shake Toukmanian in Chapter 6.

Client/person-centred theory has some way to go to elaborate the detail of client incongruence. Rogers' basic idea (1951, 1959) was that fundamental separation (incongruence) between self-concept and experience leads to denial and distortion of experience that is threatening to the self-concept which in turn leads to psychological tension and disturbance. Seeman (1983) argued that fully-functioning human personality is integrated, with free-flow of experience across all levels and between all domains. Seeman backed his conclusions with illuminating and varied research, but the concepts of 'incongruence', 'integration' and the 'flow of experience' are still largely universal, generalised and undeveloped. Gendlin's work (e.g. Gendlin, 1964/70, 1978) and the consequent field of experiential psychotherapy contributed one aspect of this emerging theoretical map — the idea of personality as a structureless experiencing process. We contend, however, that real promise also lies elsewhere, specifically in our appreciation of psychological contact and the client's experience of the therapist. In summary, the work in this volume locates Conditions One and Six at the heart of our unfolding understanding of the development of the personality, psychological distress and the detailed nature of the healing elements in the therapeutic relationship.

CONDITIONS ONE AND SIX AND OTHER THERAPEUTIC APPROACHES

Under-studied though they may have been in the person-centred approach, ideas equivalent to psychological contact and the client's perception of the therapist, receive much attention in some other therapeutic approaches. It is not possible to give any detailed description of these concepts here, much less to engage in comparative analysis, but we would briefly acknowledge the development and elaboration of equivalent concepts. Different approaches identify different core element as effective in therapy, with many putting the relationship high on the list.

Those cognitive therapists who view warmth, or UPR, as at best an irrelevance and at worst an anti-therapeutic agent, understand that the relationship is the conduit through which information, diagnosis and corrective treatment flow. For them also, psychological contact has to be minimally established and the therapist must be accepted by the client as a credible authority. Only therapists who favour very highly manualised, automated or computerised self-administered programmes of treatment might appear to eschew the relationship as a vector. However, brief scrutiny of such automated systems reveal a computer program that mimics a human relationship, striving to make contact with the client and bidding the client to experience the machine as trustworthy, authoritative and understanding — in short, *human-like*.

Psycho-analytic and psychodynamic theory pivots on the dynamics of the therapy relationship. Central to these dynamics is the transferential relationship between client and therapist. There are difficulties in separating the strands of the concept of 'authority' in such complex dynamics, but it is clear that at least in part, Rogers' initial concepts of 'non-directive' and later 'client-centred' therapy were reactions to the psychodynamic concepts of transference and countertransference and the tangle of expertism, and personal and professional authority. The psychodynamic notion of re-enacting archetypal or mythic relationships driven by hidden motives, constitutes one particular understanding of psychological contact and the client's experience of the therapist. Notwithstanding the work presented in this volume — and other contributions such as Rogers (1951) and Shlien (1984) — the edifice of transference theory is traditionally held to overshadow the comparatively lightweight client-centred and experiential offerings. In particular, Warner, in Chapter 4, reacts critically to the language used in psychology which views human experiencing in either a mechanistic way or a way which implies deep, ready-formed processes. Both Ellingham (Chapter 13) and Cameron (Chapter 14) take critical views (albeit different ones) of the concept of 'transference' and develop alternative vocabularies for experiences at the edge of awareness. All of this work comes not a moment to soon, since client-centred therapy in particular has, in the eyes of others, struggled to account for some experiences in the absence of a coherent vocabulary.

Humanistic psychotherapies, as a generic group, also put the relationship at the centre of the therapeutic process. Those humanistic therapies that emphasise somatic awareness and methods, from Gestalt through to Reichian bodywork, make distinctive contributions to the concepts of contact and the client's perception of the therapist. All such therapies have clear concepts of authentic contact between therapist and client and contact between parts of the client's psyche and soma. Good health as integration of psyche and soma via healing contact with another is a well-developed concept in these approaches. Whelton and Greenberg specifically describe a Gestalt therapy view of psychological contact and client's perception in Chapter 5, illustrated with many examples.

More recently, Neuro-Linguistic Programming, (NLP) itself a self-declared pragmatic integrative approach, configures psychological contact as a series of fleeting reciprocal hypnotic trances — an idea based on the work of Milton Erickson. When introducing the constructs of 'modes of representation' and 'tracking' Bandler and Grinder (e.g. 1979, 1982) use case examples to demonstrate making psychological contact with 'catatonic' patients. There is a striking similarity between such NLP interventions and Pre-Therapy contact reflections. The theoretical origins and subsequent explanations of the phenomena are, however, strikingly different.

A SPECIAL NOTE ON PERCEPTION — AND ALL IN ITS WAKE

At least two strands of thinking and writing have emerged in client-centred/ person-centred writing in recent years. One declares or assumes a scientific/

psychological perspective, the other a philosophical/theological perspective. The advent of humanistic psychology, with its recent phenomenological emphasis has pushed the experience of the individual to the fore as credible evidence has possibly blurred the boundaries between the viewpoints (and of course some would argue that it is a false dichotomy anyway). Each strand carries its own language, constructs and logic and other writers attempt to integrate these two strands. We are not sure whether careful announcing of the writer's viewpoint helps prevent confusion, but we are sure that these different viewpoints have revealed themselves in the first three volumes of this series. Perhaps because of the special place held by the puzzle of how we apprehend, represent, give meaning to, and understand the world[2] in both psychology and philosophy, we realise that this volume presents a particular challenge for the reader.

Many authors in this volume refer to Rogers' assertion in 1959 that, in terms of client-centred therapy theory, perception, awareness and consciousness are synonymous. The puzzle is thus extended to the further question presented by the nature of experience and consciousness. Again, we find at least two identifiable viewpoints here, the psychological and the philosophical.

We also understand that in the UK, the majority of counsellors will have little, or no, background in philosophy, psychology or the social sciences. They will rightly feel encouraged by much person-centred literature to trust their experience, yet it is the very nature (indeed in some chapters, the very trustworthiness) of this experience that is being explored in this volume. This is an exquisite conundrum, and one which, regardless of their experiments, ponderings and prayers, neither psychologists, philosophers nor theologians have been able to answer.

THIS VOLUME — OUR RATIONALE

To those of us who have enjoyed the relatively easy theoretical constructs of the therapist-provided conditions, this book may prove more of a challenge. If the person-centred approach has any maxims, then one must be that the therapist-provided, or 'core' conditions are 'easy to say and difficult to do'. However, therapists have behaved as though (a) psychological contact was probably slightly more difficult to say than it was to do, and (b) Condition Six followed automatically from the intent of the experienced therapist. We hope that the reader will find, in this volume, a challenge to the assumption that psychological contact and the client's perception of us is that we are warm, empathic and real, simply because we intend to be — and that this cannot be taken-for-granted. The authors in this volume declare that such assumptions are false and that therapists should take heed. When these assumptions are examined, we discover a rich vein of theory that has the potential to change our practice permanently. Furthermore, we hope that in critically examining these assumptions, and appreciating the resulting complexities, we will feel on stronger ground to face the criticisms and challenges that client-centred and experiential psychotherapy has already faced, and will doubtless continue to face in the near future.

---

2. By 'world' we mean the 'world of experience', which includes all external stimuli, visceral and somatic sensations, and awareness of psychological processes.

REFERENCES

Bandler, R. and Grinder, J. (1979). *Frogs into Princes*. Moab: Real People Press.

Bandler, R. and Grinder, J. (1982). *Reframing*. Moab: Real People Press.

Greenberg, L. S. and Pascual-Leone, J. (1995). A dialectical constructivist approach to experiential change. In R. Neimeyer and M. Mahoney (Eds.), *Constructivism in Psychotherapy*. Washington, DC: American Psychological Association, pp. 169–91.

Gendlin, E. T. (1964/70). A theory of personality change. In P. Wochel and D Byrne (Eds.) *Personality Change* New York: Wiley, (pp. 206–47). Reprinted In J. T. Hart and T. M. Tomlinson, (eds.) *New Directions in Client-Centered Therapy*, Boston: Houghton Mifflin, (pp. 129–73).

Gendlin, E. T. (1978). *Focusing*. New York: Everest House.

Rogers, C. R. (1951). *Client-Centered Therapy: Its current practice, implications and theory*. Boston: Houghton Mifflin.

Rogers, C. R. (1957). The necessary and sufficient conditions of therapeutic personality change, *Journal of Consulting Psychology, 21* (pp. 95—103). Reprinted in H. Kirschenbaum and V. L. Henderson (eds.) *The Carl Rogers' Reader*. London: Constable, (pp. 219–35).

Rogers, C. R. (1959). A theory of therapy, personality and interpersonal relationships as developed in the client-centered framework. In S. Koch (ed.) *Psychology: A study of a science. Vol. 3: Formulations of the person and the social context*, New York: McGraw-Hill, (pp. 184–256).

Seeman, J. (1983). *Personality Integration: Studies and reflections*. New York: Human Sciences Press.

Shlien, J. M. (1984). A countertheory of transference. In J. M. Shlien and R. F. Levant (eds.) *Client-Centered Therapy and the Person-Centered Approach: New directions in theory, research and practice*. New York: Praeger, (pp. 153–81).

1 The History of Conditions One and Six
Pete Sanders and Gill Wyatt

This chapter traces the development of the concepts 'contact' and 'perception' in client/person-centred theory, from the beginnings of the approach in the 1940s through to the present day. Our intentions in this chapter are to review the history of Conditions One and Six and to place the work of those authors in this volume whose work makes seminal contributions to this history. Readers should also turn to Barrett-Lennard (Chapter 2, this volume), for more information and a personal slant on some of the early history.

Unlike the other therapeutic conditions, Condition One (contact) and Condition Six (perception) have, until recently, been on the sidelines for most of the time since 1942. We make no claims for this to be a *complete* review of the history of these ideas since so little was written before the 1980s. However, we have tried to help the reader establish a foothold in understanding as the historical trace sometimes faded and disappeared only to reappear in an unexpected place.

THE ANTECEDENTS OF CONTACT AND PERCEPTION PRE-1957

Although Rogers did not publish work on the therapeutic conditions until 1957, it would be naïve to think that he and his colleagues had not been considering the nature of the effective elements in the therapeutic relationship before then. It is clear that the work of, amongst others, Raskin (1949), Seeman (1949) and particularly Standal (1954) contributed to the milieu which led to the publication of Rogers' 'conditions statements' in 1957 and 1959.

Many psychologists realised that the relationship itself was probably one of the curative factors in psychological therapy, but no-one had tried to analyse, delineate and operationalise the therapeutic relationship prior to Carl Rogers. Indeed the phrase Rogers used — 'therapeutic' or 'counselling *relationship*' — somewhat gives the game away. This curative event was not referred to as 'psychological treatment', or 'personality re-programming' by Rogers and his co-workers. Conditions One and Six could be seen as the 'relationship' conditions — the conditions which determine the context in which the therapist-provided Conditions of Three, Four and Five are delivered.

The term 'therapeutic relationship' was probably taken from the work of Jesse Taft (1933) whose work influenced Rogers in his 1942 publication. Taft writes in

CONTACT AND PERCEPTION

her introduction:
> The term 'relationship therapy' is used to differentiate therapy as I have experienced and practiced it, from psychoanalysis or any process in which either the analytic or the intellectual aspect is stressed... It was only gradually that I became sufficiently confident of my own difference to want to give it a label... to designate a philosophy and technique which... are... antipathetic to Freudian psychology and practice. (Taft, 1933, p. viii)

1942

So the term 'relationship' may be taken to imply and embrace contact between persons, when Gaylin (2001), for example, writes that when he identifies the 'relationship' as 'the heart of the matter' in therapy, he is stating that psychological contact is the foundation. Whilst this is now obvious to most practitioners, it is no longer assumed or taken-for-granted, as the authors in this volume will testify. In 1942, however, psychologists had not dreamed that the fundamentals of the human relationship needed to be analysed and understood down to the details that we now require.

Although Rogers (1942) was breaking new ground with his hypotheses regarding the counselling relationship, it did not occur to him to extend the detail of his delineation to the nature of the contact between the individuals concerned. He writes:
> Much well-intentioned counseling is unsuccessful because a satisfactory counseling relationship is never established. Frequently counselors and therapists have no clear-cut notion of the relationship which should exist... (p. 85)

He follows with his first attempt to define the 'Basic Aspects of a Therapeutic Relationship' (ibid, p. 87), namely (i) 'warmth and responsiveness' (p. 87); (ii) 'permissiveness in regard to expression of feeling' (p. 88); (iii) 'therapeutic limits' (p. 88) and (iv) 'freedom from any kind of pressure or coercion' (p. 89).

There is no mention here of psychological contact nor any hint that it may be one of the foundations of therapy. Elsewhere in the volume, Rogers does consider the client's capacity to be able usefully to access the therapeutic relationship, and thus indirectly is commenting on psychological contact without naming it as such. In the sections 'Can the client take help?' (p. 66) and 'Is the client of suitable age, intelligence and ability?' (p. 73), Rogers reviews the qualities that the client must bring to the relationship and concludes that the individual: (i) must want help, (ii) be able to accept it; (iii) must be intelligent enough, old enough and aware enough properly to engage in a therapeutic relationship. Such views were, we believe, very much a product of the professional mores of the time and probably related to the psychoanalytic idea that a client must be 'psychologically minded' in order to be able to benefit from therapy. However, as Rogers beat a new path in psychotherapy, he did not persist with these ideas for long and so the question of what minimal human capacities are required in order to generate psychological contact has largely gone unanswered until recently.

At this early stage of theory-building, it is clear that as Rogers scratched the surface of what constitutes effective therapy, he had yet to reveal the detail of the relationship to the level of necessary contact between therapist and client and the client's perception of the therapist. Contact between therapist and client was not yet truly on the map in its own right.

In *Counseling and Psychotherapy*, Rogers did, however, spend a considerable portion of the book looking at the therapeutic process within the client with particular reference to tendencies towards freer flow of expression and greater insight. Nowadays we might see such writing as the forerunner to his later work on the therapeutic *process* (as opposed to the therapeutic *relationship*) as experienced by the client, e.g. 'A Process Conception of Psychotherapy' (Rogers 1961) and is echoed in the work of others such as Jules Seeman's *Personality Integration* (Seeman 1983).

Parenthetically we note that these early statements regarding greater fluidity and flexibility within the personality structure certainly resonate with Garry Prouty's later work on psychological contact *within* the self structure (see this chapter, p. 19 and Prouty Chapter 3b this volume and also Zinschitz, Chapter 7 this volume). Prouty asserts that two persons essentially disconnected from themselves cannot connect with each other. Put another way, if I am not in psychological contact with myself, I cannot be in psychological contact with you. Freer flow within my own self-structure will facilitate better contact *within* me, and therefore make better contact with you possible. In this 1942 work it seems clear that Rogers and his coworkers were beginning to discover that improved intrapsychic contact, more flexible and better integrated self-structure, and accurate insight were the keys to psychological health, and the outcomes, if not the goals of therapy.

These early discoveries concerning the process nature of personality and its impact upon psychological health were later more fully articulated by Gendlin (e.g. 1964/70, 1978) whose insights created a new and complete theory of experiencing and the nature of human personality.

In summary then, we speculate that the ground for much of the later work on the process nature of personality and change, experiencing, and psychological contact with self, environment and others, was (unwittingly) prepared by Rogers in 1942.

But what evidence is there that Rogers had glimpsed the importance of the client's experience of the relationship and their perception of the counsellor (i.e. Condition Six) in this early work? Amongst the various capacities the client must possess in order to engage in effective therapy, there is no mention of whether the client must experience the therapist in a particular way. Other than taking general points about what is *not* helpful in therapy, including ordering, forbidding, exhortation, suggestion, advice and intellectualised interpretation (and so deducing that the client should experience the therapist as *not* exhibiting these behaviours) it would be stretching the text too far to claim that Rogers was aware of the possible importance of the client's perceptions of the therapist at this stage.

1951

Client-Centered Therapy: Its current practice, implications and theory (Rogers, 1951) chronicled major developments in the new approach and notably introduced the appellation 'Client-centered', as an improvement on the short-lived 'Non-directive' therapy. In this volume Rogers further developed his ideas regarding the ingredients of an effective therapeutic relationship, and these ideas begin to take a more definite shape. Some groundwork for the concepts of 'contact' and 'perception' as formulated in the 1957 and 1959 publications can be found in Chapter 3, 'The relationship as experienced by the client' built around a fascinating and illuminating diary kept by a client (Miss Cam). The chapter focused, in the main, on the client's perception of his or her own process but Rogers did include the client's perception of the therapist from the outset. In the first paragraph he noted, 'The centrality of the client's perception of the interviews has forced itself upon our recognition' (Rogers, 1951, p. 65), and later in a section titled *The Experience of Counselor Attitudes and Methods* Rogers wrote:

> When the counselor is favourably perceived, it is as someone with warmth and interest for the client, someone with understanding. Says one client of the counselor, 'She was the first person who seemed to understand how my anxieties looked to me' (ibid, p. 69).

However, other than these brief, yet crucial, mentions, the client's perception of the counsellor was never developed into a substantial element or elaborated beyond the narrative and Rogers made no theoretical points in this section relating to its importance.

Elsewhere, when briefly attempting an objective definition of the therapeutic relationship, Rogers reported a study by Miller (1949) using transcripts in which judges tried to identify how the therapists' responses had been received by the clients. The judges had to decide whether the client had perceived the counsellor's responses as 'accepting', 'supporting', 'denying' or 'neutral', and Rogers noted that this was the first study '... to make the attempt to measure the relationship from the client's point of view.' (Rogers, 1951, p. 52) Most interestingly, Rogers reports Miller's '... basic finding was that non-directive interviews were largely characterized by an experience of acceptance rather than neutrality or support.' It seems clear though, in the context of the text that this is presented more as evidence for the centrality of empathy, rather than pointing the reader towards the necessity of the client having perceived it.

When elaborating his 'Theory of personality and behaviour' (ibid., pp. 481-533) it is clear that Rogers' phenomenological approach put the client's perception *of their own world* at the centre of the development of the self-structure, the genesis of psychological tension and distress, and the therapeutic process. In similar vein, the 19 Propositions contained many telling statements regarding the individual's experience of *their own* perceptual field. Yet other than stating that positive change will take place in a primarily threat-free environment, Rogers did not make the therapist-provided elements of the therapeutic relationship, or the perception of them by the client, central to his argument.

If the theme of the client's experience of the therapist was not moved on much in *Client Centered Therapy*, then the notion of psychological contact, if only expressed in terms of being a minor facet of the therapeutic relationship, was not even evident. The fundamentals of the relationship, were briefly and obliquely touched upon, for example in Chapter 4, 'The Process of Therapy', Rogers quotes from a letter from a counsellor to Rogers regarding a largely silent client, presenting with acute shyness, who nevertheless was voted 'woman of the month' in high school at the end of therapy. The counsellor is clearly baffled as to how such progress was achieved with so little verbalisation in therapy. Rogers wrote:

> Whatever happened seems not to have happened as the result of verbal interchange... when one considers a number of cases of this sort, it seems more likely that the outcome was due to an experience in a relationship... How then, can we formulate therapeutic process in terms of a relationship? (Rogers, 1951, p. 158)

Rather than develop the theme in terms of the nature of the contact between the therapist and the client, Rogers went on to explore the process of therapy inside the client.

In summary, again we believe that the reader has to stretch the text somewhat to see any clear, unequivocal antecedents to Conditions One and Six in this 1951 work. In short, and at risk of stating the obvious, Rogers had simply not yet formulated his 'conditions statement'. He had not yet stated that clients and counsellors *must* be in (psychological) contacts, nor had he yet stated that it was *necessary* that the client should experience empathy, UPR and congruence.

THE INTRODUCTION OF CONTACT AND PERCEPTION IN ROGERS' WORK IN 1957 AND 1959

In the late 1950s Carl Rogers presented his theory of psychotherapy in two seminal publications (Rogers, 1957, 1959), as six conditions *necessary and sufficient* to the therapeutic process. Some commentators have speculated as to the meaning of the slight variations in wording between the 1957 paper and the 1959 chapter. Trying accurately to appreciate Rogers' real intentions is important, especially since the differences in wording between the two publications impinge more heavily on Conditions One and Six than on the others, as Gill Wyatt points out in her introduction to this series (this volume page iii), when she combines Rogers 1957 and 1959 statements, with the 1957 additions in parentheses and italics:

1) That two persons are in *(psychological)* contact.
2) That the first person, whom we shall term the client, is in a state of incongruence, being vulnerable, or anxious.
3) That the second person, whom we shall term the therapist, is congruent *(or integrated)* in the relationship.
4) That the therapist is experiencing unconditional positive regard toward the client.
5) That the therapist is experiencing an empathic understanding of the client's internal frame of reference *(and endeavours to communicate this to the client)*.
6) That the client perceives, at least to a minimal degree, Conditions Four and Five, the unconditional positive regard of the therapist for him, and the empathic understanding of the therapist. *(The communication to the client of the therapist's empathic understanding and unconditional positive regard is to a minimal degree achieved.)*

Not unreasonably, many have assumed that the 1959 paper represented a

refinement of Rogers' ideas. However, in an interview recorded in 1966 and published in 1970 (Hart and Tomlinson, 1970), Rogers disclosed:
> That theory formulation finally reached its climax in the chapter in Koch (Rogers, 1959) written in about 1953–4, which was of considerable value to me. However, like everything else that has *closure*, that chapter could very well be serving a deleterious purpose. Then the paper on 'Necessary and Sufficient Conditions,' I agree with you, was a real turning point toward a more general formulation of the relationship. (p. 520, original emphasis)

It appears, then, that the chapter published in 1959 was actually written in 1953–4, and represents as close to a complete and specifically therapy-related statement of his theory as he could make. The paper published in 1957 was written later, but not as a *refinement* of the previously-written chapter. Rather, it was the presentation of his ideas as a 'more *general* formulation of the relationship' (ibid, emphasis added). Indeed in the same interview Rogers went on to say how tentative he felt when giving the 'necessary and sufficient conditions' paper to a University of Michigan audience.

It is probable that Rogers did not intend to convey significantly different meanings when using 'contact' (1959) rather than 'psychological contact' (1957). This is clear as we read Rogers' further explication of terms (Rogers, 1959, p. 207):
> 27. *Contact*. Two persons are in psychological contact, or have the minimum essential relationship when each makes a perceived or subceived difference in the experiential field of another.

Further, Rogers (1959) clearly signalled his deliberate attempts to delineate the different nuances of meaning in words used in the three major contexts which concern him in that chapter, namely therapy, personality and interpersonal relationships. Therefore we need not suspect that the different use of 'contact' and 'psychological contact' either had hidden meaning on the one hand, or was an accidental oversight on the other. It was, we believe, the acceptable use of interchangeable phrases to mean the same thing, in Rogers' words 'the minimum essential relationship'.

Although there is no equivalent debate around the usage of the term 'perception' it is useful to look again at Rogers' definition of perception, not least to be reacquainted with the concept of *subception*:
> For our own definition we may say that perception is a hypothesis or prognosis for action which comes into being in awareness when stimuli impinge on the organism . . .
>
> Thus we might say that perception and awareness are synonymous, perception being the narrower term (Rogers, 1959, p. 199)

And
> 10. *Subceive, Subception*. McCleary and Lazarus[1] formulated this construct to signify discrimination without awareness. They state that 'even when a subject

---

1. McCleary, R.A. and Lazarus, R. S. Autonomic discrimination without awareness. *J. Pers.* 1949, 18, 171–7.

is unable to report a visual discrimination he is still able to make a stimulus discrimination at some level below that required for conscious recognition. Thus it appears that the organism can discriminate a stimulus and its meaning for the organism without utilizing the higher nerve centers involved in awareness. It is this capacity which, in our theory, permits the individual to discriminate an experience as threatening, without symbolization in awareness of this threat (ibid., pp. 199–200).

Rogers called upon the leading edge of psychological thinking at the time to provide a plausible mechanism for the notion of denial of threatening experience. However, in the intervening years the original empirical 'evidence' for the hypothesised sub-threshold perceptual process, subception or subliminal perception as it later became known, has been almost completely discredited in academic psychology. In the narrow sense of subception as defined by the early work of psychologists such as McCleary and Lazarus, the idea that there is any level of perception 'below' or 'beyond' perception available to full consciousness is not supported by scientific psychological evidence[2]. Most contemporary academic psychologists are deeply sceptical and would explain any remaining phenomena in terms of the selective attention capacities of the human perceptual system. In other words, stimuli are perceived, but do not come into full awareness because of the way we pay attention to the stimulus field and how we store the perceptions in memory.

It is difficult to explain why the overwhelming body of scientific evidence militating against the existence of the process of subception (as defined by McCleary and Lazarus) has been largely ignored by client/person-centred writers over the years. Integrating contemporary psychological understanding of cognitive perceptual, attentional and memory processes would only enhance person-centred theory. The person-centred community has, however, moved towards a more general understanding of a process explaining the concept of denial of experiences that are perceived to be threatening. The main task, it would appear, is to develop theory which embraces the human processes of denial of threatening experience that lie out of full awareness without wholesale capitulation to the psychoanalytic concept of the unconscious (dubbed 'a concept from hell' by John Shlien, 1994). Ellingham elaborates and proposes a resolution to the complex and contentious conflict in the relationship between subception, perception, organismic experiencing and Freud's unconscious in Chapter 12 of this volume.

Contact and perception — two sides of the same coin?

From above, we have shown that as early as 1942 Rogers first used the term 'relationship' to describe the element of 'contact', but in 1959 he conceded that

---

2. There is a huge body of literature on this subject, much of the 'positive' 'evidence' is anecdotal or lies outside the discipline of psychology, e.g. in the field of advertising and media, including 'evidence' of young people being influenced by satanic messages masked in pop music. See Dixon (1971) and Moore (1992) for reviews. An internet search will also yield many dedicated websites — some academically credible, others not.

this had led to misunderstanding. In an effort to clarify the position and move towards an operational definition of the term 'relationship' he wrote: 'The present term [contact] has been chosen to signify more clearly that this is the *least* or minimum experience which could be called a relationship' (Rogers, 1959, p. 207).

From this early writing, it seems that Rogers was keen to explain that contact is, in essence, a reciprocal interpersonal event, symbolized in awareness. In order to be effective, this minimum essential ingredient is a *re*-lationship, not a one-sided broadcasting of information regardless of whether the other person receives it, or something that can happen without either party being aware of it. So contact and perception and awareness are interdependent, reciprocal, mutually inclusive events — contact *assumes* perception and perception *assumes* awareness. One person affects or impinges upon the perceptual field of the other, in everyday life it is a wave and a wave back, a 'hello' and at least a look of recognition.

Contact
Later in his 1959 chapter, when writing about more general interpersonal relationships (in contrast to the specialised therapeutic relationship), Rogers laid out the conditions, process and outcome of both a *deteriorating* interpersonal relationship and an *improving* interpersonal relationship, pointing out:

> The most recent extension of our theoretical constructs has been the attempt to formulate the order which appears to exist in all interpersonal relationships and interpersonal communication. This formulation springs, as will be evident, primarily from the theory of therapy, viewing the therapeutic relationship as simply one instance of interpersonal relationship (pp. 235–6).

In both of these more general formulations, contact features as the necessary foundation, i.e. that a relationship has to be mindfully experienced. Rogers expressed it thus, that even in a deteriorating relationship:

> A person Y is willing to be in *contact* with person X and to receive communication from him . . .
> 2. Person X desires (at least to a minimal degree) to communicate to and be in *contact* with Y. (p. 236, original emphasis).

So, the minimal connection between two persons — before it can be said that they are 'in relationship' — is that they both have a *desire and intention* to be in contact with each other.

Perception
Rogers took care to define the terms 'perception' and 'subception' in his 1959 paper, and these definitions help our understanding of Condition Six, i.e. that the therapist communicates empathic understanding and UPR and the client perceives these to a minimal degree, as follows:

1. Rogers regarded perception and awareness as synonymous, and again, awareness as synonymous with symbolisation and consciousness. This implies that since perception and awareness are equivalent, then in therapy, the client must be consciously aware of the empathic understanding and UPR of the therapist.

2. Rogers stressed the idea of minimal requirements or the minimal extent to which something is required to happen. Some scholars have responded to this by attempting to measure this threshold amount, others take it to be a more general attempt to operationalise the irreducible requirements of the situation. Either way, to reiterate, in therapy the client's conscious awareness of the therapist's empathy and UPR is the signal that the minimal requirement has been met.
3. The further implication must be that if the client is not aware of the empathic understanding and UPR of the therapist, then the condition has not been met (regardless of the intentions or behaviour of the therapist).

So to use a culinary metaphor: if we wanted to make carrot soup and the recipe read, 'take one carrot', some might understand this to mean 'you can't have carrot soup without a carrot', whilst others would ask 'how big does the carrot have to be before it can really be called carrot soup?' Both would have to agree, though, that if there is no carrot, there is no carrot soup.

The perception of the therapeutic conditions *by the client* is, therefore, key to the whole relationship. Whilst this may be obvious to some, the fact of the matter is that little has been done to explore, document or elaborate understanding of this key element in comparison with empathic understanding, UPR and congruence. Most of us, it would appear, are content with the reverse logic contained in the assumption, i.e. that since we intend to make carrot soup, then it *must* be a carrot that we are making it with. In other words, since the therapist intends to be empathic and non-judgemental, then this is what the client is perceiving.

For the majority of the last century, much of psychology was predicated on a fundamental mistrust of the person. This was testimony to the dominance of psychoanalytic thinking as it pervaded the whole of academic psychology and its associated research procedures.[3] Later, psychology became infected with the behaviourist dogma that only that which can be 'objectively' measured has validity. The result of these influences was that any measurement of human qualities *had* to be made (i) from the external frame of reference and (ii) by qualified 'experts'. This made it difficult to do anything other than base estimation of the therapist-provided conditions on *experts'* evaluation, (e.g. Truax, 1967; Truax and Carkhuff, 1967) rather than *client* perceptions of them (e.g. Barrett-Lennard, 1962). Psychological assessment at the time *required* the opinion of expert raters in order to be even admissible, let alone credible.

Rogers' advancing of the phenomenological and existential themes in person-centred theory, his dogged insistence on the central importance of the client's perception of their own world and his anti-expert stance continued to disturb the scientific community. The Wisconsin Project (p. 15 below) saw the initiation of two strands of endeavour as the team attempted to develop and implement a client-centred research methodology which would satisfy the traditional

---

3. The unconscious drives, the *real* intentions of the person, could only be accessed by indirect measurement methods which required interpretation by experts, so the 'science' of psychometrics was born.

psychological community without violating the phenomenological core of the approach. On the one hand, proper usage of the rating scales devised by Charles Truax did not involve the opinion of the client as to the qualities of the therapeutic relationship — the correct protocol involved the use of trained expert raters. On the other, use was made of Godfrey Barrett-Lennard's effort to marry a scientific approach drawing on the statistical procedures of psychometrics, with a straightforward trust of the client's own assessment of the therapy and the therapist. (See below and in Chapter 2, this volume, by Godfrey Barrett-Lennard.)

CONTACT AND PERCEPTION (LOST AND FOUND) 1960–2002

Notwithstanding the major contributions made by Garry Prouty and Godfrey Barrett-Lennard, we might summarise the situation by saying that for much of this time whenever two or more people were in the room, then contact was *assumed*. Similarly, if expert raters (in research) or observers (in training) agreed that the therapist was communicating empathic understanding and UPR, it was *assumed* that that was what the client perceived.

When reviewing recent trends in Client-Centred work in 1970, regarding Condition One, contact, Van der Veen makes a single comment, writing:

Given these therapist conditions, and given some psychological contact between therapist and client, what qualities in the client are necessary for change? (p. 26)

So here contact is assumed, taken for granted, a 'given'. And what of Condition Six? Another passing mention:

The other element is that he [the client] *perceives the therapist conditions* to a minimal degree. He needs to have a minimal sense that the therapist is genuine, empathic and has positive regard for him . . . (original emphasis, p. 26).

We are not being critical of Van der Veen here, since it was he (see below) who, along with Barrett-Lennard, kept the concept of the client's perception afloat during the 1960s. But here he seems to swim with the tide of opinion that Conditions One and Six were the chorus line, the 'backing vocals', to the therapist-provided star conditions (later to be elevated to 'the Core Conditions') of congruence, UPR and empathic understanding. In a recent review, Bozarth (2001) blames Rogers' 1959 formulation of client-centred therapy as an 'if-then' hypothesis for the almost relentless focus on the therapist-provided conditions. The rating scales growing from this formulation, devised by Truax (1967) and popularised as a skills training tool by Truax and Carkhuff, (1967) then cemented the tendency to see the therapist-provided conditions as 'skills' and assured the relegation of contact and perception to the status of ignored or assumed conditions. Whatever the reason, one thing is certain, the spotlight was trained almost exclusively on the therapist-provided 'core conditions', with little respite, save for the work of Barrett-Lennard (1959, 1962), Prouty, (1976, 1990, 1994) and Van der Veen (1970). What was lost in these years was the focus on the relationship as 'the heart of the matter' (Gaylin, 2001).

Barrett-Lennard and the client's perception 1959/1962

Springing from his doctoral study (Barrett-Lennard, 1959), Godfrey Barrett-Lennard's relationship inventory (BLRI)[4] brought the proper study of the client's perception of the therapist to the fore (Barrett-Lennard 1962). Noticing that the emphasis of all other research was on the rating of the therapist-provided conditions by outside judges[5] Barrett-Lennard realised that the theory hinged upon the client's experience of the therapist in the counselling relationship. He set himself the task of devising a measurement instrument which would reliably tap the internal frame of reference of the client in relation to their perceptions of the therapist. Barrett-Lennard alone recognised the significance of Rogers' Condition Six, appreciated its place in research methodology, and acted upon this. In Chapter 2, this volume, Barrett-Lennard revisits, reviews and updates this work.

The study
His work involved not only attending to important strands of client-centred theory and practice, but also developing a methodology that could reliably measure such a difficult variable:
1. Careful definition of the variables to be measured was needed in order to render them measurable. Five scales were developed: empathic understanding, level of regard, unconditionality, congruence and willingness to be known.
2. It was important to ensure that client's recorded impressions of the therapist stood a realistic chance of having grown from the relationship (i.e. their experience together), and not from therapeutic change within the client. Clients were therefore asked to rate the therapists after session five. (Therapy lasted for an average of 33 sessions.)
3. 42 client-therapist pairs were studied, comprising both expert and novice therapists working with equivalent groups of clients.
4. Both clients and therapists were asked to complete the Relationship Inventory forms.
5. Whether clients did improve was measured by three scales administered to clients (for details see Barrett-Lennard, Chapter 2, this volume) as well as the judgement of the therapist.

The findings
Refraining from detailed consideration of the implications of the statistics, (for this readers are directed to Barrett-Lennard, 1962, and a more available text, Barrett-Lennard, 1998) the findings can be summarised as follows:
1. The expert therapists (on average 7 years older) were rated higher on all scales except the 'willingness to be known' scale than the novice therapists.

---
4. Referred to in various texts as either the Relationship Inventory (RI) or the Barrett-Lennard Relationship Invenotory (BLRI). See Barrett-Lennard Chapter 2 this volume.
5. In order to avoid experimenter effects, often the trained raters, were deliberately chosen to be naïve to client-centred therapy — adding 'distance' essential to the experimental method, but futher removed from possible understanding of the importance of the clients' experience.

2. A bigger proportion of clients seen by the expert therapists fell into the 'more changed' category.
3. Cases with the expert therapists had roughly twice the number of sessions as those with the novice therapists.
4. Those clients who rated the therapists most highly did show some evidence of changing/improving the most, and this was strongest for the most troubled clients.

In his 1962 psychological monograph, Barrett-Lennard concluded that there was a plausible causal connection between the client's perception of the therapist-provided conditions and change in the client.

After such a hopeful start, readers might imagine that the BLRI would become *the* principal instrument of measurement in client-centred research. This would then place the perceptions of the client — not only their unique world, but also their reception of the therapist-provided conditions — at the centre of research, training and reflective client-centred therapy practice itself. This, however, was not to be the case. Instead, client perception is forever present as a topic that enjoys a passing (but important) mention, but is never really brought to the fore (some of the few exceptions to this are presented below). It nags away — a sentence here, a phrase there — but the perception of the client never really has its day as the pivotal signifier that the relationship *is* therapeutic, rather being assumed as such by the therapist or judged by outside observers.

In 1961, Rogers tracked the progress of Barrett-Lennard's work in a paper published in the *American Journal of Psychotherapy* (Rogers, 1961b reproduced in Tomlinson and Hart, 1970). In reporting Barrett-Lennard's 1959 findings, Rogers concluded a short section on 'The Relationship as Perceived by Clients' with a 'tentative equation':

> Given a relationship [a cursory nod towards psychological contact] between therapist and client we can say:
>> Genuineness plus empathy and unconditional positive regard for the client equals successful therapy for the client.
>
> More accurately we can phrase it this way:
>> Perception by the client of genuineness, empathic understanding and unconditional positive regard in the therapist equals successful therapy for the client.
>
> Or perhaps better still:
>> The more the therapist is perceived by the client as being genuine, as having empathic understanding and an unconditional regard for him, the greater will be the degree of constructive personality change in the client. (Rogers in Hart and Tomlinson, 1970, p. 194)

This is a forceful restatement of his 1957 and 1959 hypothesis. Interestingly it de-emphasises psychological contact and emphasises the perception of the client. Other than in this brief, but unequivocal section, in this paper Rogers was mainly continuing to concentrate on the process in the client and the relationship between the therapist-provided conditions and a favourable outcome, based on empirical research. Client-centred therapy was influenced by the ideas of Taft ('relationship therapy') and though once radical, the notion that the relationship was central to therapy was becoming more accepted. There were still several important theoretical, philosophical and practice battles to be fought. If there had been progress on the 'relationship-is-important' front, it was not the case elsewhere—the notion of empathy had been consistently ridiculed, congruence/genuineness was too much of a challenge to the professional position of the 'expert' and UPR was seen as at least problematic and probably impossible.

Van der Veen and the client's perception 1961/1970

1970 saw the publication of 'Client Perception of Therapist Conditions as a Factor in Psychotherapy' by Ferdinand Van der Veen in a volume charting new directions in client-centered therapy (Hart and Tomlinson, 1970). The chapter detailed research first presented nearly a decade earlier (Van der Veen, 1961/1970) at the Annual Meeting of the American Psychological Association.

Van der Veen's data was collected in conjunction with, but incidental to, the Wisconsin Project and aimed to test the hypothesis that client perception of therapist-provided conditions was an essential aspect of effective therapy with hospitalised clients with a diagnosis of schizophrenia — a somewhat different client group from that studied by Barrett-Lennard. Other hypotheses tested by Van der Veen also gave his work a different flavour from that of Barrett-Lennard and the main Wisconsin study. Using predominantly the BLRI (but also the MMPI[6] and Q-sort,[7] and some data from the interviews used to select participants) Van der Veen reported the following results:

1. Therapists were perceived as providing more of the conditions than other significantly helpful (non-therapist) persons.
2. The more psychologically adjusted the client, the more they perceived the therapist conditions.
3. Higher therapist conditions were perceived by clients whose level of process in therapy was higher (measured on scales that measured how much they talked about their problems and referred to their own experience, and how much they related their problems to themselves).
4. The degree of client movement in therapy is positively related to the client's perception of the conditions in therapy.
5. The degree of client movement in therapy is positively related to rater-estimated levels of therapist conditions.

These results provided further evidence that client perception of the therapist-provided conditions was indeed implicated if not actually necessary for effective therapy. What neither Van der Veen nor Barrett-Lennard had shown was that positive client movement would *not* take place if the client did *not* perceive the

---

6. MMPI — The Minnesota Multiphasic Personality Inventory: a psychometric personality test *de rigeur* in positivist research. Regarded by psychologists as a valid and reliable measure of some therapy-related personality variables, but not favoured in client-centred circles.
7. The Q-sort is a statistical method devised by Stephenson (1953) and adapted initially by Butler and Haigh (1954) as a measurement of therapeutic change directly related to client-centred theory. See Shlien and Zimring (1970) for a fuller account.

therapist variables. Such a finding is needed in order to establish the *necessity* of Condition Six.

The combination of findings 4 and 5 along with findings summarised by Watson (1984) do support the idea that the therapist conditions *actually* have to be provided. It may not be sufficient for the client to experience, e.g. empathy, regardless of the therapist's behaviour. There must be some concurrence between empathy actually provided and empathy actually perceived. This is, however, not a simple matter. There is obviously a subtle interplay between empathy transmitted and empathy received, as Rogers was only too aware in his earlier presentation of the diary of Miss Cam (Rogers, 1951, p. 113). Miss Cam reports:

> You said some things that didn't seem to be quite what I meant. But far from being threatening, they were positively encouraging. It's nice to find that a misunderstanding isn't irrevocable — that I can correct it, and that you will understand and accept the correction.

This diary extract beautifully illustrates the dance between client and therapist where intention to be empathic, the actuality of inaccuracy, and the acceptance by the client of fallibility on the part of the therapist, are all perceived by the client and woven into a positive personal learning as she goes on:

> It isn't necessary to be perfectly clear and understood every time I speak. There's no need to be scared to death every time I open my mouth for fear I'll say something that's not entirely accurate and entirely beyond reproach or criticism. No need to pick my words with such care that I end up expressing myself much less clearly than if I had just said the first thing that came in to my head. (ibid, p. 113)

It seems that a wide range of therapist behaviours will be experienced and thus perceived as therapeutic by clients and we may find Bozarth's position closer to the truth in practice.[8]

Van der Veen continued to study client perception and looked at whether differences in the client's *ability* to perceive others in certain ways would affect Condition Six and therefore the successful outcome of therapy. In an unpublished study in 1965, he found that more disturbed clients perceived distinctly lower therapist conditions (with the exception of empathic understanding) than the less disturbed clients. Could this mean that certain personality disturbances might render a client less able to access therapeutic conditions?

In an associated finding, Van der Veen (1967) found that the perception of lower levels of the conditions was also related to a lower level of process in the client, to a more rigid mode of experiencing (for the sample of people diagnosed as schizophrenic). When commenting on these findings in 1970, Van der Veen wrote:

> The client's inability to *perceive others* as genuine, empathic and accepting may be a major stumbling block on his path to psychological change. This can

---

8. Bozarth takes the view that idiosyncratic, unsystematic therapist responses are just as likely to be percieved as empathic and helpful by the client. Indeed, possibly *all the more* helpful because of their unsystematic nature since they will have no pre-planned therapeutic objective. See Bozarth 1984/2001 and to a lesser extent 1993/98 for a fuller account.

be especially true when the age, background or social class of the client and therapist differ greatly. (Van der Veen in Tomlinson and Hart, 1970, p. 31, original italics.)

These findings have two implications, firstly that if the client's personality and level of process affects their ability to perceive the therapist-provided conditions, then Rogers' process conception (Rogers, 1961a) of therapy is validated at the lower stages, 1 and 2. Rogers freely admitted that therapists may not be able to help clients at stages 1 and 2. These findings suggest that one reason may be because such clients are not able to experience the therapist as genuine, empathic, warm and non-judgemental.

The second implication concerns clients and counsellor relationships where there is a cultural gap. Van der Veen's words above need little amplification. When clients and counsellors come from different cultural backgrounds, the clients ability to experience the counsellor as empathic, genuine and accepting may be a stumbling block to a good relationship. The responsibility is on the counsellor to mitigate any such effects and this has been a constant refrain in cross-cultural texts for decades, whether the cultural differences involve race and culture, social class, religious differences, disabilities or sexuality. Davies and Aykroyd explore these issues in relation to gay, lesbian and bisexual clients in this volume, Chapter 13.

The Wisconsin Project 1967 — a watershed?

Conducted at the Mendota State Hospital in the early 1960s, and published after much internal conflict in the team in 1967, what is popularly known as 'The Wisconsin Project' (Rogers, Gendlin, Kiesler and Truax, 1967) was an ambitious, groundbreaking research programme. It had as its aim the understanding of the effective ingredients of the therapeutic relationship in the most challenging of contexts, namely, with hospitalised, severely disturbed clients with a diagnosis of schizophrenia.

For the purposes of this chapter, the Wisconsin Project has significance (a) because its use of the BLRI was the first research project to use the instrument following Barrett-Lennard's development of it from 1959 onwards, and (b) because, with hindsight, the issue of psychological contact is considered central to effective therapy with many clients diagnosed as schizophrenic.

The 'life' of the project was some nine years in length from planning through to publication. There were major problems with the data (some of which mysteriously disappeared), clients (some dropped out), and disagreements within the staff team. Although the results are frequently presented as inconclusive, the study was a courageous attempt to subject psychotherapy to empirical research methods, and much was learned (albeit from 'mistakes') about planning and conducting of psychotherapy research and the development of appropriate measuring instruments.

The BLRI was one of the measures used and readers are referred to Barrett-Lennard 1998, pp. 68–9 and pp. 267–70 for a summary analysis of the results. At one point, Barrett-Lennard draws the interesting conclusion that:

Judging from all the descriptive information, they were working with persons with whom forming a relationship of understanding, trust and healing was truly a *most* uphill process ... (p. 268, original emphasis).

Although this was not directly measured nor emphasised in the report, it seems that the clients had real difficulty in perceiving the therapists in an undistorted fashion and making good psychological contact. Given that these are central to relationship establishment the results are, with hindsight, unsurprising.

After Wisconsin. Plus a digression to consider the role of Carl Rogers in generating theory

It goes without saying that Carl Rogers, and his ideas, were central to the genesis of client-centred therapy theory. During his lifetime he wrote copiously and seemed to be the engine for the development of theory. However, no substantial additions were made to the basic theory of personality and therapy after the 'Process conception of psychotherapy' is published in *On Becoming a Person* in 1961. Rogers concentrated on innovations in the *application* of client/person-centred psychology after the Wisconsin Project ended in some disarray and he moved to California. It is a salutary note that theory development effectively stopped in the early 1960s in the discipline of client-centred therapy until after Rogers' death in the mid-80s. We could be forgiven for surmising that leading thinkers in client-centred therapy and the person-centred approach deferred to Rogers in terms of theory development during his life and simply could not imagine the development of new theory without his central involvement. Since he appeared to abdicate this role in terms of therapy theory in the early 1960s, development of therapy theory more-or-less ground to a halt.

Of course we acknowledge that Gendlin's ideas gave birth to a fecund strand of theory development which continues to be lively today as 'experiential' psychotherapy — with much to contribute to our appreciation of psychological contact and client perception. However, this strand has never been accepted as a part of classical client-centred therapy and the relation of experiential therapy and client-centred therapy remains the subject of debate and controversy. Indeed Garry Prouty developed his Pre-Therapy work on psychological contact under Eugene Gendlin's wing and claims that it is 'different' from client-centred therapy, though 'rooted' in it. Prouty explains:

> Although Rogers himself believed Pre-Therapy was important, I realize the relationship with CCT is complicated. My work, although deeply influenced by Rogers, is not 'classical' CCT ... I have labeled it Pre-Therapy — because it is somewhat different from 'classical' Client-Centered Therapy. It is measured scientifically not as the core conditions, but rather as psychological contact and its consequences. It is a different principle from the core conditions although it allows their aplication. (Prouty, 2002 personal communication)

We further acknowledge the contributions to theory and practice by John Shlien, (Shlien, 1984) Laura North Rice (1974) Fred Zimring (1974) and others, but the weight of these contributions is debatable in retrospect, since they appear neither to have been assimilated into mainstream client-centred therapy theory, nor have they deviated the course of client-centred therapy theory from a mainstream emphasis on the Rogerian conditions. Also, there have been refinements, restatements and elaborations of existing therapy theory, e.g. Bozarth, 1993/98, but we would, as an acknowledged generalisation, assert that no *new* theory emerged until the late 1980s.

Not only did theory development stop, there was also a change in emphasis in the approach as it followed Rogers' interests, away from therapy, and the elaboration of detail in its major concepts, towards other applications of person-centred psychology. This change is sometimes referred to as the 'californisation' of client-centred therapy and its transformation into the person-centred approach. The therapeutic strand of the new person-centred approach focused almost exclusively on the therapist-provided conditions of empathy, unconditional positive regard and congruence, which became known as the 'core' conditions. Whatever the reasons, the sum effect of these various influences seems to have been the de-psychologising of client-centred therapy into the person-centred approach. It moved from being a psychological discipline (with all of the academic rigour implied) to an 'approach', a 'way of being' (with the blurring of the edges therein implied). Again, notwithstanding the differing interpretations of the history of the approach at this time, and accepting that our view is partial and partisan, it is clear that amongst the claimed casualties of this era were Conditions One and Six.

Some would mount a persuasive argument based on the aphorism 'if it ain't broke, don't fix it'. Some classical client-centred therapists view Rogers' chapter in Koch's epic work (Koch, 1959) as a complete statement, requiring no adjustment, refinement, addition or development, save better elaboration and exploration of the links between the theory as stated and the application of it in therapy, for example with different/new client groups. Linked to this is the view that Rogers himself considered his work in the therapy arena 'complete', or at least that he had given all he had to give. It was time to move on to new pastures and his new interest, namely working in groups, according to Barrett-Lennard (1998), began in his last year at Wisconsin.

When invited to re-state his theory some years later, in collaboration with Ruth Sanford, we note that some changes *have* occurred in this version. Of relevance to the present work, Rogers and Sanford (1984) miss out (psychological) contact altogether as a therapeutic condition and congruence is included in the client's perception (Watson also makes this point in his research review, 1984) but it is difficult to know how much weight to give to what some consider to be minor changes in wording, and others believe to be significant indicators of theory evolution.

In addition to the continued flourishing of experiential therapy approaches since Rogers' death in 1987, therapy theory development of more classical client-centred therapy as a strand of academic applied psychology/psychotherapy has enjoyed something of a renaissance. We would cite the work of Mearns (1999, 2000), and Warner (1991, 2000) as contenders to being genuine additions to the body of theory rather than revisions or new perspectives.

The Wisconsin study is implicated as the catalyst for these changes in emphasis and direction, including the move from client-centred *therapy* to person-centred *approach*. Shlien (1994, 2001) asserts that after Wisconsin, Rogers was left emotionally drained, distrustful of academia, and terminally lacking in confidence as a therapist. Whatever the exact circumstances, it is probably no surprise that he had little appetite for therapy theory development. Scrutiny of the published work, subsequently published accounts and recent correspondence, do little to clarify the puzzle and leave us with the inevitable conclusion that psychological contact (in particular) and the client's perception (to a lesser extent) as active ingredients of the therapeutic atmosphere were overlooked.

It may have been that the therapists involved did indeed get a hint that something was lacking or that some factors needed greater attention. In 1972, Rogers reflected on the Wisconsin Project in one of the chapters of *Person to Person*:

> Another simple observation. Our schizophrenics tend to be either massively silent or to engage in continuous (and not very revealing) conversation. It has been found that half of our schizophrenics, in their second interviews show either less than 1% silence or more than 40% silence . . . This sharply differed from clinic clients. Our schizophrenic individuals tended to fend off relationships either by an almost complete silence — often extending over many interviews — or by a flood of overtalk which is equally effective in preventing a real encounter. (Rogers and Stevens, 1968, p. 188)

With hindsight it is too tempting not to put this down to what Prouty subsequently called a 'contact-deficit', or that such clients were 'contact-impaired'.

According to Barrett-Lennard's estimation, one of the saving features of the published findings of the Wisconsin study was Rogers' and Gendlin's work on the construct of experiencing. Later Gendlin refined these early ideas in two chapters in the Hart and Tomlinson (1970) compilation, concluding:

> My conception of the illness: [schizophrenia] *It is not so much what is there, as what is not here*. The interactive experiential process is . . . deadened . . . in disconnection from the world (Gendlin in Hart and Tomlinson 1970, p. 288, original emphasis).

Here Gendlin clearly identifies one of the missing elements which prevents the clients from properly engaging in a therapeutic relationship. Again, we are reading an accurate description of the contact-impaired individual. This is further evidence that the experience of the Wisconsin Project continued to raise issues and shape ideas for years afterwards among members of the team. These ideas were just a few words short of being pivotal to the topics which are at the centre of the present volume. The only words missing were 'psychological contact'. We could surmise, then, that for the latter part of the study itself, and at the report-writing stage, the experience of the Wisconsin Project was so plainly upsetting for the team members due to the problems with loss of data and personal tensions within the team, that they did not have the energy for clear conclusions regarding psychological contact with the clients.

With the emphasis so clearly on the *that which could be measured* (i.e. empathy, UPR and congruence) by trained raters, the therapists and the clients themselves, it is understandable that the issue of psychological contact, since it need not then be 'measured', can be assumed, taken-for-granted and hence ignored. This, at least is the view held by Watson, who, when reviewing research into client-centred therapy in 1984, wrote:

> The omission of Condition One . . . deserves comment . . . If Conditions Two through Six are operationally defined and shown to be present — it follows then that Condition One is present, then Condition One does not require its own operational definition separate from those for the remaining conditions (Watson, in Levant and Shlien, 1984, pp. 18-19).

And there we have it baldly stated: psychological contact can be assumed, and it was. That is, until Prouty (1994, Prouty, Van Werde and Pörtner, 1998, 2002) brought to our attention that client-centred theory had made a mistake in this assumption and had neither theory nor practice to implement when psychological contact as an essential condition, was absent due to a contact-impairment in the client.

Gendlin's contribution

Throughout the early 60s, the 'traditional' structural view of mental life was challenged by both Rogers (1961) and Gendlin (1964/70) — many crediting Gendlin's earlier work on experiencing as seminal (Gendlin, 1958). Whatever the origin, entities and structures were replaced by *processes*, right up to the level of the person as an individual unique process. It is difficult now to imagine how different and revolutionary such an idea was,

Gendlin suggested that human life comprised an inner stream of pre-symbolic experience, ever present and available to awareness only if deliberately attended to (or 'focused' on). This stream of experience included hitherto unprocessed bodily processes, visceral sensations, sensed (but unnamed) energies and emotion, implicit meanings not yet articulated. Daily life consists of occasional, accidental and (unless subjected to personal discipline such as meditation) random access to this stream of experience, this inner flow. Gendlin (1978) developed a discipline for accessing this flow which he called 'focusing' — either a step-by step method for deliberate access or a schema for the therapeutic process. Increasing psychological health is understood as better access to this inner flow for the individual.

It is clear that such theory and practice are central to the ideas of contact and perception. Focusing itself may be understood as a contact-discipline. By this we mean that it forces the issue of contact and perception in two ways — contact within the individual and contact between the therapist and client. Indeed, this neatly describes the major source of conflict between the classical client centred therapists and the experiential psychotherapists, i.e. the issue of directivity. Classical client-centred therapists and some clients baulk at the 'forced' nature of focusing and the 'managed' nature of process-directed experiential therapy. There can be no doubt, though, that within experiential therapy theory and practice, contact is not assumed, it is *assured*. Intra-psychic contact and inter-psychic contact and perception are *required* and relentlessly checked for accuracy.

CONTACT AND PERCEPTION

Prouty's development of Pre-Therapy 1976-2002

Garry Prouty, encouraged by Rogers and Gendlin, pondered for over a decade before first publishing his work (1976) with people diagnosed as schizophrenic and having profound learning disability (in Prouty's North American terms, 'psychotic' and 'retarded'). Then almost 20 years later, he published the 'founding' book in Pre-Therapy (Prouty, 1994).

Since three of the chapters from that book are reproduced in this volume (see chapters 3a, b and c), Prouty's work can speak for itself. Readers will also find other authors in this volume and elsewhere (e.g. Coffeng and Van Werde in this volume and Pörtner, 2000) have developed strands of Prouty's work as both a theory of experience and a practical method.

To summarise Prouty, he suggests that in order for psychotherapy to take place (since Rogers postulated the *necessity* of the conditions, including One and Six) psychological contact must be established. This never more pressing than with those clients who have their ability to establish and maintain psychological contact with another human being impaired by illness or injury, organic or psychological. Prouty went further than the on-off, binary view of psychological contact assumed by many writers and therapists. He identified three types of contact: contact with self, contact with the environment and social contact (or contact with others). This is a *cascade* of contact, with the whole process being critically impaired if an element is missing. So, the internal economy of contact, between self and experience is as important as contact between self and other, before therapy can be effective. The links with Gendlin and experiential psychotherapy are obvious.

Prouty went further still in an effort to explain how this cascade of contact breaks down (and can be re-established) in various psychotic symptoms such as hallucination. He postulates that a combination of internal and external experiential isolation means that the individual functions at a pre-symbolic level. Pre-Therapy, then according to Prouty 'points at the concrete' re-establishing the connection between sensation, experience and self. Again, the reader is referred to Prouty's complete work (1994) and the three chapters reproduced in this volume.

Watson's review of research 1984

In 1984, Neill Watson made a major contribution when he reviewed the then current status of empirical studies into client-centered therapy. The review was near-comprehensive and contained a summary of no less than nineteen studies of client perceptions of the relationship and client evaluations of the outcome of individual therapy. He also reviewed a further eight studies where client perceptions were related to the therapist evaluations of outcome. Such studies honoured the phenomenological nature of the theory and, following Barrett-Lennard, paid due attention to the *necessity* of Condition Six. Both groups of studies used a variety of measures including the BLRI.

Tellingly, Watson writes:

. . . only two studies . . . assessed all the hypothesised conditions: client incongruence, therapist congruence, therapist unconditional positive regard, and therapist empathy. (Watson, in Levant and Shlien, 1884, p. 27)

Psychological contact doesn't figure here as a hypothesised condition. However, before we condemn this omission, we should remember that this is entirely in line with Watson's proposal that psychological contact does not need to be viewed as independent. Its presence can be *assumed* if the other conditions can be measured. This does lead to the view (we believe, often held, unstated by many client/person-centred practitioners) that psychological contact is a discrete binary condition. It is either on, or off; present or not present, and is not (can not be) a matter of degree. The concept of psychological contact as multiplex, and as a continuum, was introduced later by Prouty (1994).

Watson summarised the findings as follows:
1. Client perceptions of both therapist and outcome (nineteen studies)
    • Two studies assessed all conditions (except contact, but including client incongruence) and found that all were positively correlated with client self-ratings of improvement.
    • When studied individually or in twos and threes, all of the therapist-provided conditions *except UPR* were related to a positive client self-rated outcome.
2. Client perceptions of therapist and therapist ratings of outcome (eight studies)
    • Two studies found positive relationships between client perceptions of all therapist-provided conditions and therapist ratings of outcome, but these studies did not include client incongruence.
    • Six studies measured one or more (but not all) conditions and found that in various combinations, one or more of the therapist-provided conditions was correlated positively with therapist-rated outcome.
    • Unconditionality of regard and congruence were the conditions not found to be positively correlated in all studies.

Whatever else may be deduced from research into the therapist-provided conditions, it seems that client-perception as measured can be considered as valid as therapist-ratings and opinions when evaluating outcome. This should give heart to those who wish to apply empirical methods to phenomenological realities. Cramer (1990), noting the paucity of research into Rogers' conditions hypothesis, proposed conditions for the evaluation of client-centred therapy. In his review he gave due prominence to client perception of facilitative conditions and the need for this aspect to be explored, but in our view this plea came too late. The era of funded research into anything that didn't promise a quick-fix was over. It is difficult to predict if or when the tide might turn.

Van Werde and Pörtner: making relationships with contact-impaired persons

There used to be a common understanding that a certain level of intellectual functioning was required before therapy could be accessed by an individual. Client-centred therapy and the person-centred approach has now moved on from this. In addition to developments announced in this volume (see Chapters by Coffeng, Van Werde, Zinschitz), some practical applications of a deeper understanding of Conditions One and Six (though especially of Condition One) have been reported. There has also been a real advance in re-establishing human contact with people previously thought to be beyond help by virtue of being beyond psychological contact. Such people as those suffering from isolating psychotic conditions, learning disabilities, organic conditions such as Alzheimer's disease (and other forms of dementia), brain injury and terminal illness, all may be helped by Pre-Therapy.

CONCLUSION

After a spluttering start and being largely ignored for nearly thirty years Conditions One and Six have begun to find their place in contemporary Client-Centred and experiential therapy theory — they even get special mention in 'mainstream' professional journals as a result of theoretical agitation (for a good example in the UK, see Tudor, 2000). They are now, most certainly on the map. Indeed, we assert that they are rapidly being recognised as the coordinates of the map itself. The inability of client-centred and experiential psychotherapies to develop critically our understanding and integration of Conditions One and Six into our theory until recently has had wider implications. In our view this failure helps explain the criticism levelled from other theoretical orientations that the person-centred approach is simplistic and light on theory. Giving Condition One and Six their true significance broadens the application of client-centred and experiential therapies and allows for a more complex theory to be developed. In this new century, it may be that they will become one of the main foci of research and theory development in client centred therapy.

REFERENCES

Barrett-Lennard, G. T. (1959). Dimensions of perceived therapist related to therapeutic change. Unpublished doctoral dissertation: University of Chicago.

Barrett-Lennard, G. T. (1962). Dimensions of therapist response as causal factors in therapeutic change. *Psychological Monographs, 76.* (43, Whole, No. 562).

Barrett-Lennard, G. T. (1998). *Carl Rogers' Helping System: Journey and substance.* London: Sage.

Bozarth, J. D. (1984/2001). Beyond reflection: emergent modes of empathy. In J. M. Shlien and R. F. Levant (Eds.) *Client-Centered Therapy and the Person-Centered Approach: New directions in theory, research and practice,* (pp. 59–75). New York: Praeger. Reprinted in S. Haugh and T. Merry (Eds.) (2001). *Rogers Therapeutic Conditions:. Volume 2: Empathy.* Ross-on-Wye: PCCS Books, (pp. 190–205).

Bozarth, J. D. (1993/98). The coterminus intermingling of doing and being in person-centered therapy. *The Person-Centered Journal. 1*(1), 33–9. Reprinted in J. D. Bozarth (1998) *Person-Centered Therapy: A revolutionary paradigm.* Ross-on-Wye: PCCS Books, (pp. 97–102).

Bozarth, J. D. (2001). Client-centered unconditional positive regard: A historical perspective. In J. D. Bozarth and P. Wilkins (Eds.) *Rogers' Therapeutic Conditions: Evolution, theory and practice. Volume 4: Unconditional Positive Regard.* Ross-on-Wye: PCCS Books, (pp. 5–18)..

Butler, J. M. and Haigh, G. V. (1954). Changes in the relations between self-concepts and ideal-concepts consequent upon client-centered counseling. In C. R. Rogers and R. F. Dymond, (Eds.) *Psycxhotherapy and Personality Change,* (pp. 55–75). Chicago: University of Chicago press.

Cramer, D. (1990). The necessary conditions for evaluating client-centered therapy. In G. Lietaer, J. Rombauts and R. Van Balen (Eds.) *Client-Centered and Experiential Psychotherapy in the Nineties* (pp. 415–28). Leuven: University of Leuven Press.

Dixon, N. F. (1971). *Subliminal Perception: The nature of a controversy*. New York: McGraw-Hill.

Gaylin, N. (2001). The relationship: The heart of the matter. In N. Gaylin *Family, Self and Psychotherapy: A person-centered perspective*. Ross-on-Wye: PCCS Books, (pp. 95–104).

Gendlin, E. T. (1958). The function of experiencing in symbolisation. Doctoral dissertation, University of Chicago.

Gendlin, E. T. (1964/70). A theory of personality change. In P. Wochel and D. Byrne (Eds.) *Personality Change* (pp. 206–47) New York: Wiley. Reprinted In J. T. Hart and T. M. Tomlinson, (Eds.) *New Directions in Client-Centered Therapy* (pp. 129–73). Boston: Houghton Mifflin.

Gendlin, E. T. (1978). *Focusing*. New York: Everest House.

Hart, J. T. and Tomlinson, T. M. (Eds.) (1970). *New Directions in Client-Centered Therapy*, Boston: Houghton Mifflin.

Mearns, D. (1999). Person-centred therapy with configurations of the self. *Counselling 10*(2) pp. 125–30.

Mearns, D. (2000). The nature of 'configurations' within self, (p.101 – 119) and, Person-centred therapy with 'configurations' of self, (pp. 120–143). In D. Mearns and B. Thorne, *Person-Centred Therapy Today*. London: Sage.

Mearns D. and Thorne, B. (2000). *Person-Centred Therapy Today: New frontiers in theory and practice*. London: Sage.

Miller, H. E. (1949). 'Acceptance' and related attitudes as demonstrated in psychotherapeutic interviews. *Journal of Clinical Psychology 5*, 83–7.

Moore, T. E. (1992). Subliminal perception: Facts and fallacies. *Skeptical Inquirer*, 16, 273–81.

Prouty, G. (1976). Pre-Therapy, a method of treating pre-expressive psychotic and retarded patients. *Psychotherapy: Theory, Research and Practice, 13 (Fall)*, 290–4.

Prouty, G. F. (1985). The development of reality, affect and communication in psychotic states. *Journal of Communication Therapy, 2* (1), 99–103.

Prouty, G.F. (1990). Pre-Therapy: A theoretical evolution in the person-centered/experiential psychotherapy of schizophrenia and retardation. In G. Lietaer, J. Rombauts and R. Van Balen (Eds.) *Client-Centered and Experiential Psychotherapy in the Nineties*. Leuven: University of Leuven Press, (pp. 645–58).

Prouty, G.F. (1994). *Theoretical Evolutions in Person-Centered/Experiential Therapy: Applications to schizophrenic and retarded psychoses*. Westport: Praeger.

Prouty, G. F., Van Werde, D. and Pörtner, M. (1998). *Prä-Therapie*. Stuttgart: Klette Cotta. Engl. Transl. (in press). *Pre-Therapy*, Ross-on-Wye: PCCS Books.

Raskin, N. J. (1949). An objective study of the locus of factor in psychotherapy. Unpublished doctoral dissertation, University of Chicago.

Rice, L. N. (1974). The evocative function of the therapist. In D. A. Wexler and L. N. Rice (Eds.) *Innovations in Client-Centered Therapy*. New York: Wiley, (pp. 289–310).

Rogers, C. R. (1942). *Counseling and Psychotherapy: Newer concepts in practice*. Boston: Houghton Mifflin.

Rogers, C. R. (1951). *Client-Centered Therapy: Its current practice, implications and theory*. Boston: Houghton Mifflin.

Rogers, C. R. (1957). The necessary and sufficient conditions of therapeutic personality change, *Journal of Consulting Psychology, 21* (pp. 95–103). Reprinted in H. Kirschenbaum and V. L. Henderson (Eds.) *The Carl Rogers Reader*, London: Constable, (pp. 219–35).

Rogers, C. R. (1959). A theory of therapy, personality and interpersonal relationships as developed in the client-centered framework. In S. Koch (ed.) *Psychology: A study of a science. Vol. 3: Formulations of the person and the social context*. New York: McGraw-Hill, (pp. 184–256).

Rogers, C. R. (1961a). *On Becoming a Person*. Boston: Houghton Mifflin.

Rogers, C. R. (1961b/1970). The process equation in psychotherapy. *American Journal of Psychotherapy*, 15 (1), 27–45. Reprinted in J. T. Hart and T. M. Tomlinson, (Eds.) *New Directions in Client-Centered Therapy*, Boston: Houghton Mifflin, (pp. 190–205).

Rogers, C. R., Gendlin, G. T., Kiesler, D. V. and Truax, C. B. (1967). *The therapeutic relationship and its impact: A study of psychotherapy with schizophrenics*. Madison: University of

Wisconsin Press.
Rogers, C. R. and Stevens, B. (1968). *Person to Person: The problem of being human.* Lafayette: Real People Press.
Seeman, J. (1948). A study of the process of non-directive therapy. *Journal of Consulting Psychology, 13,* 157–68.
Seeman, J. (1983). *Personality Integration: Studies and reflections.* New York: Human Sciences Press.
Shlien, J. M. (1984). A countertheory of transference. In J. M. Shlien and R. F. Levant (Eds.) *Client-Centered Therapy and the Person-Centered Approach: New directions in theory, research and practice.* New York: Praeger, (pp. 153–81).
Shlien, J. M. (1994). Embarrassment anxiety: A literalist theory. In R. Hutterer, G. Pawlowsky, P. F. Schmid and R. Stipsits (Eds.) *Client-Centered and Experiential Psychotherapy: A Paradigm in Motion.* Frankfurt am Main: Peter Lang, (pp. 101–6).
Shlien, J. M. (1994). Untitled and uneasy. Unpublished notes for a lecture given at the 3rd ICCCEP Conference, Gmunden, Austria.
Shlien, J. M. (2001) Unpublished interview.
Standal, S. W. (1954). The need for positive regard: A contribution to client-centered theory. Unpublished doctoral dissertation, University of Chicago.
Stephenson, W. (1953). *The Study of Behaviour: Q-technique and its methodology.* Chicago: University of Chicago Press.
Taft, J. (1933). *The Dynamics of Therapy in a Controlled Relationship.* New York: Macmillan.
Truax, C. B. (1967). Appendices B1 and B2: Rating scales for therapeutic conditions. In C. R. Rogers, E. T Gendlin, D. J. Kiesler and C. B. Truax (Eds.) *The Therapeutic Relationship and its Impact: A study of psychotherapy with schizophrenics.* Madison: University of Wisconsin Press, (pp. 555–80).
Truax, C. B. and Carkhuff, R. R. (1967). *Toward Effective Counseling and Psychotherapy: Training and practice.* Chicago: Aldine.
Tudor, K. (2000). The case of the lost conditions. *Counselling 11*(1), 33–7.
Van der Veen, F. (1961/1970). Client perception of the therapist conditions as a factor in psychotherapy. In J. T. Hart and T. M. Tomlinson, (Eds.) *New Directions in Client-Centered Therapy.* Boston: Houghton Mifflin, (pp. 129–73).
Van der Veen, F. (1965). Perceived therapist conditions and degree of disturbance. Unpublished manuscript: University of Kansas.
Van der Veen, F. (1967). Basic elements in the process of psychotherapy: A research study. *Journal of Consulting Psychology, 31,* 295–303.
Warner, M. S. (1991). Fragile process. In L. Fusek (ed.) *New Directions in Client-Centered Therapy: Practice with difficult client populations (Monograph Series 1).* Chicago: Chicago Counseling Center, (pp. 41–58).
Warner, M. S. (2000). Person-centred therapy at the difficult edge: A developmentally based model of fragile and dissociated process. In D. Mearns and B. Thorne, *Person-Centred Therapy Today,* London: Sage (pp. 144–71).
Watson, N. (1984). The empirical status of Rogers' hypotheses of the necessary and sufficient conditions for effective psychotherapy. In J. M. Shlien and R. F. Levant (Eds.) *Client-Centered Therapy and the Person-Centered Approach: New directions in theory, research and practice,* New York: Praeger, (pp. 17–40).
Zimring, F. M. (1974). Theory and practice in client-centered therapy: A cognitive view. In D. A. Wexler and L. N. Rice (Eds.) *Innovations in Client-Centered Therapy.* New York: Wiley, (pp. 117–37).

2

Perceptual Variables of the Helping Relationship: A measuring system and its fruits

Godfrey T. Barrett-Lennard

A perceptual emphasis has always characterised client-centred thought, which has stressed that human beings act on and respond to reality as they experience and perceive it to be. A person's field of perception is influenced by a variety of factors, internal and external. Whatever goes into this mix, it is the person's own resulting view or estimation that directly influences them. The therapy relationship is a case in point. A therapist's response to a client could be examined by an observer, in carefully systematic vein. But it is not, reasonably, this externally assessed state of affairs but, rather, the client's own experience and perception that he or she goes by. This way of thinking has been fundamental to my approach to measuring qualities of relationship — in therapy and a spectrum of other life contexts.

This chapter focuses on my Relationship Inventory, a research questionnaire inspired by Rogers' conditions of therapy theory. I am thinking especially of his classic formulation, as published in 1957, but circulated the previous year to his graduate students and other Counseling Center colleagues. I was one of those student colleagues, and Rogers unveiled this exciting theory at precisely the time I was seriously on the lookout for a topic for my doctoral thesis. I soon decided that I wanted to test the theory. But exactly how? Especially, how was I going to measure the therapist-to-client relationship qualities discriminated? There were no established scales, and it was necessary to invent them from the ground up. This chapter includes the story of this invention and the research flowing from it. But before getting to that I want to speak of the theory which started it all off.

Rogers' 1957 formulation of his conditions of therapy theory, and its restatement as the fulcrum of his complete theoretical perspective (Rogers, 1959), burst on the psychotherapy scene with almost transformative impact. Some readers were at once highly critical, others took great heart from his striking vision; few were indifferent. For the graduate students and other close colleagues around Rogers his new formulation was exciting but did not come as a surprise, and was taken literally as a fertile hypothesis rather than revealed or final truth. This certainly was how I took it, although I did not see until later how distinctly Rogers had been on a decade-long path to this formulation.

CONTACT AND PERCEPTION

Rogers' conditions theory unfolding

The shape of the answer Rogers had been searching for was stated over ten years earlier, where he spoke carefully of certain conditions needing to be met in order to initiate and carry forward a therapeutic process with broadly predictable outcomes (Rogers, 1946). The ideas continued to work in his thought, and are re-expressed in another directly relevant paper prepared for the important book on theory and research in psychotherapy edited by O. H. Mowrer (1953). There Rogers speaks again of the surprisingly orderly process of therapy, and goes on to say:

> We know at least something of the attitudinal conditions for getting this process under way. We know that if the therapist holds within himself attitudes of deep respect and full acceptance for the client as he is, and similar attitudes toward the client's potentialities for dealing with himself and his situations; if these attitudes are suffused with a sufficient warmth which transforms them into the most profound type of liking and affection for the core of the person; and if a level of communication is reached so that the client can begin to perceive that the therapist understands the feelings he is experiencing and accepts him at the full depth of that understanding, then we may be sure that the process is already initiated (Rogers, 1953).

Two years after the likely date of writing the article for Mowrer's book, Carl Rogers framed a short, very concise statement simply titled 'Some basic hypotheses of client-centered therapy'. This evidently was never published,[1] but clearly is another stepping-stone to the 1957 paper. In it, the author speaks of the therapy relationship being optimal when the therapist is genuine/congruent (both words are used), accepting and prizing of the other, and empathically and non-judgementally understanding. (This may be Rogers' first recorded singling out of therapist congruence as a crucial condition.) These qualities are pictured as providing 'an atmosphere of safety and psychological freedom' — leading to briefly enumerated therapeutic outcomes.

Thus, the 1957 paper was not new ground in substance for Rogers himself. Rather, it was a consummation in the formulation and declaration of a perspective in which, by then, he was feeling a great deal of personal confidence. The theory is advanced as a basic hypothesis regarding the essential change-producing factors in psychotherapy generally, not only in his own approach. These are presented firmly, clearly, and with the assurance of long thought and informal testing. The conditions advanced pivot on qualities of the therapist-client relationship, and include in addition one necessary feature of the client's state or quality of functioning. This feature is that he or she needs to enter therapy 'in a state of incongruence, being vulnerable or anxious' (Rogers, 1957, p. 96). Moving from incongruence to relative congruence was viewed by Rogers as being at the core of healing change in therapy.[2] Such change is implicit in the earlier research

---

1. The mimeographed copy I have is dated by the author as August, 1954, and is not included in Rogers' own listings of his publications. He may have written it as a working paper or for a seminar, and to share at least with his graduate students and other immediate colleagues.
2. This is implied in the 1957 paper and spelled out explicitly in Rogers' broader statement of theory (1959), already available pre-publication when the 1957 paper came out.

on therapy outcome (Rogers and Dymond, 1954) However, the casting of client incongruence and its expressions *as a prerequisite condition of therapy* did not become a focus of research — in contrast to the main relationship conditions.

The first-stated of Rogers' conditions was that the two persons 'are in psychological contact', implying that they are aware of one another and that the posited context for change is a relationship. Further conditions hinge on and imply this general condition and it was not singled out for research until much later when Prouty (as indicated in this volume) brought it into strong focus. Next in Rogers' mention was the client condition of incongruence, implying a mismatch between underlying experience in some vital region and the client's conscious awareness or outward behaviour.

Rogers' other four conditions are qualities of therapist response and client perception. The therapist needs (i) to be essentially congruent (authentic, genuine, integrated) in the relationship with the client; (ii) to 'be experiencing unconditional positive regard for the client', and (iii) to be 'experiencing an empathic understanding of the client's internal frame of reference'. The final, overarching condition is that aspects (ii) and (iii) need to be communicated or at least *perceived* by the client. (The same is true of aspect (i), in my understanding.) Rogers said 'communicated' in 1957 but soon thereafter stressed that the client's perception was the crucial factor. He also acknowledged that although the conditions are described as if they are all-or-none elements they can also be viewed as existing in varying degree over a wide range (Rogers, 1959). These amendments may reflect the fact that the first two studies to test the theory, in which the conditions were quantified and measured, were by then in progress. These studies, distinct in their methodology and treatment of theory, were by Halkides (1958) and myself.[3]

Focusing the propositions for empirical study

My study rearranged the main elements in Rogers' theory, and made some logical inferences beyond his formulation. I reasoned that the relationship *as experienced by the client* would be most crucially related to the outcome of therapy. The way that therapists 'actually' responded would be relevant to the way they were experienced, and thus have an indirect relation to outcome. 'In the hypothetical case of two clients with identical characteristics, the differential response of the therapists would be wholly responsible for the different perceptions of clients and, hence, for differences in therapy outcome' (Barrett-Lennard, 1962, p. 3). Thus I did not want to interpose outside judges (as Halkides did) but to develop some systematic way of tapping the relevant perceptions of client and also therapist participants. The spotlight would be on the therapist, as viewed by each partner.

Two amendments to Rogers' formulations seemed compelling to me. First, it would be the *client's experience* of the therapist's congruence that would be directly relevant, for the same reason that it would be their experience of the

---

3. Halkides' study remained unpublished, but reference to it can be found in some of Rogers' papers (1958, 1965), and in my previous book (1998, p. 282). She initiated the method of using observer-judges to rate the conditions variables from brief segments of recorded interviews.

therapist's empathic understanding and unconditional regard that would be crucial. Second, unconditional positive regard (UPR) struck me as a very awkward concept to view and treat as a single variable. I tried to frame statements reflecting UPR and they tended either to express the element of warmth, respect, liking, etc. *or else* to convey a quality of non-judgemental receptivity that was evenhanded in respect to the diversity of feelings and self-meanings expressed by clients. Both conceptual *and* measurement issues prompted a decision to separate UPR into two distinct variables named 'level of regard' and 'unconditionality'. I also added a further relationship variable called 'willingness to be known' but this was not supported by my research, and subsequently dropped as a separate measure. (Some of its substance was then absorbed into and enriched the congruence dimension.)

Having selected the variables to measure, and having elected to call on the client and therapist partners to provide the data for this measurement, just what kind of instrument seemed both fitting and feasible? I continued to generate possible items that could be answered or compared, one group of items for each variable. As I worked at devising simple statements to reflect differing facets and expressions of each variable, the concepts themselves sharpened further in my own mind. The whole process of original development of what became the Relationship Inventory is described more fully in other places (especially, Barrett-Lennard, 1962, 1986). Suffice it to say that I finally opted for a fairly straightforward multiple-choice questionnaire format, with about half the items framed with theoretically positive wording (a simple item in the other-to-self form is 'He/she respects me'), and half with negative wording (e.g. 'His/her response to me is usually so fixed and automatic that I don't really get through to him/her'). Respondents answer each item by choosing one *either* of three possible grades of 'Yes' (strong to muted) *or* one of three possible degrees of 'No'.

Five judges, provided with my definitions of each variable, had assisted me in finalising the selection of items for each scale (Barrett-Lennard, 1962, pp. 6–7). Every statement, however answered, was to contribute in a plus or minus direction to the score on one (only) of the component scales. The definitions, in summary, of the four variables that lasted, are as follows:

1. *Empathic understanding* was conceived, first of all, to be an active process of '*desiring* to know the full present and changing awareness of another person' and '*reaching out* to receive his communication and meaning'. Doing this involved an inner processing of the other person's expressions (verbal and non-verbal) into *experienced* meaning congruent with immediately significant features of the other's awareness (Barrett-Lennard, 1962, 1981, italics added). Further expressed, empathy in this perspective is a form of knowing, a caring but disciplined opening of self to the living feelings and meanings of the other. It is the other's distinct and separate consciousness that is reached and bridged, from the self of the therapist-partner, in moments of deep empathy. Even at points of strongest resonation, the empathizing partner retains background awareness that the feelings and flow of consciousness so immediately vivid are originating in and belong to the separate other person. At any moment, this awareness can rise to focal consciousness.

My view of empathic interaction as a multi-step process occurring in a distinct sequence originated in the seventies, and is also spelled out in later papers (Barrett-Lennard, 1981, 1993, 2001a). Viewed from this framework, it is evident that different measures of empathy tap into different phases of the total empathic process. The initial phase of empathic resonation and awareness occurs in the listener's consciousness. The RI form that draws on this consciousness is the '**m**yself-to-the-**o**ther' (or MO) one. An illustrative item is 'I usually sense or realise how he/she is feeling'. In the form that the *listened-to person* answers this item reads 'He/she usually senses or realises what I am feeling'. In this case the empathy scale taps the experience of being understood, or Phase 3 empathy.

2. In defining *level of regard,* concern for clear operational meaning is especially apparent. A's level of regard for B is conceived as the net balance of all the various qualities and strengths of A's personal feelings and attitudes (positive, negative and indifferent) experienced toward and in relation to B. Positive feelings include respect, caring, appreciation, affection, and others. Negative feelings include dislike, disapproval, expressed indifference, impatience, contempt, and the like. In systematic expression, level of regard was defined as the 'composite "loading" of all the distinguishable feeling reactions of one person toward another, positive and negative, on a single, abstract dimension' of which the lower extreme 'presents maximum predominance and intensity of negative-type feeling, not merely a lack of positive feeling' (Barrett-Lennard, 1962). It became clear to me later that the scale does not reach into the *most* negative zone of possible feelings (hatred, loathing, extreme fear and aversion, etc.) that can arise between persons. Nor, at the other extreme, does it reach into the sphere of strong romantic, filial, or spiritual love experience. Nevertheless, I have not encountered any scores right at the 'bottom' end of the theoretical range, and only rarely (even in close personal relationships) is the *most* positive rating given to *all* items for this scale.

3. The aspect of *unconditionality* implies that A's personal attitude or feeling toward B holds steady regardless of what B shows of his/her inner self and its experiencing. Expressed more exactly, A's attitude does not vary contingently, that is, according to the particular self-revelations, feeling reactions or other self-expressions of B. Conversely, conditionality implies that A's regard for B does vary according to the light that B shows him/herself in, or to differing qualities that s/he spontaneously expresses (Barrett-Lennard, 1986).

   B's own acceptance of self-attributes is prone to be selective in any event, in accordance with her/his conditions of worth. To the extent that A responds conditionally, in keeping with B's own 'self-conditionality', this would tend simply to reinforce the status quo in B's functioning. Alternatively, if A responds in a strongly conditional fashion along *new* lines, this may potentiate new conditions of worth in B (Barrett-Lennard, 1978). Scores that indicate perceived non-acceptance, or significant conditionality of relation, are not uncommon in personal relationships, much less common in the therapy relationships I have studied.

4. As earlier discussed, *congruence* refers theoretically to wholeness, integration, inner consistency. More exactly, it implies consistency between the three

levels of (i) a person's primary, pre-verbal or 'gut' experience, (ii) their inner symbolic consciousness, and (iii) their outward behaviour and communication. The concept is theoretically centred on consistency between the first two of these levels — primary experience and awareness — this being considered the main potentiating condition for congruence between awareness and communication. Thus, the concept refers, first of all, to 'all-of-one-piece' congruence within the person. Outer congruency and total communication of awareness are, however, not the same thing. The crucial feature of congruent communication is that is not at odds with the person's inner consciousness, this is in turn anchored in their primary experience. As I put it originally, 'the highly congruent individual is completely honest, direct, and sincere in what he conveys, but he does not feel any compulsion to communicate his perceptions, or any need to withhold them for emotionally self-protective reasons' (Barrett-Lennard, 1962, p. 4). As in the cases of other conditions, it is the client's *founded perception* of congruence-related qualities such as the therapist's genuineness, transparency, and honesty with her/himself and the client, that would be directly critical in therapy.

The Relationship Inventory itself: Structure and fidelity

The Relationship Inventory (RI) thus contains theoretically grounded groups of items, each group a sample of statements from a domain representing one of the four defined relational variables. (I prefer the designation 'relational' variables or qualities and think it was a consequential mistake for Rogers to refer to them broadly as (therapist) 'attitudes'.) In structure, the instrument is a multiple-choice questionnaire, the answer choices being a refinement of a 'yes-no' answer system. The respondent is asked to 'mark each statement . . . according to how strongly you feel that [yes] it is true, or [no, it is] not true, in this relationship'. The three affirmative answers range from 'YES, *I strongly feel that it is true*' (coded +3) down to '(Yes) *I feel that it is probably true, or more true than untrue*' (coded +1). On the No side the corresponding answers are 'NO, *I strongly feel that it is not true*' (–3) and '(No) *I feel that it is probably true, or more true than untrue*' (–1).

In the widely used 64-item RI, eight positively worded items and eight that are negatively worded represent each of the four scales, with the items for each scale dispersed throughout the instrument. The latter feature means that similar statements do not appear consecutively and runs of items that are all positively or all negatively expressed are avoided. The answer codes of +3 to –3 are treated as item scores, except for a sign reversal in the case of negatively worded items (since 'no' to a negatively worded item has the same direction of meaning as 'yes' to a positively worded statement). After the relevant sign reversals, scale scores (for empathic understanding, say) are obtained by summing ratings for the pertinent group of items. This also means that the answer to every item can increase *or* diminish a scale score, and the *possible* range of scores is –3n to +3n, where 'n' is the number of scale items (–48 to +48, with 16 items). To add more flesh to the bones of concept and approach, following are illustrative items drawn from each scale of the other-to-self (OS) form. They are identified as R (for Level of Regard scale), E (for Empathic Understanding), U (Unconditionality), or C

(Congruence). The added + or – shows whether a Yes answer counts positively or negatively toward the scale score (and the reverse for No answers). Respondents mentally insert the name of the other person, in the underline space in each item.

U– 11. Depending on my behaviour, _____ has a better (or worse) opinion of me sometimes than he/she has at other times.

C+ 12. I feel that _____ is real and genuine with me.

R– 17. _____ is indifferent to me.

E+ 18. _____ usually senses or realises what I am feeling.

E– 22. _____'s own attitude toward things I do or say gets in the way of understanding me.

E+ 30. _____ realises what I mean even when I have difficulty in saying it.

R– 33. _____ just tolerates me.

R+ 37. _____ is friendly and warm toward me.

U+ 39. How much _____ likes or dislikes me is not altered by anything that I tell him/her about myself.
[Alternate wording] No matter what I say about myself, _____ likes or dislikes me just the same.

C+ 44. _____ is willing to express whatever is actually in his/her mind with me, including feelings about either of us and how we get along.

U+ 51. Whether thoughts and feelings I express are 'good' or 'bad' makes no difference to _____'s feeling toward me.

C– 52. There are times when I feel that _____'s outward response to me is quite different from the way he/she feels underneath.

E– 58. _____'s response to me is usually so fixed and automatic that I don't get through to him/her.

R+ 61. _____ feels affection for me.

In a two-person relationship, there are potentially at least four participant views of one person's response to the other. In therapy research, two views have been in focus: the therapist's response (i) as perceived by the client — using the OS RI form — and (ii) as self-experienced by the therapist and tapped by the 'Myself-to-Other' (or MO) RI form. In symmetrical couple relationships, the views of self and other by *both* partners, and the multiple comparisons these generate — such as her response to him as he sees it and as she sees it herself; or his view of her response compared with her view of his — can provide pertinent data.[4] The MO form itself preserves the substance of each item, reworded in self-referent form. Exact equivalence of form would make for unnatural or improbable expression in the case of some items, and a good deal of thought (and some trial and error) went toward attaining equivalent substance. The following examples correspond to several like-numbered items in the list above:

12. I feel that I am genuinely myself with _____.
18. I usually sense or realise how _____ is feeling.
33. I put up with _____.

---

4. This combination of views not only has application in research, as early demonstrated in a study by Thornton (1960), but evidently can (in judicious and well-informed usage) yield helpfully evocative information for couples in a relationship enrichment programme context.

36. [Revised] I don't show my inner impressions and feelings, with _____ .
37. I feel friendly and warm toward _____ .
51. Whether _____ is expressing 'good' thoughts and feelings, or 'bad' ones, does not affect the way I feel toward him/her.

The two forms of the RI are identically scored. However, given the different positions and frames of reference of the participants in helping relationships, actual scores from the two sources are not expected to be the same, and they may not be highly correlated. (It would raise questions of the theory and/or validity of measures if there were zero correlation in a sample with a broad spread of scores.) The detailed rationale and procedure for scoring the RI are closely described in a previous, available report of mine (Barrett-Lennard, 1986) — which is recommended as a further resource for anyone using the Inventory. That report goes on to a close examination of issues and evidence relating to the reliability and validity of the instrument.

A reliable measure should yield very similar results on different occasions if what is being measured has not changed. In the case of a relationship, even one of long duration, it is hardly likely to hold completely steady, as experienced by participants. My own initial check of test-retest reliability employed a sample of students asked to describe a close personal relationship before and after a four-week interval. At retest, respondents were separately asked whether the relationship had changed. In the final sample of 36 pairs (omitting 'changed' cases) the test-retest correlations were all high: .84 to .90 on the present scales (1962, p. 12). Another kind of reliability check does not depend on retesting. This method studies internal coherence, for example, by forming two half-length scales, correlating the half-scale scores and adjusting for the reduced length. When this was done, using my original 'client' RI data, the corrected reliabilities (.82 to .93) were more than adequate. Using 'therapist' RI data, reliabilities were higher still (1962, Table 3).

The overall picture of reported evidence on the internal and test-retest reliability of RI scales, involving a range of investigators working in a variety of contexts, was presented by Gurman (1977). Fifteen respondent samples generated the data for internal reliability assessment, using split-half and alpha coefficient methods. Results from differing RI revisions, and from therapy and other relationship samples, are included. The means of resulting coefficients are: for regard .91, empathy .84, unconditionality .74, and congruence .88. The test-retest reliabilities listed (Gurman, 1977, Table 1) are based on ten samples, yielding coefficients ranging from .61 to .95. The means across samples ranged from .80 (for unconditionality) to .85 (for congruence), with retest intervals up to 12 months.

In my 1986 report, I comment on this substantial consistency, and conclude that: 'It can safely be said that, given sound administration/data-collection procedures, existence of a very adequate level of technical reliability of the primary forms of the RI is not in question' (1986, p. 458). Careful theoretical grounding and item-selection, and high obtained reliability, establish clear *potential* for valid measurement. One of my reports (1978) details item-analyses employed in checking and refining the choice and formulation of items for the main 64-item revision of the RI. In addition to careful checking of item behaviour in several samples, judges again helped to confirm and finalise the item selection, in a preliminary form of content validation (1978, p. 14; 1986, p. 458).

Another major area of validation comes from results consistent with theoretical expectation. Besides my own research, a considerable range of independent predictive studies concerned with association between the RI-assessed qualities and outcome, in help-intended situations, cumulate to provide substantial evidence of predictive construct validation. Gurman (1977, p. 523) concluded from his searching review of pertinent research that 'it is clear... that there exists substantial, if not overwhelming evidence in support of the hypothesized relationship between patient-perceived therapeutic conditions and outcome in individual psychotherapy and counselling' (italics removed). Most of this evidence entailed use of Client/OS forms of the RI. Gurman also noted that 'On the basis of the existing data deriving from properly conducted factor-analytic studies, it appears that the RI is tapping dimensions that are quite consistent with Barrett-Lennard's original work on the Inventory' (1977, p. 513, italics removed). Gurman's two conclusions, taken together, strongly imply that the RI, at least in the Client/OS forms, yields measurements in accord with its theoretically based intention.

There are also pertinent studies of non-therapy relationships, in which expected differences between groups on RI measures have been examined. Quick and Jacob (1973), for example, found that RI scale scores from perceptions of the husbands or the wives of the other's response, were significantly lower where either or both partners were seeking counselling than for couples not evidencing distress. Even when the influence of role conflict (assessed by another test) was partialed out, the RI differences between these groups held up. Wampler and Powell (1982) collated mean score data for each RI scale as reported by a number of investigators for samples of distressed and/or non-distressed couples. For three scales, the means without exception are much higher for the assorted, non-distressed groups. For unconditionality, the overall separation was strongly in the same direction but not consistent in all studies. These reports and other research with bearing on validation of the RI are reviewed in the fuller analysis of validity issues and evidence in my 1986 report (pp. 458–62).

In concluding that there is a wide range of evidence supporting the working validity of the RI, I do not mean to imply that it is a literally perfected instrument, that it should not be tested in new ways, or that it should not be altered in any circumstance. Clearly, by now, it should not be altered lightly. The only substantial alteration I have made (and relatively recently) to the general OS and MO forms is to produce the alternate 40-item form, initially for use in survey-type studies. The structure and rationale is identical, and the change essentially is to reduce the number of items from 16 to 10 in each scale — mainly by omitting some items, merging others, and (in two or three cases) reversing the positive/negative wording of the item. Experience and judgement more than fresh data contributed to the choice of items to 'sacrifice' or modify. Reliabilities could be a little lower, given the reduced item sample. However, I have not yet seen separate statistics for this 'short' version and, so far, I favour use of the 64-item forms where the length is not a problem. Several distinct adaptations of the main Inventory forms (40 or 64 items), for particular uses or populations, have been developed — as I

CONTACT AND PERCEPTION

will further mention.

The views that focus on one person at a time in a relationship do not exhaust potential uses of the RI, even in studying two-person relationships. Each partner can also look at their twosome as a whole (for example, 'We respect one another as persons', and 'We understand each other'). Also, an acquainted third person could provide their 'observer' view of A's response to B (e.g. 'He respects her') or of the twosome ('They respect each other'). Another possibility is to ask A to anticipate how B *will see* A's response, and to obtain B's actual perception of this response. I will come back to further discussion of these and other variations. In the meantime, a brief retelling of the story of research on the therapist to client relationship is a natural starting point.

Therapy relationship research with the RI

My original study pivots on predicting client change from the measures of relationship taken relatively early in therapy. Two kinds of therapist judgements made at the start and/or end of therapy provided one estimation of change. The judgements were used to divide the sample conservatively into a 'more changed' group (with the rating evidence all positive) and a 'less changed' cluster (where evidence was less positive or mixed). Relationship scores were significantly higher for the more changed group on all four of the present RI scales when assessed from the crucial client RI data.

A second index of change was derived from three correlated self-inventory measures: Dymond's 'Q-Adjustment' scale (1954), an anxiety measure (Taylor, 1953), and the MMPI Depression scale. It turned out, however, that the initially high scorers on this composite measure had little room to increase their scores, and change was negatively correlated with starting level. To overcome this effect with minimal bias, the median *initial* score was used to divide the sample, the lower scoring half being retained for a second test of association between relationship and change. Tau correlations in the reduced sample reached significance on all present RI measures from the client data. Using therapist RI data all associations were positive, although at low significance levels.

Another part of the analysis centred on a comparison both of relationship quality and of outcome for the clients of more expert and less expert therapists. The therapist groups were distinct in level of experience and in their routes to this experience (the more expert group had been reselected for internships and staff counselling or even faculty positions, in the laboratory Counseling Center Rogers headed). The groups also differed in age, the experts averaging seven years older. Their *clients* were matched and alike by groups in ways that included ratio of males to females (plus similarity in same-sex/opposite-sex pairings with therapists), age characteristics, educational level, and pre-therapy adjustment data (Barrett-Lennard, 1962, p. 21). In accord with prediction, *RI scores from the clients with more expert therapists* (N=12) *were higher than those with non-experts* (N=15) on the four RI scales, with low probability of this being a chance occurrence (ibid., Table 16). As well, *a bigger proportion of clients with the expert therapists group fell in the 'more changed' category* (ibid., p. 22).

Another, albeit indirect, indicator of client movement applicable to the whole sample was also at hand. Other research had found that length of therapy was a useful backup indicator of change (Standal and van der Veen, 1957; Cartwright, Robertson, Fiske and Kirtner, 1961). Since the client groups were equated in various ways, any large differences in duration of therapy could scarcely be a result of the longer-running cases taking more time to make the same gain. In fact, the cases with expert therapists ran on average for twice as long as the other group, a strongly significant difference.[5]

For the sample as a whole, therapist appraisals yielded the primary criterion of change. The fact that *client*-provided relationship information best predicted *therapist* evaluations of change rules out an artifact that might have been at work if therapists had been the source of both of these associated measures. Also, the fact that therapist expertise was jointly linked to relationship quality *and* client change implied that therapists were having an interrelated impact on both levels. The thrust of the results was supportive of the theory the study set out to test. Theories are not literally proven, at least in applied psychological research, but the pattern of supporting evidence was highly encouraging, and helped to spawn many further studies.

Further research in the last four decades includes about 150 studies I know of that have used the Relationship Inventory in therapy-related investigations. The majority of the very varied reports are listed in a resource bibliography of RI studies.[6] I have not attempted to review this whole span of research, but have worked to make this bibliography useful by preparing a few lines of information about each study referenced. (Many of the studies included are dissertation reports not accessible through professional journals.) Besides investigations involving actual client-therapist relationships, this 'pool' also includes numerous 'therapy analogue' studies, where the research design governed the scope of the interaction. The Wisconsin study of therapy with schizophrenic clients, for which the original RI was reduced to a 72-item four-scale version, is an early example.

Difficulties in implementing this ambitious study resulted in serious gaps in the data. Complete RI returns were gathered both early in therapy *and* at termination for eight cases only. Early-late correlations in this small sample were quite high (Rogers et al., 1967, p. 169) and similar to reliabilities attained with less distressed clients. The four RI scales correlated more highly with each other early in therapy (mean rho = .60) than at termination (mean rho =.23), possibly implying that clients were more discriminating at the later point. Not surprisingly, these very troubled respondents saw their therapists less positively than clients did in my original study. Their concerned and perhaps optimistic therapists, on the other hand, saw their own response in a considerably more positive light (ibid., p. 170). In the analyses overall, primary use was made of judge rating scales, including a scale of 'accurate empathy' (AE), tested against the RI and correlating positively with three of the RI scales (ibid., p. 173). These correlations have doubtful meaning, however, given the limited samples and later research evidence, such as that from Kurtz and Grummon's important study (1972). This

---

5. Results from a range of secondary hypotheses expanded the picture outlined here, in a coherent total pattern of evidence and implication (Barrett-Lennard, 1962).
6. Barrett-Lennard, G. T. (current). *Relationship Inventory Resource Bibliography*. Manuscript printout of approximately 51 pages and 400 reference items in ten groups, as of mid-2001.

used six 'empathy' scales (including AE), which clearly were not measuring the same thing. The only measure of the six found to significantly predict therapy outcome was the RI E scale from client data (ibid., Table 5).

There are numerous translations of the RI prepared, for example, by investigators working in Arabic, Dutch, French, German, Greek, Italian, Japanese, Korean, Polish, Portuguese, Slovak, Spanish and Swedish languages.[7] For the most part, these have been direct translations of the 64-item RI. Lietaer's work (1976) is one of the exceptions. He added items largely on 'directivity' and used factor-analysis in preparing a Dutch-language RI, then used (for example) to compare relationships in psychoanalytic (p-a) and client-centred (c-c) therapy. P-a therapists were seen by their clients as distinctly more directive and the c-c therapists as generally more transparent (a congruence-related factor). Leaving aside 'directivity', the corresponding scores of client and c-c therapist partners correlated at low but positive levels. Correlations in the p-a group were near-zero (mean r = .06) (Lietaer, 1979, Table 7). The associations are about what one would expect in the case of the c-c group, and suggest that the p-a therapists had trouble identifying their personal response to clients *or* were less communicative on this level. Such inference ties in with their clients tending to see them as less transparent. Both this and the Wisconsin study give occasion to mention that gathering sound RI data *from therapists* is probably even more dependent on confidence between researcher and 'subject', and on the care and integrity of steps involved, than gathering the RI data from clients.

The ambitious US National Institute of Mental Health Collaborative Research Program on treatment of depression included interpersonal therapy (IPT) and cognitive-behaviour therapy (CBT). Exhaustive analyses of the many-sided outcome data showed that clients improved under both of these therapy regimes, IPT having the advantage with more severely depressed patients (Elkin et al., 1989). The therapy relationship was assessed by the RI answered by clients after the second of 12 or more therapy sessions. Outcome differences were 'generally not predicted' by type of treatment but *were linked to quality of the therapist-to-patient relation* (Blatt et al., 1996, p. 169). Thus, the conclusion that it seems 'more productive to explore dimensions of the interpersonal relationship established between patient and therapist... that affect therapeutic change than to continue to look for differences among different types of therapeutic intervention' (ibid., p. 170).

A number of other studies have focused on aspects of therapist personality which were expected to have bearing on the way clients experience the relationship. As illustration, several investigators have looked at the influence of counsellor dogmatism. In the first such study, Cahoon (1962) found that in general the lower the dogmatism score (Rokeach scale) of the counsellor the better the relationship (Client RI). The same thrust of result was more distinct in a study by Valsi (1975). In research with a different twist, Osborne (1970/71) had student 'client' and trainee counsellor respondents answer the RI *before* and after a single interview, and *both* partners also responded to the Rokeach Dogmatism Scale.

---

7. Colleagues have also used the 64-item RI in American Sign Language and, probably, in Afrikaans, Croatian and Turkish languages. *I would be pleased to hear from any reader who can confirm these or further translations.*

The before-interview RIs tapped relationship *expectancies*. Generally, dogmatism was related to client relationship scores or client-therapist congruency, both in expectancy and post-interview data. Also, low dogmatic clients and counsellors both expressed more favourable expectations of relationship.

Tosi (1970) obtained pre-therapy dogmatism scores of practicum counsellors *and* their clients, in educational-vocational counselling, and used these to predict client RI total scores after an initial interview. It was found, for example, that the ratings of relationship were most positive 'when low-dogmatic counselors were paired with medium- and low-dogmatic clients' (ibid., p. 286). In the author's overall conclusion, client ratings of the relationship increased with greater openness in the dyad (ibid., p. 287). Taken together, these studies support the very plausible idea that counsellor dogmatism and helping relationship quality are inversely related. Such evidence would have stronger meaning, however, if obtained in a context of more developed therapy/helping relationships. The RI is designed not just to tap perceived interaction but *qualities of experienced relationship.* A single interview (only 15–20 minutes in some analogue studies) could scarcely provide distinct experience in a unique relationship over the full range tapped by the RI. Even a full first interview would not reliably suffice. In a minority of the further therapy studies in my bibliography the RI data were in fact gathered after three, four or more interviews.

Applications beyond individual therapy

Small-group relations and interpersonal change occurring through intensive groups is another region for fertile research use of the RI, either in its regular form or group/plural forms (e.g. 'They respect me'). The complexity and patterning of process in small groups includes as *one aspect* the focus on evolving two-person relations, which were of particular interest to Clark and colleagues in mid-1960s work with the RI. The unique idea of this work was that *the combination of giving and receiving substantial empathy* and the other measured conditions would be especially propitious for beneficial personal change. To get at this feature, each participant completed an OS RI on the response of each other member. The RI scores generated by person A, say, were ranked, and a 'mutually therapeutic relationship' (MTR) was said to exist when another member who fell in the upper half of these ranks also placed A in the 'upper half' position. This might not happen at all, or it could happen with several others. A significant association was found between an index of change in the way a member communicated about problems and his/her number of MTRs (Clark and Culbert, 1965: 191–2). This interesting finding, however, was only weakly supported in a similar second study (Clark et al., 1969, p. 68). Given the multi-level process and individuality of groups it would seem unlikely that the connection studied would be free of dependence on any other variable factors.

My 1998 book also reports pertinent results from mid-sixties Australian workshops focusing on experiential learning in small groups. As example, the 64-item MO form of the RI was answered just before and just after the initial workshop in the series, in reference to the 'last client' to enter a therapy/helping relationship with the respondent. The second time, the directions were to answer for the same relationship as it was before the workshop began. It was thought that participants would afterwards admit further data into their awareness and/or set different personal standards for themselves, and the RI measures were examined for decrease or increase. Congruence scores diminished for 26 of the 32 members, increasing for six only, a result with very low chance probability. Almost the same proportion also diminished on the unconditionality scale, and empathy scores tended to fall as well.

Further examination of these results, coupled with similar data from a second workshop, showed that in Workshop 1, the strong effect had resulted largely from 'Group X' (one of the two experiential working groups), and that in Workshop 2, results for the group with the same leader-facilitator as Group X were in the same direction. For example, on the C scale, scores decreased for 8/11 respondents. These and further data suggested that leadership *and* member composition were jointly contributing to the varying effect across workshops and groups. The RI was used in another way in Workshop 3. Intending members nominated a current client and/or other person in close contact. These 'observers' were called on before the workshop, and again a few weeks later, to complete the OS RI on the member's response to them, and mail their returns directly to the investigator. Workshop members also answered this form of the RI *for the way they expected their observer to perceive them*. They did this after arrival at the workshop, and again a few weeks later. The 'before and after' returns from 23 member-observer pairs revealed that responding members anticipated their observers' perceptions of them more accurately following the workshop than beforehand. Interested readers would find more detail on these results and the total study in my previous book (1998, pp. 294–8).

Marques-Teixeira and colleagues (1996) used the groups'-response-to-me form of the 64-item OS RI, in Portuguese, with the members of five kinds of small group: an actual therapy (psychodrama) group, a group of psychotherapy trainees, a religious group, a close friends group and a team of workers. After the groups were well-established, participants answered for the response of their group to them. Sophisticated data-analysis supported the conclusion that an integrated 'group effect' hinged on the existence and development of empathic communication, mediated in crucial part by a facilitator.

More than two decades earlier, Cary Cooper had conducted several small-group studies, making central use of the RI Congruence scale. An illustrative study examined two kinds of possible leader-member influence, one kind pivoting on member-to-leader identification and the other on inner search and integration. Group members and their trainer/facilitators, in 12 T-groups, participated. In a word, it was found that when the trainer is seen as attractive, participants identify with him and become more like him in attitude and behaviour; when the trainer is seen as self-congruent (RI C scale) participants change toward increased personal congruence (movement of self-concept toward self-ideal) (Cooper, 1969, p. 528).

Therapy and personal development groups have also been the context of most of the further studies (about 30) in my bibliography that report use of the RI in group research. There is much scope for additional research in the same orbit, and even more for the study of group relations in 'natural' life contexts that are so much part of our world as children and adults. Pertinent research on marriage/couple and family relations includes therapy studies but has given similar attention to the patterning of experience outside explicit helping contexts. The initial studies were student thesis research studies with me, on the heels of my own PhD. As instance, Thornton's work (1960) on marriage relationships, and Rosen's (1961) on parent-child relations are outlined in my 1998 book (pp. 307–8). Although he directly studied only one-to-one relations, Rosen surmised that a total 'child-mother-father' interactive effect was operating, and suggested the relevance of knowing how the *child* sees each parent responding to the other. Related possibilities would be to target the child's view of his/her parents' twosome, or, the way members experience their family as a whole — as in later work by Gomes (1981).

Gomes investigated relational systems in intact one-child (1C) and two-child (2C) middle-class Brazilian families, using forms of the RI arranged and translated for this study. Three levels of relationship were tapped: each family member's perception of the individual response to them of each other member; their experience of the ways *pairs* of others responded (parents jointly, and parent-child combinations in 2C families); and their perception of the relational quality and feeling in the family as a whole. The data fit the idea of relationships being more homogeneous in 1C families, and of the whole-family 'We' being more distinct from other relations in the larger 2C families (ibid., 1981, pp. 63–70). Family size was linked to another kind of difference: in 2C families the children experienced mothers as responding more positively than fathers, on all RI dimensions; *not so in the 1C families* where parents were experienced more equally. The data invite further research building on the theory of multiple levels of relation (Barrett-Lennard, 1984, pp. 238–40).

Another study I previously outlined (1998, p. 310) used a measure of 'interspousal empathy' adapted from the RI, viewed in relation to marital satisfaction — before and after therapy. A more ambitious work (Wampler and Sprenkle, 1980), using the whole RI, examined effects of the Minnesota Couple Communication Program. Effects were studied using the RI and a measure of 'open' versus 'closed' communication style — which was a focus of the learning program. Initial behavioural gains in two differently sequenced groups fell away by the follow-up point. However, the experienced quality of relationship rose and held (except in a control group), with significant pre- to follow-up differences on RI scales. Thus, change toward the more open behavioural *style* did not persist but enhanced relationships evidently did (ibid., p. 581). The crucial comparisons were made for those persons who stayed with the project for the whole 33 weeks, suggesting both motivation and time for relationship quality to develop.

Colleagues who have used the RI in therapy and other research represent varied theoretical and practice orientations, including a number with strongly behavioural or CBT leaning. Others have taken an eclectic stance, focusing on skills development and/or cognitive principles. Vansteenwegen's action research on outcomes in couple therapy is a case in point, that I wrote of earlier (1998, pp. 310–11) and will mention here briefly. The outcomes he centred on included change in qualities of the couples' relationships as measured by Lietaer's revision of the RI (Vansteenwegen, 1979). Greater overall shifts in experienced relationship occurred in the treated group than in a control sample. In perception of the other's response these differences were significant across all scales (ibid., Table 1). At a two-year follow-up point, the *direction* of all of these changes was sustained (Vansteenwegen, 1982, Table 2).

The relation of teachers to students is another vital sphere of interpersonal life, and a fertile area for research use of the RI. This work began with a study by Emmerling (1961), who used a somewhat simplified adaptation of the original RI with a large sample of high-school students down to the ninth grade. The students' 20 teachers had been preselected as 'more open' or 'less open' in style, and the hypothesis that more open teachers would receive higher scores than the less open group was supported for each RI scale. The dovetailing of this and other evidence suggested that the relational qualities had bearing on teacher effectiveness. The study broke new ground in its focus and method, and probably more new questions than clear-cut answers were generated. This and a handful of other studies are outlined in my 1998 book (pp. 313–14). Limitations in quality and scope of the work with the RI reported in this area, so far, mean that the field remains wide open for further careful and inventive inquiry. To this end, up-to-date 40-item versions are available of 'student' and 'teacher' forms of the RI, designed for high-school-age children. A simpler OS Child form is also 'ready and waiting' for use in studying teacher-student and other formative relationships in the world of children.

The study of (potentially enabling) supervisory relationships, especially in education and therapy training, is another significant area of application of the RI. Cline's inquiry into the 'confirming behaviour of school executives' (1970) is an interesting example. About 700 teachers completed the OS RI on their principal's response. The principals answered the same Inventory for the way they *expected* their staff to perceive them, and also responded to the California Psychological Inventory. From CPI results, respondents and their schools were grouped in quartiles. The top quartile (Q_1) were headed by the best-functioning principals, the least well-functioning (on these data) fell in Q_4. Comparisons from the teacher RI data revealed a significantly lower average level for Q_4 principals on *unconditionality* (ibid., p. 32), seen by Cline as a key element in confirming behaviour. Prediction by Q_4 principals of how teachers experienced them were generally of lower accuracy than predictions of the Q_1 group. Cline pictured the school as a self-balancing field system and considered that his evidence overall supported 'the idea that each school faculty represents a nuclear unit with perhaps a reflected personality of its own' (ibid., p. 30).

In a later illustration, 362 teachers also answered the OS RI on their school principal, and described the organizational climate of their school on a multi-factor questionnaire instrument (Jaeger, 1989, pp. 221–3). In this case, RI Regard vied with RI Total Score as significant predictors of factors such as intellectual climate, achievement standards, and organizational effectiveness (ibid., pp. 171–85). Jaeger broadly concludes that the relationship attitudes of principals directly relate to more positive or negative school climate, and that RI-measured qualities in the teacher-principal relation affect achievement aspirations of the school. Spence (1989) chose to focus on supervision of teachers in the actual teaching process. Supervision was defined in dual terms, helping relationship dimensions and task steps, and participant satisfaction with supervision was studied in relation to these two features. For teachers, satisfaction hinged mainly on the quality of relationship response, while for supervisors it was both relationship and task achievement.

There are *many* issues in supervision that research might help to illuminate. For example, peer interchange can be a vital element in learnings through group supervision. Byrne (1983) explored reciprocal peer supervision in a practically oriented study of therapy training. Six graduate students were taped during three individual sessions with their faculty supervisor and three with their peer partner, these sessions then content analysed. The nature and categories of supervisee talk were closely explored, with 'client focus' and 'self-focus' emerging as primary categories. More 'teaching' from faculty, and more support from peers, were both expected and received. Scores on the OS-64 RI scales were 'in the positive range for both faculty and peer supervisors, with peers scoring higher on all dimensions' (1983, abstract). The results supported the use of peer supervision as a complement to working with experienced faculty.

One-to-one personal friendship relations are understudied — generally, and in terms of research that has made use of the RI. An investigator who has pursued significant work in this area is Duncan Cramer. The relation of self-esteem and the facilitative quality of friendships (measured by the RI, in regular or shortened form) has been a main axis of this work. Having established such a link in his initial studies (1985, 1987, 1989, 1990), Cramer went on to employ sophisticated statistical procedures to pin down the presumed causal influence of relationship quality on self-esteem. The most recent report I have seen of this work (Cramer, 1994) uses relationship and self-esteem data gathered twice, with a 15-week interval. In this and a previous study, unconditionality stood out in predictively affecting self-esteem (ibid., p. 332, Table 2).[8]

Studies where respondents describe a whole spectrum of life relationships or report their experience of an interpersonal milieu, is another understudied area, although it does include a few early examples of interesting work. In a study by Gross et al. (1970), patients who were near discharge after over 60 days in their hospital ward answered the RI in reference to the treatment staff generally (for example, 'How much staff members like or dislike me is not affected by anything that I think or feel'). Again, the U measure gave distinctive results. Staff members (in reference to the patients as a group) saw their response more positively than the patients did, on this scale especially; and vector analysis of patient returns showed the unconditionality dimensionally quite distinct from the other variables (ibid., pp. 543–4). Another study (Wargo and Meek, 1970/1971) examined the perceived response of the total milieu, by the client participants in a residential rehabilitation program. They answered an OS RI, worded even more broadly (item 1: 'People here respect me as a person').[9]

I conceived the idea, in the mid-seventies, of an even wider, basically redesigned form of the RI that would tap relationship quality over the whole

---

8. My previous book also provides a fuller summary of Cramer's work (1998, pp. 315–16).
9. Gilmour-Barrett (1973) used a group MO form of the RI (e.g. 'I respect them as persons') answered by child-care workers in reference to the children in their care, in residential treatment centres. Management qualities and structural-program arrangements were studied in relation to worker RI scores, with discovery of links that again highlighted the unconditionality dimension.

spectrum of the respondent's experienced interpersonal world. Specifically, a profile of measures from up to 10 or 11 experienced relationships across the person's family, friendship and vocational life would be obtained. The new form (then 42 items, now 40) was initially tested in a validity study by Holland (1976), on a sample of upper high school and university students. Reliability estimates were adequate or better for each RI scale. From *separate data*, it was evident that some subjects lived in a much more connected and supportive family/friendship environment than others did, and they were sorted into three criterion groups. Average RI scores were all higher for the top support group than the bottom one (ibid., Table 7). Higher overall RI scores were also found, as expected, for family and friendship relations than for vocational relationships.

While preparing the new form, I shared my draft work with another investigator, who proceeded with his own related study (Sundaram, 1977), using a working adaptation of only 24 items. Forty-nine young, first-year tertiary college students, men and women, rated the response of individual family members, friends, teachers, and additional significant others, for a total of *up to* 20 relationships. This was done twice, with an interval of five months. Sundaram was interested, much as Cramer was later, in the bearing of facilitativeness of life relationships on personal well-being. He deduced adjustment levels from another instrument, and hypothesised that the general quality of relationships would correlate with *change* in adjustment from test to retest (verified, 1977, pp. 34–9). Careful (step-wise multiple regression and path) analyses were used in an effort to establish causality, with a model of reciprocal causal interaction between relationship and adjustment being the best fit to the data (ibid., pp. 49–52).

I was not able at the time to follow these studies up but my new form received occasional use by other investigators, notably including Townsend (1988). She used *total score means across all relationships* as an index of experienced facilitative environment. This correlated strongly with measures of loneliness and of interpersonal self-efficacy (ibid., Table 4). Further results suggested that actual self-disclosure with partners was a function partly of overall experienced facilitation (pp. 47 ff.). Much more recently, after revision of the instrument and a further student-run validity study, added refinements were made and Form OS-S-40 is waiting for new uses — an issue I will come back to.

This chapter has grown long and I cannot here enumerate specific further examples of research already conducted, except to mention one other area in passing. A number of studies of nurse-patient relationships and communication have made research use of the RI. This work has mostly singled out nurse empathy, as experienced by patients, as the interpersonal quality of primary interest, and several studies are listed in my 1998 book (p. 319). As implied earlier, in the context of nurse-patient or any other relationships there needs to have been appreciable direct contact and opportunity for communication if the results are to be regarded as based on experience in the particular relationship and having distinctive reference to it. Despite the long and wide-ranging usage of the RI there is potential both for new kinds of application and careful studies in familiar areas.

Looking toward new paths of investigation

There appears to be a dearth of very recent or new usage of the Relationship Inventory in psychotherapy research, specifically, despite the fact that the underlying theory calls for continued investigation and refinement. One suggested focus, which no study appears to have pursued so far, would be to obtain baseline measures of client-experienced interpersonal life quality outside therapy (using RI Form OS-S-40) and to look at the client's view of the therapist's response (regular OS form) in light of this larger context. Such data would make possible a new kind of test of conditions theory: if experienced empathic understanding and the other RI-measured qualities have a central role in enabling change, their experienced presence in the client-therapist relationship surely must be at a qualitatively different level or concentration than in other current relationships in the client's life. If this were not so in instances of successful therapy, then their interaction or *combination with other factors* might well be decisive. Related is the question of whether, over the course of a productive therapy experience, relations with significant others become experienced as generally more positive. And if life relations do improve, has the 'gap' narrowed between the therapy and other relationships, and, does this narrowing (if found) have any causative relation to voluntary termination of therapy?

Depression, anxiety and other manifestations of personal-emotional stress and conflict can play havoc with a person's effective capacity for empathic contact with others, this tending to increase emotional isolation in a potentially self-reinforcing pattern. The way clients relate to their underlying experience (perhaps a self-empathic process) and their connection with the inner experience of other persons, both fall in the domain of empathy. I have explored these twin aspects and their interconnection elsewhere (Barrett-Lennard, 1997), and see a number of possibilities for research. For example, does empathic attunement become a more significant priority and source of meaning to clients, through therapy? And, does the individual's empathic sensitivity, as experienced by significant others, increase over therapy? On the second issue, clients might, for example, be asked to nominate individuals toward whom they feel some understanding. These 'understood' persons would then be called on to describe the client's response to them in empathy-relevant ways, both before and after therapy, to test for change. As an added feature, if the client's own view of his/her understanding of these persons was also obtained, client empathy seen from the outside and inside vantage points should be more congruent afterwards than before (presuming therapy had been effective in helping the client become more open to experience). The RI would be a resource in work to test such hypotheses.

As implied earlier, an experimental form of the Inventory, available for some time but used rarely, is designed to study relationships *viewed as a whole* by the participants (for example, 'We feel at ease together', 'I feel that we put on a role or act with one another', 'We like and enjoy one another', and 'We each want the other to be a particular kind of person'). I call this version Form DW–64 (Dyad-We, 64 items). It is thought that the instrument in this form would be especially suited to investigation of couple relationships, but applicable also to other family and friendship relations. The quality of the experienced *We*, via the RI, might be quite similar for the two participants or rather divergent. This similarity/difference viewed in conjunction with the score levels, would help to reveal the health and fruition of the relationship itself, and could be useful in counselling as well as opening distinctive paths of research.

Another potential usage of the RI is to call forth the respondent's view of an *ideal or desired relationship* — with a therapist, a partner, a child (by a parent, or parent by a child), a teacher, a close-knit community or group (by a member), or in another category of relationship. The theory implies that the more the better: the more positive the experienced relationship on each RI variable the more facilitating (or healing) and growthful in quality it is. But this would not be the view of therapists of all persuasions; and one would not expect it to be consistently the case among other categories of relationship. The nature of personal ideals on the unconditionality of regard dimension may be particularly variable. Personal congruence in respect, for example, to the transparency component, is not likely to be equally valued in all therapies. The RI would be applicable in comparative studies of therapy systems, not only to assess experienced therapist-to-client relationships (as in the NIMH research, for example) but to advance knowledge of the ways that process *goals* of therapists within and between alternative approaches actually vary. These and other suggested lines of study begin to illustrate a bounty of possibilities for fresh research with the RI — limited only by the thoughtful inventiveness of interested investigators.

Later thought on the helping conditions

I have touched on later developments in my thought concerning the nature and processes of empathy. Broader discussions than my own include the excellent first and last chapters, by the editors, in the volume *Empathy Reconsidered* (Bohart and Greenberg, 1997). Development of the RI took into account a number of distinct facets of empathic response. As I would restate them now, these include desiring to know *the other's* perspective and becoming absorbed in connecting with their experienced world; moving close in experiential recognition and understanding without being overtaken by triggered *self*-experience that clouds the listener's perception of what is originating and living in the other; sensing below the surface of indirect or fumbling expression to reach the other's felt meaning, and thus also responding freshly to the distinctive experience of the other *now*; and not falling into sympathetic reassurance but acknowledging the living feeling of the other, including their hurt, confusion, or felt despair when present; and, responding not only to limited parts of the other's meaning but, somehow, to the whole sum or core of it. The RI items still seem to me to tap into these facets and thus connect with most of the domain of my present concept of empathic understanding (Barrett-Lennard, 2001a).

RI-measured level and unconditionality of regard have emerged as quite distinct, only lightly correlated variables in virtually every study reporting their correlation. This evidence, my own later thought, and the uphill difficulty others have faced in addressing the concept of unconditional positive regard, affirm to me that breakdown of the construct was needed conceptually and is supported empirically. The notion of conditional regard is itself a fairly straightforward idea.

Unconditionality has an opposite meaning. It implies that the responding person's attitude is *not* contingent on the listened-to person expressing one voice or aspect of self rather than another. The experiencing self of the other is not a focus of selective or 'only-if' regard, is neither strongly praised nor condemned for its particular feeling or attitude or consciousness at any given time. By itself, unconditionality implies neither a high nor a low level of *positive regard* — either in theory or as seen in research. High unconditionality with low positive regard could be perceived as indifference or even as a generalised (non-selective) rejection of the other but would not, theoretically, produce or nurture *inner* division and conflict. To contribute to a healing, or a freeing and integratively growthful process, unconditionality would in theory need to be coupled with at least a moderate ambience of positive regard.

Contemporary exploration of unconditionality and UPR includes contributions by Lietaer (1984), Wilkins (2000), Bozarth (1998) and Purton (1998).[10] Lietaer emphasises the centrality, for unconditional regard, of true openness and receptivity on the therapist's part. He implies that, far from being passively non-judgemental, the unconditionally responsive therapist is very actively engaged with the other. Expressed personally, it 'means *that I keep on valuing the deeper core of the person*' (1984, p. 47). In other words, 'it has nothing to do with indifference but rather points to a deep involvement with and belief in the other' (p. 48). Lietaer sees this active quality expressed in the therapist especially honing in on the other's immediately *felt* experience and inner frame of reference or *personal* meaning and, in this sense, having a certain directional influence. The paradox is not resolved but appears accentuated in passages under the heading of 'confrontation and unconditionality' (pp. 54–7). All this was too much for Bozarth (1998) who, while clearly respecting his colleague's scholarly acumen and raising of issues, felt that his view of the therapist as an active, expert and at times guiding agent implies abandonment of the notion that unconditional positive regard is the basic curative factor in client-centred theory. This encounter of ideas, and the overlapping but also quite distinctive explorations by Wilkins and by Purton, imply that the conception and its implications remain live foci of debate and refinement.

Rogers' emphases both on therapist congruence and unconditional acceptance, especially when the former is interpreted simply as being genuinely oneself and the latter as being impartially receptive to the point of conveying no value direction, makes for a certain tension among principles. Congruence by itself is a challenging, interesting construct, which I once explored in an informal piece 'Notes on congruence' (1972). One issue that struck me flows from the inherent complexity of the human organism. The more adaptive and less preprogrammed an organism is, the more potential there is for incongruence. Learned patterns can be at odds with those that are more inherent, and with each other. Features of personality and behaviour can develop in ways that are not in harmony. Risk of incongruence is part of the price we humans pay for complexity, for the diversity within our make-up, for our intricate and highly

---

10. Up-to-date and illustrative teaching/learning presentations focusing on unconditional positive regard include Chapter 4 in Mearns' and Thorne's popular text (1999).

differentiated perceiving, feeling, wanting, thinking consciousness. More highly programmed organisms, 'lower' on the evolutionary scale, would have less potential for incongruence.

'Just why', I also asked in my Notes, 'is a high level of therapist congruence evidently beneficial in therapy, and in personal relationships more broadly?' There is a relatively clear answer, at least in theory, in the case of unconditionality of regard and its function in undoing acquired conditions of worth. For congruence, my working answer follows:

- Congruence facilitates trust, self-expression, self- and interpersonal exploration, perhaps in that order. The therapist's trust in disclosing immediate features of his/her responding experience with the client, and sharing his/her real self in this sense, probably helps the client to trust in turn.
- Listener congruence makes possible an openness to the full range of the other's felt expressions and meaning. It is thus a foundation for empathic understanding, and can enable active, non-judgemental response toward the sharing, exploring self of the other person.
- Positive congruency 'models' a quality of responsive openness and unguarded whole presence that may invite the trying out of response in kind, especially by a person tense and unhappy with inner constraints and controls on expression.
- Pluralistic contemporary societies may be more dissociative than earlier cultures. Highly diverse views regarding the nature of the good life, coupled with less rootedness, may work to increase guardedness and incongruence; but also give some individuals more opportunity to be responsive to their own nature (with increased congruence).
- Of course, it is possible too that our faith in the importance of congruence as reflected, say, in self-expressiveness, immediacy and openness, adds to the difference that it makes as a therapeutic condition. Confidence itself can be infectious and, in the current milieu of thought, therapist confidence and congruence may well be correlated.

In recent years several colleagues, among them Lietaer (1993) and Bozarth (1998), have published thoughtful exploratory restatements of the meaning and 'faces' of congruence, and a whole book is just out on this topic (Wyatt, 2001). Later thought has not basically altered the concept itself, although I now think of it (even) less as a personality trait and (even) more in interactive terms. My current work on the natural pluralism of self (2001b) speaks by implication to the situational variability of congruence. It implies in particular that the congruency of a person's functioning depends partly on the relational context in which the self is manifest. Research has not yet directly addressed this issue but what evidence there is from RI studies accords with the expectation that both perceived and self-experienced congruence tends to vary from one relation to another; relations that differ, for example, in implicitly felt personal-emotional safety.

Developments in theory have, for practical purposes, not much changed the interior meaning and substance of constructs that the Relationship Inventory was developed to measure. Theory and practice possibilities are, however, evolving beyond this framework. Certainly this is true in my own thought and work, for example, as further advanced in my 'extended theory of change' (Barrett-Lennard, 2002). There I propose that realisation of helping relations broadly in the Rogerian tradition depends in turn on supporting conditions in the societal and organisational frameworks that make such therapy possible and desired. Further, if the scope of our practice is expanded to new levels such as I go on to envision, it will be evident that added principles reaching beyond classical conditions theory are needed. The RI, with its track record, remains a resource not only in the familiar contexts and new applications sketched in this chapter but in ways remaining for invention in the even wider reaches unfolding.

REFERENCES

Barrett-Lennard, G. T. (1962). Dimensions of therapist response as causal factors in therapeutic change. *Psychological Monographs, 76* (43, Whole No. 562).

Barrett-Lennard, G. T. (1972). *Notes on congruence*. Privately circulated manuscript, based on a presentation to the Society for Psychotherapy Research.

Barrett-Lennard, G. T. (1978). The Relationship Inventory: later development and adaptations. JSAS *Catalog of Selected Documents in Psychology, 8,* 68. (MS 1732).

Barrett-Lennard, G. T. (1981). The empathy cycle: refinement of a nuclear concept. *Journal of Counseling Psychology, 28,* 91–100.

Barrett-Lennard, G. T. (1984). The world of family relationships: a person-centered systems view. In R. F. Levant and J. M. Shlien (Eds.), *Client-centered therapy and the person-centered approach: New directions in theory, research and practice* (pp. 222–42). New York: Praeger.

Barrett-Lennard, G. T. (1986). The Relationship Inventory now: issues and advances in theory, method and use. In L. S. Greenberg and W. M. Pinsof (Eds.), *The psychotherapeutic process: A research handbook* (pp. 439–76). New York: Guilford Press.

Barrett-Lennard, G. T. (1993). The phases and focus of empathy. *British Journal of Medical Psychology, 66,* 3–14.

Barrett-Lennard, G. T. (1997). The recovery of empathy — toward others and self. In A. C. Bohart and L. S. Greenberg (Eds.), *Empathy reconsidered: New directions in psychotherapy* (pp. 103–21). Washington, DC: American Psychological Association.

Barrett-Lennard, G. T. (1998). *Carl Rogers' helping system: Journey and substance.* London and Thousand Oaks: Sage.

Barrett-Lennard, G. T. (2001a). Unfolding the meaning and processes of empathy. In *The healing of relationship* (Chapter 4). Book manuscript, in preparation.

Barrett-Lennard, G. T. (2001b). Selves in relationship: Warp and weft. In *The healing of relationship* (Chapter 7). Book manuscript, in preparation.

Barrett-Lennard, G. T. (2002). Contextualising Rogers' helping principles: Toward an extended theory of change. Manuscript submitted for publication.

Blatt, S. J., Quinlan, D. M., Zuroff, D. C. and Pilkonis, P. A. (1996). Interpersonal factors in brief treatment of depression: further analyses of the NIMH Treatment of Depression Collaborative Research Program. *Journal of Consulting and Clinical Psychology, 64,* 162–71.

Bohart, A. C. and Greenberg, L. S. (Eds.) (1997). *Empathy reconsidered: New directions in psychotherapy.* Washington, DC: American Psychological Association.

Bozarth, J. (1998). *Person-Centered Therapy: A revolutionary paradigm.* Ross-on-Wye: PCCS Books. (Chapter 4: Unconditional positive regard.)

Buresch, M. C. (1980). Sensitivity training as a method of increasing the therapeutic effectiveness of group members. *Dissertation Abstracts International, 40,* 3383B–3384B.

Byrne, B. (1983). Trainee uses of reciprocal peer supervision and of faculty supervision in psychotherapy training. *Dissertation Abstracts International, 44,* 111A.

Cahoon, R. A. (1962). *Some counselor attitudes and characteristics related to the counseling relationship* (Doctoral dissertation, Ohio State University). University Microfilms #63-2480.

Ganley, R. M. (1989). The Barrett-Lennard Relationship Inventory (BLRI): current and potential uses with family systems. *Family Process, 28,* 107–15.

Cartwright, D. S., Robertson, R. J., Fiske, D. W. and Kirtner, W. L. (1961). Length of therapy in relation to outcome and change in personal integration. *Journal of Consulting Psychology, 25,* 84–8.

Clark, J. V. and Culbert, S. A. (1965). Mutually therapeutic perception and self-awareness in a T group. *Journal of Applied Behavioral Science, 1,* 180–94.

Clark, J. V., Culbert, S. A. and Bobele, H. K. (1969). Mutually therapeutic perception and self-awareness under variable conditions. *Journal of Applied Behavioral Science, 5,* 65–72.

Cline, E. W. (1970). Confirming behaviour of school executives. *Dissertation Abstracts, 31,* 1067A.

Cooper, C. L. (1969). The influence of the trainer on participant change in T-groups. *Human Relations, 22,* 515–30.

Cramer, D. (1985). Psychological adjustment and the facilitative nature of close personal relationships. *British Journal of Medical Psychology, 58,* 165–8.

Cramer, D. (1987). Self-esteem, advice-giving, and the facilitative nature of close personal relationships. *Person-Centered Review, 2,* 99–110.

Cramer, D. (1989). Self-esteem and the facilitativeness of parents and close friends. *Person-Centered Review, 4,* 61–76.

Cramer, D. (1990). Disclosure of personal problems, self-esteem, and the facilitativeness of friends and lovers. *British Journal of Guidance and Counselling, 18,* 186–96.

Cramer, D. (1994). Self-esteem and Rogers' core conditions in close friends: a latent variable path analysis of panel data. *Counselling Psychology Quarterly, 7,* 327–37.

Dymond, R. S. (1954). Adjustment changes over therapy from self-sorts. In C. R. Rogers and R. F. Dymond (Eds.), *Psychotherapy and personality change* (pp. 76–84). Chicago: University of Chicago Press.

Elkin, I., Shea, M. T., Watkins, J. T., Imber, S. D., Sotsky, S. M., Collins, J. F., Glass, D. R., Pilkonis, P. A., Leber, W. R., Docherty, J. P., Fiester, S. J. and Parloff, M. B. (1989). National Institute of Mental Health treatment of depression collaborative research program: general effectiveness of treatments. *Archives of General Psychiatry, 46,* 971–82.

Emmerling, F. C. (1961). A study of the relationship between personality characteristics of classroom teachers and pupil perceptions of these teachers. *Dissertation Abstracts, 22,* 1054–5.

Gilmour-Barrett, K. C. (1973). Managerial systems and interpersonal treatment processes in residential centres for disturbed youth. Unpublished doctoral dissertation (in psychology), University of Waterloo, Ontario.

Gomes, W. B. (1981). The communicational-relational system in two forms of family group composition. Unpublished Master's thesis, Southern Illinois University.

Gross, W. F., Curtin, M. E. and Moore, K. B. (1970). Appraisal of a milieu therapy environment by treatment team and patients. *Journal of Clinical Psychology, 26,* 541–5.

Gurman, A. S. (1977). The patient's perception of the therapeutic relationship. In A. S. Gurman and A. M. Razin (Eds.), *Effective psychotherapy: A handbook of research* (pp. 503–43). Oxford: Pergamon.

Halkides, G. (1958). An experimental study of four conditions necessary for therapeutic change. Unpublished doctoral dissertation, University of Chicago.

Holland, D. A. (1976). The Relationship Inventory — Experimental Form OS-S-42: a validity study. Unpublished honours BA thesis (psychology), University of Waterloo, Ontario.

Jaeger, T. K. (1989). Principal/teacher interpersonal relations and school climate. *Dissertation Abstracts International, 49,* 3571A.

Kurtz, R. R. and Grummon, D. L. (1972). Different approaches to the measurement of therapist empathy and their relationship to therapy outcomes. *Journal of Consulting and Clinical Psychology, 37,* 106–15.

Lietaer, G. (1976). Nederlandstalige revisie van Barrett-Lennard's Relationship Inventory voor individueel-terapeutische relaties. *Psychologica Belgica, 16* (1), 73–94.

Lietaer, G. (1979). De beleving van de relatie door client en therapeut in client-centered en psychoanalytisch georienteerde therapie. Een empirische bijdrage. *Tijdschrift voor Psychotherapie, 5,* 141–60.

Lietaer, G. (1984). Unconditional positive regard: A controversial basic attitude in client-centered therapy. In R. F. Levant and J. M. Shlien (Eds.), *Client-centered Therapy and the Person-centered Approach: New directions in theory, research and practice* (pp. 41–58). New York: Praeger.

Lietaer, G. (1993). Authenticity, congruence and transparency. In D. Brazier (Ed.), *Beyond Carl Rogers* (17–46). London: Constable.

Marques-Teixeira, J., Pires de Carvalho, M. M., Moreira, A. M. and Pinho, C. (1996). 'Group effect?' Implementation of the Portuguese translation of the Barrett-Lennard Inventory on five group types. In R. Hutterer, G. Pawlowsky, P. F. Schmid and R. Stipsits (Eds.), *Client-centered and experiential psychotherapy: A paradigm in motion* (pp. 585–98). Frankfurt am Main: Peter Lang.

Mearns, D. and Thorne, B. (1999). *Person-centred counselling in action* (Second Edition). London: Sage.

Mowrer, O. H. (Ed.) (1953). *Psychotherapy: Theory and research.* New York: Ronald.

Osborne, W. L. (1970/71). The relation of dogmatism to dyadic counseling relationship congruency. *Dissertation Abstracts International, 31,* 3882A. (University Microfilms No. 71-3941.)

Purton, C. (1998). Unconditional positive regard and its spiritual implications. In Thorne, B. and Lambers, E. (Eds.), *Person-centred therapy: A European perspective* (pp. 23–37). London: Sage.

Quick, E. and Jacob, T. (1973). Marital disturbance in relation to role theory and relationship theory. *Journal of Abnormal Psychology, 82,* 309–16.

Rogers, C. R. (1946). Significant aspects of client-centered therapy. *American Psychologist, 1,* 415–22.

Rogers, C. R. (1953). Some directions and end points in therapy. In O. H. Mowrer (Ed.), *Psychotherapy: Theory and research* (pp. 44–68). New York: Ronald.

Rogers, C. R. (1954). Some basic hypotheses of client-centered therapy. Mimeographed, privately circulated article.

Rogers, C. R. (1957). The necessary and sufficient conditions of therapeutic personality change, *Journal of Consulting Psychology, 21,* 95–103.

Rogers, C. R. (1958). The characteristics of a helping relationship. *Personnel and Guidance Journal, 37,* 6–16.

Rogers, C. R. (1959). A theory of therapy, personality, and interpersonal relationships as developed in the client-centered framework. In S. Koch (Ed.), *Psychology: A study of a science,* Vol. 3: *Formulations of the person and the social context* (pp. 184–256). New York: McGraw-Hill.

Rogers, C. R. (1965). The therapeutic relationship: recent theory and research. *Australian Journal of Psychology, 17,* 95–108.

Rogers, C. R. and Dymond, R. F. (Eds.) (1954). *Psychotherapy and personality change.* Chicago: University of Chicago Press.

Rogers, C. R., with Gendlin, E. T., Kiesler, T. J. and Truax, C. B. (Eds.), (1967). *The therapeutic relationship and its impact: A study of psychotherapy with schizophrenics.* Madison: University of Wisconsin Press.

Rosen, H. H. (1961). Dimensions of the perceived parent-relationship as related to juvenile delinquency. Unpublished Master's thesis, Auburn University, Alabama.

Spence, S. A. (1989). The presence of and relationships between helping elements and task steps in post-observation supervisory conferences. *Dissertation Abstracts International, 49,* 2887–2888A.

Standal, S. W. and van der Veen, F. (1957). Length of therapy in relation to counselor estimates of personal integration and other case variables. *Journal of Consulting Psychology, 21,* 1–9.

Sundaram, D. K. (1977). Psychological adjustment as a function of interpersonal relationships: a field study. *Dissertation Abstracts International, 37,* 5380–5381B.

Taylor, J. A. (1953). A personality scale of manifest anxiety. *Journal of Abnormal and Social Psychology, 48,* 285–90.

Thornton, B. M. (1960). Dimensions of perceived relationship as related to marital adjustment. Unpublished Master's thesis, Auburn University, Alabama.

Tosi, D. J. (1970). Dogmatism within the counselor-client dyad. *Journal of Counseling*

Psychology. 17, 284–8.
Townsend, M. E. (1988). Self-disclosure and psychological adjustment: Towards an understanding. Unpublished honours bachelor thesis (psychology), Monash University, Melbourne.
Valsi, A. (1975). The influence of selected personality dimensions on counselling effectiveness. *Dissertation Abstracts International, 35*, 4173A. (University Microfilms No. 74-29,877.)
Vansteenwegen, A. (1979). Residentiële partnerrelatie-therapie: Een evaluatie-onderzoek. *Tijdschrift voor Psychiatrie, 21*, 426–40. (As 'Residential couple-therapy: a controlled outcome study', presented to the Society for Psychotherapy Research meeting in Oxford, England, 1979.)
Vansteenwegen, A. (1982). Intensive psycho-educational couple therapy: Therapeutic program and outcome research results. *Cahiers des Sciences Familiales et Sexologiques*, No. 5 de L'Université Catholique de Louvain, Belgium.
Wampler, K. S. and Powell, G. S. (1982). The Barrett-Lennard Relationship Inventory as a measure of marital satisfaction. *Family Relations, 31*, 139–45.
Wampler, K. S. and Sprenkle, D. H. (1980). The Minnesota Couple Communication Program: A follow-up study. *Journal of Marriage and the Family, 42*, 577–84.
Wargo, D. G. and Meek, V. C. (1970/1971). The Relationship Inventory as a measure of milieu perception in rehabilitation center students. *Rehabilitation Counseling Bulletin, 14*, 42–8.
Wilkins, P. (2000). Unconditional positive regard reconsidered. *British Journal of Guidance and Counselling, 28*(1), 23–36.
Wyatt, G. (Ed.), (2001). *Rogers' Therapeutic Conditions: Evolution, Theory and Practice. Vol 1: Congruence.* Ross-on-Wye: PCCS Books.

3a

Pre-Therapy: An essay in philosophical psychology[1]

Garry Prouty

THE CONCRETE PHENOMENON 'AS ITSELF'

Pre-Therapy, consistent with Person-Centered Gestalt, and Experiential psychotherapies, rests within the existential phenomenological tradition. It is a 'pointing at the concrete' (Buber, 1964). Its method is based on a conception of the concrete phenomenon 'as itself'.

The concrete phenomenon as itself can be clarified in terms of first, the 'concrete attitude' of the client, and second, the concreteness of the phenomenon as 'naturalistic', 'self-indicative', and 'desymbolized'.

The concrete attitude

Gurswitch (1966) describes a phenomenological study of brain-damaged patients by Gelb and Goldstein, who found that these patients had a 'concrete attitude', as distinguished from a 'categorical attitude'. A patient with a concrete attitude experiences many shades of the same color as different colors. A person with a categorical attitude who is not brain-damaged would describe the many shades as the same color.

The brain-damaged person cannot categorize; meanings are perception-bound and not abstracted essences. Arieti (1955), also influenced by Goldstein, found the same concrete attitude among schizophrenics.

Pre-Therapy, because it primarily focuses on mentally retarded and schizophrenic clients, is especially sensitive to developing a conception of the phenomenon consistent with the concrete attitude of these populations and the extraordinarily concrete responses of Pre-Therapy.

The 'as itself'

The 'as itself' is naturalistic. Farber (1959, 1967) and Riepe (1973) propose a phenomenology that describes phenomena as they appear 'naturally' in

---

[1]. First published as Chapter 4 in *Theoretical Evolutions in Person-Centered/Experiential Therapy. Applications to Schizophrenic and Retarded Psychoses.* Westport: Praeger (pp. 31–4). Reproduced by kind permission of the Author and publisher.

consciousness.

This is done *without* the suspension of the natural attitude toward experience, or a phenomenological reduction to an essence (Jennings, 1992).[2] The concrete phenomenon is described as it manifests itself 'as itself'.

The 'as itself' is self-indicative. The concrete phenomenon is 'absolutely self-indicative' (Sartre, 1956). This means the phenomenon is 'what it is, absolutely, for it reveals itself as it is. The phenomenon can be described, as such, for it is absolutely indicative of itself.' Again, the phenomenon is described 'as itself'.

The 'as itself' is desymbolized. The concrete phenomenon is described as 'desymbolized' (Scheler, 1953). Scheler states:

> Something can be Self-Given only if it is no longer given merely through any sort of symbol; in other words, only *if* it is not meant as the mere fulfillment of a sign that is previously defined in some way or other. In this sense, phenomenological philosophy is a continual de-symbolization of the world.

In other words, the phenomenon appears non-symbolically 'as itself'.

The 'as itself': An example. The 'as itself' is a primordial, perceptual consciousness of the phenomenon. This example is drawn from a non-verbal memory I had as an infant.

The awareness of the world is of lying on my back in a crib. On my right side, at an even height with my body and at about a 15 degree angle, is a window. Through the window, at a medium distance, there is a tree. The tree is black and gray without leaves. The limbs reach toward the sky like bony fingers. The sky is gray-black, like dusk.

My awareness of self was two-fold. First, the experience 'belonged' to consciousness. Consciousness was sensed as the locus of experience. Second, consciousness was aware of itself as consciousness 'of'. Consciousness grasped itself through the act of intentionality.

The awareness of 'other' was the unrecognized figure of my mother entering the scene. The experience was of her arms picking me up and the correlated swirl of bright light. The sensation was of being wrapped in a blanket and carried on her shoulder and being rocked very slowly. The sense of 'other' was present and separate.

This primordial consciousness of world, self, and other is foundational for the development of an existential consciousness.

EXISTENTIAL CONSCIOUSNESS

Existential consciousness is characterized by: the existential structures of consciousness, existential contact, and existential autism.

---

2. Jennings, J. L. (1992). The Forgotten Distinction between Psychology and Phenomenology. In Miller, R. (Ed.), *The Restoration of Dialogue: Readings in the Philosophy of Clinical Psychology.* Washington, D.C.: American Psychological Association, pp. 293–305. This section contains a detailed discussion of Husserl's views on naturalism and 'bracketing'.

The existential structures of consciousness

Pre-reflective consciousness is described as the immediately sensed perception of lived experience, or *Erleben*, in German.

In the language of Merleau-Ponty, the world, self, or other can be described as 'Concrete A-Priori' (Merleau-Ponty, 1962; Mallin, 1979). World, self, and other are the natural and categorical 'revelatory absolutes' of immediate consciousness through which particular concrete existents manifest themselves.

The existential structures of consciousness are characterized by a pre-reflective consciousness (lived experience) of the world, self, or other (existence) as concrete phenomenon (naturalistic, self-indicative, desymbolized).

Existential contact

This contact of pre-reflective consciousness with the concrete phenomenon of the world, self, and other is described as 'existential contact'.

Husserl (Speigelberg, 1978) conceived all consciousness as 'intentional'; that is, all consciousness is consciousness of something. All consciousness 'intends' an 'object'. Existential contact is the natural, alternating movement of immediate pre-reflective consciousness toward the natural presence of the world, self, or other. Consciousness naturally and alternately moves toward existence.

Existential autism

Impairment of existential contact due to psychological or organic disorder results in existential autism (Laing, 1990; Dosen, 1983). The rich, meaningful, everyday, natural, pre-reflective consciousness is no longer 'intentional' (toward, with, or about). Consciousness is no longer contactful.

Existence becomes a 'void of significance', a failure in coherence. Consciousness becomes empty, an isolated shell of meaninglessness. Consciousness is not related to existence. It lives without the 'creation of meaning' that comes from primordial contact with the natural absolutes of the world, self, or other.

Pre-Therapy, in existential-phenomenological terms, is the movement of consciousness from existential autism to existential contact.

REFERENCES

See end of chapter 3c page 74.

3b Pre-Therapy as a Theoretical System[1]

Garry Prouty

THE MEANING OF 'PRE'

To understand Pre-Therapy, it is useful to examine the prefix 'pre'. 'Pre', in the context used here, refers to pre-conditions. Several analogies convey this functional and logical meaning.

In the field of art, painters generally use an instrument to function, such as a brush. A modern artist may use a manufactured wooden handle with bristles. A caveman might have used a wooden tree branch with leaves or moss. In either case, a brush is typically a necessary pre-condition of painting. The modern painter often uses oil paints. The artist from prehistoric times may have used berry juices or animal fats. In either situation, the function of painting requires a fluid medium as a pre-condition. Finally, the prehistoric artist would require a surface. He or she may have used a cave wall. The modern artist may purchase a manufactured canvas. Functionally, both require a relatively flat surface. This is another necessary pre-condition of painting.

Another analogy can be drawn from the field of reading development. In order to read, children must possess the psychological capacity known as symbol recognition. Second, they must have the neuromuscular capacity to move their eyes from left to right. Third, they must have the memory capacity to retain information. Symbol recognition, neuromuscular capacity, and memory function are the pre-conditions of reading.

Each of these analogies presents the meaning of 'pre' as the logically necessary conditions of their particular functions (painting or reading). What I have described are the *necessary* conditions of painting and reading.

Transposing this analysis to Rogers' work in clinical psychology one might ask: what are the *necessary conditions* of a therapeutic relationship? This, of course, *deconstructs* Rogers' conception of the 'necessary and sufficient conditions'. It enables us to ask: what is *necessary*? What is *sufficient*? This further enables us to ask: what are the necessary *pre-conditions* of a therapeutic relationship?

Many clients are not fully capable of maintaining therapeutic relationships,

---

1. First published as Chapter 5 in *Theoretical Evolutions in Person-Centered/Experiential Therapy. Applications to Schizophrenic and Retarded Psychoses.* Westport: Praeger (pp. 35–49). Reproduced by kind permission of the Author and publisher.

as is the case with the schizophrenic and retarded/psychotic populations. What are the necessary conditions to form a relationship? This deconstruction of Rogers' definition into necessary and sufficient components allows us to examine it in a new context. It allows us to think in terms of pre-relationship. What goes on before we can form a classical client-centered relationship? The first meaning of 'pre' is pre-relationship.

In a similar manner, we can examine the concept of Experiencing. As many of the schizophrenic and retarded/psychotic clients have no easy access to a therapeutic relationship; they cannot easily access their Experiencing. This is probably due to a lack of 'internal contact' resulting from a strong autistic component (Minkowski, 1970; Dosen, 1983). Prouty explains (Prouty, 1994, Chapter 3) that schizophrenic clients do not seem able to process their Experiencing. When this is the case, we face a problem similar to that which occurs with a therapeutic relationship. What is the necessary condition of Experiencing? What has to be psychologically operative before Experiencing can occur? This new train of thought leads us to the language pre-experiential.

When we think clinically about pre-relationship and pre-experiential, we are exploring how to help clients who are *relationship or experientially impaired and cannot use these functions for therapy* This is the genesis of Pre-Therapy: it describes the clinical search for a mode of treatment for those who cannot fully use relationship or Experiencing processes.

The logic of the pre-conditions of relationship and Experiencing evolves into a wider theoretical question. What are the pre-conditions, the necessary conditions of psychotherapy in general? What are the psychological functions necessary for psychotherapy? The deconstructed theory of Rogers' necessary and sufficient conditions gives us direction. Psychological contact is the necessary condition of psychotherapy. This is the foundation for an evolved Pre-Therapy.

PSYCHOLOGICAL CONTACT

Pre-Therapy is a theory of psychological contact. It is rooted in Rogers' conception of psychological contact as the first condition of a therapeutic relationship. It is also rooted in Perls' (1969) conception of ego as a 'contact function'. Pre-Therapy is the development or restoration of the functions necessary for a therapeutic relationship and Experiencing. Pre-Therapy, described in general terms, develops the *necessary psychological capacities for psychotherapy*. It assists those clients who are impaired in the psychological functions required for treatment to occur.

Psychological contact, as a theoretical system, is described as: contact reflections, contact functions, and contact behaviors (Peters, 1986b; Leijssen and Roelens, 1988).

Contact reflections refer to counselor technique. They represent evolution in the Person-Centered/Experiential method (see Prouty, 1994, Chapters 1 and 2). Reflection for Rogers embodied the attitudes; reflection for Gendlin facilitates the Experiencing process. Reflection for Pre-Therapy develops psychological contact.

Contact functions refer to the internal psychological functions of the client. They are an evolution in Perls' concept of psychological contact as an ego function[2] (see next page). They are described as reality contact, affective contact, and communicative contact.

Contact behaviors refer to specific behaviors to be measured so as to illustrate the outcome of Pre-Therapy. Reality, affective and communicative contact are the emergent behaviors that represent changes in contact.

Contact reflections

Contact reflections have the theoretical function of developing psychological contact between therapist and client when the client is incapable of reality, affective, or communicative contact. They are applied when there is not sufficient contact to implement psychotherapy.

Contact reflections are concrete in that they are extraordinarily literal and duplicative. They are empathic to the specific concrete particularity of the client's regressed efforts at expression and communication. This is the core empathy.

There are five contact reflections (Karon and Vanderbos, 1981): situational reflections (SR), facial reflections (FR), word-for-word reflections (WWR), body reflections (BR), and reiterative reflections (RR).

Situational contact refers to reflections at the client's situation, environment, or milieu. For example, a therapist may situationally reflect: 'Tom is playing with the red ball.' Another situational reflection may be: 'You are holding the chair.' These types of reflections help make reality contact. They facilitate existential contact with the *world*.

Facial contact describes reflections of facial affect. Many psychotic and retarded clients, due to psychosocial isolation, over-medication, and institutionalization, do not experience themselves as the locus of emotion or feeling. They often exist in a state of emotional autism, numbness, or absence. Often, the feeling exists in a pre-expressive form in the face. Arthur Burton (1973) suggests that the face has the phylogenetic function of emotional expressivity. It has evolved through mammalian biological development for that purpose.

Facial reflections may be demonstrated by the following: 'You look sad', or 'You look scared'. Another example might be: 'Your face looks happy'. The therapist is 'inter-humanizing' the emotion or feeling with the client. Facial contact or reflections have the theoretical function of developing affective contact or existential contact with the *self*.

Word-for-word contact or reflections mean the literal 'welcoming' repetition of singular words, multiple word fragments, or fragments of meaning that the client expresses. Many schizophrenic clients, due to their use of neologisms, word-

---

2. Perls, F. S., Hefferline, R. and Goodman, P. (1951). *Gestalt Therapy: Excitement and Growth*. New York: Julian Press, p. 229. In a structural sense, Perls sees the dynamic units constituting the system self as a form of contact (p. 224). Perls then goes on to say that reality is given in moments of good contact — a unity of awareness, motor response and feeling (p. 372). Perls further describes a definition of perceptual contact as a sequence of figures forming against grounds (p. 403); Perls, F. S. (1976). *The Gestalt Approach and Eyewitness to Therapy*. New York: Bantam Edition, p. 17. Perls describes a functional relationship between a human being and his environment in terms of a contact boundary. It is at the contact boundary that psychological events take place. Perls further states that our thoughts, acts and emotions are our way of experiencing and meeting these boundary events (p. 17); Polster, E. and Polster, M. (1974). *Gestalt Therapy Integrated*. New York: Vintage Books, p. 103. According to the Polsters. the contact boundary is the point at which one experiences the 'me' in relation to the 'not me'. Through contact, both are more clearly experienced (p. 103).

PRE-THERAPY AS A THEORETICAL SYSTEM

salads, and echolalia, are often incoherent. The same difficulties occur with the retarded/psychotic, only these difficulties are compounded communicatively by mental retardation. In either case, the client's speech seems to flow coherently, then incoherently, coherently, incoherently, and so on. For example, the client may say: '[incoherent word, incoherent word] house [incoherent word, incoherent word], tree.' The therapist would selectively reflect 'house', then 'tree'. This word-for-word reflection reinforces the client sense of self as a communicator. This is perhaps a poetic empathy as reflected in Buber's 'Response' of 'I' to 'Thou'. Word-for-word reflections develop communicative contact or existential contact with the *other*.

Body contact refers to reflections of the client's body. Schizophrenic and retarded/psychotic clients manifest echopraxia, catatonia, and bizarre body posturing. The significance of the body in the psychotherapy of schizophrenia was researched by Mauerer-Groeli (1976). From the psychoanalytic perspective, that author found improved ego functions as a result of body therapy with a large number of psychotic clients.

In Pre-Therapy, there are two kinds of body reflections. The first is an empathic body duplication by the therapist. This is illustrated by Prouty and Cronwall (1990). Cronwall describes a depressed and profoundly retarded client whose major behavior in therapy was to 'make-believe' he was turning the steering wheel of a car. There was no language or contact with the therapist. The client only drove his imaginary steering wheel. The therapist's body reflected this by turning her own steering wheel and duplicating the body movements of the client.

The second body reflection in Pre-Therapy is verbal. For example, a therapist may reflect catatonic posturing: 'Your arm is in the air. Your body is very rigid.' These kinds of body or verbal reflections help assist the client experience his body as a 'me' or self-experience. This can be the resolution of a very primitive trauma or lack of development.

Re-contact or reiterative reflections refer not to a specific technique, but to a principle. The principle is: if a specific reflection succeeds in making psychological contact, repeat it. Repeating the psychological contact maximizes the opportunity to develop a relationship or to facilitate Experiencing.

There are two types of re-contact: immediate and longer term. An example of immediate re-contact is drawn from Prouty and Cronwall (1990). A profoundly retarded client, who had no contact with the therapist, utters a word: 'Candy'. The therapist immediately re-contacts or reiterates 'Candy'. The client then responds, more intentionally, louder, 'Candy'. The client then gradually says, 'Napkin', 'Plates', 'Party'. By reiterating 'Candy,' the client's communication expanded. Van Werde (1990) describes a therapeutic sequence with a psychotic, mentally retarded girl who was diagnosed as schizo-affective. The therapist performed a longer-term, reiterative re-contact. The therapist, earlier in the session, had body reflected: 'You touched your forehead.' Some minutes later, the therapist made a reiterative reflection: 'You touched your forehead.' The client then proceeded to say, 'Grandma.' This interchange evolved into the client expressing genuine and congruent feeling about her grandmother.

Pre-Therapy, by using contact reflection, tends to reduce psychotic expression and facilitate more realistic communication embodying the world, self, or other

CONTACT AND PERCEPTION

(reality, affective, and communicative contact).

Contact functions

The contact functions, in psychological terms, represent an expansion of Perls' concept of 'contact as an ego function'. They are conceived as awareness functions and described as reality, affective, and communicative contact.

The development or restoration of the contact functions is the necessary precondition for psychotherapy. They function as the theoretical goals of Pre-Therapy.

Reality contact

Reality contact (world) is defined as the awareness of people, places, things, and events. If we describe the world as we concretely experience it, we see that we live with things. Our world is an infinite thematic field of things. Things are part of our living existence. We turn handles, we throw balls, we smell flowers, we touch stones, we use toasters, we see by electric light bulbs. Things are a definite part of our reality sense.

Even if we do not have intimate relationships, our world is peopled. Everywhere, there are people. We live with people. People are on the bus, in the airplane, at the physician's office, on the island of Tahiti, and so on. Again, there is an infinite thematic of people. Even if we live alone on an island, there are people in our heads. We would talk to them. People are a concrete part of our reality sense.

Mankind is spatially constructed. We live 'in' space. Spatiality is a concrete part of our reality. Things and people are bound up with space. The ball is here. The ball is there. I am here. You are there. These are the meanings of place. Place is a deep part of our reality sense. Spatiality is also an infinite thematic.

Mankind is also temporally constructed. We live 'in' time. Time is also a concrete part of our reality. Things, people, and places have their occurrence in time. This is the concrete meaning of event. I am here now. You are there now. We were there then. We will be married in November. Time is an infinite thematic.

People, places, things, and events are the concrete, yet infinite thematics of our 'being-in-the-world'.

Affective contact

Affective contact (self) is our response to the world or other. Affective contact is defined as awareness of moods, feelings, and emotions. Moods, feelings, and emotions are different phenomenological and concrete forms of affect.

Mood is affect that is subtle, diffuse, and general. Often, a mood is background sensing. It is a coloring of events. I can go to a football game and experience an anxious or depressed mood that feels separate from the current reality. The mood also has a low intensity to it. It often lacks direct focus.

Feeling is more pronounced affect. A feeling is clearer and it has a specific locus. It is in response to the event itself. I feel this or that about this or that. The intensity of feeling is stronger than that of a mood. It is not as subtle; it is more articulated as an affective experience. Instead of being background, it is more foreground about the event. I feel sad that my grandmother is deceased and is no longer here to care about me.

PRE-THERAPY AS A THEORETICAL SYSTEM

Emotion is affect that is considerably more intense and more clearly linked to an event. It is sharp, clear, and more detailed. Emotion has the psychological quality of being totally foreground. My emotional reaction is rage if you are attacking my child or my wife.

Moods, feelings, and emotions are an infinite thematic of our contact with existence.

Communicative contact

Communicative contact is defined as the symbolization of reality (world) and affect (self) to others.

Communicative contact is more than the transmission of information. It is the meaningful expression of our perceived world and self to others. It conveys denotative and connotative meanings from our experiential universe. It reveals to the other. It enables psychological contact with the other.

Communicative contact primarily refers to social language. We concretely live in language. It is an infinite thematic of our being-in-the-world. We think in language. We speak in language. We create in language. We even die in language, as on tombstones. One merely has to experience living in a culture with a different language to experience the psychological significance of language.

The contact functions in therapy

A therapeutic vignette illustrates contact reflections resulting in the restoration of the contact functions in a chronic schizophrenic woman. It also illustrates the restoration of psychological contact as a pre-condition of relationship.

> *Dorothy is an old woman who is one of the more regressed women on X ward. She was mumbling something (as she usually did). This time I could hear certain words in her confusion. I reflected only the words I could clearly understand. After about ten minutes, I could hear a complete sentence. (For a therapist reflection key, see page 56, para 3)*
>
> CLIENT: *Come with me.*
> THERAPIST: WWR *Come with me.*
>   *[The patient led me to the corner of the day room. We stood there silently for what seemed to be a very long time. Since I couldn't communicate with her, I watched her body movements and closely reflected these.]*
> CLIENT: *[The patient put her hand on the wall.] Cold.*
> THERAPIST: WW-BR *[I put my hand on the wall and repeated the word.] Cold. [She had been holding my hand all along, but when I reflected her, she would tighten her grip. Dorothy began to mumble word fragments. I was careful to reflect only the words I could understand. What she was saying began to make sense.]*
> CLIENT: *I don't know what this is any more. [Touching the wall: reality contact.] The walls and chairs don't mean*

CONTACT AND PERCEPTION

		anything any more. [Existential autism.]
THERAPIST:	WW-BR	[Touching the wall.] You don't know what this is any more. The chairs and walls don't mean anything to you any more.
CLIENT:		[The patient began to cry: affective contact. After a while she began to talk again. This time she spoke clearly: communicative contact.] I don't like it here. I'm so tired, so tired.
THERAPIST:	WWR	[As I gently touched her arm, this time it was I who tightened my grip on her hand. I reflected.] You're tired, so tired.
CLIENT:		[The patient smiled and told me to sit in a chair directly in front of her and began to braid my hair.]

This vignette begins to express Pre-Therapy as a therapeutic theory and philosophy. It illustrates the use of contact reflections to facilitate the contact functions (reality, affect, communication).

In existential/phenomenological terms, this vignette illustrates a resolution of existential autism (loss of contact with the world, self, and other) and the development of existential contact (contact with the world, self, and other. Clearly, the existential structures of consciousness are reintegrated with existence. This case also illustrates another dimension of Pre-Therapy: it shows the movement from a pre-expressive mode of communication to an expressive mode of communication.

Contact behaviors

Contact behaviors are the emergent behavioral changes that result from the facilitation of the contact functions through the use of contact reflections. They are the operationalized aspect of psychological contact.

Reality contact (world) is operationalized as the client's verbalization of people, places, things, and events.

Affective contact (self) is operationalized as the body or facial expression of affect. For example, a bodily expression of affect may be: 'John angrily kicks the chair.' A facial expression of affect may be: 'John looks sad.' Affective contact may also be operationalized through the use of feeling words. The client may use affective language such as 'sad', 'angry', 'happy', and so on.

Communicative contact (other) is operationalized as the client's verbalization of social words or sentences.

What is being measured is the expression of reality, affect, and communication. On a clinical level, the measurement reflects the shift in a client from a pre-expressive to an expressive level. In addition, we are measuring the client's increased expression about the world, self, or other.

Pilot studies

The measurement process is as follows. A Pre-Therapy scale is constructed for three dimensions: reality, affect, and communication. Dimension I (reality) is scorings for people, places, things, and events. Dimension II (affect) is scorings for facial expression, bodily expression, and feeling words. Dimension III (communication) is scorings for words and sentences. These three scoring dimensions measure movement from a pre-expressive to an expressive communication about the world, self, or other.

The procedural steps are: (1) Clients are tape-recorded through all sessions; (2) the recordings are transcribed to scoring sheets; and (3) raters are trained for scoring competency.

Pilot studies (Prouty, 1985), using single-case observations, present data supporting the construct validity (Christensen, 1991) of psychological contact.

Table 1 describes nine pairs of mean scores, from two independent raters, over a three-month period with a retarded schizophrenic client. Mean scores per month are compared between raters. These scores have a correlation coefficient of 0.9966, with a p-value of 0.0001, presenting strong evidence against the null hypothesis of no correlation. The pairwise t-test resulted in a value of 0.9864 with a p-value of 0.3528. These results indicate no difference between rater scorings.

Table 2 describes 24 pairs of scorings from two independent raters through a single session of Pre-Therapy with a schizo-affective, retarded client. Scores are drawn from percentiles 1–20, 40–60, and 80–100. In other words, the beginning, middle, and end of the session were evaluated. A correlation coefficient of 0.9847 with a p-value of 0.0001 was obtained. The pairwise t-test produced a value of 2.3738 with a p-value of 0.0526. These results indicate no difference between scorings at 1% or 5% levels of significance.

Table 1
RAC Mean Frequency per Standardized Sessions

	Three-Month Intervals February–October Rater 1, 2	
	Rater 1	Rater 2
February–April		
Reality	59	48
Affect	27	27
Communication	71	77
May–July		
Reality	149	175
Affect	11.5	11.5
Communication	110	100
August – October		
Reality	379	446
Affect	17	13
Communication	214	225
Correlation Coefficient 0.9966 p-value		0.0001
t-value 0.9864 p-value		0.3528

CONTACT AND PERCEPTION

An independent pilot study (De Vre, 1992) further confirmed construct validity and also developed evidence for reliability. De Vre and her colleagues, Van Werde and Deleu, utilizing the Pre-Therapy scale, measured three data samples from three clients. Two clients were described as chronic schizophrenics, and the third was diagnosed as a borderline psychotic. All three clients were measured under hospitalized conditions.

Table 2
RAC Frequencies — Single Session

	Reality				Affect		Communication	
	pe	pl	ev	th	f	b	w	s
R-1	9	3	4	6(22)	3	1(4)	3	6(9)
R-2	10	5	2	7(24)	2	1(3)	4	8(12)
R-1	43	16	31	15(105)	5	7(12)	40	17(57)
R-2	42	14	28	12(96)	5	8(13)	36	17(53)
R-1	34	6	11	4(61)	0	8(8)	19	16(35)
R-2	29	5	13	4(51)	0	8(8)	11	14(25)

Correlation coefficient   0.9847   p-value 0.0001
          t-value   2.3738   p-value 0.0526
1% or 5% Level of significance

The first measure of agreement (Cohen, 1968) between two raters was kappa 0.39. With refinement of the English to Flemish translation, the second measure, with the same raters and a second client, was kappa 0.76. A third measure, with the same raters and a third client, was kappa 0.87. These measures of agreement were statistically significant at 0.00005.

A reliability measure was developed by having two independent psychiatric nurses instructed in the use of the Pre-Therapy scale. The rating of the first data sample was 0.39. The nurses' level of agreement was kappa 0.7 at a 0.0005 level of significance.

These U.S. and Belgian pilot studies provide some indication for the valid and reliable measurability of contact behaviors.

REFERENCES

See end of chapter 3c page 74.

3c The Practice of Pre-Therapy[1]
Garry Prouty

Thus far, I have described Pre-Therapy in terms of philosophical psychology and as a theoretical system. This chapter will focus on clinical practice, presenting materials from the treatment of schizophrenics and mentally retarded/dual-diagnosed clients.

PRACTICE OBSERVATIONS

Pietrzak notes that for Pre-Therapy, the 'techniques are simple, but the practice is difficult'.[2] These practice observations are added to the techniques to enhance their usage.

Since Rogers emphasizes empathy as one of the core conditions, Pre-Therapy emphasizes 'empathic contact'. However, this empathic contact has a different focus than the client's frame of reference. The focus of empathy is the client's regressed, incoherent efforts at pre-expressive communication. *The therapist does not know the client's frame of reference.* The empathy is for the client's effort at developing coherent experience and expression, perhaps a form of concretizing the self-formative tendency during these primitive phases of therapy.

A second level of empathy concerns the concreteness of pre-expressive behavior. The contact reflections need to be extraordinarily concrete. They are not focused on the generalized 'essence' of meaning, but on the literal expressive behavior. *The empathy is for the concrete particularity of behavioral expression.*

A third level of empathy concerns the increase of psychotic expression as a function of Pre-Therapy. The client needs to get worse before she can get better. The therapist needs to be empathic to an increase in delusional and hallucinatory expression, as well as to an increase in bizarre communication (strange body postures, language disturbances, etc.). This means being empathic to the lived experience of the psychosis itself. This is, of course, the opposite of behavioral or chemical management.

Other empathic concerns involve temporality and spatiality (Binswanger, 1958).

---

1. First published as Chapter 6 in *Theoretical Evolutions in Person-Centered/Experiential Therapy. Applications to Schizophrenic and Retarded Psychoses.* Westport: Praeger. (pp. 49–64). Reproduced by kind permission of the Author and publisher.
2. Ms. Pietrzak served as Pre-Therapy pilot study coordinator. She had primary responsibility for organizing and supervising the project.

CONTACT AND PERCEPTION

Often, experiences of time and space are altered. One client reports being terrified of time stopping. Another client reports being horrified by her experience of a room shrinking. The phenomenology of time is slowed during depression and accelerated for manic episodes. The spatial phenomenology is often altered in hallucinatory states because the hallucination occupies a literal space (Havens, 1962).

Empathy for temporal and spatial experience is very important in approaching chronic regressed clients. Very often they are frightened of contact. Spatiality becomes a sensitive dimension. One forward step too close can be overwhelming and disrupt relationship formation.

The tempo of contact is also a sensitive dimension. Rapidly given reflections may overwhelm the client. Multiple reflections, given at one time, can also alienate the client. Conversely, too few reflections, expressed too slowly, may cause the loss of contact. It is important to understand that the therapist is entering a phenomenological 'world' and that one needs to be empathic to the experiential structures of that world.

CLIENTS

The first case history concerns a young, catatonic, schizophrenic male who had been treated with electro-shocks, as well as multiple chemical interventions. The treatment vignette is drawn from a 12-hour period during which the therapist was able to restore verbal communication.

The second case history involves a mentally retarded, schizophrenic young woman. The description is about the resolution of a psychotic episode and presents Pre-Therapy as a form of crisis intervention.

The third case is about an institutionalized, severely retarded young man who was also diagnosed as depressed. Although the case did not evolve into psychotherapy, as we classically understand it, improvements were sufficient to maximize institutional services. This illustrates another application of Pre-Therapy.

CATATONIA

Prouty and Kubiak (1988a) describe the application of Pre-Therapy to a catatonic schizophrenic client.[3] The client was a 22-year-old Caucasian male who had had several hospitalizations.

Vignette

> *The client was one of 13 children. His parents were farmers of Polish ethnicity. His mother had been hospitalized several times for schizophrenic problems. Family observation revealed at least one sibling who, although not hospitalized, displayed psychotic symptoms. The family brought the client*

---

3. This case history was presented at a symposium with Carl Rogers, Eugene Gendlin, Natalie Rogers, and Nathaniel Raskin at the University of Chicago in September 1986. The videotape is available at the Center for the Studies of the Person, La Jolla, California.

to the United States for evaluation. A preliminary observation confirmed that the client was potentially responsive to Pre-Therapy

According to psychiatric documents, the client had been described as: 'mute', 'autistic', 'catatonic', 'making no eye contact', 'exhibiting trance-like behavior', 'stuporous', 'confused', 'not establishing rapport', 'delusional', 'paranoid', and finally, 'experiencing severe thought-blocking'.

He had been diagnosed variously as: manic-depressive, hysterical reaction, hebephrenic schizophrenic, paranoid schizophrenic, catatonic schizophrenic, profound schizophrenic, schizophrenic, affective type. He had received six electro-shock treatments, as well as numerous chemical interventions including Stelazine, Diazepam, Imipramine, Chlorpromazine, Anafranil, Phenothiazine, Haldol, and Trifluoperazine.

The client was returned to his home for several months while plans for residential care and legal details were arranged. My associate therapist arrived and found that the client, kept at home for several months, had deteriorated into psychosis. The parents had not rehospitalized him. He was in a severe catatonic state, having withdrawn to the lower portion of the three-story home. He did not eat meals with the family, only creeping out at night to use the family refrigerator. He had lost considerable weight and his feet were blue from being cramped and stiffened due to his lack of movement and circulation.

The contact work. This vignette describes segments of a 12-hour process that illustrates the application of contact reflections, the successful resolution of the catatonic state, and the development of communicative contact (without medication).

The patient was sitting on a long couch, very rigid, with arms outstretched and even with his shoulders. His eyes were straight ahead, his face was mask-like, and his hands and feet were blue-gray.

The therapist sat on the opposite side of the couch, giving no eye contact to the patient. Reflections were given five to ten minutes apart.

Segment I   (approximately 2:00 p.m.)

THERAPIST:	SR	I can hear the children playing.
THERAPIST:	SR	It is very cool down here.
THERAPIST:	SR	I can hear people talking in the kitchen.
THERAPIST:	SR	I'm sitting with you in the lower level of your house.
THERAPIST:	SR	I can hear the dog barking.
THERAPIST:	BR	Your body is very rigid.
THERAPIST:	BR	You are sitting very still.
THERAPIST:	BR	You are looking straight ahead.
THERAPIST:	BR	You are sitting on the couch in a very upright position.
THERAPIST:	BR	Your body isn't moving. Your arms are in the air.
CLIENT:		[No response, no movement.]

She brought a chair and sat in it directly in front of the patient and mirrored his body exactly as she saw it.

CONTACT AND PERCEPTION

Segment II (approximately 3:30 P.M.)

THERAPIST:	BR	Your body is very rigid. You are sitting on the couch and not moving.
		[approximately 15-20 minutes later]
THERAPIST:		I can no longer hold my arms outstretched. My arms are tired.
CLIENT:		*[No response, no movement.]*
THERAPIST:	BR	Your body is very stiff.
THERAPIST:	BR	Your arms are outstretched.
THERAPIST:	BR	Your body isn't moving.
CLIENT:		*[Put his hands on his head, as if to hold his head, and spoke in a barely audible whisper.]* My head hurts me when my father speaks.
THERAPIST:	WWR	My head hurts me when my father speaks.
THERAPIST:	BR	*[Therapist put her hands as if to hold her head.]*
THERAPIST:	RR/WW	My head hurts when my father speaks.
CLIENT:		*[Continued to hold head for two to three hours.]*

Segment III (approximately 8:00 P.M.)

THERAPIST:	SR	It's evening. We are in the lower level of your home.
THERAPIST:	BR	Your body is very rigid.
THERAPIST:	BR	Your hands are holding your head.
THERAPIST:	RR/WW	My head hurts when my father speaks.
CLIENT:		*[Immediately dropped his hands to his knees and looked directly into therapist's eyes.]*
THERAPIST:	BR	You've taken your hands from your head and placed them on your knees. You are looking right into my eyes.
CLIENT:		*[Sat motionless for hours.]*
THERAPIST:	RR/BR	You dropped your hands from your head to your knees.
THERAPIST:	SR	You are looking straight into my eyes.
CLIENT:		*[Immediately, he speaks in a barely audible whisper.]* Priests are devils.
THERAPIST:	WWR	Priests are devils.
THERAPIST:	BR	Your hands are on your knees.
THERAPIST:	SR	You are looking right into my eyes.
THERAPIST:	BR	Your body is very rigid.
CLIENT:		*[He speaks in a barely audible whisper.]* My brothers can't forgive me.
THERAPIST:	WWR	My brothers can't forgive me.
CLIENT:		*[Sat motionless for approximately an hour.]*

Segment IV (approximately 1:45 a.m.)

THERAPIST:	SR	It is very quiet.

THERAPIST:	SR	You are in the lower level of the house.
THERAPIST:	SR	It is evening.
THERAPIST:	BR	Your body is very rigid.
CLIENT:		[Immediately, in slow motion, put his hand over his heart and talks.] My heart is wooden.
THERAPIST: BR/WW		[In slow motion, put her hand over her heart and talks.] My heart is wooden.
CLIENT:		[Feet start to move.]
THERAPIST:	BR	Your feet are starting to move.
CLIENT:		[More eye movement.]

The therapist took the patient's hand and lifted him to stand. They began to walk. The patient walked with the therapist around the farm and in a normal conversational mode spoke about the different animals. He brought the therapist to newborn puppies and lifted one to hold. The client had good eye contact. The client continued to maintain communicative contact over the next four days and was able to transfer planes and negotiate with Customs officers on the way to the United States. He was able to sign himself into the residential treatment facility, where he underwent classical Person-Centered / Experiential psychotherapy.

This vignette illustrates the function of Pre-Therapy, which is to restore the client's psychological contact enabling treatment. Very clearly, this client's reality and communicative contact were improved sufficiently to enter psychotherapy.

Pre-expressive verbal communication

It should be reported that apparently meaningless statements, in the psychotic processing, proved to be very germane to the etiology of the psychosis.

'My head hurts when my father speaks': this statement became clarified when anger about physical and emotional abuse emerged in therapy.

'Priests are devils': this meaning became clearer when it was discovered that the family priest made homosexual overtures toward the client. This was the event that precipitated the psychosis.

'My brothers can't forgive me': this referred to a homicidal attempt on his brother's life. The client ran over his brother with a farm tractor. He had a delusional belief that his brother was a Communist.

These non-explicated, out-of-context, highly relevant statements illustrate the pre-expressive nature of psychotic communication.

CRISIS

Prouty and Kubiak (1988b) report the use of Pre-Therapy as a form of crisis intervention. The client was a mentally retarded female, diagnosed as hebephrenic schizophrenic. She lived in a residential treatment facility. The paraprofessional therapist (now a professional counselor and college instructor) was taking a group of clients on a community visit. The psychotic reaction occurred

CONTACT AND PERCEPTION

while they were driving in a van.

Vignette

The client was one of seven on an outing from a halfway house. She was seated in the rear seat of the van. As I looked in the rear-view mirror, I observed the client crouched down into the seat with one arm outstretched above her head. The client's face was filled with terror and her voice began to escalate in screams.

I pulled the van off the road and asked the volunteer to take the others out of the van. I sat next to the client, sharing the same fear.

CLIENT:		[In rising voice.] It's pulling me in.
THERAPIST:	WWR	It's pulling me in.
CLIENT:		[Continuing to slip farther down into the seat, with left arm outstretched. Eyes still closed.]
THERAPIST:	BR	Your body is slipping down into the seat. Your arm is in the air.
THERAPIST:	SR	We are in the van. You are sitting next to me.
CLIENT:		[Screaming.]
THERAPIST:	FR	You are screaming, Carol.
CLIENT:		It's pulling me in.
THERAPIST:	WWR	It's pulling you in.
THERAPIST:	SR	Carol, we are in the van. You are sitting next to me.
THERAPIST:	FR	Something is frightening you. You are screaming.
CLIENT:		[Patient screaming.] It's sucking me in.
THERAPIST:	WWR	It's sucking you in.
THERAPIST:	SR/BR	We are in the van, Carol. You are sitting next to me. Your arm is in the air.
CLIENT:		[Beginning to sob very hard. Arms dropped to lap.] It was the vacuum cleaner.
THERAPIST:	WWR	It was the vacuum cleaner.
CLIENT:		[Direct eye contact.] She did it with the vacuum cleaner. [Continued in a normal tone of voice.] I thought it was gone. She used to turn on the vacuum cleaner when I was bad and put the hose right on my arm. I thought it sucked it in. [Less sobbing. It should be noted that daily, this patient would kiss her arm up to her elbow and stroke it continually.]
THERAPIST:	WWR	Your arm is still here. It didn't get sucked into the vacuum cleaner.
CLIENT:		[Smiled and was held by therapist.]

Later that afternoon, a psychotherapy session was held and the client began to delve into her feelings about punishment received as a child. The kissing and stroking of the arm ceased. This vignette illustrates how the client was helped to deal with the acute episode in a psychologically beneficial manner *without medications. The client was able to experience how her symptoms of arm kissing and stroking related to a negative childhood emotional trauma of her mother threatening her with a vacuum cleaner. In addition, the client was able to use this newly integrated material as a basis for further therapy concerning her mother.*

PROFOUND RETARDATION AND DEPRESSION

Psychiatric treatment of the severely depressed and retarded has been achieved with lithium carbonate (Sovner and Hurley, 1983). Prouty and Cronwall (1990) report a successful psychological treatment utilizing Pre-Therapy.

Vignette

Client X was a 21-year-old male and a custodial resident of a state institution. He was diagnosed as profoundly retarded on the basis of Stanford Binet testing. His mental age was two years and four months. His IQ was 13.

Because of the severity of symptoms, he was not eligible for vocational or educational training. In addition, he was ineligible for field trips or cottage activities. His symptoms included crying, psychomotor retardation, mood swings, and obsessive stereotypic grass-pulling.

Medical records indicate the client had minor cerebral palsy and a history of slow motor development, sitting up at 14 months and walking at 22 months. The parents were of lower socioeconomic status. The father, an alcoholic, physically and emotionally abused the boy during his first five years of life. This resulted in divorce and the boy being placed in the institution. The mother remained in good contact with the youngster and became involved in parent advocacy at the state facility.

The case is significant because the psychological treatment was completed without medications, thus allowing a clearer assessment. The client had previously been treated with Prolixin, Thorazine, Melleril, and Vistaril. All medications were stopped at the beginning of Pre-Therapy.

As a result of treatment, symptoms decreased and the client exhibited more realistic communication. This increase in realistic communication was confirmed by objective data, and the client became eligible for programmatic services within the institution.

Early Treatment: Autistic Phase — Therapist Report. *Treatment sessions were 30 minutes, twice weekly. 'During our first sessions, X would come loping into the room, sit down in a chair, and start driving an imaginary car. He would hold his hands and arms as on a steering wheel. (I later introduced a toy steering wheel.) He made clicking noises (turn signals) and engine noises ('Vroom') over and over during the session. He would pretend to turn the wheel and bend sideways until he was touching the floor with his hand, shoulder, or arm. Sometimes he would make great crashing noises and say, 'Beep-beep.' He drove continually and constantly during sessions for approximately the first year. There was very little eye contact during this time.*

CONTACT AND PERCEPTION

Typical Session

Therapist:		Hi, X.
Therapist:	SR	You're looking at the steering wheel.
Therapist:	SR	X is sitting in the chair, holding the steering wheel.
Therapist:	SR	We're both sitting in brown chairs.
Client:		Vroom.
Therapist:	WWR	Vroom.
Client:		Click, click.
Therapist:	WWR	Click, click.
Therapist:	SR	X is turning the steering wheel.
Therapist:	BR	Arms crossing. [Crosses arms.]
Therapist:	BR	Body bending in chair. [Bends.]
Client:		Vroom, vroom.
Therapist:	WWR	Vroom, vroom.
Therapist:	SR	Our heads are touching the floor.
Therapist:	BR	We are bending over.
Therapist:	FR	You are looking.
Therapist:	SR	You are looking at the steering wheel.
Client:		Eee, kruss, sss.
Therapist:	WWR	Eee, kruss, sss.
Therapist:	SR	You're making crashing noises.
Client:		Click, click.
Therapist:	WWR	Click, click.
Therapist:	SR	You're making signal noises.
Therapist:	SR	We're sitting in a big room.
Therapist:	SR	The sun is shining.
Therapist:	BR	We're facing each other.
Therapist:	BR	Your arms are turning.
Therapist:	BR	[Hands on steering wheel.]
Therapist:	BR	You do, I do.
Therapist:	FR	X is smiling.
Therapist:	SR	X has been driving for a long time.
Therapist:	RR	Last time we were together, we were in a small room.
Therapist:	FR	You look sad.
Therapist:	SR	You are making crashing sounds.
Therapist:	BR	You do, I do.
Client:		Vroom, vroom.
Therapist:	WWR	Vroom, vroom.
Client:		Beep, beep.
Therapist:	WWR	Beep, beep.
Therapist:	RR	Last time we were together, you had a red shirt on.
Therapist:	SR	Today you have a yellow shirt.
Client:		Vroom, vroom.
Therapist:	WWR	Vroom, vroom.
Client:		Vroom, vroom.
Therapist:	WWR	Vroom, vroom.

THE PRACTICE OF PRE-THERAPY

Mid Treatment: Relatedness Phase—Therapist Report. *Gradually, the client became aware that I was reflecting his verbalizations and body movements. As we started to make contact, he would drive, giving me eye contact and smiling as I did contact reflections. He would contort his body so his head was on the floor; however, he was seated in the chair, making driving sounds and actions. He would look to be sure I was giving contact reflections. We spent a lot of time driving, turning corners so that our upper bodies were almost on the floor, while our backsides remained in the chairs.*

As the driving behaviors slowly decreased he would play with cars and other toys. I brought a large unbreakable mirror to the sessions. He would make faces into it and simultaneously watch his image while watching my reflections of his facial expressions. We played with a toy whose different shapes fit into holes of the same shape. At first, he played only with the basic toy and he had trouble fitting the shapes successfully From there he moved to fitting the shapes in easily and then became uninterested in the toy altogether. He liked to draw and continued to enjoy playing with cars. His crying behavior was diminishing in the cottage. During all this time I used only Pre-Therapy contact reflections.

THERAPIST:		Hi, X.
CLIENT:		Hi, Mimi.
THERAPIST:	SR	You looked at Mindy when you said hi.
THERAPIST:	SR	You sit in chair.
THERAPIST:	SR	You're looking for the steering wheel.
THERAPIST:	FR	You look all around.
THERAPIST:	SR	You picked up steering wheel.
THERAPIST:	FR	You're smiling.
CLIENT:		Vroom, vroom.
THERAPIST:	WWR	Vroom, vroom.
THERAPIST:	FR	You watch Mindy.
THERAPIST:	SR	The big mirror is on the table.
THERAPIST:	FR	You stick out your tongue.
THERAPIST:	RR	You do, I do.
THERAPIST:	FR	You smile when Mindy sticks out her tongue.
THERAPIST:	SR	We are both looking in the mirror.
THERAPIST:	BR	X and Mindy are sitting next to each other.
THERAPIST:	SR	X and Mindy look in the mirror.
THERAPIST:	FR	X smiles.
THERAPIST:	FR	You smile, I smile.
THERAPIST:	FR	Your lips are turned down.
THERAPIST:	SR	You are looking at X in the mirror.
THERAPIST:	FR	X is frowning.
CLIENT:		Here.
THERAPIST:	WWR	Here.
THERAPIST:	FR	Now your lips turned up.
THERAPIST:	FR	You do, I do.

CONTACT AND PERCEPTION

Therapist:	FR	X is smiling.
Therapist:	SR	You pick up the steering wheel.
Client:		Vroom, vroom.
Therapist:	WWR	Vroom, vroom.
Client:		Vroom, vroom.
Therapist:	WWR	Vroom, vroom.
Therapist:	SR	You look in mirror.
Therapist:	RR	You used to drive all the time.
Therapist:	SR	Now you drive sometimes.
Therapist:	SR	You pick up the red and blue toy.
Therapist:	SR	You're turning the toy around in your hands.
Therapist:	SR	You hand me the toy.
Client:		Open.
Therapist:	FR	You look.
Therapist:	FR	You look at Mindy.
Therapist:	SR	You want to take the shapes out of the toy.
Therapist:	FR	You watch.
Therapist:	RR	Last time we were sitting in the chairs.
Therapist:	RR	Last time it was raining.
Therapist:	SR	Today the sun is shining.
Therapist:	RR	Before, X said. 'Open.'
Client:		Here.
Therapist:	WWR	Here.
Therapist:	SR	You want the triangle in the hole.
Therapist:	FR	X smiles.
Therapist:	BR	You do, I do.

Ending Treatment: Expressive Phase —Therapist Report. *In the ending phase of therapy, X's driving behavior was extinct, as was his crying behavior. He no longer tore up the grass and he took part in a pre-vocational program. He went home from our sessions without the aid of staff. During our sessions he was more verbal and more assertive, expressing higher self-esteem. He would walk around the room and ask basic questions. He would express emotions appropriately and knew when he was happy or sad. He was able to attend field trips. He would even talk about other people, showing much improved reality contact and social communication.*

Therapist:		Hi, X.
Client:		Fine.
Therapist:		How are you today?
Client:		Fine.
Therapist:	WWR	Fine.
Therapist:	SR	You're taking off your coat.
Therapist:	SR	You are looking at Mindy.
Client:		Hang up?
Therapist:	WWR	Hang up?
Therapist:	SR	You want to know what to do with your coat. You can

		put it over there.
THERAPIST:	SR	*You put your coat on the chair.*
THERAPIST:	SR	*You're walking across the room.*
THERAPIST:	BR	*You sit down.*
THERAPIST:	SR	*You put your arms on the table.*
THERAPIST:	BR	*You do, I do.*
THERAPIST:	SR	*You reach in the bag.*
THERAPIST:	SR	*X takes out the green car.*
CLIENT:		*Vroom, vroom.*
THERAPIST:	WWR	*Vroom, vroom.*
THERAPIST:	SR	*X pushes the car off the table.*
THERAPIST:	SR	*It flies across the room.*
THERAPIST:	FR	*X laughs.*
THERAPIST:	BR	*X stands up.*
THERAPIST:	SR	*X pushes chair back.*
THERAPIST:	SR	*X picks up car.*
THERAPIST:	SR	*You're walking to the candy machine.*
THERAPIST:	SR	*You're rattling the handle.*
CLIENT:		*Candy.*
THERAPIST:	WWR	*Candy.*
CLIENT:		*Candy (louder).*
THERAPIST:	WWR	*Candy.*
THERAPIST:	SR	*X wants candy.*
THERAPIST:	SR	*No candy now, X.*
THERAPIST:	SR	*You're looking at Mindy.*
THERAPIST:	BR	*You're walking.*
THERAPIST:	SR	*You're looking at the stuff on the counter.*
CLIENT:		*Plates.*
THERAPIST:	WWR	*Plates.*
CLIENT:		*Napkins.*
THERAPIST:	WWR	*Napkins.*
CLIENT:		*Party?*
THERAPIST:	WWR	*Party.*
THERAPIST:	SR	*You want to know if there is going to be a party?*
THERAPIST:	SR	*Christmas is coming.*
CLIENT:		*Santa.*
THERAPIST:	WWR	*Santa.*
THERAPIST:	SR	*Santa comes at Christmas.*
THERAPIST:		*What are you doing for Christmas?*
CLIENT:		*Going home in car.*
THERAPIST:	WWR	*Going home in car.*
CLIENT:		*See Mom.*
THERAPIST:	WWR	*See Mom.*
THERAPIST:	RR	*You'll see Mom when you go home for Christmas.*
THERAPIST:	RR	*Before you laughed when you pushed the car off the table.*
THERAPIST:	FR	*You smiled when Mindy says that.*

CONTACT AND PERCEPTION

>   THERAPIST: Is someone coming to take you back to your house?
>   CLIENT: No.
>   THERAPIST: Good-bye, X.
>   CLIENT: Good-bye, Mimi.

A four-year follow-up review showed a stabilized and improved adjustment. The client was still without psychiatric medications. Institutional records indicate the client's accessibility to programmatic services. He participates in vocational, educational, and social activities. However, records also indicate instances of crying and verbal aggression.

An interview with his mother revealed her impressions: 'He's improved a lot... I really think it helped him a lot... We can bring him home now for longer periods of time without as much stress... It worked great.'

Most interestingly, she reported, 'It helped him see himself.' His mother also wished the treatment could have continued longer if circumstances could have permitted.

REFERENCES

Arieti, S. (1955). *Interpretation of Schizophrenia.* New York: Robert Brunner.
Binswanger, L. (1958). The existential analysis school of thought. *Existence: A New Dimension in Psychiatry and Psychology* (p. 194). New York: Basic Books.
Buber, M. (1964). Elements of the interhuman. In Friedman (Ed.), *The Worlds of Existentialism* New York: Random House. (Pp. 229–547).
Burton, A. (1973). The presentation of the face in psychotherapy. *Psychotherapy, Theory and Research, 10(4),* 301.
Christensen, L. B. (1991). *Experimental Methodology,* 5th edn. Boston: Allyn and Bacon.
Cohen, J. (1968). Weighted kappa: Nominal scale agreement with provision for scaled disagreement or partial credit. *Psychological Bulletin,* 70, 213–20.
De Vre, R. (1992). *Prouty's pre-therapié,* Master's Thesis. Ghent, Belgium: Department of Psychology, University of Ghent.
Dosen, A. (1983). Autism and disturbances of social contact in mentally retarded children. Vienna, Austria: Paper presented to the VII World Congress of Psychiatry.
Gurswitch, A. (1966). Gelb-Goldstein's concept of concrete and categorical attitude and the phenomenology of ideation. In J. Wild (Ed.), *Studies in Phenomenology and Psychology.* Evanston, Ill: Northwestern University Press, (pp. 359–89).
Farber, M. (1959). Consciousness and natural reality. *Naturalism and Subjectivism,* Albany, NY: State University of New York Press, p. 87.
Farber, M. (1967). Descriptive philosophy. *Phenomenology and Existence: Toward a Philosophy within Nature.* New York: Harper Torchbooks, pp. 14–37.
Havens, L. (1962). The placement and movement of hallucinations in space, phenomenology and theory. *International Journal of Psychoanalys is, 43,* 426–35.
Karon, B. and Vanderbos, G. (1981). *Psychotherapy of Schizophrenia.* New York: Aaronson.
Laing, R. D. (1990). Minkowski and schizophrenia. In K. Hoeller (Ed.), *Readings in Existential Psychology and Psychiatry.* (Special issue of *Review of Existential Psychology and Psychiatry.*) Seattle, Wash.: 195–8.
Leijssen, M. and Roelens, L. (1988). Herstel Van Contactfuncties Bij Zwaar Gestoorde Patienten Door Middel Van Prouty's Pre-Therapie (The contact functions of Prouty's Pre-Therapy) (pp. 21–34). Belgium: *Tijdsch rift Klinische Psychologie.*
Mallin, S. B. (1979). *Merleau-Ponty's Philosophy.* New Haven, Conn.: Yale University Press.
Maurer-Groeli, Y. A. (1976). Korperzentrierte Gruppenpsychotherapie bei akut schizophren Erkrankten *Arch. Psychiat. Nervenkr.* 221,259–71.

Merleau-Ponty, M. (1962). The phenomenal field. In T. Honderich (Ed.), *The Phenomenology of Perception* (p. 60). London: Routledge and Kegan Paul.

Minkowski, E. (1970). Schizophrenia. In J. Wild (Ed.), *Lived Time* (pp. 281–2). Evanston, Ill.: Northwestern University Press.

Perls, F. S. (1969). The ego as a function of the organism. *Ego, Hunger and Aggression* (p. 139). New York: Vintage Books.

Peters, H. (1981). *Luisterend Helpen: Poging Tot een Beter Cm gaan Met de Zwakzinnige Medemes*. Lochem/Gent, Netherlands: De Tijdstroom.

Peters, H. (1986b). Prouty's pré-therapie methode en de behandeling van hallucinaties een versiag (Prouty's Pre-Therapy methods and the treatment of hallucinations) (pp. 26—34). Netherlands: RUIT (Maart).

Prouty, G. (1985). The development of reality, affect and communication in psychotic retardates. Unpublished manuscript.

Prouty, G. (1994). *Theoretical Evolutions in Person-Centered/Experiential Therapy. Applications to Schizophrenic and Retarded Psychoses*. Greenwood, CT.: Praeger.

Prouty, G. and Cronwall, M. (1990). Psychotherapy with a depressed mentally retarded adult: An application of pre-therapy. In A. Dosen and F. Menolascino (Eds.), *Depression in Mentally Retarded Children and Adults* (pp. 281–93). Leiden, Netherlands: Logan Publications.

Prouty, G. and Kubiak, M. (1988a). The development of communicative contact with a catatonic schizophrenic. *Journal of Communication Therapy*, 4(1), 13–20.

Prouty, G. and Kubiak, M. (1988b). Pre-therapy with mentally retarded/psychotic clients. *Psychiatric Aspects of Mental Retardation Reviews*, 7(10), 62–6.

Riepe, D. (1973). *Marvin Farber and the program of naturalistic phenomenology. Phenomenology and Natural Existence*, (pp. 26–48). Albany: State University of New York Press.

Sartre, J. P. (1956). *Being and Nothingness*. New York: Washington Square Press.

Scheler, M. (1953). Phenomenology and the theory of cognition. *Selected Philosophical Essays*. Evanston, Ill.: Northwestern University Press.

Sovner, R. and Hurley, A. (1983). Do the mentally retarded suffer from affective illness? *Archives of General Psychiatry*, 40, 61–7.

Spiegelberg, H. (1978). The pure phenomenology of Edmund Husserl. *The Phenomenological Movement: A Historical Introduction*, Vol. 1, 2nd edn. (p. 107). Boston: Martinus Nijhoff.

Van Werde, D. (1990). Psychotherapy with a retarded schizo-affective woman: An application of Prouty's pre-therapy. In A. Dosen, A. Van Gennep and C. Zwanikken (Eds.), *Treatment of Mental Illness and Behavioral Disorder in the Mentally Retarded: Proceedings of International Congress, May 3rd and 4th, Amsterdam, The Netherlands* (pp. 469–77). Leiden, The Netherlands: Logon Publications.

4   Psychological Contact, Meaningful Process and Human Nature.
A Reformulation of Person-Centered Theory

Margaret S. Warner

The person-centered approach to psychological contact offers a humanizing alternative to views of severe disturbance that are prevalent in clinical psychology. And, while the concept of contact is often ignored, this first 'necessary and sufficient condition of personality change' (Rogers, 1957) can be seen as forming a foundation for the rest of the person-centered view of human nature. To fully realize this potential, however, I believe that the person-centered conceptualization of psychological contact needs to be clarified and elaborated.

In this paper I will offer a reformulation of the concept of 'psychological contact'. This reformulation aims to clarify the relation of psychological contact to human actualization in a way that captures the courageous persistence with which clients strive to establish and maintain contact with reality, while attempting to avoid pitfalls implicit in the theories of other psychological approaches. To do this I will first review some of the issues relating to psychological concepts and theories that need to be addressed in order to maintain the distinctive power of the Person-Centered Approach. I will summarize the two main definitions of 'psychological contact' within person-centered theory — that of Carl Rogers and that of Garry Prouty, considering the strengths and weaknesses of each formulation.

Following this, I will offer a slightly altered definition of psychological contact, one that I believe resolves some of the issues implicit in the earlier formulations. Using this definition as a base, I will consider ways that psychological contact and normative ways of processing meaning function interdependently. To do this, I propose that human beings are predisposed to conceptualize experience using 'soft meanings', a term that allows us to connect person-centered theory with some of the newer developments in the human sciences relating to evolutionary psychology and the negotiation of meaning.

SOME BROAD ISSUES IN THE LANGUAGE OF PSYCHOLOGY

Early psychological theories often described human phenomena as if they were mechanical (e.g. stimulus-response sequences) or as if there were fully formed 'deeper' meanings under the surface (e.g. repressed or unconscious meanings) that could be determined by experts in a relatively unilateral way. In recent years, many of the assumptions behind such language have been challenged in philosophy, sociology and linguistics (Greenberg and Pascual-Leone, 1997; Gendlin, 1995, 1997).

Few psychologists or counselors today would claim to hold these assumptions in their more extreme and simplistic forms. Yet, I believe that aspects of such assumptions still permeate clinical psychology. Often, psychological theories are used to buttress the idea that the client's own version of his or her experience is insignificant in comparison to that of experts. When unchallenged, such assumptions have a particularly strong effect on the most vulnerable clients — those who are poor, stigmatized, developmentally challenged or severely disturbed. Such clients are often treated as if they were incapable of doing serious work on psychological difficulties or of having a meaningful voice in choices affecting their own lives. In the process, they are often treated as if outwardly conventional social behavior were the only index of mental well-being.

Work in narrative psychology (Spence, 1982; Sarbin, 1986) abandons many of the mechanistic, authority-driven assumptions of psychology, advocating a co-construction of meaning by therapist and client. Yet, such work sometimes goes to another extreme, speaking as if meaning were an arbitrary construction or invention. Many therapies are trying to find a collaborative alternative between these two positions, one that recognizes ways that issues are deeply embedded in the totality of clients' lived experience, without assuming that the therapist should operate as an expert capable of unilaterally decoding the meaning of client situations (Stolorow and Atwood, 1992; Miller, 1997; Mitchell, 1988).

Rogers' (1957, 1959) theory offers a third alternative, one which offers a much better fit with these recent, more collaborative forms of therapy and with recent work in philosophy and linguistics. Rogers proposes that human beings have an organismically grounded impetus to explicate the meaning of their situations (which is developed within and facilitated by authentic, empathic, prizing relationships) that operates in the service of actualization. Gendlin's work (1968, 1970, 1995, 1997) greatly deepens the philosophic underpinnings of Rogers' work, and connects it to recent work in philosophy, biology and linguistics.

The concept of contact is central to a person-centered model of human nature, particularly as it relates to work with severely disturbed clients. Yet, I believe that psychological contact and its relation to the ongoing negotiation of meaning characteristic of human beings is vague and contradictory as currently formulated within person-centered theory. Given this, I think that it is worth the theoretical effort to clarify and further articulate our understanding of the term.

INITIAL FORMULATIONS OF PSYCHOLOGICAL CONTACT: CARL ROGERS AND GARRY PROUTY

The first of the 'necessary and sufficient' conditions of therapeutic personality change — that 'two persons are in psychological contact' — is quite minimal as Rogers (1957) formulates it:

> All that is intended by this first condition is to specify that the two people are to some degree in contact, that each makes some perceived difference in the experiential field of the other. Probably it is sufficient if each makes some 'subceived' difference, even though the individual may not be consciously aware of this impact (cited in Kirschenbaum and Henderson, 1989, p. 221).

CONTACT AND PERCEPTION

Rogers (1957) notes that contact, as he has defined it, is such a basic condition that he would label it as an 'assumption' or a 'precondition' (p. 222). In another statement of the conditions of the therapeutic process (Rogers, 1959), he offers an even shorter version of this criterion, stipulating only that 'two persons are in contact'.[1]

Notably, Rogers' definition of contact deals with perceptions and has nothing to do with any meaningful organization of such perceptions. Yet, the everyday meaning of 'contact' goes beyond simple alterations in the experiential field. People feel out of contact with each other when they can't sense the other person as meaningfully present. For example, therapists are likely to feel out of contact when clients seem strikingly incoherent, irrational, inattentive or unpredictable. Both therapists and clients often experience intense distress and therapeutic difficulty when they are unable to be in contact in such everyday ways. Rogers' minimalist definition of contact makes no attempt to address the quality of such contact or its impact on the therapy process.

Garry Prouty (1994) considers the issue of contact at considerable length in connection to his work with clients who are experiencing schizophrenia or retarded psychoses. Prouty notes that, when contact is impaired,

> The rich, meaningful everyday natural pre-reflective consciousness is no longer 'intentional' (toward, with, about) ... Existence becomes 'void of significance', a failure in coherence. Consciousness becomes empty, an isolated shell of meaninglessness. It lives without the 'creation of meaning' that comes from contact with the natural absolutes of world, self or other (p. 34).

Prouty suggests that when clients' contact with self, world or other is impaired therapists can develop connection using 'contact reflections' that stay very close to the client's exact words and gestures.

> Contact reflections are concrete in that they are extraordinarily literal and duplicative. They are empathic to the specific concrete particularity of the client's regressed efforts at expression and communication (p. 38).

Prouty proposes that 'pre-therapy' using contact reflections tends to strengthen 'contact functions':

> Pretherapy ... tends to reduce psychotic expression and facilitate more realistic communication embodying world, self or other (reality, affective or communicative contact) (p. 40).

Once contact functions are strengthened, more ordinary therapy can proceed.

In general, Prouty seems to view most psychotic material as potentially realistic forms of experience that have been partially processed or processed in aberrant ways. However, Prouty (2000) also suggests that some retarded and psychotic clients give indications of having a surprisingly developed, realistic and coherent 'pre-expressive self' that emerges at certain moments without seeming to go through extended processing.

Prouty critiques Rogers' definition of 'contact' as one of the necessary and sufficient conditions:

---

1. For the purposes of this paper I will use the terms 'contact' and 'psychological contact' interchangeably.

> Unfortunately, Rogers provides no theoretical definition of psychological contact.
> Additionally, he does not provide any technique for restoring psychological contact if it is impaired. Last, he proceeds theoretically as if contact between therapist and client were assumed. In essence, Rogers does not provide any theoretical or clinical guidance for psychological contact, often a major problem for these clients (p. 26).

Prouty is addressing an important issue here, but in the process he is shifting definitions somewhat. Rogers' definition of contact as cited above is clear. To be in contact, the therapist only needs to make some perceived, or perhaps even subceived, difference in the client's experiential field. Rogers makes no requirement that contact be elaborated, that it be reality oriented or that it come in any particularly process-rich form. The psychotic and developmentally disabled clients that Prouty is working with in Pre-therapy meet Rogers' criteria of contact almost by definition. Notably, if the therapist didn't make some difference in the client's experiential field, it is hard to see that there would be any way for the 'contact reflections' advocated by Prouty to have any impact on the client.

While Prouty (1994, 2000) has shifted away from Rogers' original definition of contact, I believe that the expanded definition implied in Prouty's writings makes theoretical sense given Rogers' other necessary and sufficient conditions of constructive personality change. Notably, Rogers states in his sixth condition that the therapist's empathy and unconditional positive regard need to be at least minimally communicated (1957) or perceived by the client (1959). Any full sort of communication and perception of empathy would seem to require a client to have some meaningful sense of having a personal existence him- or herself. Some moderately unified sense of self would seem necessary for a client to be able to perceive that another person exists in the world, to be aware that the other person has a phenomenal reality, and to believe that the other person could be empathic. This is not to say that significant perceptions and connections may not happen without fully developed psychological contact. Contact can be viewed as a continuum, in which quite minimal levels of contact are sufficient for Rogers' core conditions to work to some degree. And, Prouty (1994) suggests that responses that convey empathy for clients' contact-impaired expressions tend to increase the levels of psychological contact that are available to that person.

Given these considerations, I think that the shift in definition implied in Prouty's writings has significant advantages. Still, Prouty leaves psychological contact explicated in language that carries many of the philosophical problems of earlier theories. While Prouty's broader theory (1994, 2000) is clearly phenomenological, his actual definitions of contact are worded as if the client were accessing phenomena that had a definite and pre-existing reality under the surface. For example, world, self and other are described as 'natural absolutes' (Prouty, 1994, p. 34). 'Affective contact' is described as 'the awareness of moods, feelings and emotions'; 'communicative contact' is defined as the 'symbolization of reality (world) and affect (self) to others' (Prouty, 2000, p. 69). These definitions are worded as if 'emotions', 'reality', 'world', 'affect' and 'self' and the like were pre-existing phenomena under the surface with which one could be in contact.

This sort of reified wording is common within psychology, and at times it can be useful in formulating researchable hypotheses. Still, I think that such language is problematic as a way of conceptualizing phenomena in person-centered theory, since it de-emphasizes the dimension of existential freedom in the human processing of meaning. In the process, it begs the question, which I think is central to person-centered theory, of how meaningful contact is formed if there isn't a preformed version of reality already existing somewhere in the human organism. In this paper I attempt to develop a theoretically clear account of the sorts of meaningful contact implied by Prouty (1994, 2000) without using language implying that a pre-determined version of reality already exists under the surface.

PSYCHOLOGICAL CONTACT REFORMULATED

The expanded definition of 'psychological contact' that I want to explore in this paper is as follows: 'Contact is a fundamental adaptation of the human organism that allows human beings to feel that they are meaningfully present[2], both verbally and non-verbally, to themselves and to each other'. In personal interactions one ordinarily has a sense of being in contact with a person who is present in a regular, culturally normative way. Even sitting non-verbally with another person, one has a sense of this sort of psychological contact. For example, if one were sitting with a relative who had had a stroke and was unable to speak, one might still have the sense of being in contact with a meaningful person just by the look in the person's eye, or the intention conveyed by a hand gesture.

Yet, the elements that go into this sort of contact are exceedingly complex if looked at closely. Take, for example, an interaction at the beginning of a session in which a client looks at the therapist and says in a hurt tone of voice, 'I thought we were going to meet at three today. Did you forget?' The client has made non-verbal connection in a way that is easily sensed as personally intended. She has formed a comprehensible statement in grammatical language which represents some apparently genuine feeling in the moment. She conveys that she knows who you are, who she is and what you are both doing there. She seems to have a unitary sense of self that she is able to speak out of when she says 'I'. And, from that unitary perspective, she is able to consider some aspects of what your frame of reference and intentions might be. She is able to feel some level of distress without a level of intensity that would bring her to bang her head against the wall or to physically attack you.

'Psychological contact', as defined here, is both a way that individuals represent themselves to themselves that allows them to experience and speak from a personally meaningful subjective self and it is a way that individuals represent themselves to each other that allows them to convey a sense of meaningful presence to each other. I propose that, to have such a personally meaningful subjective self, an individual needs to have a moderately coherent narrative version of his or her life experience, one that is organismically grounded and that serves a number of species-common, cultural and idiosyncratic purposes simultaneously. I will discuss these various elements involved in the

---

2. There are, of course, varying degrees and kinds of meaningful presence. The 'presence' that Rogers refers to in his later writings (Rogers, 1980) seems to be a particularly valuable form of meaningful presence that occurs when the core conditions come together in relational depth (Mearns,1997).

formation of psychological contact at greater length in later sections of this paper.

I suggest that these capacities coming together in ordinary moment-to-moment interactions create a sense of psychological contact that is characteristic of human nature and is basic to the functioning of human culture. Because human beings are adapted to expect basic levels of this sort of 'meaningful presence' within themselves and in relation to others, they tend to feel intense discomfort when they are unable to achieve it. To explore this hypothesis further, let us consider some recent thinking about 'human nature' within evolutionary psychology and relate this thinking to ordinary experiences within person-centered therapy.

HUMAN NATURE, ACTUALIZATION AND EVOLUTIONARY PSYCHOLOGY

A considerable amount of work has been done re-conceptualizing the role of human nature in the understanding of psychology and culture in recent decades. Tooby and Cosmides (1992) make a strong case that: '. . . the species-typical organization of the psychology and physiology of modern humans necessarily has an evolutionary explanation and an evolutionarily patterned architecture' (p. 55), and '. . . if one is interested in uncovering intelligible organization in our species-typical psychological architecture, discovering and describing adaptations is the place to begin' (p. 55).

Those adaptations that are basic to human nature are thought to have occurred in the millions of years that humans lived as hunter gatherers in the Pleistocene era. Evolutionary psychology, then, would suggest that any distinctively human aspects of the actualization tendency will involve a process or cluster of processes that enhanced human survival in the Pleistocene era.

Evolutionary psychologists note that such adaptations do not unfold independently from the environment. Rather the biology of the organism is evolved to expect a certain sort of 'environment of evolutionary adaptedness' that is essential to its unfolding:

> Adaptations evolve so that they mesh with the recurring structural properties of the environment in such a way that reproduction is promoted in the organism or its kin. Like a key in a lock, adaptations and particular features of the world fit together tightly to promote functional ends (p. 69).

We would expect any species-wide psychological tendencies to emerge in conjunction with those early childhood family experiences that are relatively universal. Parental nurturance and the attachment processes of early childhood are likely candidates (Stern, 1985).

Some evolutionary psychologists have held that the mind consists almost entirely of multiple 'domain-specific' intelligences. Such intelligences have been compared to an array of functionally dedicated computers[3], each dealing with a separate area of life, having, for example,

---

3. Gendlin (1995, 1997, 2001 (in draft)) elaborates on such separations of capacities, but suggests that comparisons with computers and machines are highly misleading when applied to living organisms.

... procedures, representational formats, or content primitives that evolved especially to deal with faces, mothers, language, sex, food, infants, tools, siblings, friendship ... (Tooby and Barkow, 1992, p. 94).

Others (Samuels, 2000) have proposed that more domain-general capacities emerged at some point in human evolution. Mithen (2000) notes that:
... the central role of the brain in understanding the mind has been saved by the claim that there occurs a change in the structure, rather than the size of the brain at 60,000 years and it is this that lies at the root of the modern mind ...

That new types of thinking emerge cannot be doubted, and I am confident that these relate to cross-domain thinking — the integration of knowledge and ways of thinking that had previously been isolated within separate intelligences (p. 211).

This emergence of cross-domain thinking is closely tied to the development of 'public language' which allows the human mind to use culture to expand beyond the resources that any individual mind could develop:
Once people communicate with language it makes little sense to conceive of the mind as being constituted within the body of a single person, as each person draws upon, exploits, and adds to, the ideas and knowledge within other people's minds (Mithen, 2000, p. 213).

Clark and Chalmers (1998, cited in Mithen, 2000) speculate that:
The intellectual explosion in recent evolutionary time is due as much to this linguistically enabled extension of cognition as to any independent development of our cognitive resources (p. 213).

We are so accustomed to living within our own human natures, that it can be difficult to see the magnitude of this shift into integrative forms of meaning and to notice the ways that the processes by which such meanings are developed in a day-to-day way. Let us take some time, then, to look closely at the ways that ordinary human interactions accomplish this quite extraordinary feat. The non-directivity of person-centered therapy gives us a particular chance to reflect on human capacities and predilections which are basic to human nature without the confounding effects of interventions that come from outside the clients' frames of reference. And, seeing the way that these phenomena operate in human nature should help clarify the nature of change within therapeutic processes in general and person-centered therapy in particular.

CROSS-DOMAIN PROCESSING OF MEANING

Clients in person-centered psychotherapy ordinarily do a great deal of cross-domain processing of experience. Such processing crosses subject areas as well as a variety of quite different ways that such experience is organized within the human organism — such as images, words, or the felt sense of situations (Warner, 1997; Rice and Greenberg, 1984; Gendlin, 1964, 1968, 1974, 1990; Rice, 1974; Wexler, 1974). Clients tend to feel a sense of relief when they feel understood about something that is important to them within relationships that are experienced as authentic and prizing (Warner, 1997). With that sense of relief, spontaneous change and reorganization of experience often occurs. New thoughts, feelings images, memories, and the like emerge in awareness. These new experiences come in a variety of forms, which probably engage quite different parts of the brain. Clients typically attend further to newly emerging aspects of their experience and reformulate them in words that better express the meaning of those experiences. This cross-domain thinking enables people to put words to whole clusters of experience. And, in the process of putting words to experience, the felt quality of the experiences themselves tends to change.

Notably this evolved way of creating meaning is simultaneously personal and public — allowing humans to integrate experiences that had previously been separate and to do this in terms that connect to group processes that developed over large spans of time and space. This way of creating meaning is deeply relational, requiring a public language that is grounded in culture and learned in early attachment relationships. And, on the other hand, human beings can't be in relationships with each other without such meaningfully organized languages.

Psychological contact and the ability to process meaning across domains seem to be mutually necessary aspects of the culturally-based group functioning that is characteristic of human beings. Adult forms of psychological contact develop within attachment relationships of early childhood in which children develop the ability to process meaning in culturally normative ways. This ability to process meaning continues to be necessary to maintain psychological contact, and some amount of psychological contact with other human beings is necessary to continue to process meaning.

I propose that this intimate relation between psychological contact and the ability to process meaning is maintained by a particular sort of 'soft' meanings. Such soft meanings are particularly adapted to the creation of versions of experience that carry forward the wide range of different sorts of experience implicit in the human organism. While such versions of experience are intimately related to the totality of organismic experience, they do not involve any simple representation of pre-exiting realities 'under the surface'. Let us explore the nature of such soft meanings in more depth.

SOFT MEANING AS THE BASIS OF PSYCHOLOGICAL CONTACT AND THE NEGOTIATION OF MEANING

Many clusters of experience are organized in terms of a particular sort of concept that I would call 'soft meanings' which are applied to a sort of phenomena that I would call 'soft phenomena' (Warner, 1983). Soft meanings apply to humanly formulated intrapsychic phenomena such as self, intentions, purposes, attributes of character and the like, as well as to various cultural forms. Soft meanings have a number of qualities that I will explore at some length. But, let me briefly state their core attributes here. (1) Soft meanings are open to ongoing negotiation and change so that they don't have the sort of stable reality over space and time expected of 'hard' phenomena. (2) Separate observers of soft phenomena don't necessarily converge on a single way of conceptualizing soft phenomena. (3) Yet, human beings are adapted to conceptualize experience in terms of soft phenomena and soft phenomena tend to feel extremely 'real' under certain circumstances. (4) Soft phenomena have as much or more impact on people's lives as more hard phenomena. 'Hard' meanings, on the other hand, apply to phenomena that have a 'thing-like' character, such as physical objects and extremely stable cultural processes. Let us explore these phenomena in more depth.

Soft phenomena such as self, intentions, purposes, emotions or attributes of character are interpreted in varying ways by different individuals at different times. One person may say a comment was a joke, another may think that it really was an intentional insult. A person may think that he is committed to a project and later believe that he was just avoiding spending time at home with his wife. A person may express anger when drunk but later feel that that emotion didn't come from his real self. Hard phenomena, on the other hand, tend to be identified in the same way by differing observers and the attributions tend to remain stable over time. Two people in a room that see a table are likely to agree that it is a table and persist in that belief at a later time. Most people will agree on whether they have been to a wedding or whether a soldier was saluting, for example.

Soft phenomena tend to feel real to human beings, while in a certain sense they are constructs of the imagination. As a person is labeling a soft phenomenon, that labeling often feels very real and solid. For example, at the moment when a person says, 'I want a hot-fudge sundae so much that I can taste it', or 'I thought I had forgiven my father, but I realize now that I have hated him my whole life', this coming together of a variety of experiences may feel as solid and convincing as any physical event in her life. And, since human social life tends to be organized in terms of soft phenomena, these phenomena have as much or more impact on the concrete events of people's lives as more solid 'hard' phenomena. For example, if I decide that I don't really love my fiance, I may decide not to get married. If a jury decides that I intentionally pushed someone off a bridge rather than accidentally falling against that person, I may have to go to prison for the rest of my life.

Given the evolutionary importance of this sort of culturally-based, cross-domain thinking, I suspect that soft phenomena feel 'real' because human beings are adapted to construing life in those sorts of categories. Yet, if looked at closely, soft phenomena don't have any solidness of existence. If I say 'I am truly sorry' or 'I'm not my true self today' or 'you are irresponsible', those phenomena don't exist in any concrete place.

While soft phenomena are defined by criteria that are broadly shared within a culture, particular instances of a phenomenon are likely to be named differently by different people. One juror may think that an accused person is 'genuinely remorseful' while another thinks that he is 'coldly cynical'. And, individuals or subcultural groups may vary in the exact criteria of attribution used. What seems 'loyal' to a Yankee Protestant, may be quite different from what seems 'loyal' to an Italian from Sicily. And, given the many dimensions of such attributions, any attribution can sensibly be disputed or changed at a later time.

It is notable to me that clients who try to formulate and reformulate their experiences typically use soft meanings to create a coherent narrative. In forming these narratives they are usually trying to accomplish a number of quite different purposes at once. Clients typically try to develop a narrative version of experience that fits the totality of their own lived experience, one that is culturally and linguistically sensible, and one which offers some predictive fit with the reality the person finds herself in.[4] And, they try to do this in a way that maintains their subjective sense of viability, looking for ways of construing their experience that don't leave them so overwhelmed or demoralized that they have no incentive to continue living in ways that they value.

I suspect that at the point of evolution at which human beings developed a 'public language' that language (and the biological organism supporting such language) was structured to serve multiple purposes simultaneously in the ways cited above. People developed public language within a culture and were evolved to feel the need to 'fit' or be seen as sane within a culture. Yet the purpose of that same language was to integrate very disparate kinds of information from within individuals' own experience. One core advantage of this personally integrative, culturally-based language was an improved ability to predict what was going to happen next in the material world — something that is sometimes called 'reliability for truth' (Samuels, 2000, p. 188). Yet with their expanded ability to consider possibilities and to foresee outcomes, human beings evolved a capacity for destructive rage and despair that is beyond that of other animals. It is sensible that human beings would have an evolutionarily-based tendency to avoid ways of construing their situations that were so overwhelmingly painful or demoralizing that they would come to threaten their own lives or those of close associates.

The sorts of multipurpose narratives that I am describing here allow individuals to organize and represent complex and disparate clusters of experience in relatively unified ways that allow them to have a sense of psychological contact. Individuals can have a sense of who they are, what they are doing and why they are doing it that can be communicated to other people of the same culture. This is not to say that everything is known or that everything is communicated. But, psychological contact offers a beginning point from which more could be known and more could be communicated in words, gestures or other sorts of action. And this beginning point, this sense of meaningful presence, tends to offer the reassuring conviction that one is dealing with a regular, sane person, a person with whom one can expect to continue interacting in a culturally comprehensible way.

While the multiple purposes of human narratives can be separated for the purpose of analysis, actual human beings tend to feel the totality of their lived experience in more holistic ways. Gendlin (1995) notes that multiple elements come together into a single organismic implying:

> A great many factors *cross* in a single felt sense. Some have been separated out before, many have not. Your felt sense (of this presentation) implicitly contains all you have heard me say, but also much that you have thought and read about these topics over the years, and your own work in all of its many relevances — and much more all *crossing* so each implicitly changes, *governs and gives relevance to* the others (p. 552).

---

4. These first purposes could be seen as paralleling Prouty's (1994) three content areas of contact — contact with 'self', 'world' and 'other'. Conceptualizing them as purposes offers some theoretical flexibility in that it is less likely to be construed as implying the existence of a single right 'reality'.

CONTACT AND PERCEPTION

Gendlin proposes that only some words or expressions work to 'carry forward' the implicit multiplicity of lived experience. When this happens, an individual has an intuitive felt sense of the rightness of the words:

> ... what is implicit is changed by explicating it. But not just any change. The explication releases that tension that was the ____. But, what the blank was is not just lost or altered, rather that tension is *carried forward* by the words ... (p. 549).

Usually, there are many versions of a person's experience available that would be culturally sensible or realistic. Yet, only a very few of these will be congruent with the lived experience of the person at that particular moment, offering a felt sense of rightness to the person him- or herself.

This view of psychological contact makes sense of the particular power that can be found in therapies that encourage self-directed processing. If psychological contact is structured by multipurpose narratives sensed in holistic ways by the individual, there can be no single right way of construing reality that can be determined from the outside. Of course, few psychological professionals would say that they want to impose a single version of reality on their clients. Yet, the presumption of the existence of a pre-existing reality is built into much of the language of psychology and counseling. Emotions are described as being 'buried', 'unconscious', 'cut off' or 'under the surface' as if there were a single right reality already there for the client to dig up. Or, the person's experience is seen as altered by 'defense mechanisms' as if a pre-existing right version of reality existed (that an outside expert might ascertain) that had gone through some sort of distortions. Descriptions of the archaic defense of 'projective identification' often seem to suggest that unconscious realities can be transferred directly from one person's body into that of another person in ways that are both mysterious and inexorable. The word 'mechanism' itself implies a rigid, cause-effect sequence of predictable outcome. When psychologists and counselors use this sort of language, they easily slip into believing that the meaning of clients' situations already exists inside them in a preformed way and that the 'real' meanings of such situations could be unilaterally determined from the outside.

In talking about multipurpose narratives we can acknowledge that particular ways of construing experience may work better in serving one purpose or another — such as resonating with a person's bodily felt experience or predicting what is likely to happen next — without saying that any single version of the person's experience is authoritatively right. We can acknowledge that some clusters of experience have an aptness for particular sorts of construal. And we can acknowledge that a few core purposes are central to human nature as it has evolved, so that most people will find life exceedingly difficult if they are systematically thwarted. But this does not imply that any single construal is right for any particular purpose, much less that we know which of these purposes should be most important to a client at any given moment.

Metaphorically speaking, one could see flour, eggs, butter, milk, baking powder and sugar on a kitchen table and say that those ingredients have particular potential to become a cake. But a cook could also make scrambled eggs and biscuits. Or, the cook might not want to bake anything at all. One would not say that the ingredients constitute a buried cake or a repressed cake or a cake under the surface. Language that implies a single right outcome de-emphasizes the personal process and existential choice of the person who must decide what to make of the ingredients at hand. While I think that casual use of such 'reality under the surface' language is problematic for psychology in general, I think that it is particularly treacherous for therapists who want to stay centered on the phenomenal reality of the client.

If anything, I think that the complexity of the evolved purposes of human narratives may have intensified the human experience of subjectivity and choice. At any given moment, most people have versions of their experience that only partially meet all of the narrative purposes I have listed above. A person may sensibly say, 'I know that this seems crazy, but I feel as if I will die if I become successful in my work.' Or, she may say, 'I think it's better right now to just ignore what I feel about this situation and just go ahead anyway.' Or, 'Thinking about this is overwhelmingly painful and reminds me of what the original abuse felt like, but I want to try to stay with it anyway.'

Person-centered therapists have pointed out the value of staying receptive to aspects of experience that don't fit well with ordinary narrative purposes — that seem crazy or unrealistic or different from anything that the person identifies with as themselves. They observe that when received empathically, such experiences tend to go through changes that carry them forward, ultimately coming together in new organismically grounded formulations that come much closer to meeting the various narrative purposes that are relevant to the person.

Individuals have existential choice as to which purposes are given greater weight than others at any given moment. They have choice among a variety of mental faculties that can be brought to bear as they process experience. They have choice as to whether to go ahead with a version of experience that is partially satisfactory or whether to ponder it further in the hopes of coming to a better understanding. And, the availability of multiple possible ways of understanding situations also opens various possibilities of strategy in human discourse. People may choose one way of construing a situation over another based on its impact on others in their environment — for example, to flatter or deceive or comfort (Warner, 1983, 1989).

Additionally, individual people may sensibly choose to go against ways of responding that are deeply embedded in human nature. In the same way that a person might choose to be celibate or to live in solitude, a person may decide to avoid making any kind of public sense (perhaps as a Beat poet), or to minimize attention to some aspects of their personal lived experience in formulating an understanding of their situation (perhaps as a Stoic or a practitioner of Zen). They may have other more idiosyncratic purposes for their own accounts of meaning in their lives, that are different from or added to more adapted, species-common purposes.

CAPACITIES RELATED TO PSYCHOLOGICAL CONTACT AND THE NEGOTIATION OF MEANING

A number of capacities have been noted in the client-centered and experiential literature that allow multipurpose narratives to emerge from and differentiate organismic experience. Such narratives organize soft phenomena in ways that allow human beings to feel a sense of psychological contact with themselves and each other. The following is a partial, somewhat overlapping list of such capacities:

(1) an ability to hold experience in attention, and to direct attention to aspects of experience that are felt to be most relevant (Warner, 1997);

(2) an ability to attend both to complex, multifaceted aspects of felt-sense experience and to more verbal, linear, logical-propositional ways of knowing (Gendlin, 1964, 1968, 1970, 1974, 1990);

(3) an ability to form and attend to images that literally or metaphorically capture the immediacy of experience (Rice, 1974; Rice and Greenberg, 1984);

(4) an ability to make use of one or more alternate ways of integrating experiences that are available within the organism; or to use a variety of modes of integrating experience sequencing them in ways that allow the person to use the strengths of different mental capacities (Warner, 1997; Greenberg and Pascual-Leone, 1997);

(5) an ability to moderate the intensity of reactions in such a way that the person can get information about the affective significance of experiences without being traumatized or losing control of their actions in the process (Warner, 1991, 1997, 2000);

(6) a capacity to move back and forth among various kinds of logical categories to determine those that are relevant to various narrative purposes and to use culturally coherent systems of causation to check the validity of particular versions of experience (Prouty, 1994; Warner, 2002 (in press));

(7) an ability to dissociate from experiences that are traumatically painful and overwhelming (Warner, 1991, 1997);

(8) an ability to integrate narratives in ways that create a subjective sense of self (or selves) that is relatively stable and coherent (Rogers, 1951, 1959; Wexler, 1974; Mearns and Thorne, 2000).

I suspect that there are innumerable other capacities that we take for granted in ordinary, day-to-day interactions that are relevant. The 'domain general' capacities that go into formulating narratives, integrate great numbers of more 'domain specific' capacities that are being identified by clinical and evolutionary psychologists. It seems likely, therefore, that breakdown in any number of those more domain-specific capacities could endanger contact. For example, Baron-Cohen et al. (1995) suggest that autistic children have difficulty with a particular evolved capacity to have a 'theory of mind' that predisposes people to experience others as having intentions. Others have noted that 'prosopagnosic' clients, who have damage to the occipitotemporal areas of the brain, lose specialized capacity for the emotional recognition of faces (Murphy and Stich, 2000, p. 79).

PSYCHOLOGICAL CONTACT AND DIFFICULT PROCESS

While individuals may choose to limit certain elements of psychological contact for personal reasons, I believe that the situation is quite different when a person is unable to be in contact in usual human ways. Ordinarily, multiple species-common purposes come together in a moderately unified version of experience that lets one human being feel that he or she is in contact with another human being.

When individuals are unable to formulate versions of reality that meets those purposes they are likely to feel the consequences in ways that are exceedingly hard to bear. Metaphorically speaking, one could say that the human situation 'talks back'. When a person is unable to form a version of reality that predicts what will happen next, reality talks back as painful, unexpected events happen. When a person is unable to formulate experience in ways that are culturally sensible, the culture talks back by shaming, rejecting and isolating the person. When a person is unable to find a way to formulate experience in ways that are organismically grounded, the body talks back with emptiness, anxiety and somatic pain. If a person is unable to find a way to formulate experience that makes life tolerable and offers some hope, he or she may find death to be a preferable solution. For all of these reasons, being blocked from psychological contact is almost always experienced as an affliction. Person-centered writers have described several forms of process that make contact difficult at length elsewhere so I will only describe them briefly here.

Some clients experience 'fragile process' (Warner, 1991, 1997, 2000) in such a way that they have difficulty holding experience in attention at moderate levels of intensity. As a result, they tend to have difficulty starting and stopping experiences that are personally significant or emotionally connected. And, they are likely to have difficulty taking in the point of view of another person while remaining in contact with such experiences. For example, a client may talk circumstantially for most of a therapy hour and only connect with an underlying feeling of grief at the very end. She may then be afraid that she will cry forever and find herself unable to return to work for hours afterward. She may want to talk to the therapist about the intense vulnerability of her feelings and to have them understood. Yet, if the therapist attempts to understand in a way that doesn't catch her feelings in exactly the right words, she may feel that the therapist has annihilated her experience.

All of these elements of fragile process can make psychological contact difficult. A sense of self — which, of course, is a soft phenomenon — involves a coming together of a sense of organismically grounded coherence in relation to one's lived experience. Such a sense of self usually develops within a mutually reinforcing cycle in which one represents oneself to oneself and one's experience is received and accepted by other human beings. The vulnerability, intensity and shame that emerge when a person touches fragile aspects of experience can easily lead a person to avoid the sorts of processing necessary to the development of such an organismically grounded, coherent version of experience. And, the shame and relational touchiness characteristic of fragile process can easily stop a person from having the sort of relational interchanges that would support any sense that the person's experiences are socially real or acceptable. I believe that it is very hard to hold onto a sense that experiences are personally real without such a sense of their being socially real. Also, such relational difficulties can make it hard to receive feedback from others, leading to a sort of tunnel vision in which the person only formulates experience from his or her own point of view.

Given all of these aspects of fragile process, the person may have difficulty forming a personally grounded, predictively realistic or culturally coherent version of experience. Clients who have a fragile style of processing often experience their lives as chaotic or empty. If clients with fragile process choose to stay connected with their experience in personal relationships, they are likely to feel violated and misunderstood a lot of the time. When they express their feelings, other people in their lives are likely to see them as unreasonably angry, touchy and stubborn. These others are likely to become angry and rejecting in return, reinforcing clients' sense that there is something fundamentally poisonous about their existence. If, on the other hand, they give up on connecting or expressing their personal reactions, they are likely to feel frozen or dead inside. Many alternate, holding in their reactions while feeling increasingly uncomfortable and then exploding with rage at those around them.

Useful styles of working with clients experiencing fragile process or other closely related sorts of process have been described by a number of person-centered and experiential psychotherapists (Bohart, 1990; Eckert and Biermann-Ratjen, 1998; Eckert and Wuchner, 1996; Lambers, 1994; Leijssen, 1993, 1996).

Clients who experience 'dissociated process' go through periods of time when they quite convincingly experience themselves as having selves that are not integrated with each other (Warner, 1998, 2000; Roy, 1991; Coffeng, 1995). As a result, they either experience disunity of self that is likely to feel 'crazy' to themselves and to others or they have periods of forgetfulness of times when other 'parts' were dominant. This kind of dissociated process virtually always results from severe early-childhood trauma. Young children who haven't developed alternative ways of distancing themselves from overwhelmingly intense experiences, stumble on an ability to move into trance-like states that diminish immediate experiences of trauma. These trance-like states develop into clusters of experience that are subjectively experienced as independent selves. Clients tend to move into such 'parts' experiences when original trauma memories threaten to return. Such separate selves seem to offer a way to avoid being flooded by the original memories.

Dissociated process, then, impedes psychological contact by leaving crucial aspects of experience separate from each other in ways that make it difficult for them to be processed into a meaningful whole. As a result, the person processing in a dissociative way may experience a great deal of vagueness as to how and why s/he acted in particular ways. At some moments the client may convey aspects of parts in ways that seem chaotic and disorganized to the point of seeming psychotic to others. Or, when a particular part is more fully present, a therapist can feel very much in contact with the subset of the person's reactions, motives and memories related to that part but have almost no contact with reactions, motives and memories associated with other parts.

Prouty (1990, 1994) describes psychotic clients as having impaired contact with 'self', 'world' and 'other'. The clients he describes have difficulty forming narratives about their experience that make sense within the culture or which offer a predictive validity in relation to their environment. Some experience a kind of inner void or deadness. They often have experiences in the form of voices or hallucinations that are neither culturally accepted nor are easy to process (Prouty, 1977, 1983, 1986, 1994). When such core narrative purposes are impeded, the person loses an ability to develop a coherent, meaningful version of their own experience and/or to convey a coherent, meaningful version of their experience to others.

Still, Prouty maintains that psychotic experiences are meaningful and have the potential to process into more reality oriented forms. He elaborates on contact functions, contact reflections and contact behaviors relevant to therapeutic work and research relating to 'contact-impaired' clients. A number of person-centered therapists (Pörtner, 1974; Van Werde, 1990, 1998; Deleu and Van Werde, 1998; Warner, 2002 (in press)) have experienced success applying and elaborating on Prouty's work with varying populations and settings. Other person-centered therapists have reported success in working with psychotic clients in more broadly defined versions of person-centered therapy (Raskin, 1996; Rogers, 1967; Binder, 1998).

DIFFICULT PROCESS IN PERSON-CENTERED THERAPY

While the forms of process that make contact difficult are quite different on the surface, some similar therapeutic patterns have been cited by a number of person-centered therapists. Therapists are struck by how strong the desire for psychological contact is even when it is exceedingly difficult to establish (Prouty, 1994, 2000; Warner, 1998, 2000, 2001, 2002 (in press)). The intensity and persistence with which clients work to develop psychological contact makes sense when the central role of psychological contact within human evolution is understood. Clients who have the greatest cognitive and emotional difficulty staying in contact still struggle to make sense of their experience and to communicate it to other people. In this, Rogers' image of a potato that will keep growing a shoot toward a faint source of light from a window high above in a cellar is apt.

As noted earlier, the person-centered process literature elaborates many different mental faculties that are available for making sense of experience in normative ways. And, if these faculties fail or are compromised in some way, individuals develop alternate ways of trying to express and understand experience — such as hallucinations, thought disorders, personality 'parts', or voices. Client-centered therapists have come to welcome such aberrant forms of expression as personally meaningful attempts at contact.

In general, client-centered therapists have found that when they can successfully convey empathy and prizing to clients, this tends to encourage and stimulate the use of whatever capacities for contact are available. This often requires efforts on the part of the therapist to understand the client based on expressive efforts that are quite limited or hard to understand. Sometimes the exact words or gestures of the client are all that the therapist has to relate to (Prouty, 1994). And, the clients' difficulties with processing often make it difficult for them to receive or to understand complex communications from the therapist. As a result, several person-centered therapists have noted that they have found it helpful to simplify the forms in which they express understanding, looking for styles of expression that are less demanding of complex processing manoeuvres by the client. Prouty (1994) has advocated word-for-word reflections and naming of exact gestures and facial expressions in response to out-of-contact psychotic experiences. Warner (1991, 1997, 2000) and Roy (1998) have noted that clients in the middle of fragile or dissociated process often require silence or empathic responses that are very close to their exact words to feel understood.

Given client expressions that may be very limited or very different from more normative experiences, therapists often find that they need to work to develop process sensitivity. Therapists can easily distort their understanding of the client by making it more similar to things they know of from their own experience. Thus, therapists can go a long time not hearing that clients are experiencing separate 'parts' or the degree of vulnerability that is involved in fragile process. And, therapists often find a need to process their own feelings about pain, despair and strangeness in order to be able to emotionally tolerate staying in contact with clients who are having extreme forms of such experiences.

While most clients struggle to establish contact, some clients have felt extremely traumatized and manipulated in their attempts to develop psychological contact early in life. They may be tempted to give up or they may see any attempts at contact a threat to their existence. Under these circumstances, therapy that intensifies bodily felt experience or that invites clients to trust other human beings may not be experienced as a good thing by the client. Therapists find that they need to be able to understand the exquisite ambivalence of clients who are tempted to give up on contact or who pull away from contact at some points. Yet, the wish for contact is so basic to human beings that such a choice is seldom unambivalent or permanent. Therapists' willingness to understand and stay with clients as they pull away from psychological contact often turns out to be a deciding factor in the clients' developing the desire and the courage to re-engage.

The human need for psychological contact is strong enough that even moderate increases in psychological contact are of great personal and psychological value to clients. If a client connects with another human being while he or she is making sense in some ways but not others, this in itself is likely to bring a lessening of that client's existential aloneness and anxiety. Even a partial ability to make sense of one's experience tends to lower a variety of psychological and behavioral symptoms (Prouty, 1994; Warner, 2001). And, if anything, clients who have difficulty establishing or maintaining contact have greater need to have someone stay with them while they struggle to find their own voice. Honoring the existential freedom to decide what matters and why it matters becomes more important in therapeutic relationships in which contact is difficult given the fact that these clients find this sort of respect, freedom and personal connection so hard to come by in the rest of their lives.

REFERENCES

Binder, U. (1998). Empathy and empathy development in psychotic clients. In B. Thorne and E. Lambers (Eds.) *Person-centred therapy: A European perspective*. London: Sage Publications.
Bohart, A. C. (1990). A cognitive client-centered perspective on borderline personality

development. In G. Lietaer, J. Rombauts and R. Van Balen (Eds.), *Client-centered and experiential psychotherapy in the nineties* (pp. 599–621). Leuven, Belgium: Leuven University Press.

Clark, A. and Chalmers, D. (1998). The extended mind. *Analysis*, 58 (1), (pp. 7–19).

Coffeng, T. (1995, May). Experiential and pre-experiential therapy for multiple trauma. In R. Hutterer, G. Pawlowsky, P.F. Schmid, and R. Stipsits (Eds.), *Client-centered and experiential psychotherapy: A paradigm in motion* (pp. 499–511). Frankfurt am Main: Peter Lang.

Deleu, C. and Van Werde, D. (1998). The relevance of a phenomenological attitude when working with psychotic people. In B. Thorne and E. Lambers (Eds.), *Person-centred therapy: A European perspective*. London: Sage Publications.

Eckert, J. and Biermann-Ratjen, E. (1998). The treatment of borderline personality disorder. In L. Greenberg, J. Watson, and G. Lietaer (Eds.), *Handbook of experiential psychology* (pp. 349–67). New York: The Guilford Press.

Eckert, J. and Wuchner, M. (1996). Long-term development of borderline personality disorder. In R. Hutterer, G. Pawlowsky, P.F. Schmid, and R. Stipsits (Eds.), *Client-centered and experiential psychotherapy: A paradigm in motion* (pp. 213–33). Frankfurt am Main: Peter Lang.

Gendlin, E. T. (1964). A theory of personality change. In P. Worchel and D. Byrne (Eds.), *Personality Change* (pp. 100–48). New York: John Wiley and Sons, Inc..

Gendlin, E. T. (1968). The experiential response. In E. Hammer (Ed.), *Use of interpretation in treatment* (pp. 208–27). New York: Grune and Stratton.

Gendlin, E. T. (1970). A theory of personality change. In J. T. Hzart and T. H. Tomlinson (Eds.), *New directions in client-centered therapy* (pp. 129–74). Boston: Houghton Mifflin.

Gendlin. E. T. (1974). Client-centered and experiential psychotherapy. In D. Wexler and L. N. Rice (Eds.), *Innovations in Client-Centered Therapy* (pp. 211–46). New York: John Wiley and Sons.

Gendlin, E. T. (1990). The small steps of the therapy process: How they come and how to help them come. In G. Lietaer, J. Rombauts, and R. Van Balen (Eds.), *Client-centered and experiential psychotherapy in the nineties* (pp. 205–24). Leuven, Belgium: Leuven University Press.

Gendlin, E.T. (1995). Crossing and dipping: Some terms for approaching the interface between natural understanding and logical formulation. In *Minds and Machines*, Vol. 5, Issue 4. (pp. 547–60).

Gendlin, E.T. (1997). How philosophy cannot appeal to experience, and how it can. In D. M. Levin (Ed.), *Language Beyond Postmodernism* (pp. 3–41). Evanston, Illinois: Northwestern University Press. .

Gendlin, E. T. (2001 — In draft). *The process model*. (Available on the Focusing Institute website: http://www.focusing.org.)

Green, M. F. (1998). *Schizophrenia from a neurocognitive perspective*. Boston: Allyn and Bacon.

Greenberg, L. S. and Pascual-Leone, J. (1997). Emotion in the creation of personal meaning. In M. Power and C. R. Brewin (Eds.), The transformation of meaning in psychological therapies (pp. 157–73). New York: John Wiley and Sons.

Kirschenbaum, H. and Henderson, V. L. (Eds.) (1989) *The Carl Rogers Reader*. New York: Houghton Mifflin Company.

Lambers, E. (1994). Borderline personality disorder. In D. Mearns (Ed.), *Developing person-centered counseling* (pp. 110–12). London: Sage Publications.

Leijssen, M. (1993). Creating a workable distance to overwhelming images: comments on a session transcript. In D. Brazier (Ed.), *Beyond Carl Rogers* (pp. 129–47). London: Constable.

Leijssen, M. (1996). Characteristics of a healing inner relationship. In R. Hutterer, G. Pawlowsky, P.F. Schmid, and R. Stipsits (Eds.), *Client-centered and experiential psychotherapy: A paradigm in motion* (pp. 427–38). Frankfurt am Main: Lang.

Mearns, D. (1997). Person-centred counselling training. London: Sage (pp. 16–29).

Mearns, D. and Thorne, B. (2000). *Person-centred therapy today: New frontiers in theory and practice*. London: Sage Publications.

Miller, J. B. (1997). *The Healing Connection: How Women Form Relationships in Therapy and in Life*. Boston: Beacon Press.

Mitchell, S. A. (1988). *Relational Concepts in Psychoanalysis*. Cambridge, Massachusetts: Harvard University Press.

Mithen, S. (2000). Mind, brain and material culture: An archeological perspective. In P. Carruthers and A. Chamberlain (Eds.), *Evolution and the human mind*. Cambridge: Cambridge University Press.

Murphy, D. M. and Stich, S. (2000). Darwin in the madhouse: Evolutionary psychology and the classification of mental disorders. In P. Carruthers and A. Chamberlain (Eds.), *Evolution and the human mind*. Cambridge: Cambridge University Press.

Pinker, S. and Bloom, P. (1992). Natural language and natural selection. In J. H. Barkow, L. Cosmides, and J. Tooby (Eds.), *The adapted mind: Evolutionary psychology and the generation of culture*. New York: Oxford University Press.

Pörtner, M. (1974). Client-centered therapy with mentally retarded persons: Catherine and Ruth. In G. Lietaer, J. Rombauts, and R. Van Balen (Eds.), *Client-centered and experiential psychotherapy in the nineties* (pp. 559–69). Leuven, Belgium: Leuven University Press.

Power, M. J. (1997). Conscious and unconscious representations of meaning. In M. Power and C. R. Brewin (Eds.), *The transformation of meaning in psychological therapies*. New York: John Wiley and Sons.

Prouty, G. (1977). Protosymbolic method: A phenomenological treatment of schizophrenic hallucinations. *Journal of Mental Imagery*, 1(2 Fall), pp. 339–42.

Prouty, G. (1983). Hallucinatory contact: A phenomenological treatment of schizophrenics. *Journal of Communication Therapy*, 2 (1), pp. 99–103.

Prouty, G. (1986). The pre-symbolic structure and therapeutic transformation of hallucinations. In M. Wolpin, J. Schorr and L. Krueger (Eds.), *Imagery*, Vol. 4 (pp. 99–106). New York: Plenum Press.

Prouty, G. (1990). Pre-therapy: A theoretical evolution in the person-centered/experiential psychotherapy of schizophrenia and retardation. In G. Lietaer, J. Rombauts, and R. Van Balen (Eds.), *Client-centered and experiential psychotherapy in the nineties* (pp. 645–58). Leuven, Belgium: Leuven University Press.

Prouty, G. (1994). *Theoretical Evolutions in Person-Centered/Experiential Therapy*. Westport, Connecticut: Praeger.

Prouty, G. (2000). Pre-therapy and the pre-expressive self. In T. Merry (Ed.), *Person-centred practice: The BAPCA Reader*. Ross-on-Wye: PCCS Books.

Raskin, N. J. (1996). Client-centered therapy with very disturbed clients. In R. Hutterer, G. Pawlowsky, P.F. Schmid, and R. Stipsits (Eds.), *Client-centered and experiential psychotherapy: A paradigm in motion* (pp. 529–31). Frankfurt am Main: Peter Lang.

Rice, L. N. (1974). The evocative function of the therapist. In D. A. Wexler and L. N. Rice (Eds.), *Innovations in Client-Centered Therapy*. New York: John Wiley and Sons, pp. 289–311.

Rice, L. N. and Greenberg, L. S. (Eds.) (1984), *Patterns of change*. New York: The Guilford Press.

Roelens, L. (1996). Accommodating psychotherapy to information-processing constraints: A person-centered psychiatric case description. In R. Hutterer, G. Pawlowsky, P.F. Schmid, and R. Stipsits (Eds.), *Client-centered and experiential psychotherapy: A paradigm in motion* (pp. 533–43). Frankfurt am Main: Peter Lang.

Rogers, C. R. (1951). *Client-centered therapy*. Boston: Houghton Mifflin.

Rogers, C. R. (1957). The necessary and sufficient conditions of therapeutic personality change. *Journal of Consulting Psychology*, Vol. 21, No. 2, pp. 95–103. Reprinted in H. Kirschenbaum and V. L. Henderson (Eds.) (1989) *The Carl Rogers Reader*. New York: Houghton Mifflin Co.

Rogers, C. R. (1959). A theory of therapy, personality, and interpersonal relationships as developed in the client-centered framework. In S. Koch (Ed.), *Psychology: A study of a science, Vol. 3. Formulations of the person and the social context*. New York: McGraw-Hill.

Rogers, C. R. (Ed.) (1967). *The therapeutic relationship and its impact: A study of psychotherapy with schizophrenics*. Madison, Wisconsin: University of Wisconsin Press.

Roy, B. (1991). A client-centered approach to multiple personality and dissociative process. In L. Fusek (Ed.), *New directions in client-centered therapy: Practice with difficult client populations (Monograph Series 1)* (pp. 18–40). Chicago: Chicago Counseling and Psychotherapy Center.

Roy, B. (1998). An illustration of memory retrieval with a dissociative identity disorder client. Unpublished manuscript.

Samuels, R. (2000). Massively modular minds: Evolutionary psychology and cognitive architecture. In P. Carruthers and A. Chamberlain (Eds.), *Evolution and the human mind*. Cambridge: Cambridge University Press.

Santen, B. (1990). Beyond good and evil: Focusing with early traumatized children and adolescents. In G. Lietaer, J. Rombauts and R. Van Balen (Eds.), *Client-centered and experiential psychotherapy in the nineties,* pp. 779–96. Leuven, Belgium: Leuven University Press.

Sarbin, T. R. (Ed.) (1986). *Narrative psychology: The storied nature of human conduct*. New York: Praeger.

Schore, A. N. (1994). *Affect development and the origin of the self*. Hillsdale, NJ: Lawrence Erlbaum Associates, Publishers.

Spence, D. P. (1982). *Narrative truth and historical truth*. New York: W.W. Norton and Company.

Sroufe, L. A. (1996). *Emotional development: The organization of emotional life in the early years*. New York: Cambridge University Press.

Stern, D. N. (1985). *The interpersonal world of the infant*. New York: Basic Books, Inc.

Stolorow, R. D. and Atwood, G. E. (1992). *Contexts of being: The intersubjective foundations of psychological life*.

Swildens, J. C. (1990). Client-centered psychotherapy for patients with borderline symptoms. In G. Lietaer, J. Rombauts and R. Van Balen (Eds.), *Client-centered and experiential psychotherapy in the nineties* (pp. 623–35). Leuven, Belgium: Leuven University Press.

Tooby, J. and Cosmides, L. (1992). The psychological foundations of culture. In J. Barkow, L. Cosmides, and J. Tooby, (Eds.), *The adapted mind: Evolutionary psychology and the generation of culture* (pp. 19–136). New York: Oxford University Press.

Van Werde, D. (1990). Psychotherapy with a retarded schizo-affective woman: An application of Prouty's pre-therapy. In A. Dosen, A. Van Gennep, and G. Zwanikken (Eds.), *Treatment of mental illness and behavioral disorder in the mentally retarded: Proceedings of international congress*, May 3rd and 4th Amsterdam, The Netherlands (pp. 469–77). Leiden, The Netherlands: Logon Publications.

Van Werde, D. (1998). Anchorage as a core concept in working with psychotic people. In B. Thorne and E. Lambers (Eds.), *Person-centred therapy: A European perspective*. London: Sage Publications.

Warner, M. S. (1983). Soft meaning and sincerity in the family system, *Family Process, Vol.* 22, (December).

Warner, M. S. (1989). Empathy and strategy in the family system, *Person-Centered Review*, Vol. 4, No. 3 (August).

Warner, M. S. (1991). Fragile process. In L. Fusek (Ed.), *New directions in client-centered therapy: Practice with difficult client populations* (pp. 41–58). Chicago: Chicago Counseling and Psychotherapy Center, Monograph I.

Warner, M. S. (1997). Does empathy cure? A theoretical consideration of empathy, processing and personal narrative. In A. C. Bohart and L. S. Greenberg (Eds.). *Empathy reconsidered: New directions in psychotherapy* (pp. 125–40). Washington, D.C.:American Psychological Association.

Warner, M. S. (1998). A client-centered approach to therapeutic work with dissociated and fragile process. In L. Greenberg, J. Watson, and G. Lietaer (Eds.), *Foundations of experiential theory and practice: Differential treatment approaches*. New York: Guilford Press.

Warner, M. S. (2000). Client-centered therapy at the difficult edge: Work with fragile and dissociated process. In Dave Mearns and Brian Thorne (Eds.), *Person-centred therapy today: New frontiers of theory and practice*. Thousand Oaks: Sage.

Warner, M. S. (2002). (In press). Luke's dilemmas: A client-centered/experiential model of processing with a schizophrenic thought disorder. In Watson, J., Goldman, R. and Warner, M. S. (Eds), *Client-centered and experiential psychotherapy in the 21st century: Advances in theory, research and practice*. Ross-on-Wye: PCCS Books.

Wexler, D. A. (1974). A cognitive theory of experiencing, self-actualization and therapeutic process, in D. A. Wexler and L. N. Rice (Eds.), *Innovations in client-centered therapy*. New York: Wiley.

5 Psychological Contact and Perception as Dialectical Construction
William J. Whelton and Leslie S. Greenberg

In a classic paper Rogers postulated six necessary and sufficient conditions for effective therapeutic change (1957). The first of these is that there be 'psychological contact' by which Rogers meant a 'minimal relationship' (1957, p. 96), the indispensable context for the provision of the other conditions. The sixth condition states that the empathy and unconditional positive regard of the therapist must be perceived by the client 'at least to a minimal degree' (Rogers, 1959, p. 213). The first and sixth conditions share a close logical connection because they are integrated and inseparable aspects of the relational environment, which is the required framework for the effective provision of the other conditions. Twice Rogers used the word 'minimal' to describe these conditions and he seems to have been emphasizing that if these (along with the other) conditions are satisfied to even the slightest degree, therapy will often still produce beneficial results. Perhaps Rogers (1959) was making this point again when he later dropped the word psychological from his formal description of the first condition, although contact still clearly meant some type of encounter between persons. With these conditions, however, Rogers is acknowledging that an encounter or relationship, however slight, in which the client attends sufficiently to the therapist to perceive and experience the therapist as understanding and unconditionally positively regarding, is an essential requirement for effective therapy. The meaning of these complex terms and ideas is not as self-evident as might appear to be the case and this chapter will examine some inherent difficulties with them.

We will begin by trying to unravel some of the difficulty and complexity of the concepts of psychological contact and perception. Contact has been defined as touching, meeting, or communicating (*The Concise Oxford Dictionary*, 1990, R. E. Allen, p. 247). The third or communicative aspect of the above definition of contact seems most apt to the notions of contact and perception. Psychological contact means that a person is *minimally* aware of the presence of another person and *to some degree* attends to *what they are* communicating. Perception of the conditions adds to this that the person construes the therapist's communications as empathic and unconditionally positive regarding. Furthermore, this condition implies a receptivity in the person to being understood and prized in this way. A major difficulty with the concepts of psychological contact and perception is that awareness and attention in humans are variable processes of active meaning constructing agents, to some degree under their explicit control and to some degree automatic. Contact and perception thus are always in the eye of the beholder. A student, for example, may be listening in a restless way to what registers as the dreary, monotone rambling of a professor she feels is bludgeoning the class with inanities. She is clearly in contact, however half-hearted or distracted that contact might be. But suddenly, with no apparent change in the professor, she hears the word 'Marx' and she comes alive. Her body is brought erect, her gaze becomes focussed, and she is 'all ears', attending carefully to the professor, trying to gauge the professor's take on one of the few thinkers who mean anything to her. The quality of her contact is so transformed that it hardly seems possible that what she had been previously experiencing could be called contact. Evidently, to begin with, there is a great deal of qualitative variation in the category we are designating as 'psychological contact'.

In terms of understanding these more elaborate dimensions of contact it is useful to look at Gestalt Therapy (Perls, Hefferline and Goodman, 1951), which has long emphasized the notion of contact. The Gestalt approach sees the 'capacity for' contact and the 'quality of' that contact to be mutually determining and integrally linked. It is not simply an issue of having or not having contact: it is the degree or quality of contact that is important. It might be better to talk about the type of contact or its quality rather than its presence or absence. One provocative idea that emerged from Gestalt Therapy was that contact *is* the self, that the self waxes and wanes according to the rhythm of contact and withdrawal (Greenberg, 1995; Perls, 1969). Contact is a matter of awareness and the forming of a figure of contact against a ground of possibilities. Psychological contact, then, is essential to the very existence of the self, and to its health and development. In addition, the self's degree or type of contact become the focus of therapy rather than a precondition.

An example might clarify some of the complexity entailed in the concepts of contact and interpersonal perception. In Act 1 of Shakespeare's (1608/2000) famous play, King Lear is in psychological contact with his daughter Cordelia. He expresses his genuine rage and disappointment at what he perceives to be her lackluster filial performance, failing entirely to see her honesty and sincere love. The issue raised here is with what is he in psychological contact and what does he perceive? Through blind autocracy and self-absorption he fails to perceive the devotion that lies behind her honest communication. He had contact with her and still in some fundamental sense he missed her. Suffering and loss gradually and painfully awaken Lear from his moral stupor and his contact with Cordelia at the end of the play is imbued with passion, love and intense presence.

Lear is very authentically 'himself' at both points in time and an important element of the classic drama consists in the changes within him that allow him to enter into a new relationship with Cordelia. But, as observers, it is hard for us not to see the later perception as fundamentally more in touch with what really 'is' than the earlier perception. It would seem that obstacles and misunderstandings have been removed, allowing these two people more direct and trusting access to the way they genuinely feel about each other. But as will be elaborated later in this paper, given that perception determines reality no one has direct access to 'reality'. All versions of reality involve subjective interpretation built on a foundation of essentially unexaminable, a priori assumptions; so it is unclear, in many contexts, how one perception can be judged to be 'more realistic' than another. This is one of many complex problems associated with the concept of perception. If all interpersonal perceptions are constructed and perspectival are there any criteria by which these perceptions may be judged to be more or less realistic or accurate and how are we to determine whether what is intended is received?

Based on our dialectical constructivist perspective on human functioning, outlined later, three propositions will be advanced in this paper. The first is that psychological contact, which is intended to include here both the mere fact of psychological contact and all the possible varying degrees of quality of that contact (e.g. presence, intensity, brightness, liveliness), and perception are inextricably related to the functioning of the self. The self in this view is the unifying psychological construct, the basic sense of agency, ownership and identity that draws together all of a person's experience so that it might potentially be assigned some order and meaning. The self, understood as a dialectical constructivist process, is always involved in and is at the center of contact and perception.

The second proposition is that the self is a process and is a dynamic self-organizing system that functions through the dialectical construction of meaning. This involves a process in which various levels of information are synthesized to render a felt sense of oneself in the world (Greenberg and Pascual-Leone, 1995, 1997, 2001; Whelton and Greenberg, 2001). The primary dialectic of importance in therapy is that between automatic emotional experience and deliberate cognitive and interpretive processes. In this chapter, the contention will be made that this same dialectical process through which the self and its meanings are constructed can contribute substantially to an understanding of the processes involved in psychological contact and interpersonal perception.

A third proposition will be advanced which is a corollary to the sixth condition of Rogers' from the larger perspective of the negotiated therapeutic enterprise. This proposition asserts that the client must not only be *capable* of contact and perception, as implied in these conditions, but also must *desire* to be in contact and *desire to receive* empathy and unconditional positive regard. These conditions must be negotiated, at least implicitly, in the form of a working alliance. The therapist's provision of empathy and unconditional positive regard are effective only if the client as part of a working alliance has implicitly or explicitly agreed to their use.

The chapter will first examine the notions of psychological contact and the perception of the conditions of therapy as they were first articulated by Rogers (1957, 1959) and developed by Prouty (1994), as well as the ideas about contact that have been developed within Gestalt Therapy (Perls et al., 1951; Yontef, 1993). Next, the theory of dialectical constructivism will be offered as a means to understand both the nature of psychological contact and of clients' perceptions of the conditions. The two major components of dialectical constructivism will be presented. Constructivism will be discussed as a corrective to naïve realism (Mahoney, 1991). This is important since all contact and perception is, to a degree, a construction. Then some recent theory and research pertaining to emotion will be summarized (e.g. LeDoux, 1993). An understanding of the neuropsychologically distinct nature of emotion as an information-processing system is important for an appreciation of its influence on perception and meaning construction and for an understanding of the dialectic between emotion and cognition in dialectical constructivism (Greenberg, 2002). Having discussed the relevance of a dialectical constructivist perspective for contact and perception, a few thoughts will be offered about the implications of recent social cognitive research in interpersonal perception to these processes.

THE ROGERIAN VIEW

Rogers (1959) expressed a keen awareness that for the central conditions of empathy, unconditional positive regard and genuineness to work, a framework is required for their delivery and impact. These conditions need to be nested within a personal encounter in which certain circumscribed psychological processes of attention, awareness and interpersonal perception are functioning, and this is what Rogers spelled out in the first and sixth conditions. The first condition of effective therapeutic change, the concept of psychological contact, refers to the basic psychological processes required for a person to be conscious of engaging in a direct, often verbally communicated, exchange with another person:

> The first condition specifies that a minimal relationship, a psychological contact, must exist . . . All that is intended by this first condition is to specify that the two people are to some degree in contact, that each makes some perceived difference in the experiential field of the other . . . if each is aware of being in personal or psychological contact with the other, then this condition is met . . . (Rogers, 1957, p. 96).

Making psychological contact is simply a question of possessing the basic psychological wherewithal necessary to have an encounter with another person and using those faculties to attend at least minimally to the therapist. Ordinarily, according to Rogers (1957), a person could simply tell you whether they were or had been in psychological contact with another person. Rogers observed that the contact 'or relationship' must often be 'of some duration before the therapeutic process begins' (1959, p. 213). The sixth condition adds something fundamental to the first condition. It says that the client must 'perceive' the therapist's empathy and unconditional positive regard. When viewed in conjunction with the first condition, this expands the notion of contact to include a communicative process in which the client is aware of, and open to, the therapist's efforts at communicating understanding and regard. Rogers says, 'it is not enough for the therapist to communicate, since the communication must be received' (1959, p. 213). The full implications of this statement tend to support the argument to be made later in this paper: that perception and reception are inexorably related to the functioning of the self and linked to the establishment of a working alliance. In other words, if the client wants to be unconditionally positively regarded and understood, or perceives this as relevant, he or she will be open and receptive to the perception of these attitudes in the therapist.

CONTACT AND PERCEPTION

Prouty (1994) has elaborated both a theory and a practice of 'pre-therapy' based on an integration of ideas from Rogers' (1957) notion of psychological contact as a precondition of therapy, Gendlin's (1961) concept of Experiencing, and the Gestalt Therapy concept of ego and contact functions (Perls et al., 1951). According to this view, some people have lost basic contact and live in existential autism, a fascinating metaphor for a 'failure in coherence' in which 'consciousness becomes empty', a state in which, according to Prouty, the fundamental, primordial contact with self, world, and other is lost. Such persons need pre-therapy to bring them from existential autism to existential contact.

However, it seems to us too dichotomous to suggest that one either has or does not have sufficient 'psychological contact' to begin therapy. Rather, *one person contacts another psychologically in the manner that is possible given the degree of development and organization of their self.* Contact, if successful at all, is successful within a 'proximal zone of development' of the self of the person who is engaged in the contact (Vygotsky, 1986). What is required from the therapist will vary with the client's self-organization, needs, and current capacity for contact, and may include the therapist's understanding (Rogers, 1957), the 'mirroring empathy' spoken of in Self-psychology (Kohut, 1977), or the word-for-word reflections of Prouty (1994); essentially, whatever is needed to further the growth (construction) of the self. It, however, makes more sense to us to conceptualize contact as existing on a continuum rather than as either/or, a position with which Rogers seems to have agreed for all the conditions except contact:

> The greatest flaw in the statement of these conditions is that they are stated as if they were all-or-none elements, whereas conditions 2 to 6 all exist on continua ... the more marked the presence of conditions 2 to 6 ... the greater the degree of reorganization which will take place ... (Rogers, 1959, p. 215).

THE GESTALT THERAPY TRADITION

Contact is one of the central concepts in Gestalt Therapy (Perls, Hefferline and Goodman, 1951). Gestalt theorists have elaborated in some depth the qualities and dimensions of interpersonal encounters and their relationship to self-processes and it is our contention that Rogers was attempting to clarify very similar phenomena with his conditions of contact and perception. What has been done in Gestalt can be of some assistance in expanding the context in which these conditions are interpreted and in elucidating their meaning. The origins of the Gestalt idea of contact can be found in domains as diverse as field theory, phenomenology, and physiology. Living organisms are structured systems that are aspects of fluctuating fields and they continue to exist by an unending exchange of elements within those fields. While we see organisms as discrete, bounded units, field theory suggests that such a view is a byproduct of the automatic organizing function of our perceptual apparatus, and that all such reification should be held tentatively. The discrete organism and its field are not as truly separate and bounded as they might appear; they are, rather, part of each other in a continuous co-constitutive process. Contact for complex systems such as human beings is the content of experience, both the form and the process of the continual encounter between the organism and its environment. Gestalt Therapy models have tended to emphasize the 'contact boundary', which is easily visualized as the 'place' of encounter, such as the skin for touch, but such a metaphor best suggests that in countless ways an organism is continuously exchanging matter and energy (often what we call 'information') with its environment and certain functions or processes must serve as the vehicles or locus of this exchange:

> ... the contact-boundary ... is essentially the organ of a particular relation of the organism and its environment ... this particular relation is growth ... contact is awareness of the field or motor response in the field ... (Perls et al., 1951, p. 229).

The notion here of growth emphasizes the complexity and the dynamic nature of this interaction. The word 'growth' implies an increase in the complexity, differentiation, and development of an organism produced by what Perls et al. (1951) called 'assimilating novelty', encountering something new at the boundary and rendering it useful.

The favourite example of these processes for Perls (1947) was eating. Eating requires discrimination in the field of that which is toxic from that which is nourishing and edible. A number of sensory and motor processes enable the organism to find and prepare what is to be eaten and, at the contact boundary, it is tasted, ingested and destructured in order to be rendered assimilable by the organism and transformed into usable energy. This example serves to highlight a number of relatively generic features of contact. Perls most liked it for two reasons: first, because learning to eat is one of the earliest tasks of infancy, it acted, in his view, as a template for further forms of contact; and second, because it accentuated the necessity of some degree of aggression, however mild, in contact if an organism is to maintain its integrity. But the main overarching theme of contact is *awareness* and that is clearly displayed here, as well. In healthy functioning, conscious awareness serves to organize the internal and external environments so that what is needed is figural. And healthy contact also entails the ability to act responsibly to meet these aware needs. In this example, contact involves the discriminatory functions of sight, smell and taste and an element of aggression. The food contacted is either accepted or rejected and once accepted it must be changed and destructured in order to be assimilated.

Contact necessarily involves the curiosity, vulnerability and flexibility required to allow the self to contact that which is 'other'. Contact is the meeting of differences (Yontef, 1993; Latner, 1992). Such an encounter requires a balance between a commitment to one's own integrity and an openness to change and to an acceptance of what is, a process that Perls et al. (1951) called creative adjustment. These early developers of Gestalt Therapy identified a number of interruptions, blocks or resistances to contact. Introjection, confluence, and projection, for example, are processes that block an awareness of the boundaries between self and other that are necessary for healthy contact. The Polsters (1973) worked to delineate and expand the idea of 'contact functions', the means whereby contact is achieved. Essentially, these are the sensory or motor mechanisms that mediate encounter with the external environment: seeing, hearing, tasting,

CONTACT AND PERCEPTION

smelling, touching, talking, and moving. When these are blocked, dampened, or in anyway diminished contact itself is diminished (Polster and Polster, 1973). This is the first of two points to be emphasized in relation to the Gestalt Therapy view of contact. Gestalt Therapy is focussed on processes of contact and awareness and good contact is considered a hallmark of healthy functioning. For this reason, there is an acute sensitivity in this approach to the *quality* of contact. Contact is about having sufficient self-support to truly encounter what is of interest in a situation: '…a charge of excitement exists within the individual which culminates in a sense of full engagement with whatever is interesting at that moment…' (Polster and Polster, 1973, p. 130). This is contact undertaken with full awareness, 'the process of being in vigilant contact with the most important event in the individual/environment field with full sensorimotor, emotional, cognitive and energetic support' (Yontef, 1993, p. 205). A great deal of human contact has become suffused with various degrees of avoidance and contact without aliveness and interest tends to stultify into a deadened process of habit. Second, in the Gestalt Therapy view, contact is firmly linked to the self, though more than one view of the self has been proposed by Gestalt (Greenberg, 1995; Perls et al., 1951). In the most radical process view of the self advanced by Goodman, the self essentially is the process of contacting and withdrawing from the environment. Gestalt views the self as a process not an object thus their view is strongly phenomenological and subjective. The self is the fluid, aware process of experiencing, and what fuels experience is contact. Contact in this view cannot be divorced from the self. In a similar manner, the self is ineluctably involved in the conditions of contact and perception that are described by Rogers. The self is organized in the very process of making contact and communicating with another, and the form which that contact takes and what is perceived within that contact are to some degree a function of the self's organization. How this happens and the psychological processes involved will be elaborated next.

DIALECTICAL CONSTRUCTIVISM

Dialectical Constructivism (Greenberg and Pascual-Leone, 1995, 1997, 2001; Pascual-Leone, 1987, 1989, 1990; Pascual-Leone and Irwin, 1994; Pascual-Leone and Johnson, 1991; Watson and Greenberg, 1996; Whelton and Greenberg, 2001) is a theory that endeavours to explain both the construction of the self and the construction of a sense of personal meaning out of the ceaseless welter of an individual's experience. This theory makes a number of assertions. The most fundamental of these is that while the stream of our conscious experience often appears to be unified and coherent, it is in fact a complex synthesis of many levels of processing produced by a variety of mental operations on many levels of information, most of which are out of awareness (Pascual-Leone, 1987, 1989, 1990). There are two basic streams of information that contribute to consciousness: the conscious, deliberate conceptualisation through which thinking and reflection occur and the automatic, visceral flow of immediate emotional experience. Emotion is neuropsychologically independent of cognition (e.g. LeDoux, 1989) and both emotion and cognition work dialectically to produce a felt sense of self and world from moment to moment. Both contact and perception thus ultimately come about from the synthesis of a variety of levels of tacit processing.

Two major components of this approach, constructivism and emotion, will be discussed briefly below.

Constructivism

A central belief in all constructivist epistemologies is that the direct, unmediated access to the 'real' world that might lead to certain knowledge is impossible. Even a sensory process such as vision involves the constructive activity of perception: that is, the mind actively uses the neural connections already developed through experience and culture to organize and structure new sense data so that they are meaningful and interpretable (Mahoney, 1991). Constructivism posits that what any of us take to be reality is an interpretation and that other interpretations are always possible. Radical constructivists would argue that there is no 'reality', that the legitimacy of various worldviews is entirely relative, and that in the sea of possible interpretations there are no objective criteria by which to prefer one to another. Social constructionism is a variant position that, in viewing culture (especially language) as the major constitutor of personal realities differs from constructivism, which focuses on the more internal mental processes that determine perception. Social constructionism, however, is similar to radical constructivism in holding that there is no social reality, only socially constituted perspectives. More moderate constructivists contend that there is a reality but that human knowledge of that reality will always be indirect, incomplete, and fallible. Such thinkers generally contend that the essential criterion for knowledge is pragmatic, that is, what is adaptive and functional given all else that is known in a given time and place. Reality itself will impose some constraints (such as death or furniture into which one inevitably will bump) on clearly misguided interpretations (Mahoney, 1991).

Some knowledge of constructivist perspectives is necessary for an understanding of the nature of psychological contact and perception, which involve varying degrees of awareness and symbolization, and the active construction of meaning on the part of the receiver. That this process is fundamentally a dialectical construction will be shown later. In order to appreciate the dialectic between emotion and cognition a quick review of current research on emotion is helpful.

Emotion

There is an increasing accumulation of both physiological (LeDoux, 1989, 1993) and psychological (Epstein, Lipson, Holstein and Huh, 1992; Epstein, 1993; Winkielman, Zajonc and Schwarz, 1997; Zajonc, 2000) evidence that there are two distinct systems of information-processing: one is rapid, automatic, affective and out of awareness; the other is slow, cognitive, conscious and analytic. The mind is accustomed to integrate and synthesize these systems in ways that allow for a coherent sense of self, so they are not easy to tease apart (Greenberg and

Pascual-Leone, 1995).

One of the core brain structures involved in the emotion system is the amygdala, which computes the significance of sensory stimuli processed through the thalamus (Kolb and Whishaw, 1996; LeDoux, 1989). Neuropsychological evidence demonstrates that the amygdala can bypass the neo-cortex and hippocampus to produce an emotional reaction to the ambiguous features of an unidentified stimulus (LeDoux, 1989). These lightning emotional processes initiate action faster than conscious thought would allow when the life or integrity of the self is at stake. The emotion system, then, is a rapid, automatic, partially independent system of ancient evolutionary origins which can function without conscious awareness and whose principal function is enhancing the integrity of the organism through a computation of the environment's most primitive meaning to the self and the reflex instigation of self-preservation or appetitive action (Lang, 1995). With the evolution of the neo-cortex an array of complex interactions between cognition and emotion have developed producing the conscious, cognitive-affective experience of feelings and more richly-textured emotional experiences such as pride or shame (Greenberg and Paivio, 1997).

Frijda (1986) offers one of the most complete evolutionary theories of emotion, at the core of which lies the pivotal notion that emotions are fundamentally adaptive. Emotions are vitally linked to action: they are changes in readiness or disposition to act in ways relevant to an individual's concerns (Frijda, 1986; Lang, 1995). Emotions are a form of information-processing which orients people to their welfare and disposes them to act on their behalf in a given environment (Frijda, 1986; Greenberg, 2002; Greenberg and Safran, 1987; Greenberg and Paivio, 1997; Schwarz, 1999; Schwarz and Clore, 1983). Feelings give people valuable informational help about what is significant to their well-being and help to orient them in their environment. Emotions are thus a primary meaning system (compare Teasdale and Barnard, 1993). One study showed that fear and anger impact people quite differently, fear informing them about risk, and anger about the blameworthy actions of another person (Schwarz, 1999). This is not logical, factual or conceptual information. It is a qualitatively different kind of information because it conveys a sense of the situation's meaning to a particular individual, given that individual's fundamental needs and goals and within the parameters of their learning history. This latter point is crucial. While primary emotions are adaptive, a given learning history can distort the experience and expression of these emotions (Greenberg, 2002; Greenberg and Paivio, 1997).

THE DIALECTICAL CONSTRUCTION OF MEANING

The Theory of Constructive Operators (Pascual-Leone, 1987), at the base of the dialectical constructivist perspective, delineates in abstract and formal terms how a person constructs meaning (Greenberg and Pascual-Leone, 1995, 1997, 2001). This complex theory has been elaborated and tested over a number of years. Three core ideas will be emphasized here. The first is that there is no homunculus or foundational ego hidden behind our experience, no conductor directing the orchestra of selfhood. The sense of agency and self-direction that people experience (which are *not* thereby illusory) are themselves constructed from the dynamic synthesis of diverse psychological elements. Second, affect plays a key organizing role in the production of a sense of self-experience and of personal meaning. The felt sense of self in the world, while mediated by cognitive interpretations, is largely the product of emotion schemes. Third, while the two fundamental streams of cognition and emotion are synthesized in this dialectical process, each is informed by a whole array of more basic building-blocks, including the salience of environmental stimuli, the views and reactions of others, sensory and kinaesthetic processes, and both emotional and conceptual information. Many of these processes are automatic but it does not follow from this that the construction of meaning is an essentially passive affair. The construction of meaning is a highly engaged and active undertaking in which people choose what it is they will attend to and how they will edit and interpret their experiences and identities.

Dialectical constructivism as applied to psychotherapy (Greenberg and Pascual Leone, 1995, 1997, 2001; Greenberg and van Balen, 1998) recognizes the importance of consciousness in psychological functioning. Consciousness is pivotal for selecting the sources of information to which attention will be directed, and the interpretation of this information which is to be favoured. It is in the arena of consciousness that we are represented to ourselves and then to others using culturally-derived symbolic resources such as words, images and stories. But consciousness is strongly influenced, even over-determined, by many sources of information, which have already been extensively processed. It is the final arbiter of dynamic syntheses of many other levels of information that are not in conscious awareness.

In this system these levels of information-processing are dynamically synthesized over a number of stages. This means that both hardware and software processors selectively attend to sensory, kinaesthetic, emotional and conceptual data organizing it into new emergent experience. The most important subjective (software) processors are schemes, particularly emotion schemes. Schemes are structures which synthesize bodily, emotional and cognitive information rapidly and automatically, preparing and orienting the person for action. Emotion schemes are fundamental generators of meaning and experience. While the affect system is a hardwired, neurophysiological response system generating automatic emotional responses from immediate perceptual appraisals, it is shaped by associative and conceptual learning such that emotion schemes are developed through experience. An emotion scheme synthesizes sensory, perceptual, cognitive, and emotional processes into a global feeling state, a self-organization primordially rooted in emotion, a sense of oneself in the world.

Schemes alone, though, cannot account for the possibility of new performances within the system. Novelty necessitates not only schemes (software) but also several metasubjective, innate, hardware operators. Hardware processors determine which schemes will dominate in a given dynamic synthesis. These operators include affect, mental effort, and a field closure factor. Affect, as has been mentioned, begins as an innate, neurophysiologically-based response system that through learning and the introduction of cognitive experience, comes to produce complex, emotional experiences (Greenberg and Safran, 1987). Executive schemes guide the processing of mental effort that consists of two basic tracks: a scheme-boosting attentional mental energy component and a scheme-interrupting attentional general inhibition mechanism. An executive scheme is not some unified agency with a fully developed plan to implement. There are a variety of executive schemes, which represent bits of plans, and they are boosted or interrupted themselves in the emerging synthesis. But when activated in a situation an executive scheme guides attention and mental energy resources in the service of an affective goal. Another hardware operator is the field closure factor which functions on the Gestalt simplicity principle inducing the closure of experience as a totality (Greenberg and Pascual-Leone, 2001).

There are five basic dialectical steps in the construction of a momentary performance or experience, be it contact, perception or meaning (Greenberg and Pascual-Leone, 2001). Three of these are automatic and out of awareness, though each of them consists of a dynamic synthesis, which involves the operation of editing or selection mechanisms. The first moment is an automatic sensory or motor (or other physiological) process in response to an input or stimulus. The second moment, generated by these bodily processes, is an affective response resulting in an affective goal or goals. The third step is the activation of pre-executive and executive schemes and their attendant plans of action and mechanisms for governing hardware operators. These three steps in the sequence result in a bodily felt sense or a self-organization, which is passively experienced by the subject. This subjective flow of experiencing is felt to just 'happen', and it is experienced as an entirely automatic process. It contains and expresses the fundamental meaning of a situation for an individual. The last two steps which involve conscious effort and deliberation and which result in the final experience or performance follow these early stages. These final steps involve complex conceptual tasks such as the symbolization of experience in language and story.

In this dialectical constructivist approach, meaning does not emerge intact from some revelatory, full-formed internal experience. Nor, indeed, does it emerge from the external imposition (or internalisation) of socially-constructed, cultural rules or symbols which simply apply meaning as if from the outside. It is a personal and unique synthesis in which these elements and more are part of the process of both the discovery and construction of meaning. On one hand it emerges from an awareness of the complex internal world of feeling and sensation that, blended with out of awareness learning and cognition, forms our emotional experience. Only a portion of this internal world is ever attended to and brought into conscious awareness and symbolized with words, that portion which tends to have the best fit with one's preferred conscious view of self. The important dialectic in therapy is between this largely emotional internal world of experience and the cognitive, conceptual and deliberate world of conscious thought. The latter serves to symbolize and explain the emotional experience which forms the core of one's felt sense of self in the world. This cognitive and conscious side of the dialectic creates rational and narrative accounts of the self and is deeply shaped and influenced by the symbolic, narrative and moral sources of meaning in one's culture. Thus, what we make of our experience makes us who we are (Greenberg, 2002).

THE DIALECTICAL CONSTRUCTION OF PSYCHOLOGICAL CONTACT AND PERCEPTION

In a recent movie the popular actor Tom Hanks plays a courier service executive castaway on a tiny Pacific atoll. Though Hanks' character in the movie is resolute and exceptionally resourceful, the island is bleak and inhospitable, and he becomes ever more desolate and lonely. One way he responds in an effort to adapt to his situation is by painting a face on a white volleyball and giving it a name (Wilson). He carries on lengthy conversations with Wilson and clearly forms an emotionally-charged attachment to 'him'. In a sense such a scheme seems freakish and perhaps even a little psychotic but part of the dramatic charm of the movie is to make the improbable take on life and seem, under the circumstances, credible and real. It is a powerful dramatic depiction of the human need for contact. The self is somehow constructed by the internalisation of a matrix of intimate relationships and this movie conveys the difficulty of sustaining a self, of continuing to strive to exist as a self, outside of relationship.

No doubt a number of psychological theories and interpretations can be brought to bear on this story. Self-psychologists might point out that Wilson serves as a self-object (Kohut, 1977). Object relations theorists might argue that Hanks' character has regressed to a level of magical thinking in service of ego integrity and that Wilson is the transitional object helping to maintain that integrity (St. Clair, 1986). Such explanations tend to obscure more than they clarify. The central issue is that the self exists in relationship. Infant research describes the attunement of the young infant to the human face. The Jewish Parisian philosopher Levinas has worked out a phenomenological ethics based on what it means to gaze into another person's face. To do so is to recognize the otherness and the infinite mystery of their humanity, which holds one captive and hostage in one's moral duty to them (Levinas, 1961/1969). The relation of the self to the other certainly entails a profound ethical dimension but the key point in this context is psychological: if, in relation to another, one can surpass oneself, it is also in relationship that one finds oneself, or more primordially, that one is even constructed as a self. It is as a self that one has psychological contact. The type of contact that is called 'psychological' is the type of contact that a human self has with another human self. Since we view the self as a process, and since psychological contact is also a process, the self rises and falls, forms and reforms, again and again in and through psychological contact. The self is an identity formed from the dialectical construction of automatically boosted emotionally-anchored self-organizations and conceptual beliefs and narratives about the self and so these are the processes through which psychological contact is achieved, if it is achieved, and in whatever form it is achieved.

Thus, there is no a priori, universal structure or form of human contact and communicative awareness which can exist mechanically apart from a self and its culture and experience, and onto which these personal elements can be grafted. Where there is psychological contact, there is a communicating self in action. For this very reason, psychological contact may still be difficult, or even impossible, for someone whose physical organs of contact (e.g. sight, voice) are perfectly sound and intact. This is what makes contact, 'psychological' contact.

CONTACT AND PERCEPTION

As Prouty (1994) implies in his work on the concept of pre-therapy, if the self is profoundly fragmented or disorganized, as in the case of a person with autism or schizophrenia, there is often little or no indication of communicative awareness or psychological contact. Prouty's concrete reflections seem to sometimes help such individuals by diminishing the 'otherness' of the responsive other, offering a type of pure mirroring that may reduce anxiety and begin to soothe and organize the self.

Less distressed individuals arrive for therapy and enter into psychological contact according to their current state and their immediate and automatic perception of the therapist while in that state. Some at least minimal level of contact can usually be achieved but this contact is informed and greatly coloured by the nature and possibilities inherent in the client's current self-organization. A given client may be distant, or distracted, or cold, or obsequious, or curious, or excited, or fearful, or hostile in the manner of their contact, according to the emotion schemes evoked in the moment and the way in which they explain and interpret these to themselves. Emotion schemes are often fundamentally interpersonal, that is they function to automatically organize the self in response to a perception (i.e. construction) of the other. So, for example, a client may construe the therapist as an 'authority figure' based on certain perceived elements in the therapist's appearance and manner, say, the 'stern' look on the therapist's face, the expensive suit she is wearing, and a certain quality of power and decisiveness in her voice. It seems fairly uncontroversial that such a perception is based, at least in part, on selective attention and implicit interpretation. The issue of whether it is true or false or both is impossibly thorny and complex and beyond the scope of this paper. The relevant point is that one person's construction of another is based on an immediate perception synthesized from a variety of levels of information-processing. Such a perception of the other will, in a given individual, be linked to an emotion schematic organization of the self, perhaps as small, anxious, and weak in the face of authority. In the moment, it is unlikely that there will be any clear cognitive interpretation of these feelings, but the motivational content of the emotion scheme might be commands along the lines of 'be careful with this person' or 'don't show much to her, she's trouble'. The quality of this hypothetical client's psychological contact will be shaped by this perception and dialectical self-organization, probably in the direction of being limited, closed, suspicious and somewhat self-conscious and myopic.

It may be argued that such a conceptualisation goes well beyond the mere fact of psychological contact, that all Rogers intended was to exclude from therapy people unable to attend to and communicate with another person. But this 'mere fact' cannot be abstracted from a self; it is always formed and modified by the organization of the self in response to context and to a perception of the other. In many relatively healthy and non-distressed people, psychological contact will appear to be much more 'neutral', that is, a much more tentative, curious, open approach to another. But excitement, curiosity and interest are emotional states that reflect and express a strong self-organization.

Allowing for such a dialectical constructivist picture of what psychological contact means, the first and sixth Rogerian conditions appear to be very closely linked in both conceptual and practical terms. The sixth condition posits that the client must minimally perceive the understanding and positive regard of the therapist. Rogers (1957) observes that the perception of an attitude is necessarily indirect, that the client must interpret the words and actions of the therapist as expressing understanding and acceptance. Logically, the form of the client's psychological contact with the therapist must be a central determinant of such a perception, along with the attunement and responsiveness of the therapist to the nature and limits of the client's psychological contact. In difficult situations there is the need for extraordinary interpersonal sensitivity and skill to successfully achieve such a bridge. If, for example, the contact is tenuous or fraught with anxiety, distrust, or guardedness, effective responsiveness essentially means communicating a presence that the client is capable of receiving as positive given their closed or fearful self-organization. The perception of the conditions entails the effective negotiation of the working alliance, a matter to which we will now turn.

PERCEPTION OF THE CONDITIONS

Constructivism posits that what any of us take to be reality is an interpretation and that other interpretations are always possible. A similar view is articulated in the Rogerian notion that it is not what the therapist does, but the client's perception of what the therapist does, that is crucial for therapeutic change. Psychotherapy research attests to this idea: it is client perceived empathy that best predicts outcome, and client-perceived empathy does not necessarily correlate with observer-rated empathy (Horvath and Greenberg, 1994). In his sixth condition, Rogers has formulated the principle that clients actively interpret the words and gestures of therapists and that being empathic, unconditionally positively regarding and genuine is of no avail unless the client construes one's words and actions as such.

Empathy can be experienced by some people as painful and intrusive or as being some kind of game or power trip the therapist is playing. For example, a highly fragile self may experience symbolization of internal experience as overwhelming. Or a prison convict may interpret a therapist as institutionally mandated to exercise power by 'changing' him or her. A person in this latter situation might well interpret the therapist's efforts at empathy as an invasion of the last refuge of their freedom and self-determination: their private feelings and their inner life. True empathy, of course, would lead one to recognize this and back off. The point stands though. Not everyone wants to be accurately understood anymore than everyone wants to be interpreted or behaviourally modified, or any other therapeutic process.

It seems that perceiving the conditions is dependent on a prior condition — that of a working alliance structured on the formation of an appropriate bond and on perceived agreement on the goals and tasks of therapy (Horvath and Greenberg, 1994). In person-centered therapy the goal is to set up an understanding relationship and the main client task is to receive the genuine understanding and prizing of the therapist and to explore the self. Empathy and unconditional positive regard are helpful only if one wishes the other to be empathic and prizing, and, as an extension of this, if it fits with what one needs at the moment and can be affectively tolerated. It is not simply a matter of offering the conditions because they will provide no therapeutic benefit if the client does not wish to open themselves to receive them. And it is not simply that the client needs to be in contact because a person can be in good contact and wish to maintain a boundary and not wish for empathic understanding or positive regard from a particular person at a particular time.

It seems, then, that there is a further necessary condition for effective therapy. This condition is that the client desires empathy and positive regard from the therapist and collaborates with the therapist in the task of being understood and prized. Only then will the empathy be perceived as empathic and the positive regard experienced as such. Seeing the relevance of, and wishing to engage in, being understood and prized will determine whether empathic efforts and positive regard will be therapeutically beneficial. There are many situations in which clients may not wish to be understood for fear of losing what at that time is more important — autonomy. This is often the case with adolescents as they are attempting to establish their identities autonomously.

INTERPERSONAL PERCEPTION

The role of the client's past interpersonal experience on the client's perception of the therapist has been a controversial issue. Transference, as outlined in classical psychoanalysis, is not a congenial concept in Rogerian or experiential therapy for several reasons, which have been thoughtfully articulated by Shlien (1984) and Spinelli (1995). Transference as viewed by traditional analysts tends to reduce new, creative and living encounters to the status of a prop theater in which the client is manipulated by mysterious forces to re-enact his or her formative relationships in the present. This phantom theater casts the client essentially as a puppet tossed about unwittingly by alien and unconscious drives. The therapist, in turn, is viewed as the seer, empowered to divine the client's true thoughts and motivations. Such a view, however, negates the freedom, liveliness, self-determination, and dialogue, which is the mark in experiential or phenomenological therapies of an authentic therapeutic encounter. Recent research, however, has supported some aspects of the influence of past experience on current interpersonal perception within a broad social-cognitive model of interpersonal perception (Glassman and Andersen, 1999). It seems timely and appropriate to address the relevance of these findings for experientially oriented therapies.

These findings bear closely on the views of self and perception presented in this chapter. They suggest that past experiences influence how the client will perceive the therapist. Since the past affects the client's perceptions of the therapist it also influences whether and how the sixth condition is met. Susan Andersen and colleagues (e.g. Andersen, Reznik and Manzella, 1996; reviewed in Glassman and Andersen, 1999) offer robust and consistent experimental evidence for a universal, normal, fundamentally healthy social process whereby mental representations of past significant others are encoded in memory with heavy emotional associations. These representations in turn influence current perceptions of new people who seem to possess similar traits and features. This is highly consistent with our dialectical constructivist view of functioning. These perceptual processes are individualized in that the specific content of the representations are unique to each individual, being a schematic encoding from significant personal relationships. In this view, what has been called 'transference' is not specific to therapeutic settings but is a socially ubiquitous phenomenon. Transference, conceptualized in this way, essentially means that through learning more is perceived in a newly encountered individual than is known to be there (at a first meeting), that this 'more' is projected from schematic memories of key individuals in one's life, and that the projection is triggered when the new individual shares obvious features and traits with the significant other in memory. Nothing at all is being said here about psychodynamic, infantile, unconscious fantasies or wishes, although all the processes being described are considered to happen 'out of awareness'. Therefore, how the client perceives the therapist's provision of empathy and unconditional regard will be influenced by the client's interpretations of the therapist's behaviour, and these are influenced in part by the client's past experience.

The experimental evidence of Andersen and her colleagues is consistent with the dialectical constructivist view of how self and other are perceived. An important difference, however, is Andersen's apparent belief that the principal factor in interpersonal perception is cognition. In our view cognitive processes, that go on out of awareness to detect features of a person deemed to be relevant and important in a given person's experience, are essentially functioning at the service of emotion and emotional memory. Emotion is the primary automatic barometer of what matters to or concerns an individual in a situation. Emotional experience is core in the organization of the self and in interpersonal relationships.

This is not to downplay the crucial role of cognition but to differentiate levels and functions of cognition. At one pole of the dialectic in dialectical constructivism, conscious cognition, and its powers of language, logic and abstraction, is the primary arbiter of meaning. This conscious level, however, is not a significant factor for Andersen, who sees perception as influenced by tacit cognitive processes. In the dialectical constructivist model, however, many types of information influence perception, including the unconscious cognitive processing of situational and interpersonal cues that trigger the emotion schemes. Emotional memory and affective experience, however, are the crucial arbiters of much automatic information-processing and when all levels of information are synthesized, the effect is a felt sense of oneself in the world. This level of experiential meaning, as compared to purely conscious conceptual meaning, is centrally about a person's global feeling of motivated selfhood, the sense of being a living developing self with something that matters personally at stake in the process. More than anything, emotion is what orients and organizes this sense of being an engaged, desiring self.

In a dialectical constructivist model, identifying and interpreting the schematic interpersonal phenomena that psychoanalysis terms 'transference' is not considered pivotal to the therapeutic process. Transference is basically another way of speaking about an aspect of the everyday experience of constructing interpersonal experience (Greenberg, 2002). The influence of our past learning on our present experience does not constitute the creation of a false or distorted relationship that can be readily contrasted with one that is real or true. If elements of an individual's perceptions or experiences are being filtered through maladaptive emotion schemes, those experiences and perceptions, and the relationship that flows from them, are still reality as constructed and experienced by that individual in the moment. In addition, what matters most for change is not the understanding of how one sees the world, but rather the activation of the relevant emotion schemes in therapy, so that in their activated state the schemes are open to new emotional and cognitive experience. Thus, it is working toward the client perceiving the therapist as empathic and positively regarding that often is the work of therapy itself.

Given that all of us construe others through the lens of our idiosyncratic schematic construal system, how clients perceive their therapist's empathy and unconditional positive regard will be influenced by the perceptual lenses they bring to therapy. All perceptions are perspectival. For the sixth condition to be achieved, a complex coordination of therapist intentions and action with the client's perspective of these has to occur. Ultimately dialogue is necessary. This involves going beyond simply understanding each other toward developing a shared outlook and a common understanding and language.

Rather than a provision of a set of therapist conditions, what must occur is a true dialogue between the client and the therapist involving the co-construction of a negotiated interpersonal reality. It is only when this occurs that the client can possibly perceive the therapist as empathic and positively regarding and the sixth condition be satisfied.

CONCLUSION

In our view the attainment of the first and sixth conditions are at the heart of the therapeutic process itself. This pushes us towards a dialogical view of therapy rather than a view of therapist-offered conditions. The type of contact made and the client's perceptions are expressions of their self-organizing process and are themselves an important focus of therapy. How people construct their contact and perceptions determine the type of alliance they form and the type of process in which they will engage.

REFERENCES

Allen, R. E. (Ed.). (1990). *The Concise Oxford Dictionary* (8th ed.). New York: Oxford University Press.
Andersen, S. M., Reznik, I. and Manzella, L. M. (1996). Eliciting facial affect, motivation, and expectancies in transference: Significant-other representations in social relations. *Journal of Personality and Social Psychology, 71,* 1108–29.
Epstein, S. (1993). Emotion and self-theory. In M. Lewis and J. M. Haviland (Eds.), *Handbook of emotion*. New York: Guilford, (pp. 313–26).
Epstein, S., Lipson, A., Holstein, C. and Huh, E. (1992). Irrational reactions to negative outcomes: Evidence for two conceptual systems. *Journal of Personality and Social Psychology, 62,* 328–39.
Frijda, N. H. (1986). *The Emotions*. Cambridge: Cambridge University Press.

Gendlin, E. T. (1962). *Experiencing and the creation of meaning: A philosophical and psychological approach to the subjective*. New York: Free Press of Glencoe.

Glassman, N. S. and Andersen, S. M. (1999). Streams of thought about the self and significant others: Transference as the construction of interpersonal meaning. In J. A. Singer and P. Salovey (Eds.), *At play in the fields of consciousness: Essays in honor of Jerome L. Singer*. Mahwah, NJ: Erlbaum, pp. 103–40.

Greenberg, L. S. (1995). The self is flexibly various and requires an integrative approach. *Journal of Psychotherapy Integration, 5,* 323–9.

Greenberg, L. S. (2002). *Emotion-focused therapy: Coaching clients to work through their feelings*. Washington, DC: APA Press.

Greenberg, L. S. and Korman, L. (1993). Integrating emotion in psychotherapy integration. *Journal of Psychotherapy Integration, 3,* 249–65.

Greenberg, L. S. and Paivio, S. (1997). *Working with emotions in psychotherapy*. New York: Guilford.

Greenberg, L. S. and Pascual-Leone, J. (1995). A dialectical constructivist approach to experiential change. In R. Neimeyer and M. Mahoney (Eds.), *Constructivism in psychotherapy*. Washington, DC: American Psychological Association, pp. 169–91.

Greenberg, L. S. and Pascual-Leone, J. (1997). Emotion in the creation of personal meaning. In M. Power and C. Bervin (Eds.), *Transformation of meaning*. Chichester: Wiley, pp. 157–74.

Greenberg, L. S. and Pascual-Leone, J. (2001). A dialectical constructivist view of the creation of personal meaning. *Journal of Constructivist Psychology, 14,* 165–86.

Greenberg, L. S. and Safran, J. D. (1987). *Emotion in psychotherapy: Affect, cognition, and the process of change*. New York: Guilford Press.

Greenberg, L. S. and Van Balen, R. (1998). The theory of experience-centered therapies. In L. S. Greenberg, J. C. Watson, and G. Lietaer (Eds.), *Handbook of experiential psychotherapy*. New York: Guilford, pp. 28–59.

Horvath, A. O. and Greenberg, L. S. (1994). *The working alliance: Theory, research, and practice*. New York: Wiley.

Kohut, H. (1977). *The restoration of the self*. New York: International Universities Press.

Kolb, B. and Whishaw, I. Q. (1996). *Human neuropsychology* (4th ed.). New York: W. H. Freeman.

Latner, J. (1992). The theory of gestalt therapy. In E. C. Nevis (Ed.), *Gestalt Therapy: Perspectives and applications*. New York: Gardner Press, pp. 13–56.

Lang, P. (1995). The emotion probe: Studies of emotion and attention. *American Psychologist, 50,* 372–85.

LeDoux, J. E. (1989). Cognitive-emotional interactions in the brain. *Cognition and Emotion, 3,* 267–89.

LeDoux, J. E. (1993). Emotional networks in the brain. In M. Lewis and J.M. Haviland (Eds.), *Handbook of emotions*. New York: Guilford, pp. 109–18.

Levinas, E. (1969). *Totality and infinity* (A. Lingis, Trans.). The Hague, Netherlands: Nijhoff. (Original work published 1961.)

Mahoney, M. (1991). *Human change processes*. New York: Basic Books.

Pascual-Leone, J. (1987). Organismic processes for neo-Piagetian theories: A dialectical causal account of cognitive development. *International Journal of Psychology, 22,* 531–70.

Pascual-Leone, J. (1989). An organismic process model of Witkin's field-dependence-independence. In T. Globerson and T. Zelniker (Eds.), *Cognitive style and cognitive development*. Norwood, NJ: Ablex, pp. 36–70.

Pascual-Leone, J. (1990). Reflections on life-span intelligence, consciousness and ego development. In C. Alexander and E. Langer (Eds.), *Higher stages of human development: Perspectives on adult growth*. New York: Oxford University Press, pp. 258–85.

Pascual-Leone, J. and Irwin, R. (1994). Noncognitive factors in high-road/low-road learning: I. Modes of abstraction in adulthood. *Journal of Adult Development, 1,* 73–89.

Pascual-Leone, J. and Johnson, J. (1991). The psychological unit and its role in task analysis: A reinterpretation of object permanence. In M. Chandler and M. Chapman (Eds.), *Criteria for competence: Controversies in the assessment of children's abilities*. Hillsdale, NJ: Erlbaum, pp. 153–87.

Perls, F. S. (1947). *Ego, hunger, and aggression: A revision of Freud's theory and method.* Highland, NY: The Gestalt Journal Press.

Perls, F. S. (1969). *Gestalt therapy verbatim.* Moab, UT: Real People Press.

Perls, F. S., Hefferline, R. and Goodman, P. (1951). *Gestalt therapy.* New York: Dell.

Polster, E. and Polster, M. (1973). *Gestalt therapy integrated: Contours of theory and practice.* New York: Vintage Books (Random House).

Prouty, G. (1994). *Theoretical evolutions in person-centered/experiential therapy: Applications to schizophrenic and retarded psychoses.* Westport, CT: Praeger.

Rogers, C. R. (1957). The necessary and sufficient conditions of therapeutic personality change. *Journal of Consulting Psychology, 21,* 95–103.

Rogers, C. R. (1959). A theory of therapy, personality, and interpersonal relationships, as developed in the client-centered framework. In S. Koch (Ed.), *Psychology: A study of a science.* New York: McGraw-Hill. (Vol. 3, pp. 184–256).

St. Clair, M. (1986). *Object relations and self-psychology: An introduction.* Monterey, CA: Brooks/Cole.

Schwarz, N. (1999). Feelings as information: Informational and motivational functions of affective states. In E.T. Higgins and R. M. Sorrentino (Eds.), *Handbook of motivation and cognition: Foundations of social behavior.* New York: Guilford. (Vol. 2, pp. 527–61)

Schwarz, N. and Clore, G. L. (1983). Mood, misattribution, and judgements of well-being: Informative and directive functions of affective states. *Journal of Personality and Social Psychology, 45,* 513–23.

Shakespeare, W. (2000). *King Lear.* (S. Wells, Ed.). New York: Oxford University Press. (Original work published 1608.)

Shlien, J. M. (1984). A countertheory of transference. In R. Levant and J. M. Shlien (Eds.), *Client-centered therapy and the person-centered approach.* New York: Praeger, pp. 153–81.

Spinelli, E. (1995). An existential-phenomenological counter-theory of transference. *Counselling Psychology Quarterly, 8,* 269–77.

Teasdale, J. D. and Barnard, J. P. (1993). *Affect, cognition, and change: Re-modelling depressive thought.* Trowbridge, England: Redwood Books.

Thelen, E. and Smith, L. B. (1994). *A dynamic systems approach to the development of cognition and action.* Cambridge, MA: Massachusetts Institute of Technology Press.

Vygotsky, L. (1986). *Thought and language.* Cambridge, MA: MIT Press.

Watson, J. and Greenberg, L. S. (1996). Emotion and cognition in experiential therapy: A dialectical-constructivist position. In H. Rosen and K. Kuehlwein (Eds.), *Constructing realities: Meaning-making perspectives for psychotherapists.* San Francisco, CA: Jossey-Bass, pp. 253–76.

Whelton, W. J. and Greenberg, L. S. (2001). The self as a singular multiplicity: A process-experiential perspective. In J. C. Muran (Ed.), *Self-relations in the psychotherapy process.* Washington, D.C.: APA Press, pp. 87–106.

Winkielman, P., Zajonc, R. B. and Schwarz, N. (1997). Subliminal affective priming resists attributional interventions. *Cognition and Emotion, 11,* 433–65.

Yontef, G. M. (1993). *Awareness, dialogue and process: Essays on gestalt therapy.* Highland, NY: Gestalt Journal Press.

Zajonc, R. B. (2000). Feeling and thinking: Closing the debate over the independence of affect. In J. P. Forgas (Ed.), *Feeling and thinking: The role of affect in social cognition.* New York: Cambridge University Press, pp. 31–58.

6 Perception: The core element in person-centred and experiential psychotherapies

Shaké G. Toukmanian

I know you believe you understand what you think I said but I am not sure you realize that what you heard is not what I meant.
Author Unknown

The term 'perception' is commonly used in the current psychological literature to refer to the mental activity that is centrally involved in the integration and interpretation of information in the immediate present based on one's past transactions with the world (Neisser, 1976; Rumelhart, 1984; Weimer, 1977). Perceiving, thus, is viewed as a dynamic and inferential process. It is the construction of 'reality' not as it actually is but as it is represented and interpreted as being 'meaningful' by the individual. This portrayal is consistent with the fundamental premise of all humanistic psychotherapies (e.g. Mahoney, 1991; May, 1961; Perls, 1969; Rogers, 1959, 1961) that reality resides within the person's subjective experience, that people see what their experiential frameworks allow them to see and they make sense of what they see by developing ways of knowing and creating a version of reality that gives meaning, continuity, and coherence to their view of self, others, and events in their everyday functioning.

Perception is a key construct that permeates all aspects of Rogers' theory of therapy and personality change. Even when it is not explicitly dealt with or recognized, perception looms large in his emphasis on the primacy of subjective knowing, his existential view of the person, his conception of the nature of the therapeutic relationship, and his definitions of many of the theory's foundational constructs. Perception is also a central component of Rogers' 'necessary and sufficient conditions' of therapeutic change, although the concept is addressed directly only with reference to Condition Six. This condition stipulates that the client must, at least to some degree, perceive the therapist as being empathically understanding and unconditionally accepting for the therapeutic process to occur (Rogers, 1957, 1959). By invoking this condition, Rogers makes it clear that the client is an important player in determining the potential course of therapy. Yet, neither in his subsequent writings nor in the vast majority of the theoretical and empirical literature on person-centred therapy has the subject of the impact of clients' perceptions of the attitudinal qualities of the therapist on the *process* of therapy been dealt with adequately.

I will begin this chapter with an overview of the research into three of Rogers' conditions for positive therapeutic change, the therapist's congruence, empathy, and unconditional positive regard. This will be followed by a brief discussion of how the client's perception of the therapist is significantly implicated in his conception of the therapeutic relationship. I will argue that to be clearly understood, this phenomenon needs to be seen as being an integral part of the client's perceptual-processing system and that it is the level of clients' in-therapy perceptual functioning that influences their view of the therapist and the degree to which these conditions are received. In the final section, I will discuss this perspective in relation to ways of therapist responding that are likely to enhance the communication of empathic understanding and unconditional positive regard to the client. In my discussions, I will focus mainly on Rogers' 1957 and 1959 papers, as these are considered to be the most rigorous statements of his theory.

PERCEPTION AND THE THERAPEUTIC RELATIONSHIP

True to his belief in the fundamental predominance of the subjective and his belief in theory as being 'aimed toward the inner ordering of significant experiences', Rogers developed and refined his theory of psychotherapy based ostensibly on his systematic observations of what he *perceived* to be *meaningful*, in terms of both his own sense of himself as a therapist and whatever insight he gained into the meaning of therapy, in his transactions with clients. Thus, it is not surprising that his view of the therapist's attitudinal qualities, as experienced and conveyed to the client in the therapeutic relationship, came to be of central importance in person-centred therapy. Rogers maintained all along that the therapist's congruence in the therapeutic relationship (Condition Three), experience of unconditional positive regard for the client (Condition Four), and empathic understanding of the client's internal frame of reference (Condition Five) are critical components of successful therapy. He further asserted that it is only when the client *perceives* or experiences the therapist's empathic understanding and acceptance that positive therapeutic change can occur (Condition Six), thus implying that the phenomenon is both experientially-based and transactional (that is, bi-directional and hence, non-linear) in nature.

Despite this implication, in Rogers' theory of psychotherapy the functional relationship between the therapist's facilitative qualities and treatment outcome is conceptualized as being linear, wherein the greater the degree to which these conditions exist, 'the deeper will be the process of therapy, and the greater the extent of personality and behavioral change' (Rogers, 1959, p. 220) in the client. In view of this assertion, one can only assume that for Rogers the therapist is the main contributor to the client's experience of the therapeutic relationship and, by implication, to the outcome of therapy. Indeed, as Barrett-Lennard (1998) aptly notes, there is no recognition in Rogers' conditions statement of 'any necessary property of the client beyond the broad requirement of being "vulnerable or anxious"' (p. 79). This omission is particularly troublesome in the context of a theory that, although built on the fundamental premise of the primacy of human experience, pays very little attention to the client's agency in the therapeutic relationship, nor to factors impinging on the client's perceptions of what is being heard in the moment that are likely to influence his/her subsequent transactions and ultimately, and quite possibly, the therapeutic experience as a whole. Although Rogers offers a compelling and, what appears to be, a carefully articulated perspective on the process of therapy, I am inclined to believe that his attempt to capture complex, transactional phenomena in a theory that is of 'the if-then variety' is inconsistent with the general thrust of his humanistic perspective and that it is the theory's general neglect of the role of the dynamic interplay between the client and therapist that is likely the reason for the confusion that exists in the research literature on person-centred therapy.

Selected review of the research literature

For more than four decades, the Rogerian concept of the therapeutic relationship and the three therapist attitudinal conditions of empathy, unconditional positive regard, and genuineness have been the subject of considerable research interest. Most reviewers of this literature agree that, while there is evidence indicating that a positive client-therapist relationship is critical to successful therapy, support for Rogers' hypothesis that these therapist conditions play a causal role in 'constructive change' is modest at best, or inconclusive (e.g. Asay and Lambert, 2002; Greenberg, Elliott and Lietaer, 1994; Gurman, 1977; Lambert, DeJulio and Stein, 1978; Mitchell, Bozarth and Krauft, 1977; Orlinsky and Howard, 1986; Patterson, 1984; Sachse and Elliott, 2002). This ambiguity in results has been attributed to a variety of factors. Some argue that the Rogerian hypothesis has not yet been adequately tested because of the use of inappropriate research designs that do not address the *reciprocal nature of client-therapist transactions* (Cramer, 1990; Cramer and Takens, 1992). Others, on the other hand, believe that the confusion stems fundamentally from the general lack of conceptual and definitional clarity of the Rogerian constructs (e.g. Duan and Hill, 1996; Haugh, 2000; Hill and Nakayama, 2000; Wilkins, 2000).

For example, in their review of the current status of empathy research, Duan and Hill (1996) identify three different conceptualizations of empathy and indicate that Rogers has used all three meanings of the term in his various writings: empathy as a trait or general ability (Rogers, 1957), as a situation-specific cognitive-affective state wherein one perceives the emotional components and meanings of another's private world as if it were one's own (Rogers, 1959), and as a phase of the therapist's experiential process that involves sensing the client's inner world in the moment and communicating that sense to the client (Rogers, 1975). Barrett-Lennard (1981) offers a process conception of empathy and distinguishes between empathic resonation, expressed empathy, and received empathy, while Greenberg and Elliott (1997) believe that there are at least five different forms of empathic responding: empathic understanding, empathic evocation, empathic exploration, empathic conjecture, and empathy-based interpretation. The terms 'intellectual empathy' and 'empathic emotions (Duan and Hill, 1996) or 'cognitive' and 'affective' empathy (Gladstein, 1983) have also been used as a way of distinguishing between empathy as communicated and empathy as experienced by the therapist.

The meaning of the term 'unconditional positive regard' has also been debated in the literature (e.g. Bozarth, 1998; Lietaer, 1984; Wilkins, 2000). Rogers (1959) associated the term with the therapist acceptance and prizing of 'the whole person of the client'. For him, experiencing unconditional positive regard meant 'to value the person, irrespective of the differential values which one might place on his [or her] behavior' (p. 208). However, the term has also been interpreted and used widely to refer to the therapist's respect, warmth, non-judgmental attitude, and acceptance of the client, including the contents of the client's expressions. Lietaer (1984) sees Rogers' characterization of unconditionality problematic and contends that acceptance and congruence are essentially parts of a more basic relational attitude of 'openness', with congruence reflecting openness to one's self and unconditional positive regard as openness to another. Bozarth (1998) believes that empathy, unconditional positive regard, and congruence 'are really, ultimately and functionally one condition' (p. 80). And while Wilkins (2000) views unconditional positive regard as a crucial factor, he argues that, ultimately, the key to effective psychotherapy is 'the extent to which the therapist is able perceptively to extend unconditional positive regard to the client' (p. 23).

Researchers also seem to agree that we lack reliable and valid measures of therapist relational attitudes because we are still unclear about what it is that is being measured (e.g. Duan and Hill, 1996; Lambert et al., 1978). For example, the literature indicates that empathic understanding, when viewed as the ability of the therapist to understand the client, is a significant predictor of therapy outcome (Sachse and Elliott, 2002), suggesting that this conception of empathy is likely easier to operationalize and assess through self-report questionnaires and rating scales than when empathy is defined as an inner experience. The perspective from which the therapist attitudes are measured is another important methodological consideration. There is now considerable evidence demonstrating that studies, in which the therapist attitudinal qualities and therapy outcome are evaluated from the vantage point of the client rather than that of objective raters, show consistently more positive results (e.g. Barrett-Lennard, 1962; Gormally and Hill, 1974; Lambert et al., 1978). However, there is also evidence showing that clients vary in what they perceive to be an empathic therapist response. Bachelor (1988) has found, for example, that some clients consider 'cognitive' empathic responses as being the most helpful, whereas others report that 'affective' type of empathic responding is the most meaningful. These results seem to imply that how empathy is perceived and experienced is likely the function of what is salient for the clients in the therapy hour. The fact that therapists also vary in their interpersonal skills and effectiveness with different clients (e.g. Beutler, Machado and Neufelt, 1994; Elkin, 1999; Lafferty, Beutler and Crago, 1991; Lambert and Okishi, 1997) further suggests that, while important in facilitating constructive client change, the therapist's empathic understanding and unconditional positive regard cannot be viewed as being independent of the client's contribution to the therapeutic process and outcome.

Indeed, the emerging evidence from qualitative studies on clients' experiences of psychotherapy demonstrates that clients are far from being passive recipients of therapist-offered facilitative conditions. Rennie's (1990, 1992, 1994a, 1994b) application of the grounded theory method of qualitative analysis on interviews conducted with clients has shown that 'clients in therapy are self-aware agents' and that the most salient and consistent aspect of their therapy experience is of moments in which they are 'self-aware and deliberative both in thought and in dialogue with the therapist' (Rennie, 1994a, p. 427). Rennie conceptualizes this overarching, core property of experience as client's reflexivity which subsumes four main categories: (a) client's relationship with personal meaning, (b) client's perception of the relationship with the therapist, (c) client's experience of the therapist's operations, and (d) client's experience of outcomes. Overall, his analyses have revealed that clients' experiences are mainly covert and not expressed, even when they have a good relationship with their therapist. When engaged in self-reflection, clients attend to their feelings and thoughts from moment to moment; they exercise their agency in deciding whether or not to disclose any thought or feeling or whether to pursue or avoid entering inner experience or meaning, depending on the contingencies of the moment; they value and pay more attention to their relationship with the therapist than to the therapist's techniques; they respond in their own ways to the therapist's operations, depending on what they want and what they feel they can safely say; and they have a strong tendency to defer to the therapist's authority (Rennie, 1990, 1992, 1994a, 1994b, 2002). Apparently, as Rennie (2002) points out, 'Clients may rail inwardly against *any* approach, depending on their preferences, without letting the therapist know about their discontent because of the power dynamics entailed in the relationship with the therapist' (p. 136).

In a similar vein, Hill and her colleagues (e.g. Hill, Thompson and Corbett, 1992; Hill, Thompson, Cogar and Denman, 1993; Thompson and Hill, 1991) have also found that clients hide negative reactions to specific therapist interventions from their therapists, keep secrets or choose not to disclose certain experiences, facts, or feelings to their therapists, and often leave things unsaid because of overwhelming emotions, desire to avoid dealing with the disclosure, and fear that the 'therapist would not understand' (Hill et al., 1993). The importance of clients' perceptions of negative experiences in therapy has also been emphasized by Hatcher and Barends (1996) who found that, despite frustrations in treatment, clients maintain a good relationship with their therapist but often at the price of not being able to express disagreement and gaining less from their therapeutic experience. Finally, Paulson, Everall and Stuart's (2001) qualitative study on client perceptions of hindering experiences has shown that clients are not openly revealing of what is going on for them during therapy, that they perceive the power differential between them and their therapist as being a barrier to feeling understood and their lack of readiness and need to be motivated as factors contributing to their slow progress.

In summary, the collective returns from this body of research point to the following general conclusions: (1) that there is as yet no clear evidence showing a cause-effect relationship between the therapist's offered facilitative conditions and therapy outcome and that this appears to be due to the theory's lack of conceptual clarity regarding the client's role in and contribution to the course and outcome of therapy; (2) that clients are active, self-aware, and agential participants in the therapy process; and (3) that clients' perceptions of the therapist and the therapeutic relationship exert considerable influence on how the therapy is construed and experienced. This latter, I believe, is at the core of person-centred and experiential psychotherapies in that, while recognizing the client's contribution to the therapeutic process, it also highlights the multi-faceted nature of the Rogerian conditions as being both intrapersonal *as well as* relational phenomena.

View of perception

In view of the importance of the concept of perception in Rogers' theory of psychotherapy, I have long been troubled by the lack of clarity in his treatment of this construct. To illustrate, in his 1959 theory paper, Rogers considers perception and awareness to be synonymous and views both as constructions based on past experiences and hence as being 'transactional in nature'. Yet, Rogers goes on to define awareness as 'the symbolic representation . . . of some portion of our experience' (p. 198) and perception as 'a hypothesis or prognosis for action which comes into being in awareness when stimuli impinge on the organism' (p. 199). He further distinguishes between the two by stating that 'perception [is] the narrower term, usually when we wish to emphasize the *importance* (italics provided) of the stimulus in the process, and awareness the broader term, covering symbolizations and meanings which arise from such purely internal stimuli as memory traces, visceral changes, and the like, as well as from external stimuli' (p. 199). In addition, he invokes the construct 'subception' to denote the organism's capacity to 'discriminate a stimulus and its meaning' outside of awareness (p. 200). In making these distinctions, Rogers appears to be intent on specifying the nuances entailed in his notion of experience, but it is not clear whether he is referring to different kinds of processes or to the subtle variations of a single, fundamental process. Considering that all three concepts imply the involvement of inference, it would seem that the core phenomenon alluded to here is *perception*. In other words, what is perceived, symbolized in awareness, or subceived is the meaning or the importance that a particular event has for the individual, which is the characteristic property of perception. In this sense, it is likely that Rogers is attempting to distinguish the degree of attentional allocation to the impact of an event that is perceived on some level as being personally meaningful.

The lack of clarity in Rogers' view of perception is also evident when we consider his definition of experience, one of the pivotal constructs of his theory. Rogers defines experience as everything that is going on within the person at any given moment that is 'potentially available to awareness' (Rogers, 1959, p. 197). In other words, experience is seen to embody the impact of all that exists in the person's 'phenomenal field' — the influence of external events, such as sights and sounds, as well as that 'of memory and past experience, as these are active in the moment, in restricting or broadening the meaning given to various stimuli' (p. 197) — and 'to experience' to mean 'simply to receive . . . the impact of the sensory and physiological events which are happening in the moment' (p. 197). In the absence of an explanation as to what the term 'to receive' actually entails, it would be plausible to assume that the phenomenon that Rogers is referring to is perception and that experience, as implied in his definition, is a construction or an inference derived from and constituted of the sum total of the meanings of everything that is going on internally at any given moment. Taking this perspective a step further, Rogers may be interpreted as suggesting that what one perceives at any given moment *is* his/her experience.

This conceptual ambiguity is also reflected in Rogers' generous use of the term 'perception' in his definitions and elaborations of many of his other foundational constructs (e.g. experiencing a feeling, self-concept, internal frame of reference, maturity, etc.). A detailed discussion of these is beyond the scope of this paper. Suffice it to say, however, that regardless of how perception has been dealt with, if we accept Rogers' proposition that '. . . the effective reality which influences behavior is at all times the perceived reality' (1959, p. 223), then it can be argued that perception is the *core* element of person-centred and, experiential psychotherapies (e.g. Greenberg, Watson and Lietaer, 1998; Mahoney, 1995; Toukmanian, 1992). Furthermore, if we accept that as a helping/healing relationship psychotherapy is a dynamic encounter between two individuals or between two 'perceived realities' of the world, then it can also be argued that perception is structurally inherent to the therapy situation and that each participant's complex network of personal meanings plays a significant role in therapeutic transactions. Thus, it would seem that if we are to understand how the client's perception of the therapist influences the process of therapy, we need to go beyond Rogers' descriptive portrayal of this phenomenon and delineate the nature of inferential processes that mediate clients' perceptions as they occur in the context of the therapeutic relationship. This, I believe, would help enhance our understanding of the client's contribution to the therapy process and provide a possible explanation as to why therapy fails or is less successful with some clients. This perspective is discussed in the section that follows.

A MODEL OF CLIENT PERCEPTUAL-PROCESSING

As the focus of this chapter is on Rogers' Condition Six, the question of particular importance here is: What impact does the *client's* perceptual-processing system have on the therapeutic relationship? Or more to the point, how does the client's level of in-therapy perceptual functioning affect his/her view of the therapist as being empathic and unconditionally accepting? I will attempt to address this issue in the context of an experiential model of client perceptual organization and change that offers a schematic developmental perspective on clients' in-therapy process and a framework for examining factors contributing to clients' perceptions of the therapist from the vantage point of their cognitive-affective processes and structures.

Conceptual framework

As elaborated upon elsewhere (Toukmanian, 1990, 1992, 1996), the perceptual-processing model is based on three fundamental propositions: that (a) perception is a schema-driven construction that, at any given moment in time, reflects the perceiver's capability to detect, organize, and give meaning to information on the basis of past transactions with the world (e.g. Neimeyer and Mahoney, 1995; Neisser, 1976); that (b) people are capable of engaging in a variety of mental operations and ways of perceiving that are learned through experience (Neisser,

1967); and that (c) people's perceptions play a significant role in how they act and interact with their environment.

Briefly, the model maintains that the perceptual-processing system is where people's meanings regarding self and the world develop (e.g. Guidano, 1995; Kelly, 1955; Mahoney, 1991). This system is viewed as consisting of two interactive components: the *structural* component entails the perceiver's network of schemata or meaning structures relevant to the event being perceived; and the *operational* component, the particular mode of information processing involved in the event's construction. The model contends that using an *automated* (very rapid, pre-reflective, and undiscriminating) mode of processing hampers schematic development while a *controlled* (slow, reflective, and deliberate) mode leads to 'structural transformations' (Neisser, 1976) and to an increasing complexity of the network of schematic structures, resulting in fundamental changes in the way in which a given event is perceived (Shiffrin and Schneider, 1977) and, hence, experienced.

Based on this schematic developmental view of perception, the model proposes that psychological dysfunctions (or 'client incongruences' stated in terms of Rogers' developmental theory of psychopathology) are, by and large, difficulties associated with people's inability or failure to process the cognitive-affective components or elements of their experiences in ways that would help them generate new and potentially more functional perspectives. In other words, they are conceived of as being the function of client construals that are formulated through a predominantly automated mode of processing applied to simple or less developed networks of schemata that preclude the processing of new and unfamiliar information. In this regard, automated construals of self and self-relevant events are considered to be crucial therapeutic targets because they constitute a consistent and readily available source of autobiographical information. When invoked, they automatically feed into and become inextricably embedded in the client's idiosyncratic constructions of intra- and interpersonal events and, in doing so, play a critical and often a pervasive role in determining how events are perceived and acted upon in a wide range of every-day life situations. In other words, it is argued that clients come to therapy with locked-in rigid self-perceptions that constrain the generation of alternative perspectives for adaptive responding. And because change occurs at the level of clients' inferential or meaning-making processes, therapy must help clients learn to process these in a slow and reflective manner, so that their habitual ways of construing can be modified. The contention here is that engaging clients in a controlled mode of processing creates a means by which self-schemata are further elaborated and reorganized, leading to the creation of new meanings, a fuller and more differentiated sense of self, greater flexibility in construals of self and self-in-relation to others, and to increased adaptiveness in functioning (Toukmanian, 1990, 1992).

In a series of studies conducted within this conceptual framework, Toukmanian (1996) and colleagues have demonstrated that clients change their processing strategies in the manner and direction specified by the model. For example, there is evidence supporting the hypothesis that productive segments or sessions of therapy are characterized by client construals that are formulated predominantly through internally focused, differentiating, re-evaluating, and integrating modes of processing (e.g. Missirlian, 2002; Sinclair, 1990; Toukmanian and Jackson, 1996) and that clients who gain more from their therapeutic experience on measures of self-concept, depression, and anxiety are more likely to engage in these processing operations than those for whom therapy is less successful (Day, 1995; Zink, 1990).

Although this evidence is not related directly to clients' perceptions of the relational qualities of the therapist, it is consistent with the findings of past social psychological research on person perception which indicate that people's level of cognitive complexity is strongly implicated in the processes by which they make judgments about self and others. Studies (e.g. Crockett, 1965; Leventhal and Singer, 1964; Taguiri and Petrullo, 1958; Tripodi and Bieri, 1964) have demonstrated, for example, that individuals who possess relatively undifferentiated cognitive/schematic structures tend to make fewer inferences when forming impressions, perceive more similarities between self and others, view others on univalent dimensions, and be concerned more with overt 'surface' cues and with consistencies and regularities in perceiving others, while those with clearly articulated and complex structures tend to make more inferences from a given set of information, pay more attention to inner psychological states, and incorporate both positive and negative qualities in their perception of others. Results from more recent studies further indicate that individuals high in self-complexity show less reactivity to stressful life events (Linville, 1985, 1987) and less resistance to feedback that challenges their established view of self than low-complexity individuals (Stein, 1994).

As noted earlier, a basic assumption of the perceptual-processing model is that psychological problems stem from rigid client construals (particularly those of self and interpersonal relationships) that are based on an automated mode of processing of a narrow range of readily detectable information. Indirect support for this hypothesis comes from a number of studies in which the quality of clients' past relational experiences has been shown to be associated with their ratings of the strength of the therapeutic alliance (relationship). For example, there is evidence indicating that clients with histories of problematic or stressful interpersonal relationships (Kokotovic and Tracy, 1990) and distrust in the dependability of others (Satterfield and Lyddon, 1995) tend to view and evaluate the strength of the alliance as being low or negative early on in therapy, as do clients with memories of strained, intrusive and controlling relationships with fathers (Mallinckrodt, Gantt and Coble, 1995). Transient client internal states, such as pre-session mood (Hill, O'Grady et al., 1994), perceived intensity of symptoms (Brykczynska, 1990), and cultural values (e.g. Dahlquist and Fay, 1983; Sue and Sue, 1990) have also been identified as factors influencing client judgments of therapist helpfulness and therapy outcome.

Overall, this research literature suggests that individual differences in perception are likely due to factors implicit to the perceiver more than to the characteristics of the perceived person or the situation and that such differences are likely the function of the kinds of inferential processes that people have learned to use in their construals of others and interpersonal situations. Thus, it may be argued that clients who come to therapy with a rigid system of processes for dealing with self and relational information would tend to view the therapist and the therapeutic encounter, particularly in the early phases of therapy, in a manner consistent with their narrow and often dysfunctional 'hypotheses' about interpersonal relationships — or stated in terms of the perceptual-processing model, *the degree to which clients are able to perceive the attitudinal qualities of the therapist is predicated on the level of their in-therapy perceptual functioning.* Furthermore, to the extent that perception is a transactional phenomenon, it may also be argued that individual clients' perception of the therapist will likely have a different meaning and manifest differently depending on context and, consequently, influence the client-therapist transactions differently at different times during the course of therapy.

A perspective on the process of clients' perceptions of the therapist

It should be clear from the foregoing that an understanding of the client's subjective world as it is experienced at any given moment in therapy requires a recognition that what is perceived in the here and now is embedded in a broader network of personal meanings that serves to filter what is being perceived and experienced in the moment. This implies that even when the therapist is able to communicate his/her empathic understanding and unconditional acceptance of the client, the client's construal of the therapist will embody, and hence be 'coloured' by, all that is subjectively accessible to the client in the moment. This view should not be taken to mean that these attitudinal conditions are of secondary importance. Quite the contrary. It simply means that, given their presence in the therapeutic encounter, their relative impact at any given moment will depend on the manner and extent to which this information is actually being processed which, in turn, is seen to be the function of the client's past record or history of learned patterns of processing interpersonal situations. Let me elaborate.

Most psychotherapists acknowledge that therapy is not a smooth and uneventful journey, that some sessions progress better than others, and that breakdowns in the flow of client-therapist transactions can and often do occur in all helping relationships, regardless of therapeutic orientation. Indeed, such disjunctions would seem to be inevitable when we consider that each therapy participant approaches the therapeutic task with a different set of anticipations or 'hypotheses' as to what therapy means. For therapists, who have come to recognise the importance of introspection, self-understanding, self-awareness, and self-initiated action as avenues for solving problems, resolving intra- and interpersonal conflicts, and attaining a healthy or a 'mature and extensional' way of functioning, the presupposition is that when clients seek therapy they will talk about their difficulties by disclosing and exploring their feelings, thoughts, behaviours, and recollections of problematic events and circumstances in their life. If this 'view' is not shared by the client, it will likely create communicational disjunctions, at least early on in therapy. However, even when it is shared, admitting to having personal difficulties will have a different meaning for different clients, depending on each client's unique experiential history. For some, it may mean exposing oneself as being weak and needy; others may construe it as a threat to their established view of self as self-sufficient and self-reliant individuals;

still others may see it as an act of betrayal or disloyalty to significant people in their life, and so on. And to the extent that such construals are part of a rigid system of personal meanings, they will have an influence on how the therapist and the therapy situation is processed and perceived by the client.

Clients' maladaptive patterns of processing interpersonal situations may also be at play in what has often been referred to as 'hindering events' in psychotherapy. Take, for instance, the phenomenon of client resistance which has been portrayed in the literature in a variety of ways, depending on the particular theoretical orientation from which it is viewed. From a psychodynamic perspective, resistance is seen as an unconscious transferential phenomenon that is typically manifest in various kinds of client oppositional reactions to the therapist and/or to the therapeutic endeavour (Mahalik, 1994) such as, reluctance to self-disclose or recall painful events, lack of involvement and motivation to change, non-compliance to therapeutic tasks, sidetracking or engaging in defensive behaviour. However, resistance can also be a conscious phenomenon resulting from misunderstandings, not wanting to respond to or comply with therapist expectations, or as a reflection of the constraints clients feel against challenging the authority of the therapist (Rennie, 1994). In either case, resistance is an expression of the clients' perception of the 'reality' of the therapeutic situation and, as such, it may be seen to reflect their learned ways of processing and making sense of all that is subjectively accessible and salient for them in that context in the moment. Thus, more than being an oppositional reaction to the therapist or to the idea of change *per se*, resistance may be seen to be symptomatic of clients' inability to deal with the exigencies of an unfamiliar interpersonal situation — a situation wherein the person with whom they are interacting is being understanding and unconditionally accepting of them despite their many shortcomings. Oppositional behaviours typically occur during the early phases of therapy and change slowly over time. This suggests that, as therapy progresses and as clients gradually learn to modify their rigid ways of processing intra- and interpersonal events, they are likely to be able to 'receive' or accept more of that which exists in their 'phenomenal field' (including the attitudinal qualities of the therapist) and, consequently, perceive self-in-relation to the therapist differently.

The foregoing illustrations are based on the presupposition that the Rogerian attitudinal conditions are to some degree present in the therapeutic relationship. It is not possible, however, to speak of the therapist providing unconditional acceptance and empathic understanding to the client without considering how these attitudes are conveyed to the client in actual practice. For in-as-much as it is important to understand how clients' level of perceptual functioning affects their view of the therapist, it is equally important to recognize that the therapist's manner of communicating also plays a crucial role in how clients will perceive the therapist in the therapeutic relationship. It is this issue that I turn to next.

The communication of relational conditions

A fundamental premise of person-centred theory is the view that there is a causal relationship between the therapist's empathic understanding and acceptance of the client and therapeutic personality change. In his 1957 paper, Rogers states that for change to occur it is necessary that:

> the client perceives, to a minimal degree, the acceptance and empathy which the therapist *experiences* for him [her]. Unless some *communication* of these attitudes has been achieved, then such attitudes do not exist in the relationship as far as the client is concerned ... [and] ... Since attitudes cannot be directly perceived, it might be more accurate to state that therapist *behaviors and words* are perceived by the client as meaning that to some degree the therapist accepts and understands him [her] (italics provided, p. 99).

This portrayal clearly indicates that Condition Six is constituted of two distinct 'subconditions': that the therapist (a) must experience acceptance and empathy for the client and (b) must maintain and communicate these attitudes in words and action to the client over a period of time. Each of these dimensions represents a complex phenomenon, the implementation of which may prove to be problematic in psychotherapy practice.

It is important to recognise that there is a difference between a therapist's *experience* of empathy and acceptance and the actual *articulation or communication* of the complexity of this experience to the client. Experiencing is both an intrapersonal as well as a relational phenomenon, while the articulation of experience is an interpersonal and co-constructive process. The former requires a high level of self-awareness on the part of the therapist — an awareness of not only one's needs, values, and beliefs but also of how one's background and experiences play into the perception of the client and the therapeutic encounter. This means that the therapist must have a complex and relatively well-differentiated network of self and relational schemata to be able to process and make sense of all that which is internally accessible and externally available (transactions with the client) in the moment. This level of functioning is crucial, however, it neither automatically leads to nor guarantees that the therapist is capable of communicating his/her empathic and accepting attitude perceptively to the client.

The communication of experience, on the other hand, is an ability. It requires that the therapist not only be attuned to what the client is attempting to convey in any given moment as fully and accurately as possible, but also to have the *ability to translate* what is actually being heard into words that capture the meaning of what lies behind the client's expression. It is here that the therapist's personal/attitudinal conditions merge with the expressive/behavioural components of therapy practice and I submit that it is this ability to integrate and communicate the intra- and the interpersonal that is of critical importance to effective person-centred and experiential psychotherapies. In other words, the therapist-attributed cause of therapeutic change does not reside in the therapist's experience of the attitudinal conditions but rather in his/her manner of responding, regardless of the type of therapist response. For even when the therapist is empathically understanding and accepting of the client, the therapeutic value of a given response can be determined only when viewed in terms of *both* its contextual appropriateness and the clarity with which it articulates what is experientially salient for the client and the therapist in the moment (e.g. Gordon, 1999; Sachse, 1993).

Specifically, to the extent that psychotherapy is an interactive and co-constructive process, there will always be a constant, bilateral or reciprocal influence between client and therapist on communication. This is because what therapists say and how they express themselves will reflect their construal of their experiencing self as much as their perception of the client's experience, and what clients say and how they respond to the therapist, in turn, will reflect their own construction of what has been heard (or not heard) which, as noted earlier, will depend on their 'willingness' and/or 'perceptual readiness' to receive that which is being communicated to them in the moment. In this ongoing process, each therapy participant is both a sender and a receiver of 'messages'; each reconstructs and responds to the other person's communication based on what is *perceived* to be salient to self and to the other at any given time within the therapeutic relationship; and each is an active contributor to the process of therapy. Thus, when and how therapists communicate (or fail to communicate) their empathic understanding and unconditional acceptance of the client must be seen and understood as being an integral part of this interactive, client-therapist perceptual field.

From the standpoint of the perceptual-processing model (Toukmanian, 1990, 1992) described earlier in this chapter, my position on this issue is that (a) what therapists intend to communicate and what they actually end up communicating to the client is the combined function of their *self-awareness*, their *awareness of how the client is processing his/her experiences in the moment*, and their *ability to convey* this awareness in a tentative but clear, concise, and easy to follow manner, and that (b) disjunctions in communication occur at any one or all levels. For example, if the therapist is 'incongruent' or is functioning with a rigid perceptual-processing system and is unable to transcend this *perceptual mind frame*, he/she is likely to misperceive or be unaware of what is salient or not salient for the client and hence respond in ways that lead to what Wyatt (2001) calls 'a diminishing level of relational congruence between therapist and client' (p. 234). Similarly, when the therapist's responses are ambiguous and poorly structured, they are likely to be confusing to the client and therefore may run the risk of fostering client misconstruals and breakdowns in communication which, when maintained over a period of time, may create an atmosphere wherein the client may feel misunderstood, lose trust in the therapist's credibility as a helper, and ultimately benefit less from the therapy experience. A state of 'relational incongruence' may also arise when therapists *assume*, based on the surface meaning of clients' verbalisations, that they understand what is being communicated to them when in fact they may not. And it is here that the therapist's awareness of the client's processing strategies becomes of crucial importance.

To elaborate, it should be recognized that therapeutic transactions have multiple meanings that often are not readily apparent to the participants. This is particularly true of clients' expressions for, although the common semantic meaning of words may be obvious to the therapist, the clients' choice of words and the way in which they formulate them to express inner experiences, thoughts, and feelings will be idiosyncratic to individual client's manner of processing and making sense of what is going on for them in the therapy situation (Toukmanian,

1990, 1992). If we accept the view that therapeutic change occurs at the level of clients' inferential or meaning-making processes and that clients' processing strategies change (or fail to change) as therapy progresses, then it is to be expected that these changes will be manifest in the way clients construe and talk about their experiences during the course of therapy. In fact, studies conducted within the perceptual-processing conceptual framework (e.g. Day, 1995; Gordon, 1999; Zink, 1990) indicate that clients' manner of processing is discernible from the differential quality of their verbal expressions and that therapist responses directed at 'markers' that are reflective of processing dysfunctions help deepen the clients' self-exploration (for a fuller description of this approach the reader is referred to Toukmanian, 1990). An awareness of whether or not and in what way client expressions change can thus serve to inform therapists of 'where the client is at' with respect to his/her level of perceptual functioning and, in so doing, help them respond in a *contextually appropriate* manner (Toukmanian, 1990). This awareness, as I see it, is a key element of empathic understanding and other 'following' responses commonly used in person-centred and experiential therapies.

Specifically, in acknowledging the critical importance of Rogers' Condition Six, this experiential perspective goes a step further by proposing that (a) to be able to communicate in an empathic and accepting manner, therapists must be *trained* in ways of responding that will make these attitudes perceptible to the client and (b) in order to achieve this, training must help them develop habits of listening to and becoming aware of the developmental level of their clients' self and relational perceptual-processing system.

As I have indicated elsewhere (Toukmanian, 1990, 1996), the intent here is to get the therapists to think in 'process' terms, that is, to help them (1) shift attention away from the content and onto the quality of the clients' discourse, (2) adopt a questioning stance (e.g. What is this person trying to say? Do I really understand the meaning of his/her expressions? Is the client's construction superficial, stereotypic, and abstract or detailed, personalised, and idiosyncratic? Is the source of information being processed and construed internal or external to the client?) as a way of developing more discerning habits of listening for ambiguities of meaning and to recognise 'markers' indicative of dysfunctional patterns of processing in clients' expressions, and with this awareness, (3) respond to the meaning or to what lies beneath the client's expressions. A major advantage of this approach is that it helps therapists maintain a constant focus on the client's inner experience. And when therapists are attuned to the client's manner of processing moment-by-moment, they are likely to rely less on their own subjectivity of what is or is not salient for the client and be guided more by the client's agency or 'directivity' of the therapy process. This in turn will allow them to respond in ways that are likely will convey their openness to and desire to understand the client from his/her 'internal frame of reference'.

CONCLUSIONS

The main goal of this chapter has been to demonstrate the centrality of the concept of perception in Rogers' theory of therapy particularly as it relates to his conceptualization of the therapeutic relationship. It was pointed out that a fundamental problem in person-centred theory is that, while emphasising the primacy of the client's subjectivity and acknowledging that perception is a dynamic, experientially-based, and transactional phenomenon, it fails to recognize that the client is a major player in determining the potential course of therapy. Considering that each therapy participant has a unique experiential history and ways of construing reality, it was argued that the therapist-attributed cause of therapeutic change must be considered in light of what is experientially salient for both the client and the therapist at any given time within the therapeutic relationship. The degree to which and how clients come to perceive the therapist as being empathically understanding and unconditionally accepting was discussed in light of a schematic-processing model of client perceptions. It was concluded that this phenomenon can best be understood in relational terms and as being the combined function of the therapist's self-awareness, awareness of the client's attained level of in-therapy perceptual functioning, and ability to communicate this awareness clearly to the client. This framework offers a perspective that explicitly recognizes the client's agency in the therapeutic relationship and, as such, upholds Rogers' fundamental premise that the therapist's trust in and understanding of the subjectivity and uniqueness of the client's experiencing is of paramount importance to successful therapy.

REFERENCES

Asay, T. P. and Lambert, M. (2002). Therapist relational variables. In D. J. Cain (Ed.), *Humanistic psychotherapies: Handbook of research and practice*. Washington, DC: APA, pp. 531–57.

Bachelor, A. (1988). How clients perceive therapist empathy: A content analysis of 'received' empathy. *Psychotherapy: Therapy, Research and Practice, 25*, 227–40.

Barrett-Lennard, G. (1962). Dimensions of therapy response as causal factors in therapeutic change. *Psychological Monographs, 76*, 1–33.

Barrett-Lennard, G. (1981). The empathy cycle: Refinement of a nuclear concept. *Journal of Counseling Psychology, 28*, 91–100.

Barrett-Lennard, G. (1998). *Carl Rogers' helping system: Journey and substance*. London: Sage.

Beutler, L., Machado, P. and Neufeldt, S. (1994). Therapist variables. In A. Bergin and S. Garfield (Eds.), *Handbook of psychotherapy and behavior change* (4th ed.), NY: Wiley, pp. 229–69.

Bozarth, J. D. (1998). *Person-Centered Therapy: A revolutionary paradigm*. Ross-on-Wye: PCCS Books.

Brykczynska, C. (1990). Changes in the patient's perception of his therapist in the process of group and individual psychotherapy. *Psychother Psychosom, 53*, 179–84.

Cramer, D. (1990). Towards assessing the therapeutic value of Rogers' core conditions. *Counselling Psychology Quarterly, 3*, 57–66.

Cramer, D. and Takens, R. J. (1992). Therapeutic relationship and progress in the first six sessions of individual psychotherapy: A panel analysis. *Counselling Psychology Quarterly, 5*, 25–36.

Crockett, J. (1965). Cognitive complexity-simplicity and predictive behavior. *Journal of Abnormal and Social Psychology, 51*, 263–8.

Day, S. M. (1995). Self-concept, schematic processing and change in perceptual-processing experiential therapy. Unpublished master's thesis, York University, Toronto, Ontario.

Dahlquist, Z. M. and Fay, A. S. (1983). Cultural issues in psychotherapy. In C. E. Walkes (Ed.), *Handbook of Clinical Psychology*. Homewood, IL: Dow-Jones Irwin, pp. 1219–55.

Duan, C. and Hill, C. (1996). Theoretical confusion in the construct of empathy: A review of the literature. *Journal of Consulting Psychology, 43*, 261–74.

Elkin, I. (1999). A major dilemma in psychotherapy outcome research: Disentangling therapists from therapies. *Clinical Psychology: Science and Practice, 6*, 10–32.

Gladstein, G. A. (1983). Understanding empathy: Integrating counseling, developmental, and social psychology perspectives. *Journal of Counseling Psychology, 30*, 467–82.

Gordon, K. (1999). Is how it is said important? The association between quality of therapist intervention and client in-session processing. Unpublished master's thesis, York University, Toronto, Ontario.

Gormally, J. and Hill, C. (1974). Guidelines for research on Carkhuff's training model. *Journal of Counseling Psychology, 21*, 539–47.

Greenberg, L. S. and Elliott, R. (1997). Varieties of empathic responding. In A. C. Bohart and L. S. Greenberg (Eds.), *Empathy reconsidered: New directions in psychotherapy*. Washington, DC: APA, pp. 167–86.

Greenberg, L. S., Elliott, R. and Lietaer, G. (1994). Research on experiential therapies. In A. E. Bergin and S. L. Garfield (Eds.), *Handbook of Psychotherapy and Behaviour Change*. New York: Wiley, pp. 509–39.

Greenberg, L. S., Watson, J. and Lietaer, G. (1998). *Handbook of experiential psychotherapy*. NY: Guilford.

Guidano, V. F. (1995). A constructivist outline of human knowing processes. In M. J. Mahoney (Ed.), *Cognitive and constructive psychotherapies*. NY: Springer, pp. 89–102.

Gurman, A. S. (1977). The patient's perception of the therapeutic relationship. In A. S. Gurman and A. M. Razin (Eds.), *Effective psychotherapy: A handbook of research*. NY: Pergamon, pp. 503–43.

Hatcher, R. L. and Barends, A. W. (1996). Patients' view of the alliance in psychotherapy: Exploratory factor analysis of three alliance measures. *Journal of Consulting and Clinical Psychology, 64*, 1326–36.

Haugh, S. (2000). The difficulties in the conceptualisation of congruence: A way forward with complexity theory. In G. Wyatt (Ed.), *Rogers' therapeutic conditions: Evolution, theory and practice, Vol. 1: Congruence*. Ross-on-Wye: PCCS Books, pp. 116–30.

Hill, C. and Nakayama, E. Y. (2000). Client-centered therapy: Where has it been and where is it going? A comment on Hathaway. *Journal of Clinical Psychology, 56*, 861–75.

Hill, C., O'Grady, K. E., Balenger, V., Busse, W., Falk, D. R., Hill, M., Rios, P. and Taffe, R. (1994). Methodological examination of videotape-assisted reviews in brief therapy: Helpfulness ratings, therapist intentions, client reactions, mood and session evaluation. *Journal of Counseling Psychology, 41*, 236–47.

Hill, C., Thompson, B. J. and Corbett, M. H. (1992). The impact of therapist ability to perceive displayed and hidden client reactions on immediate outcome in first sessions of brief therapy. *Psychotherapy Research, 2*, 143–55.

Hill, C., Thompson, B. J., Cogar, M. C. and Denman, D. W. (1993). Beneath the surface of long-term therapy: Therapist and client report of their own and each other's covert processes. *Journal of Counseling Psychology, 40*, 278–87.

Kelly, G. (1955). *The psychology of personal constructs*. New York: Norton.

Kokotovic, A. M. and Tracy, T. J. (1990). Working alliance in the early phase of counseling. *Journal of Counseling Psychology, 37*, 16–21.

Lafferty, P., Beutler, L. and Crago, M. (1991). Differences between more and less effective psychotherapists: A study of select therapist variables. *Journal of Consulting and Clinical Psychology, 57*, 76–80.

Lambert, M., DeJulio, S. S. and Stein, D. M. (1978). Therapist interpersonal skills: Process, outcome, methodological considerations and recommendations for future research. *Psychological Bulletin, 85*, 467–89.

Lambert, M. and Okishi, J. C. (1997). The effects of the individual psychotherapist and implications for future research. *Clinical Psychology: Science and Practice, 4*, 66–75.

Leventhal, H. and Singer, D. L. (1964). Cognitive Complexity, Impression Formation and Impression Change. *Journal of Personality, 32*, 210–26.

Lietaer, G. (1984). Unconditional positive regard: A controversial basic attitude in client-centered therapy. In R. F. Levant and J. M. Shlien (Eds.), *Client-centered therapy and the person-centred approach: New directions in theory, research and practice*. NY: Praeger.

Linville, P. (1985). Self-complexity and affective extremity: Don't put all your eggs in the cognitive basket. *Social Cognition, 3*, 94–120.

Linville, P. (1987). Self-complexity as a cognitive buffer against stress related illness and depression. *Journal of Personality and Social Psychology, 52*, 663–76.

Mahalik, J. R. (1994). Development of the Client Resistance Scale. *Journal of Counseling Psychology, 41*, 58–68.

Mahoney, M. J. (1991). *Human change processes: The scientific foundation of psychotherapy.* New York: Basic Books.

Mahoney, M. J. (1995). *Constructive psychotherapy.* New York: Guilford.

Mallinckrodt, B., Gantt, D. L. and Coble, H. M. (1995). Attachment patterns in the psychotherapy relationship: Development of the Client Attachment to Therapist Scale. *Journal of Counseling Psychology, 42*, 307–17.

May, R. (1961). *Existential psychology.* NY: Random House.

Missirlian, T. (2002). *Depressed clients perceptual-processing emotion episodes: How does processing relate to outcome?* Unpublished master's thesis, York University, Toronto, Canada.

Mitchell, K. M., Bozarth, J. D. and Krauft, C. C. (1977). A reappraisal of the therapeutic effectiveness of accurate empathy, non-possessive warmth and genuineness. In A. S. Gurman and A. M. Razin (Eds.), *Effective psychotherapy: A handbook of research.* NY: Pergamon, pp. 482–502.

Neimeyer, R. A. and Mahoney, M. J. (1995). *Constructivism in psychotherapy.* Washington, DC: APA.

Neisser, U. (1967). *Cognitive psychology.* NY: Appleton-Century-Crofts.

Neisser, U. (1976). *Cognition and reality.* NY: Appleton-Century-Crofts.

Orlinsky, D. E. and Howard, K. I. (1986). Process and outcome in psychotherapy. In S. Garfield and A. Bergin (Eds.), *Handbook of psychotherapy and behavior change* (3rd ed.). NY: Wiley, pp. 311–81.

Patterson, C. H. (1984). Empathy, warmth and genuineness: A review of reviews. *Psychotherapy, 21*, 431–8.

Paulson, B. L., Everall, R. D. and Stuart, J. (2001). Client perceptions of hindering experiences in counselling. *Counselling and Psychotherapy Research, 1*, 53–61.

Perls, F. S. (1969). *Gestalt therapy verbatim.* Moab, UT: Real People Press.

Rennie, D. L. (1994a). Clients' deference in psychotherapy. *Journal of Counseling Psychology, 41*, 427–37.

Rennie, D. L. (1994b). Clients' accounts of resistance in counselling: A qualitative analysis. *Canadian Journal of Counselling, 28*, 43–57.

Rennie, D. L. (1990). Toward a representation of the client's experience of the therapy hour. In G. Lietaer, J. Rombauts and R. Van Balen (Eds.), *Client-centered and experiential psychotherapy in the nineties.* Leuven, Belgium: Leuven University Press, pp. 155–72.

Rennie, D. L. (1992). Qualitative analysis of the client's experience of psychotherapy: The unfolding of reflexivity. In S. Toukmanian and D. Rennie (Eds.), *Psychotherapy process research: Paradigmatic and narrative approaches.* Newbury Park, CA: Sage, pp. 211–33.

Rennie, D. L. (2002). Experiencing psychotherapy: Grounded theory studies. In D. J. Cain (Ed.), *Humanistic psychotherapies: Handbook of research and practice.* Washington, DC: APA, pp. 117–43.

Rogers, C. R. (1951). *Client-centered therapy.* Boston: Houghton Mifflin.

Rogers, C. R. (1957). The necessary and sufficient conditions of therapeutic personality change. *Journal of Consulting Psychology, 22*, 95–103.

Rogers, C. R. (1959). A theory of therapy, personality and interpersonal relationships as developed in the client-centered framework. In S. Koch (Ed.), *Psychology: The study of a science (Vol. III).* NY: McGraw Hill.

Rogers, C. R. (1961). *On Becoming a Person.* Boston: Houghton Mifflin.

Rogers, C. R. (1975). Empathic: An unappreciated way of being. *The Counseling Psychologist, 5*, 2–11.

Rumelhart, D. E. (1984). Schemata and the cognitive system. In S. R. Wyer and T. K. Srull (Eds.), *Handbook of social cognition* (Vol. 1). Hillsdale, NJ: Lawrence Erlbaum, pp. 161–8.

Sachse, R. (1993). The effects of intervention phrasing of therapist-client communication. *Psychotherapy Research, 3*, 260–77.

Sachse, R. and Elliott, R. (2002). Process-outcome research on humanistic therapy variables. In D. J. Cain (Ed.), *Humanistic psychotherapies: Handbook of research and practice*. Washington, DC: APA, pp. 83–115.

Satterfield, W. A. and Lyddon, W. J. (1995). Client attachment and perceptions of the working alliance with counselor trainees. *Journal of Counseling Psychology, 42*, 187–9.

Shiffrin, R. M. and Schneider, W. (1977). Controlled and automatic human information processing: II. Perceptual learning, automatic attending and a general theory. *Psychological Review, 84*, 127–50.

Sinclair, L. M. (1990). Metaphor and client perceptual-processing. *Dissertation Abstracts International, 51*, 4608B.

Stein, K. F. (1994). Complexity of the self-schema and responses to disconfirming feedback. *Cognitive Therapy and Research, 18*, 161–78.

Sue, D. W. and Sue, S. (1990). *Counseling the culturally different*. New York: Wiley.

Taguiri, R. and Petrullo, L. (1958). *Person perception and interpersonal behavior*. Stanford, CA: Stanford University Press.

Thompson, B. J. and Hill, C. (1991). Client perceptions of therapist competence. *Psychotherapy Research, 3*, 124–30.

Toukmanian, S. G. (1990). A schema-based information processing perspective on client change in experiential psychotherapy. In G. Lietaer, J. Rombauts, and R. Van Balen (Eds.), *Client-Centered and Experiential Psychotherapy Towards the Nineties*. Leuven, Belgium: Leuven University Press, pp. 304–26.

Toukmanian, S. G. (1992). Studying the client's perceptual processes and their outcomes in psychotherapy. In S. G. Toukmanian and D. L. Rennie (Eds.), *Psychotherapy process research: Paradigmatic and narrative approaches*. Newbury Park, CA: Sage, pp. 77–107.

Toukmanian, S. G. (1996). Clients' perceptual-processing: An integration of research and practice. In W. Dryden (Ed.), *Research in counselling and psychotherapy: Practical applications*. London: Sage, pp. 184–210.

Toukmanian, S. G. and Jackson, S. (1996). An analysis of clients' self-narratives in brief experiential psychotherapy. In R. Hutterer, G. Pawlowsky, P. Schmid, and P. Stipsit (Eds.), *Client-centered and experiential psychotherapy: A paradigm in motion*. New York: Peter Lang, pp. 113–27.

Tripodi, D. and Bieri, J. (1964). Information transmission in clinical judgments as a function of stimulus dimensionality and cognitive complexity. *Journal of Personality and Social Psychology, 32*, 119–37.

Weimer, W. B. (1977). A conceptual framework for cognitive psychology: Motor theories of the mind. In R. Shaw and J. Bransford (Eds.), *Perceiving, Acting and Knowing: Toward ecological psychology*. Hillsdale: Lawrence Earlbaum, pp. 267–311.

Wilkins, P. (2000). Unconditional positive regard reconsidered. *British Journal of Guidance and Counseling, 28*, 23–36.

Wyatt, G. (2001). Congruence: A synthesis and implications. In G. Wyatt (Ed.), *Rogers' therapeutic conditions: Evolution, theory and practice. Vol. 1: Congruence*. Ross-on-Wye: PCCS Books, pp. 229–37.

Zink, D. A. (1990). Change in anxiety in the context of perceptual-processing experiential therapy: Process and outcome research. Unpublished master's thesis. York University, Toronto, Ontario.

7   'You really understand what I'm talking about, don't you?'
Basic Requirements for Contact and Perception in Person-centred Therapy and the Implications for Clients with Learning Disabilities
Elisabeth Zinschitz

1. CONTACT AND PERCEPTION

When Rogers formulated the six conditions that are necessary for a relationship that can facilitate therapeutic change, he started and ended with two very basic elements of the human capacity for social interaction and being in the world. According to Rogers, a therapeutic relationship requires persons to be in contact and to perceive each other. So when we discuss *contact* and *perception* we are paying attention to the therapeutic relationship. In what follows I will discuss whether, in the case of clients with a learning disability, contact and perception, as formulated in the first and the sixth conditions, are essentially different from the case of other clients — and, if so, what these differences mean for the therapeutic relationship.

In his formulation of the first condition, Rogers (1957) speaks about contact between 'two persons'. In the sixth condition, however, he only refers to the client having to be aware of the conditions offered to him or her by the therapist. In the case of contact, therefore, we will look at both persons being involved in a similar activity. In the case of perception our focus will be on the client who is receiving, whilst the therapist, who is sending, provides empathy and unconditional positive regard. The fact that perception is a 'receiving-end activity' is relevant when we look at which specific capacities are needed.

In these reflections I draw from client-centred psychotherapeutic theory and philosophy. Though developmental perspectives are not really part of traditional person-centred thinking, I also refer to knowledge of human biological and psychological development. As will become clearer below, a learning disability has a huge impact on the personality development of a person.

In the case of clients with a learning disability, cognitive, and sensory, capacities may be impaired in very diverse ways. The chapter starts with an overview of how contact and perception are defined within the person-centred approach so as to understand what is necessary in order to establish and maintain contact and to perceive the attitude of the therapist. Similarly, I also refer to the development of sensory and cognitive capacities. I then look at the implications of a learning disability for the first and sixth conditions.

CONTACT AND PERCEPTION

1.1 Contact and perception in person-centred psychotherapy theory

A comprehensive review of how these two phenomena are viewed within person-centred literature is beyond the scope of this chapter, so I selected three authors whose reflections would be most relevant to the topic. Rogers' theoretical writings have been included; de Haas' work is examined because of his dynamic focus on the two-way nature of contact; and Prouty is considered because he offers a very detailed philosophy of contact, which in turn expands the possibilities of working with clients who appear to present only a basic level of 'contact-ability'.[1] For the sake of clarity I will pay attention to the different but overlapping ways these authors use the terms *perception*, *awareness* and *consciousness*.

1.1.1 Contact

Rogers (1959, p. 207) writes in definition 27, 'Two persons are in psychological contact, or have the minimum essential of a relationship, when each makes a perceived or subceived difference in the experiential field of the other'. Thus Rogers refers to contact being immediately linked to perception. Rogers further sees contact as a fundamental element, even a starting point of relationship. He notes (p. 207, ibid.), 'The present term has been chosen to signify more clearly that this is the least or minimum experience which could be called relationship'.

More on this subject can be found in de Haas (1991, pp. 370–1) who describes relationship as consisting of a contact dimension:

> Two persons are in contact with each other provided they open up towards each other. Contact implies a readiness to let yourself be influenced by the other. Contact is interrupted when one of the two closes up . . . By opening up for or closing towards each other, human beings regulate the intensity as well as the nature of their contact. Good contact . . . requires a subtle tuning in to the other person while opening up as well as while closing.

and an interaction dimension:

> We speak of interaction when two (or more) persons try to tune in to each other with regard to their verbal or non-verbal behaviour to such an extent that we can speak of mutual influence on the one hand or adaptation on the other. One person's action can lead the other to react who then in turn influences the first person.

As de Haas focuses on therapeutic interventions, he only refers to the therapist's effort to open up for the client in order to accept him or her. He does not focus on the client, nor does he explore how this opening up comes about. He gives us a little more insight into the implications of Rogers' first condition by describing contact as an activity — opening or closing up — and as a movement towards the other person.

The interaction dimension brings us to the sixth condition whilst also adding something. Rogers does not use the term 'interaction' in the formulation of the

---

[1]. For a more detailed account of Prouty's work see this volume chapters 3a, b and c..

sixth condition. He looks only at *one direction* (from the therapist to the client), whilst de Haas emphasises the dynamic character — his interaction dimension being a *movement back and forth* between two persons as long as the contact lasts.[2] When the client perceives the therapist's attitude towards him or her, i.e. is open for empathy and unconditional positive regard (contact dimension), he or she can let him- or herself be influenced by them (interaction dimension). Perception, even though not explicitly included in these reflections, still is implicit. The therapist's way of interacting is characterised by their effort to be empathic and accepting. The client is influenced by this as soon as he or she perceives this, and the quality of this influence is defined by the meaning the client gives to what he or she perceives.

De Haas further states that contact needs interaction, as contact without interaction in the long run is interrupted as the participating persons may experience the situation as oppressive. For example when there is a long silence, at some point one will start to do or say something, or the contact will be lost. On the other hand, interaction is not possible without contact because the continuous movement of action and reaction is interrupted when contact fails. This explains the primacy of psychological contact as well as the relevance of the sixth condition for the psychotherapeutic relationship: contact generates relationship and the interaction defines its quality.

Prouty suggests that existential contact[3] starts with simple observation and intentional consciousness. He refers to Merleau-Ponty (1962) who differentiates three levels as the structure of the phenomenal field of lived experience: '. . . ordinary, everyday, natural consciousness can be understood as coming from, moving towards and connected with World, Self and Other' (Prouty et al., 1998, p. 30). Thus, according to this view, we move towards and connect with awareness of objects around us, conditions of environment, consciousness of self, and consciousness of being intentionally focused on others.[4]

1.1.2 Perception

From the above we can conclude that contact and perception cannot be disconnected. As soon as there is some contact there is perception (or subception or, as Prouty calls it, consciousness).

Rogers (1959, p. 199) defines perception as 'that which comes into consciousness when stimuli impinge on the organism', adding that it is synonymous with awareness. In definition six, Rogers describes *awareness* 'as the symbolic representation of some portion of our experience. This representation may have varying degrees of sharpness or vividness, from a dim awareness of something existing as ground, to a sharp awareness of something which is in focus as figure' (ibid, p. 198).

---

2. It is to be expected that in any therapeutic relationship not only the client will undergo a change, but also the therapist will not be the same person when the relationship draws to a close.
3. 'Existential contact is the natural, alternating movement of immediate pre-reflective consciousness toward the natural presence of the world, self or other' (Prouty, 1994, p. 34).
4. For a philosophical view of contact and being in the world with others, see Rogers, C.R. and Schmid, P.F. (1991).

Further, Rogers states that perception is
> a hypothesis or prognosis for action which comes into being in awareness when stimuli impinge on the organism. When we perceive 'this is a triangle', 'that is a tree', 'this person is my mother' it means that we are making a prediction that the objects from which the stimuli are received would, if checked in other ways, exhibit properties we have come to regard, from our past experience, as being characteristic of triangles, trees, mother (p. 199).

Perception, as the narrower term, refers to 'the importance of the stimulus in the process', whereas 'awareness [is] the broader term, covering symbolisations and meanings' (ibid., 1959, p. 199). So, perception takes place on a more basic level involving mainly our senses, whereas awareness is closely connected to meaning and therefore requires higher cognitive capacities. This will turn out to be relevant later in this chapter when clients with lower cognitive capacities will be looked at.

1.1.3 Perception, awareness, consciousness

The use of the terms *consciousness, perception* and *awareness* may cause some confusion, as they seem to refer to the same phenomenon. For the sake of clarity, it seems appropriate to pay some attention to this and to see what this implies for the contact definition.

In definition six, Rogers refers to consciousness as being synonymous with awareness (1959, p. 198). The slight difference lies only in consciousness being considered as the *act* of symbolisation, whereas awareness is the *result* of symbolisation. When we look at Prouty's understanding of consciousness[5] it becomes obvious that he speaks of something more basic. He refers to *pre-reflective consciousness* which is described as 'the immediately sensed perception of lived experience, or *Erleben,* in German' (1994, p. 33). Reflective consciousness would require the activity of higher nerve centres to enable us to reflect about ourselves and our life history. According to Husserl, upon whom Prouty draws, both are intentional: 'All consciousness "intends" an "object"' (ibid., p. 34).

Looking at how these terms are used in the various contact definitions, it is possible to summarise that Rogers' psychological contact includes reflective consciousness, while Prouty's existential contact is much more basic and refers to concrete phenomenology. It is true that when Rogers elaborates on the first condition, he does include clients with a subliminal perception of the presence of the therapist and the difference that makes for him or her. But in discussing the sixth condition he does not even consider clients who have a lower level of perception or awareness (Rogers, 1957). This would mean that, if *existential contact* were included in the first condition, not only clients who are able to reflect about themselves would profit from empathy and unconditional positive regard, but also those who are in a pre-reflective state of mind.[6]

At this point it is suggested that there might be a connection between Prouty's

---

5. Prouty also says that 'consciousness naturally and alternately moves toward existence' (1994, p. 34) which seems to imply that it is a function of the actualising tendency.
6. That is where lies the importance and the potential of Prouty's Pre-Therapy. See Prouty (1994)

pre-reflective consciousness and Rogers' *subception*. Rogers defines *subception* as a

> construct to signify discrimination without awareness ... it appears that the organism can discriminate a stimulus and its meaning for the organism without utilising the higher nerve centres involved in awareness. It is this capacity which, in our theory, permits the individual to discriminate an experience as threatening, without symbolisation in awareness of this threat (1959, p. 200).

If we continue by asking which capacities and skills are required for the above defined phenomena, it seems that there is a hierarchy with regard to the required capacities for subception, perception and awareness. We will look into this more closely in the following section.

1.2 Contact and perception seen from within the developmental framework

Perception and contact as general human capacities can both be defined on a physical as well as on a psychological level. As we will see in the following, in our development, the physical level serves as a basis for psychological contact and for the perception of psychological elements within that contact. In order to organise and process our contact experiences we need cognitive abilities, which enable us to understand social interactions.

1.2.1 Physical contact

In order to be able to perceive ourselves as being in contact, we are dependent on our senses. Also as we have seen, Rogers includes sensory functioning in his definition of perception: 'Perception is that which comes into consciousness when stimuli, principally light or sound, impinge on the organism from the outside' (Kelly in Rogers, 1959, p. 199). Perception takes place through our senses. Contact on all sensory levels helps us to gradually experience the boundaries that divide us from other people and objects as well as the world around us, and therefore to develop an *awareness of self, others and world* (see above: Merleau-Ponty).

The growth of the organs necessary for perception is completed between the eighth and the twelfth week of gestation (Oerter and Montada, 1987, p. 132). As a result, synapses and axons developed between sensory cells and the brain enable the foetus to take in and transfer information. The first contact we ever have in life is experienced through the ears and the tongue, and to a lesser degree also through eyes and skin. Experiments have shown that while still in the uterus, the foetus can already distinguish sounds like the mother's heart beating and different flavours in the amniotic fluid. Contact with environment through smell and sight increases after birth,[7] during the first days and weeks (Oerter and Montada, 1987, p. 147).

The taking in of stimuli through our senses can be likened to de Haas' *opening up*. Throughout development, the infant unfolds and opens up for more and

---

7. The best distance for a newborn child's visual acuity is at 19–25 cm (see Oerter and Montada, 1987, p. 147).

more increasingly complex stimuli. The contact with others in that first phase, for example, takes place in the form of touch or skin contact. In the course of development, this conveys an awareness of a boundary, of a difference between me and something or someone else. It means 'I know where I begin and end and where you begin and end'. The same is achieved through eye contact by looking at each other, through the ears by hearing the sounds the significant other makes, and so on. Motor development contributes to the child's capacity to become more receptive to outside world stimuli and it enhances the infant's range of exploration. Initially, the possibility of moving the head in one direction or another offers a wider range of visual experiences. Then the motor development of the hand enables the child to grasp, thus enhancing a cognitive 'grasping' ability.

These many stimuli improve the development of new contacts in the neuronal networks. This leads, in turn, to an enhancement of perceptive and cognitive capacities and simultaneously to a change of contact behaviour.

A prerequisite for this development is that the organs of perception are present and functioning well, and the motor capacities are available and coherent. Furthermore, there has to be a 'neurological consciousness' which means that the brain has to be open to stimuli. Finally, adequate cognitive processing of the received stimuli has to take place.

All this implies that contact and perception are also closely linked phenomena on the developmental level, as well as in therapy theory (see above). Put simply, there is no perception if there is no contact (i.e. stimulation of our sensory nerves) and there is no contact when it is not perceived by *both* persons involved. I can touch the other person with my hand, but if he or she does not feel it, it will make no difference for him or her (see Rogers' definition 27, 1959, p. 207). In order for it to have a meaning, and therefore to have an effect on that person — as the sixth condition implies — it is necessary that he or she sees or hears that I am touching him or her. They must perceive it, add a meaning to it and in so doing be influenced or affected by it. Perception and cognition give meaning to the experienced contact, which then leads us to the level of psychological contact.

1.2.2 Psychological contact

With the unfolding of their capacities, infants move from an undifferentiated way of being in the world towards a more active way of relating to the world.

When we look at which abilities are required in order to be able to be in contact, we also see on a psychological level, at different stages of life, that different capacities are developed which define the infant's way of relating, i.e. of taking up contact with self, others and the world. Binder points out the importance of social contact for the development of the infant's perception of these three elements: 'The relational activities of the infant are crucial for the development of the self . . . , of self-awareness and awareness of others.' (Binder and Binder, 2001, p. 165).

It is remarkable to see how quickly a large potential for social interaction develops at a very early stage in life. The newborn child shows a clear preference for stimuli which are closely connected with social interaction. Eyes focus on the mothers' eyes and follow moving objects. Movements follow the sound of human speech in synchrony. Heads turn towards the source of the acoustic or olfactory stimulus. Infants calm down when they are picked up and rocked, etc. They turn away their heads or stiffen up their bodies to signal that the contact is interrupted — they close up (see de Haas above).

All this shows that an infant at his or her birth is not only equipped for the intake of food, but also for social interaction. It confirms the fact that contact is one of the existential human needs (Oerter and Montada, 1987, pp. 150–1). Originally, in classical psychoanalytic development theories, infants were seen as living in a 'normal autistic' state. They were therefore presumed to go through a longer period of an undifferentiated state of being in which social contact is only present to the extent that others take care of their needs. Infant observation has generated new ways of understanding the baby's relatedness at a very early stage of life. Relatedness is seen as existing for its own sake and is not based on physiological states of neediness (Stern, 1992, p. 70).

An infant's way of being in contact and of perceiving is dependent on the different stages of his or her development. Stern (1992)[8] observed children from the perspective of social activity and experiencing and seems to follow a phenomenological approach, distinguishing an *emerging self*, a *core self*, a *subjective self* and a *verbal self*.

1.2.2.1 Contact and perception in the phase of the emerging self
According to Stern, the phase of the *emerging self* starts at birth, before qualitative changes in the child's way of being in the world, such as direct eye contact and smiling, become visible. In the first two months of life the infant lives in a kind of pre-social, pre-cognitive phase which lacks organisation. Infants actively work their way to this emerging self by taking in stimuli while they are in a state of so-called 'alert inactivity'. They are focused on obtaining sensory stimulation. They have clear preferences and dislikes, which implies that they are able to distinguish differences. They are busy exploring boundaries in order to get an organismic concept about the make-up of their self and of others. They repeat experiences as often as necessary, so they seem to create hypotheses about what happens in the world and check these before they integrate or reject them. Cognitive processes are immersed in affective processes: the child *is* his or her affects, and does not *have* them yet.

Stern suggests that infants start out in a state of undifferentiated experiencing, but with innate capacities for learning (i.e. organisation) which facilitate their development. This learning takes place through contact with, and perception of, sensory stimuli. That is, learning has its starting point in relatedness. Infants' innate capacity to distinguish between stimuli in the long run enables them to transfer their experience from one object to another, that is, to abstract. For example, the child can eventually 'understand' a smile whether it is given by his or her mother or by another person.

This 'understanding' does not take place on a cognitive level but rather as the experiencing of a body tension. The child has the same physical reaction to each

---

8. All page numbers for Stern refer to the German translation. In the original book this part can be found under the section on The Development of Self-Awareness. The rest of this section is a summary of what can be read in the book.

smile. There is no separate awareness of cognitive activities and affective processes.

In this phase *contact* and *perception* are experienced as one and as taking place on a physical level.

1.2.2.2 Contact and perception in the phase of the core self

Between the second and the sixth month, children start to perceive themselves as physically whole and separate from their parents. They develop a sense of experiencing affects as well as of a continuous self (memory). They are able to separate between their own actions and those of others and to expect consequences as a result of their behaviour.

They become aware that there is a *core self* and a *core other* and discover that self and other have feelings, motives and intentions, which lie behind the physical events. Integration of the different sorts of self-awareness takes place — of the self that acts, the self that feels and the self that perceives his or her body and what it does. All this leads to infants relating on a more personal level.

Children experience the other in their interactions as someone who regulates their self-experiencing by evoking inner reactions (see de Haas' interaction dimension). This is about experiences the child could never induce on his or her own. According to Stern (p. 150), at this age, a large part of the entire affective spectrum which the infant is able to perceive can only be experienced in the interactive presence of the other person (p. 150). The social behaviour of this other who regulates the infant's self obviously influences the child's experiences.

In their *contact behaviour* the children become more active and purposeful. Their *perception* of others is characterised by the awareness of separateness. This means the performance of both functions is gradually moving from the physical level to the psychological level. Cognition and affects seem to become separate processes.

1.2.2.3 Contact and perception in the phase of the subjective self

The period between the seventh and the ninth month is one of great discoveries: the child becomes aware of a *subjective self* and a *subjective other* and that feelings can be shared with that other and by others. Intersubjectivity — fundamental for the development of empathy — becomes possible. Communication starts to play a more important role. The core self, which is characterised by an awareness of separateness, remains as a necessary prerequisite for sharing subjective experiencing while at the same time the child's self-awareness expands and their relatedness becomes intersubjective. The infant becomes capable of intimacy and starts to become aware of the empathy offered by the significant other. Repeated attunements lead to the development of a sense that others can share the infant's feelings. It can be deeply upsetting when the parents are misattuned to their child (Goleman, 1995, p. 101).

All this development is beautifully illustrated by the fact that the child looks at the object the significant other points at instead of at his or her pointing finger. The child is aware of the fact that the finger belongs to the other person, secondly that it points to an object they can both look at, thus sharing a joint attention, and thirdly that the other person or the object is evoking a reaction in the child.

At this stage of the development of the self the child initiates *contact* in order to share an experience and *perceives* the other person as a separate sharing being who evokes and regulates reactions in the infant. There is a clear separation between cognition and affect.

1.2.2.4 Contact and perception in the phase of the verbal self
By the age of about fifteen months the development of language makes symbolisation possible. An enrichment of the awareness of self and other takes place as self and other now have a means of developing common meanings. At this point where the *verbal self* comes to the fore, children learn to act in a symbolic way (in play) and to reflect about and refer to themselves as objective entities as well as to communicate about objects or persons who are not present.

It is important to see that the three initial selves (emerging, core and subjective self) remain present throughout life, but they are reduced to a subordinate position through the development of the *verbal self*. Language is only partially able to include the experiencing which takes place on the other three levels.

Contact at this level of development is initiated through language. *Perception* focuses on the meaning of language.

1.3 Required minimum capacities for contact and perception

I have described how contact and perception are understood within person-centred therapeutic thinking and how the potential for their functioning develops throughout the first two years of life. By combining these perspectives it becomes possible to examine at which developmental level the client can meet the conditions for therapeutic change and from there conclude which capacities are required to do so.

As previously noted, the definitions of contact contain four elements: (1) 'opening up toward' (de Haas), (2) 'making a subceived or perceived difference to each other's experiential field' (Rogers) and (3) 'a natural, alternating movement of immediate pre-reflective consciousness toward the natural presence of the world, self or other' (Prouty). When contact is established the interaction is carried by the empathy and the acceptance the therapist offers and as such influences the client (4).

1. It is not by coincidence that I put *opening up* in the first position. It seems that for this to be possible the most basic capacities are sufficient. Well-functioning sensory organs are the windows to the mind through which stimuli can enter like sun rays promoting development and growth. Clearly the nature of contact changes with every stage as the cognitive and social capacities of the infant are enhanced, but the basic functions are available in the phase of the *emerging self*.
2. Rogers' formulations require a more differentiated exploration, as he distinguishes two levels of perception and includes awareness. If the *difference* the other person *makes* in one's experiential field is *subceived*, this discrimination takes place without awareness, so without symbolisation and meaning. It seems that this capacity for subception starts with the *emerging self* where the infant is already able to distinguish differences. *Perception*

implies a consciousness of stimuli impinging on the organism. This consciousness comes to a full expression in the phase of the *core self* where clear boundaries between self and other become conscious. Rogers further writes that perception includes the capacity to make a prediction about the properties of the perceived objects and that, for this, we draw from past experience. Therefore we need a memory about the result of our repeated experiences. This also points to the stage of the *core self* where the self starts to be experienced as something continuous and so, in turn, memory develops. Referring to the hierarchy mentioned in section 1.1.3, *awareness* involves higher functioning levels which facilitate the development of meaning and symbolisation. The required capacities emerge in the phase of the *subjective self* in which the infant becomes aware of what the significant others offer (as for example empathy) and find their full expression in the phase of the *verbal self* in which the development of common meanings as well as symbolisation become possible.

3. In his definition of existential contact, Prouty includes *pre-reflective consciousness* which is characterised by a *movement toward*, i.e. *intentionality*, and *observation*. I would place this in the phase of the *core self* for the following reasons. Observation requires sensory functioning, but is also a purposeful activity. Intentionality is an orientation towards other and world, and therefore requires awareness of separateness. Both functions — purposeful action and awareness of separateness — are available from the second month on. In comparison, a *reflective* consciousness includes the capacity to think about oneself and one's history. It therefore includes symbolisation and meaning and can be positioned in the phase of the *verbal self*.

4. De Haas stresses the interconnection of contact and *interaction,* the latter of which implies that the two participants *influence* each other. The sixth condition states that the client has to perceive the offering of empathy and unconditional positive regard in order for personality change to become possible, so he or she has to be open to the therapist's influence. Subception or perception of this influence, i.e. the effect of empathy and acceptance offered by significant others, already becomes possible at the stage of the *emerging self* and the *core self* when the experience of separateness develops. The description of the development of experience, sharing (see 1.2.2.3), however, suggests that the stage of the *subjective self* needs to be reached in order to be aware — in the sense of Rogers' definition of awareness — of the received empathy and acceptance, because that is when there is awareness that the other functions and experiences separately. The ability to reflect on the implications of such a relationship for the client, the verbal self, seems necessary.

Table 1: Required functions for contact and availability

First condition elements	Maximal functions required	Available at stage of
Opening up	Sensory organs Receptivity for sensory stimuli (on the level of the organs and the brain)	*emerging self*
Subceive *the difference the other person makes in one's experiential field*	Distinction of differences of stimuli	*emerging self*
Perceive *the difference the other person makes in one's experiential field*	Distinction of separateness	*core self*
Being aware of *the difference the other person makes in one's experiential field*	Awareness of sharing with significant other Development of symbolisation and meaning	*subjective self*
Pre-reflective consciousness	Observation + intentionality: purposeful action and awareness of separateness	*core self*

Table 2: Required functions for perception and availability

Sixth condition elements	Maximal functions required	Available at stage of
Perception	Distinction of separateness	*core self*
Interaction	Experience of acceptance and empathy Awareness that the other person evokes something in me	*emerging self* and *core self* *subjective self*

1.4 The importance of significant others for contact and perception

The continuous development of our capacities for contact and perception is not guaranteed simply because the appropriate organs are present, in working order and used. More than just that is needed. Even if some of the required capacities in this learning process are innate, an external source is still necessary to provide the stimuli, thus enabling us to become acquainted with these innate capacities and to develop them further. In order to integrate our learning experiences we need to be able to repeat these until they are finally integrated. This means we need other human beings as well as objects and situations in order to 'train' our contact and perception capacities.

In the first years of life, significant others provide this opportunity. They will react to our way of being and reinforce it by their way of reacting. In this they have a quantitative as well as a qualitative influence. Gabbard, offering 'a neurobiologically informed perspective on psychotherapy', reports that research findings suggest that whatever is genetically defined not only responds to the nature of the stimuli offered by the environment, but also influences them: 'The individual's genetic endowment influences the parenting he or she receives and this development input from parents and other figures in the environment may, in turn, influence the further read-out of the genome' (2000, p. 118). This means that the parents' social behaviour toward the child is impacted by the child's 'way of being' and their expectations and understanding of that; and this again shapes this 'way of being'. 'Gene-environment interactions become a reverberating "hall of mirrors" that cannot easily be dissected' (ibid.).

In the following section we will take a closer look at the situation of and the implications for clients with a learning disability. Their disability will have influenced the parenting behaviour of the significant others in their environment. So their contact behaviour and level of perception is the result of their capacity to take in and to process stimuli as well as of the experiences made with their environment until that point in their lives.

As psychotherapists we will try to establish contact in ways that correspond with the result of this development process: the 'contact-ability' and the perception capacity of the client. Understanding the implications of the disability and of the social experiences of a client with a learning impairment, will improve our competence in establishing a therapeutic relationship, which contains a potential for personality change and for healing in a broad sense of the word.

2. CONTACT AND PERCEPTION WITH CLIENTS WITH A LEARNING DISABILITY

2.1. How to define learning disability

Definitions of disability have been formulated from different perspectives. For example, the definitions for learning (or intellectual) disabilities found in ICD10 (of the WHO) and DSM-IV (APA) include three criteria: (1) a certain level of intellectual competence, measured in IQ; (2) adaptive behaviour skills; (3) the age (before 18) at which these first two criteria were displayed (Weber, 1997, pp. 19–21). The American Association on Mental Retardation focuses on an interaction between personal skills on the intellectual and social level, mental and emotional factors, biological impairment, environment and available support measures (Weber, 1997, p. 21). Special education looks at the extent to which education measures aiming at autonomy become difficult because of the disability (Schmutzler, 1994, p. 19) and sociology emphasises the aspect of 'being different' according to the criteria valid in society (Cloerkes, 1997). And finally, systemic theory defines disability as an 'information . . . which breaks into the life of the disabled person and his or her family as well as society in a very tragic way' (Sorrentino, 1988, p. 19).[9] Sorrentino stresses that here diagnoses merely have a descriptive value which is relative to the one who receives the information.

The WHO differentiates between (1) an impairment pointing to a problem on an organic level, (2) a disability which describes a problem on the personal level and (3) a handicap which is seen as a disadvantage which limits or hampers the person in taking over roles on a social level (Cloerkes, 1997, pp. 4–6). So according to this definition the clients discussed in this paper may have an organic impairment (genetic or congenital) and therefore be disabled in their learning capacity, which leads to handicaps in life areas like school, work, relationships, etc.

Consequently, for the perspective of psychotherapeutic relationships the term 'disability' would be adequate, since the client (because of his impairment) is likely to have problems in his or her capacities to establish contact and to perceive what is happening within that contact. At the same time, disability is not to be seen as a 'fait accompli', depending only on the organic impairment but, rather, can to a large degree, be improved or worsened depending on the efforts of the other person — as we have seen above in section 1.4. So, the 'contact-dis-ability' is to be seen as an aspect which is connected with the learning disability and which is likely to be the result of an organic impairment and the quality of the interactions the disabled person has experienced throughout life with environmental stimuli and with significant others.

2.2 Disabled contact and perception

The psychological development of persons with a learning disability which defines their 'contact-ability' and perception capacities, is determined by two levels: a physical cognitive and a socio-emotional one. For the physical level, the degree and nature of the cognitive impairment on the one hand and the (genetic) disposition of the person on the other are both relevant. For the socio-emotional level the experiences the person gained in social interactions with significant others throughout his or her life are essential.

2.2.1 The person involved: receptivity and processing capacity

A client with a sensory impairment has a reduced capacity for taking in visual or acoustic stimuli. This, in turn, can lead to a cognitive disability. A cognitive impairment, however, reduces or alters the processing of stimuli. The origin of a cognitive impairment can be found on the level of (a) neuro-anatomy (structural changes of the brain, for example due to haemorrhage or morphological changes of parts of the brain), (b) neuro-physiology (impaired functioning of the brain, for example by a disturbed co-operation within neuronal networks) or (c) neuro-biology (genetic disorders, or neuro-chemical problems which impair the transmission of stimuli).

This can result in disabilities in various forms: stimuli are not received and processed by the brain; there are difficulties in distinguishing differences between stimuli and in organising them; the person has a reduced capacity of abstraction

---
9. Translated from German by the author.

and of cognitive creativity. Also speech can be impaired.

Provided a client with a learning disability does not also have a sensory impairment, the degree of his or her cognitive impairment will be relevant to determine the extent to which they possess the required capacities in order to fulfil the first and sixth condition (see Tables 1 and 2). Before we can take a closer look at this, the impact of the 'other side', i.e. the sender, needs to be examined.

2.2.2 The significant other: interaction quality

The fact that an infant has an organic impairment, and therefore a disability, influences the other people around them and their way of interacting with him or her. At the extremes of a continuum, the attitudes of others can oscillate between overprotection and neglect. An overprotective attitude can be understood as an effort to overcome the insecurity which parents,[10] or other caretakers, are confronted with. Neglect can be a reaction to the flood of demands that comes over them due to the disability.

> It is not always possible to fall back on experiences they have gained until that moment through interactions with other children. There is insecurity about what role they have.
>
> ... The child's incomprehensible way of expressing him- or herself increases this insecurity. Children with a disability react differently from what they expect ... The parents do not understand their own children and do not receive any feedback about whether their own behaviour is adequate or is rejected (Finger, 1992, p. 79).[11]

The adequate fulfilment of the human need for safety and belonging (need for integration) on the one hand and for going out and exploring (the need for differentiation)[12] on the other — needs which are immanent in the actualising tendency and promote the development of the self stages (see 1.2.2) — requires the balancing skills of a tightrope walker, and even more so when the infant's way of being is so very different. The contact functions of the child aim at fulfilling these two needs in order to foster development[13]: 'Contact functions ... reflect the fundamental polarity between the basic human needs for belonging and independence' (Stumm and Pritz, 2000, p. 365). A good result can be achieved when the environment provides a safe framework — responding to the need for integration — within which the child then can have some *space* to experiment and explore.[14] In this way he or she can try things out within a safe and clearly defined environment and thus become aware of his or her capacities and boundaries.

Overprotective parents do not give enough space for the disabled child to experiment and gain control. We could say the child has a 'disabled self-determination'. The child's, and later the adult's, life is determined by others, and

---

10. For further reading see Zinschitz, 2001a, pp. 200–2 and Zinschitz, 2001b, pp. 311–14.
11. Translated from German by the author.
12. See Kegan, 1982, p. 107; and also Zinschitz, 2001a, pp. 199–200.
13. The equivalent psychological functions of the infant are the capacity for awareness of separateness and of sharing (see self stages, 1.2.2).
14. See Pörtner, 1996, p. 27 (page refers to the German version); and also Zinschitz, 2002.

he or she grows up with a self-concept which does not include competence and self-responsibility. Neglecting parents do give space, but no safe framework, or at least not enough of it. This results in the child being flooded by impulses and impressions which it cannot process, and therefore the experience is one of being overwhelmed by anxiety. The further result is induced helplessness and (auto-) aggression: a client with a very severe physical disability and a moderate mental impairment displaying strong auto-aggressive behaviour reported how he was physically taken care of by his parents in every possible way, but when those tasks were done, they put him in front of the television and that was all. He was severely deprived of social experiences and had no strong emotional attachment to his parents nor his siblings.

The lack of stimuli experienced in the case of parental overprotective behaviour, as well as the flooding of stimuli and the incapacity to organise them adequately, lead to difficulties in the above defined contact and perception functions (see Tables 1 and 2).

3. IMPLICATIONS FOR PSYCHOTHERAPY

3.1 Frequently occurring phenomena

There is widespread agreement in person-centred literature about the nature of the problems typically experienced by persons with a learning disability. My own experiences are in accord with these descriptions.

Luchterhand and Murphy (1998) list some features which many adults with a learning disability display. These are:
- difficulties in learning or understanding (cognitive difficulties),
- a decreased or altered expression of emotions (see also Zinschitz, 2001b, p. 304),
- a tendency to respond in a positive manner,
- their behaviour (rather than their words) is indicative of their true feelings,
- they have a sense of connection to others that is not obvious (see p. 16).

Describing her psychotherapeutic work with this group of clients, Badelt (1990) reports that they are often not able to draw conclusions and develop solution strategies, and do not have much power to influence their environment and to change their life circumstances. Their speech may be impaired, and they lack autonomy.

Psychotherapists who intend to work with these clients need to be prepared for the following problems: a low level of self-initiated communication (Weber, 1997, p. 109), i.e. contact behaviour of these clients is rather passive; a slow rhythm and endless repetition of contents which seem to have no meaning (Pörtner, 1990, pp. 662–7); a lack of immediate response to what the therapist says (Pörtner, 1990, p. 663; Zinschitz, 2001b, p. 306); a strong need of physical contact (Pörtner, 1990, p. 663); decreased capacity of speech (Zinschitz, 1998, p. 215; Zinschitz, 2001b, p. 305); a difficulty in abstracting concepts from their behaviour and to discover patterns (Zinschitz, 1998, p. 215); a tendency to manipulate others due to a decreased sense of their ability to influence the environment (Zinschitz, 2001b, p. 293); a lack of frustration tolerance (Zinschitz, 2001a, p. 202); a frequently painful awareness of their disability (Pörtner, 1996, p. 91).

3.1.1 'Contact-ability'

A possible expectation about the work with these clients is that with a certain degree of learning disability, there might be no contact at all. This is certainly not the case. Experience (but also the definitions by Rogers, de Haas and Prouty) suggests that there is always some level of contact, it is merely the quality of this contact that is different. Summarising some of the characteristic features described in the previous paragraph, the quality of the contact can be *passive, slow, repetitive, physical, non-verbal or at a simple verbal level, concrete.*

This quality of the contact behaviour of a person with a learning disability who comes to therapy, will be defined by the level of self-development that each particular client has reached. With clients who seem to be functioning on the level of the emerging self, or the core self, psychotherapy in the usual sense of the word will hardly be possible. The client often does not speak, but will utter sounds. He or she can hold eye contact and may react to the words the other person expresses. At this stage there is hardly any awareness of separateness nor of sharing; a minimum degree of opening up is possible; interaction can take place on the level of pre-reflective consciousness (see Tables 1 and 2). Pre-therapy, a method developed by Prouty to establish psychological contact,[15] seems to be indicated, since for these clients the concrete pre-therapeutic reflections — which are similar to early empathic reflections in childhood (Zinschitz, 2001c, p. 47) — are helpful. This kind of contact can improve the client's life quality and sometimes also strengthen some self-awareness. In the best case it even can help the client to develop to the next stage, the one of the subjective self.

The stages of the subjective self and the verbal self provide more differentiated contact possibilities. The client will give clear signals of being in contact and aware of the presence of the other person. He or she will up to a certain degree initiate some interaction, and react to what the therapist offers. Even if the client's speech is impaired, he or she may *function* on the level of the verbal self, as long as he or she has developed an understanding of language. His or her contact behaviour does not necessarily take place by means of words — body language will also be put into action.

To illustrate this I would like to introduce two clients of mine, Christa and Marina.[16]

Christa (23) started out by having pre-therapy sessions with her assistant since she hardly ever reacted to any interaction effort by others. She would sit with her head hanging down, mumbling to herself and rocking her upper body. In her development she seemed to be at the level of the emerging self. After ten sessions a clear change had occurred: she started looking her assistant straight in the eye, took initiatives for role playing and expressed her satisfaction about the sessions. The subjective self stage had been reached and also, to a certain degree, the verbal

---

15. See Prouty, 1994. (Chapters 4, 5 and 6 reproduced in this volume as chapters 3a, b, and c.)
16. The names were changed for reasons of discretion.

self, as she symbolised her content about the role playing. She then came to therapy sessions with me in which she initiated a lot of role playing giving me very clear directions. So she was aware of my presence and also of me being a separate human being whom she could make do something. She did not address me directly by my name, nor did she always look at me or give clear signs of hearing me. She seemed to give her directions to whomever was there or even to the wall. Yet, whenever I diverged from her instructions, she would correct me very firmly. As the process went along she started to address me directly, even taking and guiding my hand at times. In summary, her way of being in contact was not completely open and direct, but there was some access and a possibility for interaction. In this interaction she was certainly not passive nor slow, but definitely repetitive, concrete, functioning at a very simple verbal level, and clearly responding to me.

Marina (26) at first was very shy and almost shaking when she came to see me. But after a period of building up trust she became more and more open and was very well able to express her worries and concerns. Her eye contact was almost constant, she clearly always heard me and responded to what I said, addressing me directly and on a rather differentiated verbal level. At times when she was insecure she would wait for me to begin. Her interactions were not more repetitive than sometimes is the case with other clients. She would remain focused on me and on what we were talking about. The process could be called slow, but it certainly was thorough.

3.1.2 Perception of empathy and acceptance

As was pointed out in 1.2.2.3, awareness of empathy, and presumably also of acceptance, offered by the significant other becomes possible in the stage of the subjective self (Stern, 1985, p. 181; see table 2) when awareness of separateness and sharing is developed. On the level of the verbal self, he or she will also be able to talk and reflect about what he or she perceives (see 1.2.2.4).

Research has shown that the expression of emotions and attitudes as well as ability to interpret facial expressions is partly innate to human beings and partly the result of ubiquitous social and cultural factors. 'From clinical neuro-psychological research we know that cerebral dysfunctions impede the correct interpretation of emotionally relevant stimuli' (Weber, 1997, P. 132). Findings imply that damage in certain parts of the brain (impairment) may lead to difficulties in understanding another person's emotions and attitudes like empathy and acceptance (disability). An overall view of research done with learning disabled children and adults (Weber, 1997, p. 130), in the context of decoding emotions from facial expressions as well as from spoken statements, indicates that persons with a medium learning disability have (slightly) more trouble in decoding the visual or acoustic expression of emotions and attitudes than non-disabled individuals. Persons with a severe disability were not able to decode them at all.

Judging by the progress she made, Christa, who has a severe learning disability, must at some level have been reached by the empathy and acceptance which her assistant conveyed to her by means of pre-therapy reflections. She does not seem to confirm the research findings. Her assistant, and later I as her therapist, clearly made a subceived, and sometimes even perceived, difference to her experiential field. She became more and more aware of our presence (as separate beings) and of what we were saying. Her verbal reactions seldom gave clear evidence about that, but her facial expression showed a certain tension while she was waiting for a reaction to what she said. And she usually corrected us if we said or did something which was not what she had intended or expected. Also her progress led us to assume that our attitude had an effect on her. It seemed as if she gradually moved out of her egocentric world and was touched by the presence of the other person. She changed in her social behaviour, her stereotypical movements decreased considerably, as did her frequent masturbation in public.

Marina, in her relationship with me and later with her environment, became more and more confident. Her main problem was her anxiety about whether she was a good girl and about other people's anger at her. In the therapy session she was in contact with me like any other client, although on a much more concrete level. Her immediate responses to my remarks, but also the fact that her shyness gradually disappeared, indicates that she felt accepted and understood. Certain changes in her showed that she let herself be influenced by my way of interacting with her, i.e. by my offering empathy and unconditional positive regard (see 1.1.1., de Haas). She gradually showed who she really was, with all her anxieties, her fantasies and her playfulness. She started to initiate sessions with issues that bothered her and stopped being so tensely polite. Even though I clearly was an important person to her whom she could consult and learn from, at the same time she treated me like an equal whom she really trusted. My impression was that she had really understood how she could profit from the interaction I offered to her and she 'used' it in an almost pragmatic way. Her ability to reflect about herself, as well as to speak about her feelings, increased. She was also able to symbolise very adequately that she felt I was empathic with her: in one of the early sessions, when she started to grasp what I was doing and what psychotherapy could mean to her, she said to me, 'You really understand me, don't you?' It sounded as if she had just discovered something wonderful which she had never experienced before.

3. 2 The therapist's work approach

In order to support the client to be open for contact and in letting him- or herself be influenced by the offered empathy and acceptance, the therapist being in the role of the significant other has to adapt his or her way of interacting to the stage of development of the client.

Clients with a learning disability need more guidance. The therapist will have offered empathy by understanding the client's need for clear structures and by taking contact initiatives because the client might otherwise feel at a loss (see Pörtner's *framework* and *space* in section 2.2.2). This can, for example, be done by offering and accepting physical contact, but also by reacting with concreteness and clarity and, more than usual in person-centred psychotherapy, with direct suggestions. References to their every-day situation may be repeated as often as necessary.

Contact and the perception of empathy and acceptance will improve when the therapist adapts his or her speech level to the client's speech capacity, on the one hand on the phonetic level (for example dialect or idiolect expressions), but also by using concrete images and examples (Pörtner, 1996, p. 75). A very important technique which can be applied when the therapist is not sure whether he understands the client is the exact repetition of whatever the therapist understands.[17] This way the client can check how much the therapist grasps from what he or she has said (Zinschitz, 2001b, p. 305) and his or her reaction gives the therapist a clue whether the client feels understood.

For these clients, change is only possible through experiencing (Pörtner, 1996, p. 35). Therefore the therapist has to focus on helping the client to experience empathy and unconditional positive regard. Here, creativity is needed; the interaction should not be restricted to pure talking. Other means, like role playing, drawing, dancing are allowed and required.

In order to reach the client, the therapist also will have to adapt to the client's rhythm. Expectations and impatience would put a client with a learning disability, who may be inclined to try and fulfil the other person's assumed needs and wishes, under a huge pressure. This can lead to distress and to a closing up, i.e. to contact interruption.

Naturally, it is essential that the therapist opens up as well and lets him- or herself not be hampered by prejudices towards disabled persons or by the wish to help and change the client's life. Therefore it is necessary that the therapist is congruent with regard to his or her inner reactions to this specific issue (Zinschitz, 2001b, p. 302). Also a belief in the actualising tendency, *even when the person is impaired*, is a prerequisite for a therapeutic attitude which supports the communication of empathy and acceptance (Zinschitz, 2001a, p. 192).

What makes the person-centred approach appropriate par excellence to establish and maintain contact with clients with disabilities (as well as to support their perception of empathy and unconditional positive regard), is the fact that it focuses on a relationship between persons of equal value. As Rogers and Schmid (1991, p. 149) puts it, 'the person-centred way of thinking and its clinical practice confirms the assertion that human beings are persons, irrespective of their state of mind, and confirms the equal value of persons, not only in normal cases, but also in crisis situations with "disordered" persons'.[18] Person-centred therapists are not deficit-oriented. They work in the first place with human beings.

REFERENCES

Badelt, I. (1990). Client-centered psychotherapy with mentally handicapped persons. In Lietaer, G. Rombauts, J., Van Balen, R. (1990). *Client-Centered and Experiential Psychotherapies in the Nineties*. Leuven: Leuven University Press, pp. 671–81.

Binder, U. and Binder, J. (2001). A theoretical Approach to Empathy. In Haugh, S. and Merry, T. *Rogers' Therapeutic Conditions: Evolution, Theory and Practice. Vol 2: Empathy*. Ross-on-Wye: PCCS Books, pp. 163–91.

---

17. Compare with the word-for-word reflection in Pre-Therapy (Prouty, 1994).
18. Translation from German by the author.

Cloerkes, G. (1997). *Soziologie der Behinderten: eine Einführung.* Heidelberg: Edition Schindele.
Finger, G. (1992). *Frühförderung zwischen passionierter Praxis und hilfloser Theorie.* Freiburg im Breisgau.
Gabbard, G. O. (2000). A neurobiologically informed perspective on psychotherapy. *British Journal of Psychiatry, 177,* 117–22.
Goleman, D. (1995). *Emotional Intelligence.* New York: Bantam Books.
Haas de, O. (1991). *Psychotherapeutisch interveniëren binnen de clientgerichte benadering.* In Swildens, H., Haase de, O., Lietaer, G. and Van Balen, R. (1991). *Leerboek Gesprekstherapie. De cliëntgerichte benadering.* Utrecht: De Tijdstroom, pp. 355–76.
Kegan, R. (1982). *The Evolving Self. Problem and Process in Human Development.* Cambridge, MA, London: Harvard University Press.
Luchterhand, Ch. and Murphy, N. (1998). *Helping Adults with Mental Retardation Grieve a Death Loss.* Philadelphia, PA, Bristol: Accelerated Development.
Oerter, R. and Montada, L. (1987). *Entwicklungspsychologie. Ein Lehrbuch.* 2nd edition, München-Weinheim: Psychologie Verlags Union.
Pörtner, M. (1996). Client-centered therapy with mentally retarded persons: Catherine and Ruth. In Lietaer, G. Rombauts, J. and Van Balen, R. (1990). *Client-Centered and Experiential Psychotherapies in the Nineties.* Leuven: Leuven University Press, pp. 659–70.
Pörtner, M. (1996). *Ernstnehmen — Zutrauen — Verstehen. Personzentrierte Haltung im Umgang mit geistig behinderten und pflegebedürftigen Menschen.* Stuttgart: Klett-Cotta. Engl. Transl. (Trust and Understanding) Ross-on-Wye: PCCS Books.
Prouty, G. F. (1994). *Theoretical Evolutions in Person-Centered/Experiential Therapy. Applications to Schizophrenic and Retarded Psychoses.* Westport: Praeger Publishers.
Prouty, G. F., Van Werde, D. and Pörtner, M. (1998). *Prä-Therapie.* Stuttgart: Klette Cotta. Engl. Transl. (2002). (Pre-Therapy, in press.) Ross-on-Wye: PCCS Books.
Rogers, C. R. (1957). The necessary and sufficient conditions of therapeutic personality change. In: *Journal of Consulting Psychology, 21*(2) 95–103.
Rogers, C.R. (1959). A theory of therapy, personality and interpersonal relationships, as developed in the client-centred framework. In Koch, S. (Ed.). *Psychology: A study of science.* Vol III, New York (McGraw Hill) 1959, pp. 184–256.
Rogers, C. R. and Schmid, P. F. (1991). *Person-zentriert: Grundlagen von Theorie und Praxis.* Mainz: Mathias-Grünewald-Verlag.
Schmutzler, H.-J. (1994). *Handbuch heilpädagogisches Grundwissen.* Freiburg, Basel, Wien: Herder Verlag.
Sorrentino, A. M. (1988). *Behinderung und Rehabilitytion. Ein systemischer Ansatz.* Dortmund: verlag modernes lernen.
Stern, D. (1985). *The Interpersonal World of the Infant.* New York: Basic Books. German Transl. (1992): Die Lebenserfahrung des Säuglings. Stuttgart: Klett-Cotta.
Stumm, G. and Pritz, A. (Eds.). *Wörterbuch der Psychotherapie.* Wien: Springer Verlag.
Weber, G. (1997). *Intellektuelle Behinderung. Grundlagen, klinisch-psychologische Diagnostik und Therapie im Erwachsenenalter.* Wien: WUV.
Zinschitz, E. (1998). The Person-Centred Approach in Work with Disabled Persons. *Counselling.* The Journal of the British Association for Counselling. 9 (3), 210–16.
Zinschitz, E. (2001a). Understanding what seems unintelligible. In Haugh, S. and Merry, T. *Rogers' Therapeutic Conditions: Evolution, Theory and Practice. Vol 2: Empathy.* Ross-on-Wye: PCCS Books, pp. 192–205.
Zinschitz, E. (2001b). Working with Clients with a Mental Disability and Their Families in a Person-Centered Way: Challenge for the Belief in the Actualizing Tendency. In Bower, D. W. (Ed.). *The Person-centred Approach: Applications for Living.* Lincoln, NE: Writers Club Press, pp. 286–316.
Zinschitz, E. (2001c). *Prä-Therapie — eine Antwort auf eine lange nicht beantwortete Frage.* Person, Zeitschrift für Klientenzentrierte Psychotherapie und personzentrierte Ansätze. 2001(1), 44–51.
Zinschitz, E. (2002). *Aus kleinen Menschen werden große . . . Frühförderung als Prävention für sekundäre Behinderungen im Erwachsenenalter.* To be published.

8   Contact in the Therapy of Trauma and Dissociation
Ton Coffeng

INTRODUCTION

Contact is a central issue for dissociating and traumatized clients. Due to lack of contact, they suffer in isolation and consequently they suffer more. They avoid people because of negative experience and have poor contact with reality and themselves. They have no contact with their feelings: their 'experiencing' (Gendlin, 1964) is frozen and so they cannot integrate their trauma.

Therapeutic contact is the client-centered answer to traumatic experience and flashbacks. It provides a foundation for the processing of feelings and the facilitation of change, so should have priority over other techniques or medication. The way it is offered depends on the phase of therapy (Coffeng, 2002). The following theoretical concepts are discussed: 'psychological contact' (Prouty, 1994), 'attachment' (Bowlby, 1969) and 'containment' (Pesso, 1988b; Winnicot, 1965). Attention will be given to the question of how clients perceive therapeutic contact.

1. GENERAL REMARKS ABOUT CONTACT

1.1. Effects of traumatic contact

When a child is sexually abused, she/he[1] undergoes sudden harmful contact: a violation of body and ego boundaries. A caregiver she trusted, changes into a perpetrator. Her notion of safe contact is broken. Unable to avoid the perpetrator, she is forced to endure abuse repeatedly. She dissociates in order to cope by the mechanism of 'peritraumatic dissociation' (Marmar, Weiss and Metzler, 1998). This way, she loses contact with herself and the world. As perpetrators usually mention false moral rules to justify their behaviour, the child becomes confused losing the right words for things. Because she may not cry or talk about it, she avoids people, and hides physical traces of the abuse. Unable to share her experience with others, she loses contact with people and becomes a stranger to

---

1. 'She' is used for the victim and 'he' for the perpetrator, but 'she' could be 'he' and vice versa. Although most victims being girls and perpetrators men, there is growing evidence of male victims and female perpetrators. When 'he' is used for the therapist it could be 'she'; when 'she' is used for the client, it could be 'he'.

herself. According to Gendlin (1964) her mental functioning becomes frozen or 'structure bound'. She turns in circles with her mind, blaming herself. She may develop symptoms like stammering or performing poorly at school, and since these symptoms are not recognized as signs of abuse, she may be blamed by others and become stigmatized. When abuse and neglect are repeated — being often the case — her dissociation may become permanent and may develop into a severe form, such as a Dissociative Identity Disorder or Multiple Personality Disorder (Ross, 1997). In the latter case she will have several identities inside, with different ages, genders, characters and memories, each identity carrying a trauma-fragment. These identities are not aware of each other due to dissociative and amnestic barriers. The client's memory and sense of time become disrupted by dissociative switches. She loses track of the day, misses appointments, needing much time and concentration for even routine activities.

Clients may also suffer from nightmares and 'daymares' (Prouty and Pietrzak, 1988) in which they re-experience the trauma as if it happens again. Flashbacks are triggered by cues (image, smell, sound) which remind them of the trauma. Flashbacks come from their 'traumatic memory' or not integrated memory of the trauma (van der Kolk et al., 1996), which differs from normal 'narrative, declarative or autobiographic memory'. Frequently, dissociative mechanisms split the memory of the trauma into part-incidents, by which the client re-experiences a part of the trauma; being amnestic for the rest. Dissociation may also split the trauma experience into its different aspects (Braun, 1986). Flashbacks then contain a trauma-fragment without context, images without feelings, or physical sensations without images. Clients don't recognize such fragments any more as parts of their trauma and suppose they are crazy. Ashamed, they don't talk about it. They do everything to prevent flashbacks: they switch into a person who doesn't feel or remember. Self-mutilation, substance abuse, eating disorders or suicide attempts are other ways to cope with it. They avoid people for fear of new traumatic relationships. Trying to control their life, they fail to have control. In trying to keep their balance they drift in isolation, and, indeed, it is a miracle when some find courage to seek therapeutic help.

1.2. The importance of contact for trauma clients — theoretical aspects

1.2.1. Experiencing is related to contact

Gendlin's concept of 'experiencing' (Gendlin, 1964) refers to a feeling process about one's contact with a given situation. The whole experience is felt at one spot in the body. What is felt is the 'implicit felt meaning' or 'felt sense': a vague feeling in the middle of the body (stomach or chest), which is specific for that situation. It contains one's perceptive and affective reactions, while previous (similar) experiences function in it as well. A felt sense is different from a thought since it can be felt, and from an emotion since it is a vague feeling. It is not felt immediately, but it is there when one relates to it. It is pre-conceptual, i.e. it has no words yet. When the right word is found for it, a relief or 'experiential shift' is felt: the felt sense changes, the changed feeling needs new words and so one sees the same situation with a fresh look, and reacts to it in a new way. The 'shift' is not limited to one's felt sense (of that situation), but involves the whole person, who now feels and thinks differently. 'Experiencing' is the process of being in the world, sensing, expressing it, and feeling the inner change. Gendlin (1964) related experiencing to change. For therapists, he introduced 'experiential responses' which point to this process of their clients; for clients, he introduced the method of 'focusing', which helps them to stay in touch with this process themselves.[2]

When people lose contact, their 'experiencing' stops. It happens to prisoners when they are isolated from people and the outside world. Many become 'crazy'. They lose contact with themselves, their feelings and bodily felt awareness of experience. Their mind goes in circles, which they cannot stop. They don't realize any more that they are thinking, are anxious or hungry. Their experiencing becomes frozen or 'structure bound' (Gendlin, 1964, p. 164): they function in a stereotyped way. Some may commit suicide, whilst others seek ways to get a glimpse of the world. Experiencing needs contact (a) with oneself, to relate to feelings, to give words to feelings, and (b) to communicate with others. Contact with a person carries experiencing forward so that the process can move. Responses from a person interrupt the 'structure bound' functioning of individuals, removing their isolation and bringing them back to themselves. Even the individual and introspective activity of focusing is more successful when another person is present (Gendlin, 1996).

1.2.2. 'Psychological contact' (Prouty)

Prouty (1976, 1994) underlined the importance of psychological contact, the first of Rogers' six conditions to facilitate change (Rogers, 1957). He called it a 'contact function' of human beings: it is a function to have contact, to feel contact and to realize it is contact. Prouty distinguishes three dimensions of contact: 'reality contact': contact with the world (people, places, events); 'affective contact': contact with oneself and one's feelings, and 'communicative contact': ability to express experience to others. These aspects of contact are fundamental. We need contact with the world. Elderly people deteriorate when they are hospitalized. They improve as soon as they have their feet on the ground or can see other people outside through their window. Reality, affective and communicative contact, are interrelated. When reality contact changes, it influences affective and communicative contact. When reality contact is interfered with, e.g. by medication, and clients lose contact with the world, they also lose contact with their feelings and fail to communicate. Conversely, when clients get better reality contact, their affective and communicative contact improve too. And finally, when communicative contact improves, contact with reality is restored, another person becoming the link between client and reality.

---

2. 'Experiential responses' (Gendlin,1968) point specifically to the client's experiencing, capture the felt sense under his words and follow the direction of the underlying felt process. Responses are checked by the client and corrected by the therapist until they fit (Gendlin, 1980). The exchange facilitates small change steps (Gendlin, 1990). Connected with 'experiencing' is the inner act of 'focusing'. Clients, who related to their felt sense and checked their words against it, were sucessful in therapy (Gendlin et al., 1968). Gendlin(1969) called this typical and crucial introspection 'focusing'. He developed a method of steps to teach this skill to others (Gendlin, 1981a). It is a special concentration between alertness and relaxation (Iberg, 1981). It involves a friendly attitude to one's feelings, which is enhanced by a client-centered listener (Gendlin, 1984; 1996).

CONTACT AND PERCEPTION

1.2.3. Contact with the ground
Basically, one needs contact with the ground before one is able to have contact with one's feelings. The six steps of focusing (Gendlin, 1981a) are preceded usually by a grounding exercise (Coffeng, 2000a; Olsen, 1982/3;, 1983).[3] Contact with the ground and the chair precedes contact with one's body. Contact with the body precedes contact with feelings. The helper is the link between the world and the focuser, whose attention is turned inside themselves. He connects the focuser with the world, while protecting her from being distracted by the outside world or inner thoughts. As the helper reflects feelings of the focuser, those feelings become 'real' and connected with the world. Grounding can be helpful for trauma clients, in that victims, rescued from a disaster, often regain contact with themselves as soon as they have their feet on safe soil. Before, they couldn't feel, having to survive. And afterwards, when they are upset by traumatic flashbacks, grounding helps to release anxiety. The helper assists the victim to contact the ground, he is the link with reality. Like a lightning conductor, he connects by verbal or physical contact, and anxious feelings can flow to the ground. Sometimes, both sit on the ground as shown in some video demonstrations (Coffeng, 1994, 1997a; Gendlin et al., 1986; Prouty, 1985). Grounding is more helpful than relaxation because victims may be afraid to relax in case they lose control (which happened during the trauma). They expect to become prey to flashbacks when they relax, so they postpone sleep fearing nightmares.

1.2.4. Contact with a place
Since teaching focusing, I have come to realize the significance of a *place*. The right place enables a person to focus, in the same way that the right place enables chickens to lay eggs.[4] At workshops, participants need their place to focus (Coffeng, 1997b; Gendlin, 1981b). When allowed to change their seat and to check inside themselves, they look around. Some find they need a different chair; others choose the ground. In this situation a helper provides a place for the focuser and he protects it as a 'placemate'. When the place feels OK, the focuser gets contact with the ground, his body and feelings. In my own practice, I encourage clients to find their place and placemate (Coffeng, 1997c). Instead of a place in reality, clients can imagine a place where they would feel safe. In their imagination they go to that place and sit there to focus (Grindler, 1982/83; McGuire, 1982/83; Olsen, 1983). The therapist/helper becomes a placemate of that imaginary place.

---

3. A person is asked if she can feel contact between her feet and the ground. Then, if she can feel her feet, ankles and knees from inside. Then to feel contact between her body and the chair; to feel that the chair carries the weight of the body. Finally, to feel other parts of the body from inside (stomach, respiration). One waits after each question till the other person nods. It takes some time. This way, the person gets contact with the ground, body and herself.

4. Giovacchini(1993) gave a nice example of the right place (illustrating a 'holding environment'). A client was sent to him, who had a severe form of Crohn's disease. The man had no notion of therapy. After some introduction to psychoanalysis, he lay on the couch. A long silence followed so the therapist became worried. When he looked, he found the client asleep. At the end of the hour, he woke the client and handed his bill. Next sessions were alike. The therapist was criticized by colleagues who supposed the client to be resistant; but the client assured him he had never had such a good sleep before. Gradually the client discussed dreams he had during therapy. The therapy went well, and after one year the client's disease was in remission!

1. 2. 5. Human contact and trauma-clients

In order to help the client regain contact with the ground and world, the therapist offers a safe place. Victims may also have difficulty with affective and communicative contact. Having hardly any access to feelings, they have no words to explain their suffering. It helps if another person simply keeps the client company providing simple human contact, taking an existential and human position. The other person can offer understanding of how hard it is to feel or to describe what happened. The helper trusts that this can happen later. Then, he will be willing to listen, contrary to many others who don't want to listen or who even question that the trauma happened. Such inappropriate reactions may well retraumatize the client (Keilson, 1979). When one is willing to be truly present, human contact is the best that can be offered.

2. SPECIFICS OF CONTACT THERAPY

The aim of therapy is to offer contact and to reach the client.[5] The ways of making contact depend on the client's ability to feel, to receive and to make contact, and this capacity changes over time. Two distinct phases of therapy will be described with their corresponding modes of contact, as well as techniques which assist the client to handle contact.

2. 1. First phase of contact — therapy

2. 1. 1. Pre-experiential aspect of dissociative process

Dissociative clients are subject to a barrage of vivid flashbacks attacking them. It is as if the trauma happens again and again. Images and sensations evoke anxiety, without bringing change or process. This 'non-process' has kinship with that of psychotic clients, which is called 'pre-experiential' (Prouty, 1976) in that it precedes experiential process. It is slow, primitive and repetitive. Psychotic clients are supposed to be 'pre-expressive', because they are unable yet to express feelings. Their condensed words become understood only afterwards. Instead of 'adjusting' psychotic patients to him, Prouty 'adjusts' himself to them, translating empathy, congruence and positive regard into their language (Prouty, 1994; Rogers, 1957). Gradually, a process evolves and the utterings of clients become understandable. Eventually, their process becomes experiential and therefore accessible to client-centered/experiential therapy.

Prouty (1976), introduced the method of Pre-Therapy to restore the psychological contact of clients. Pre-Therapy consists of 'contact reflections'. These respond to remnants of contact clients have, without any additions: they support the rudiments of the clients' functioning. Contact-reflections refer to reality, affective and communicative contact. There are five types of reflections.

---

5. Other elements of this therapy, such as the use of focusing, imagery, Pesso-techniques, etc. have been discussed elsewhere (Coffeng, 1996, 1998, 2002). The approach, from a client-centered/experiential perspective, considers the client as the expert; it differs from the official (medical and directive) guidelines of the International Society for the Study of Dissociation (Barach, 1994). Clinical aspects of dissociation were described by Chu(1994) and Ross (1997). Specifics of PTSD were given by Herman(1992) and van der Kolk(1996).

CONTACT AND PERCEPTION

(1) *Situational reflections* point to reality contact: 'We are in this room', 'I hear cars outside'. (2) Body *reflections* reflect the body posture of the client: 'You are sitting on the chair', 'Your body is tense'. One can 'mirror' the same posture with one's body. It assists the client's body awareness and reality contact. (3) Facial *reflections* describe what is visible on the client's face: 'You look scared', 'You look surprised'. It is neutral description, assisting affective contact. (4) Word-for-word *reflections* repeat literally words as they are uttered, in the same sequence: 'Fire . . . people . . . running'. One repeats remnants or fragments of clients' sentences supporting their communicative contact. (5) Reiterative *reflections* repeat reflections which were followed by response or change of the client. 'I said: "your body is tense", and then you looked at me.' These reflections support and reinforce change.

Contact reflections are realistic and simple. They mention things which are there in the present. The attention of the therapist is directed to the client's spot of attention. When the client looks at the window, the therapist mentions that, following the track of the client: 'You looked at the window, and then you looked at me'. Flexibility is also needed towards the dimensions (reality, affective and communicative) of contact. Situational reflections directed to reality, influence affective contact also. The client smiles: one responds to that. It is a slow process. It takes time before reflections reach the client and he is able to respond. The effect of reflections is not direct. It takes time before change is visible. Repetition is another characteristic. Repetition may seem a standstill, but it is acknowledged that something is seeking to be expressed: it knocks on the door until it opens. So in this case, repetition is not a circle: instead by being reflected it becomes a spiral movement. Rather like a screw for metal, it needs many turns to sink deeper into it. Repeated reflections reinforce the process and assist clients to keep their track and to stay in contact with themselves. Prouty (1999) stresses that Pre-Therapy should not consist of just techniques, but involve rather a person-centered attitude.

When clients get better contact with themselves, they get access to psychotic content and begin to talk about it. At this stage, some clinicians wrongly assume that clients are getting worse. The contrary is true: clients don't *become* psychotic but rather they get contact with their psychosis. Their hallucinations enter a 'Pre-Symbolic' process (Prouty, 1977, 1990).

In the case of trauma, the process of dissociating clients could be called 'pre-experiential' since their emotional turmoil with trauma flashbacks is without 'experiencing': a process is not moving. Their process is static and repetitive: flashbacks recur and evoke the same cul-de-sac of emotional arousal. Psychological contact is impaired by dissociative switches: they have poor reality, affective and communicative contact. They are unable to give words to their traumatic experience: they are 'pre-expressive', having 'alexithymia' (Hyer et al., 1991). Two things happen: first, contact reflections reconnect them providing a foundation; and second, the slow speed of helper responses respects the fragility of their process and slows down the hectic arousal. Eventually this facilitates change from a non-process into a process. Contact reflections and the consequent improvement of contact have the effect that clients get access to traumatic content. Clinically, they seem to get worse. They can't avoid the trauma any longer and they become upset, when their memory of trauma becomes complete. With the dissociation subsiding, clients cannot switch as easily as before so they are likely to need extra support from the therapist. Contact reflections and other supportive techniques may be needed which will be discussed later.

2.1.2. Pre-Symbolic aspect of dissociation

Prouty characterized hallucinations of psychotic patients as 'pre-symbols'. He recommends reflecting the hallucinations literally and patiently, in order to get access to them. This way, the hallucinations enter a 'Pre-Symbolic Process' (Prouty, 1977, 1991, 1994). They begin to change, appear to imply affect, and evolve gradually into returning memories of traumatic life events. These old experiences can then be worked through with client-centered/experiential therapy, the process becoming symbolic.

Initially, flashbacks of dissociative clients are recurrent sensations without image, or images without context. These fragments are not connected with complete 'experiencing'. Clients cannot express it in symbolic language either: their process seems pre-symbolic too. These fragments can be attended to by pre-symbolic processing in which the expressions of clients are followed with literal and slow reflections, which don't go into the content of trauma, but just reflect what is heard and nothing more. The slow speed of reflecting has the effect of slowing down the hectic arousal of the client. By reflecting *all* of the different and dissociated trauma fragments, the client is assisted to find any possible links between them.

2.1.3. Perception of clients of pre-contact

It is hard to gauge if clients perceive or 'subceive' contact reflections (Barrett-Lennard, 1988) since, usually, clients will not report it. They are not yet able to do so: they are pre-expressive. However, it can be observed indirectly by change in their 'contact behaviour'. For example, if they change their body posture after a body reflection we may infer that they have regained some awareness of their body. Similarly when a client looks at the therapist after a situational reflection, we could assume that reality contact is improved and there is eye-contact. Rogers (1967) suggests that contact is noticed somehow by the client on a visceral level, but may not be fully experienced.

Dissociative clients are particularly sensitive to the therapist's presence. They experience traumatic transference easily, whereby they may perceive the therapist as a former perpetrator. They may expect the therapist to be impatient or to force them to do things, fearing repetition of trauma. They may imagine the therapist looks through them not allowing them private thoughts, or suppose he is not interested. Contact reflections simply report the therapist's observation and refer to reality. The therapist becomes real and safe. It helps the client to make a distinction between inner experience and outside reality, which was previously mixed up. Making contact with reality, and a real therapist, establishes a safe basis from which clients can look at their trauma.

CONTACT AND PERCEPTION

2.2. Second phase of contact-therapy — experiential and symbolic contact

2.2.1. Theories about symbolic contact

When clients enter the second phase of therapy, their process becomes experiential and symbolic (Coffeng, 2000b, 2002). They are able to express feelings, which makes their language symbolic and understandable. Therapists can then respond with symbolic and person-centered/experiential reflections, and communication improves. In this phase, however, clients may encounter particular problems. As dissociation subsides, their memory loses its fragmentation and becomes complete: they remember the *whole* trauma instead of parts. Though complete, it is still in the form of a flashback: the trauma is not yet *integrated*. Clients may be shocked as they face it. Trapped, they cannot leave or run away, not knowing how to handle strong feelings. Concrete support is needed, so that their trauma can become integrated, and the flashback will change into a narrative memory of the trauma.

Bowlby (1969) described the attachment between mother and child. A young child learns to associate maternal contact with a pattern of stimuli (smell, touch, sound, images, affective atmosphere), and to recognize it. It is an interactive pattern in which the mother responds to the child and vice versa. The 'sophisticated web' (Stern, 1985) leads to an affective bond or attachment. Attachment is a basis from where the child explores the world (Mahler, Pine and Bergman, 1975). When contact is disrupted, the child reacts with protest and anxiety. He looks for the mother until contact is restored. This reaction, observed in humans and animals, becomes the onset of grief, if the mother does not return (Bowlby, 1961, 1980).

Winnicot introduced the concepts of 'containment' and 'holding' (Cluckers, 1989; Winnicot, 1965). When a mother holds her child, there is physical contact between her skin and that of the child. She defines the boundary between them and she supports the ego-skin of the child. It is reinforced by an affective atmosphere of cuddling and fondling. Being connected with the ground, the mother is a link between the child and reality. When a child is overwhelmed by emotions, he fears he might burst and loses contact with reality. To prevent him from exploding, the mother contains the child. She protects his ego-skin. She is connected with the world and the ground, so anxiety can flow down. Acting as a shock-absorber, she contains the strong emotions of the child. She does not stop the emotions: her containment and soothing are accepting and empathic. Containment is physical, emotional, and it is assisted by words: it is both concrete and symbolic. With her hands she holds the child, with her heart she resonates empathically, and with her voice she gives words to the feelings. The child learns that his emotions can be contained, that they can be expressed as words and can be responded by another person.

Pesso (1988b) uses the psychomotor technique of 'holding and containment', when clients, overwhelmed by strong emotions, fear they may explode and lose their boundaries. Groupmembers act as supportive figures and hold the client, forming an 'ego-wrapping' and connection with the ground. They offer physical contact and simultaneously explain to the client what they are doing: 'We hold you to protect you from exploding', 'We contain your emotions and help you to endure them', 'We connect you with the ground'. Holding and containment is both physical and symbolical (Pesso, 1984). The helping figures, acting symbolically, assist ego functions of the client. By this support the client is enabled to feel the essence of her emotions, to process them and to give words to them.

2.2.2. Practice and ethics of symbolic contact

Clients, facing their trauma fully, are afraid that they might disintegrate. They need more than verbal support. 'Holding and containment' gives this extra support in Pesso-groups. However, when therapists want to hold in individual therapy, they are confronted with ethical problems, since physical contact is considered by some to be controversial.[6] It can become safe and professional, when surrounded by preconditions. Such a precondition is the concept of 'the boundary' (Olsen, 1983). It is a spatial circle around a person, defining the border of her territory. The territory has physical, emotional and spiritual boundaries, which can be felt by focusing (Gray, 1990). In exercises, the client tries to find the right distance between her and her therapist. For example, she can move her chair or ask the therapist to move. She checks in her body which distance is right and then is invited to indicate a line (boundary) between her and the therapist. Her definition is unique: she is the only one who can feel it. The therapist helps to restore her boundary: to feel, to indicate and to protect it. He declares his respect for her boundary which he will not cross without her explicit permission. This distance is not static but can change over time, so the checking is repeated. When the client assesses her boundary frequently, she may feel free to move and sit where she wants. She may notice that she needs more distance one moment and less in another. When she experiences that her boundary is respected, she will start to trust the therapist.

Within the context of the boundary, physical contact like Pesso's techniques, above, can be introduced as follows. When the client feels ready to try it, the therapist might touch her arm so she can test if it connects her with the ground in a comfortable way. The therapist should explain the 'holding and containing' technique. Only when the client is ready, can it be tried. She is asked how she wants to be held, and the therapist follows her instructions. He continues to explain what he is doing, asking the client to check. She may refuse or withdraw at any moment or ask the therapist to withdraw. It is essential to understand that these techniques are only a possibility (Pesso, 1988a) and not a must.

Physical contact should not come out of the blue. During the first part of

---

6. Traditionally, physical contact it is considered to be unethical. Analysts warn that it would disturb the symbolic nature of therapy and neutrality of therapists. It could evoke acting-out of therapists or regression of clients (Brown and Fromm, 1986; Cluckers, 1989; Giovacchini, 1993; Herman, 1992; Kernberg, 1984; Loewenstein, 1993; McCann and Coletti, 1994; McCann and Pearlman, 1990). Others find childhood trauma responds better to body therapies than verbal therapy (Pesso, 1988b; Souget, 1985). Ogden highlights inhibited body reactions to trauma, which she approaches with psychomotor techniques (Ogden and Minton, 2001). Physical contact is essential: it can be as symbolic as verbal contact (Pesso, 1984). Others (Bohun et al., 1990; Durana, 1998; Hunter and Struwe, 1998) distinguish between therapeutic and non-therapeutic touch, stating that touch can become professional and ethical and that some precautions are esential. It is a skill therapists must learn before they use it. It should be discussed with the client and it needs her feedback. Monitoring (supervision, co-therapists, tapes, etc.) preserves its therapeutic character.

161

therapy, a relationship or attachment is growing. As contact-reflections are repeated and extra contact is offered between sessions, the therapist establishes a reliable pattern and becomes predictable. He corrects his responses whenever they don't fit. The therapist might mention the Pesso group as an example of a safe environment, when the hostile atmosphere of abuse is discussed and he may invite the client to imagine such a safe alternative. Some clients reach a point where they don't accept imaginary supportive figures any longer and they want the therapist himself to hold them (Coffeng, 1994). Other clients don't want to be touched, or become upset when it is mentioned. Their boundary must be respected, as well as their space. Some prefer to sit on the ground, in a corner of the room, or lean on the table between them and therapist for contact and grounding. The therapist might mention holding figures of Pesso groups (without intending to actually hold the client) as an imaginary alternative, which the client may consider if they have never experienced safe holding.

The therapist may have conflicting feelings. On the one hand he respects the client's boundary, but seeing his client in a miserable state, he cannot stay paralysed and may feel pressure to act. He may offer to hold or to sit near the client, and he waits. The client will need time and space to respond. Just the possibility of contact, the *offer* may suffice and the client no longer feels alone, in a vacuum. This condition may enable a client to approach trauma memory: she knows the therapist is around and she perceives his willingness to be present. When he holds the client, he explains that he holds her to help endure the horror of her trauma. He helps to express feelings. He testifies that what happened was bad. He points to the difference between the trauma and the present safe contact, from where she looks at the past. After such an intensive session, the therapist should check again with the client to ascertain whether the physical contact was acceptable.

This therapeutic process has been illustrated in a video (Coffeng, 1997a). The client was silent and she used only few words. She was assisted with contact reflections. After ten minutes, she expressed that she wanted to sit on the floor, more precisely: under the desk (the desk being a symbolic roof to protect her from dissociating). She asked the therapist to sit there too. He had to sit first, before she joined him. Then, she asked to lean against the therapist. For 15 minutes she explored how to sit, and how the therapist should hold her. Finally, she sat in front of the therapist and needed his arms around her. He made a verbal commentary, explaining what he did. She confirmed it was the right position, relaxing with a deep sigh. Then she could say whole sentences and discuss her fears. She was able to make a drawing of her dissociative state, which was pre-symbolic. Finally she showed a drawing of the therapist at home: staying in his garden, sitting in his house and sleeping in bed. She had made it to keep his presence, whenever she would feel lost between sessions. In psychodynamic terms, she had made a transitional object: the drawing was symbolic.

2.2.3. Countertransference of contact

When a therapist holds a client who re-experiences her trauma, he may be shaken by the impact of it. The therapist may make contact on two levels: empathizing with his own mind and feelings, and resonating with his body. He feels intensely how the client is affected. Being so close makes it hard to keep a distance, risking trauma contamination and burnout. Wilson and Lindy (1994) discuss 'empathic strain', which may lead to withdrawal (intellectualizing) or enmeshment (overidentification) (Loewenstein, 1993). There are several ways to cope with this. The therapist can ask a co-therapist to hold like a groupmember in Pesso-therapy, or meet a colleague for debriefing afterwards. A network of therapists and supervision can also provide support. Another way to keep a balance is through focusing. When the therapist holds a client, he tries to feel the ground and creates an inner space for himself, next to the empathy for the client. He keeps his attention flexible, by switching frequently from the reality of the trauma to the reality of the present. When he can no longer stand the trauma or be near to the client, he may indicate that he needs to withdraw for a while. It is human to have a break. It is better to be honest than pretending to listen. Hopefully it will be reassuring to the client that the therapist takes the trouble to protect himself and the client will not feel guilty afterwards (Gendlin, 1992).

This account of the therapeutic use of physical contact should not give the impression that it dominates therapy. Most of the time is spent in verbal exchanges and imagery, to integrate the trauma and to restore moral rules. The client develops a vocabulary for the experience: she is finding the truth, even though she might have been made to believe that the trauma did not happen.

2.2.4. Ways in which clients perceive symbolic contact

In the second phase, contact can be symbolic when offered in both concrete and verbal ways. As a result, clients perceive both actual contact and the possibility of contact: they know the therapist is around. As they feel contact they dare to face traumatic content and to pursue their process. Their new experience confirms that severe emotions can be endured and expressed. They feel the power of their own new truth: to find out what actually happened and to say what should have happened instead. They discover their own strong moral rules regarding what is right and wrong. This is a tough process, as they may feel they want to stick to old beliefs. Loyal ties with former abusive caregivers and their rules can be strong. Clients may find it hard to realize they were betrayed and they are likely to be angry if they believe it is the therapist who has confronted them with it. They may have to grieve before they can attach to new and reliable persons. In this process, the therapist is the most likely pivot between the old and the new.

Contact with reality and affect being better, clients can express feelings. Being able to focus, they can describe in detail if they feel contact and how they experience it. They indicate when it changes, which they couldn't before. There is the possibility for exchange and mutual feedback, which increases the therapist's ability to understand and empathize. The exchange becomes a spiral movement or 'dance of empathy' (McCann and Coletti, 1994): with every turn of the spiral, feedback is followed by better understanding. The relationship and attachment becomes stable. Clients are not upset any longer when a therapist is

---

7. An exception is the initial critical episode of the second phase, when clients begin to integrate and feel as if they disintegrate (Coffeng, 2002). They are in a vacuum. Then therapists need to be available for contact.

one minute late. They don't need to call between sessions, and can stand holidays. They hold his presence with transitional objects (dolls, drawings, letters) having symbolic energy.[7]

3. CONCLUSION

As a consequence of traumatization, victims become isolated and isolate themselves. This reinforces recurrent flashbacks: it seems as if their trauma continues. Human contact interrupts this chain, as it reconnects the victim with a place and a person (Coffeng, 1999) and this therapeutic contact facilitates recovery. Contact reflections initially support psychological contact and trauma-fragments, not accessible to semantic language, are reflected literally and slowly. The process is pre-experiential and pre-symbolic. Gradually, amnestic barriers decrease and the trauma-memory becomes complete. Clients enter a new phase: they get access to experiential feelings and can express them: their process becomes experiential and symbolic. The new episode starts with a turmoil as the full extent of the trauma is faced. At this confrontation, clients need strong support, sometimes also physical contact. Gradually, the truth of the trauma can be told and integrated. Proper moral rules are learned, so that the trauma becomes a serious mistake and not an example of normal human contact.

Contact is the basis of therapy. It may involve contact between sessions, more sessions a week, phone calls, letters, etc. It cannot be replaced by drugs. The purpose of this is to maintain contact (so that the client can hear the therapist's voice, or feel her therapist's presence) rather than providing crisis-help. Contact with a fixed co-therapist during holidays also preserves continuity and helps to prevent crises or admissions.

The therapy is intensive and long (6–10 years), which requires investment from client and therapist. Therapists need support from colleagues and employer. Support is rare, as many professionals and institutions still ignore the existence of sexual abuse (Herman, 1992). The managed health-care system is another obstacle (Sussman, 1995). Therapists who deal with trauma are tolerated at best, work often in isolation and risk burnout. They need a network (Coffeng, 1997c, 2000c; Wilson and Lindy, 1994). Clients should also have their network of people to phone, or to join them in hospitals or other places they fear. These networks and a client-centered climate enable client and therapist to walk the small steps of a long therapeutic road, without psychiatric interventions.

REFERENCES

Barach, P. M. (1994). *ISSD Guidelines for Treating Dissociative Identity Disorder (Multiple Personality Disorder) in Adults*. Skokie, IL: International Society for the Study of Dissociation.

Barrett-Lennard, G. T. (1988). Comment on Gendlin (1990), The small steps of the therapy process: how they come and how to help them come. In Lietaer, G., Rombauts, J. and Van Balen, R. (Eds.) *Client-centered and experiential psychotherapy in the nineties*. Leuven: Leuven University Press, pp. 223–4.

Bohun, E., Ahern, R. and Kiely, L. (1990). 'The use of therapeutic touch'. Unpublished paper, 7th Ann. Conference on Dissociation and Multiple Personality Disorder, Chicago.

Bowlby, J. (1961). Childhood mourning and its implications for psychiatry. *Am. J. of Psychiatry*, 118, 481–98.
Bowlby, J. (1969). *Attachment and Loss* Vol. I: *Attachment*. London: Hogarth Press.
Bowlby, J. (1980). *Attachment and Loss* Vol. III: *Separation*. London: Hogarth Press.
Braun, B. G. (1986). Issues in the Psychotherapy of Multiple Personality Disorder. In Braun, B. G. (Ed.), *Treatment of Multiple Personality Disorder*. Washington DC: Am. Psychiatric Press, pp. 3–28.
Brown, D. P. and Fromm, E. (1986). *Hypnotherapy and hypnoanalysis*. Hillsdale NJ: L. Erlbaum Associates.
Chu, J. A. (1994). The rational treatment of multiple personality disorder. *Psychotherapy*, 31 (1), 94–100.
Cluckers, G. (1989). 'Containment' in de therapeutische relatie. In Vertommen, H., Cluckers, G. and Lietaer, G. (Eds.), *De relatie in therapie*. Leuven: Leuven University Press, pp. 49–64.
Coffeng, T. (1994). *The delicate approach to early trauma. Video*. International Conference of Client-Centered and Experiential Psychotherapy, Gmunden, Austria.
Coffeng, T. (1996). Experiential and pre-experiential therapy for multiple trauma. In Esser, U., Pabst, H. and Speierer, G-W. (Eds.) *The Power of the Person-Centered Approach*. Köln: GwG, pp. 185–203.
Coffeng, T. (1997a). *Pre-experiential contact with dissociation. Video*. ICCCEP, Lisbon.
Coffeng, T. (1997b). 'Effect of teaching Focusing'. Pilotstudy. Bouman, T., Fischer, J., Smit, J. and Tijssen, H. Univ. of Groningen. Unpublished manuscript.
Coffeng, T. (1997c). 'Who takes care of the therapist?' Unpubl. paper. Workshop Amsterdam.
Coffeng, T. (1998). Pre-experiencing: a way to contact trauma and dissociation. *The Folio*, 17 (1), 43–53. German (2000) in Feuerstein, H. J., Müller, D. and Weiser Cornell, A. (Eds.), *Focusing im Prozess*. Köln: GwG, pp. 51–61.
Coffeng, T. (1999). *Rogerian aspects of recovery from trauma*. Lecture, Flemish Association Client-Centered Therapy, Leuven.
Coffeng, T. (2000a). Focusing en de experiëntiële dimensie. In Trijsburg, W., Colijn, S., Collumbien, E. and Lietaer, G. (Eds.), *Handboek integratieve Psychotherapie*. Maarssen: Elsevier/De Tijdstroom, IV 2. 2, 1–26.
Coffeng, T. (2000b). *Two phases of dissociation, two languages*. 3 videotapes. ICCCEP, Chicago.
Coffeng, T. (2000c). 'Network-principle in the treatment of trauma and dissociation'. Leeuwarden. Unpublished paper.
Coffeng, T. (2002). Two phases of dissociation, two languages. In Watson, J. et al., (Eds.), *Client-centered and experiential psychotherapy in the 21st Century: Advances in theory, research and practice*. Ross-on-Wye: PCCS Books (in print).
Durana, C. (1998). The use of touch in psychotherapy: ethical and clinical guidelines. *Psychotherapy*, 35 (2), 269–80.
Gendlin, E. T. (1964). A theory of personality change. In Worchel, P. and Byrne, D. (Eds.), *Personality Change*, 4. New York: Wiley, pp. 100–48.
Gendlin, E. T. (1968). The experiential response. In Hammer, E. (Ed.), *The use of interpretation in treatment*. New York: Grune and Stratton, pp. 208–28.
Gendlin, E. T. (1969). Focusing. *Psychotherapy: Theory, Research and Practice*, 6 (1), 4–15.
Gendlin, E. T. (1980). Client-centered therapy as a frame of reference for training: the use of focusing in therapy. In de Moor, W. and Wijngaarden, H. (Eds.) *Psychotherapy: training and research*. Amsterdam: Elsevier Biomedical Press, pp. 279–97.
Gendlin, E. T. (1981a). *Focusing*. New York: Bantam.
Gendlin, E. T. (1981b). *Focusing*. 1st Intern. Weeklong Intensive, Chicago.
Gendlin, E. T. (1984). The client's client. In R. F. Levant and J. M. Shlien (Eds.) *Client-centered therapy and the person-centered approach*. New York: Praeger, pp. 76–107.
Gendlin, E. T. (1990). The small steps of the therapy process: how they come and how to help them come. In Lietaer, G., Rombauts, J. and Van Balen, R. (Eds.) *Client-centered and experiential psychotherapy in the nineties*. Leuven: Leuven University Press, pp. 205–24.
Gendlin, E. T. (1992). *Focusing in the interactional space*. Therapists' workshop, Chicago.
Gendlin, E. T. (1996). *Focusing-oriented Psychotherapy*. New York: Guilford.
Gendlin, E. T., Beebe, J., Cassens, J., Klein, M. and Oberlander, M. (1968). Focusing ability in

psychotherapy, personality and creativity. In J. M. Shlien (Ed.) *Research in psychotherapy*, Vol. 3. Washington DC: APA, pp. 217–41.

Gendlin, E. T., Köhne, F. and Wiltschko, J. (1986). *Focusing*. Videoband. Garmisch-Partenkirchen: MP Mediateam Psychologie.

Giovacchini, P. L. (1993). *Borderline patients, the Psychosomatic Focus and the Therapeutic Process*. Northvale NJ: J. Aronson.

Gray, L. (1990). The function of the boundary in facilitating experiential focusing. *The Focusing Folio*, 9 (3), 112–27.

Grindler, D. (1982/83). Clearing a space with a borderline client. *The Focusing Folio*, 2 (1), 5–10.

Herman, J. J. (1992). *Trauma and recovery*. New York: Basic Books.

Hunter, M. and Struwe, J. (1998). *The ethical use of touch in psychotherapy*. London: Sage.

Hyer, L., Woods, G. and Boudewyns, P. (1991). PTSD and alexithymia: Importance of emotional clarification in treatment. *Psychotherapy*, 28, 129–38.

Iberg, J. R. (1981). Focusing. In Corsini, R. (Ed.) *Handbook of innovative psychotherapies*. New York: Wiley, pp. 334–61.

Keilson, H. (1979). *Sequentielle Traumatieserung bei Kinder*. Stuttgart: Ferdinand Enke Verlag.

Kernberg, O. (1984). *Severe personality disorders*. New Haven/ London: Yale University Press.

Kolk, B. van der, McFarlane, A. C. and Weisaeth, L. (Eds.)(1996). *Traumatic Stress*. New York: Guilford.

Loewenstein, R. J. (1993). Post-traumatic and Dissociative Aspects of Transference and Countertransference in the Treatment of MPD. In Kluft, R. P. and Fine, C. G. (Eds.), *Clinical Perspectives on Multiple Personality Disorder*. Washington DC: American Psychiatric Press, pp. 51–85.

Mahler, M. A., Pine, F. and Bergman, A. (1975). *The Psychological Birth of the Human Infant*. New York: Basic Books.

Marmar, C. R., Weiss, D. S., and Metzler, T. (1998). Peritraumatic Dissociation and Post-traumatic Stress Disorder. In Bremner, J. D. and Marmar, C. R. (Eds.), *Trauma, Memory and Dissociation*. Washington DC: American Psychiatric Press, pp. 229–52.

McCann, I. L. and Coletti, I. (1994). The dance of empathy. In Wilson, J. P. and Lindi, J. D. (Eds.), *Countertransference in the treatment of PTSD*. New York: The Guilford Press, pp. 87–121.

McCann, I. L., and Pearlman, L. A. (1990). *Psychological Trauma and the adult survivor*. New York: Brunner/Mazel.

McGuire, M. (1982/83). Clearing a space with two suicidal clients. *The Focusing Folio*, 2 (1), 1–4.

Ogden, P. and Minton, K. (2001). 'Sensorimotor Sequencing: one method for processing traumatic memory'. Unpublished paper, workshop Driebergen, The Netherlands.

Olsen, L. (1982/83). How I do body work. *The Focusing Folio*, 2 (3), 1–8.

Olsen, L. (1983). *Focusing and Imagery*. Workshop Breda (Holland).

Pesso, A. (1984). Touch and action: the use of the body in psychotherapy. *Bewegen en Hulpverlening*, 1 (4), 254–9.

Pesso, A. (1998a). Ego development and the body. *Bewegen en Hulpverlening*, 5, 239–48.

Pesso, A. (1988b). Sexual abuse, the integrity of the body. *Bewegen en Hulpverlening*, 5, 270–81.

Prouty, G. F. (1976). Pre-Therapy, a method of treating pre-expressive psychotic and retarded patients. *Psychotherapy: Theory, Research and Practice*, 13 (3), 290–4.

Prouty, G. F. (1977). Proto-symbolic method: A phenomenological treatment of schizophrenic hallucinations. *J. of Mental Imagery*, 1 (2), 339–42.

Prouty, G. F. (1985). *Pre-Therapy*. Video, workshop Breda, The Netherlands.

Prouty, G. F. (1990). Pre-therapy: A theoretical evolution in the person-centered/experiential psychotherapy of schizophrenia and retardation. In Lietaer, G., Rombauts, J. and Van Balen, R. (Eds.) *Client-centered and experiential psychotherapy in the nineties*. Leuven: Leuven University Press, pp. 645–59.

Prouty, G. F. (1991). The pre-symbolic structure and processing of schizophrenic hallucinations: the problematic of a non-process structure. In Fusek, L. (Ed.), *New directions in client-centered therapy. Practice with difficult client populations*. Chicago: The Chicago Counseling Center, pp. 18–40.

Prouty, G. F. (1994). *Theoretical Evolutions in Person-Centered/Experiential Therapy. Applications to schizophrenic and retarded psychoses.* New York: Praeger.

Prouty, G. F. (1999). *Restoration of Contact.* Symposium and workshop. Leeuwarden, The Netherlands.

Prouty, G. F. and Pietrzak, S. (1988). The pre-therapy method applied to persons experiencing hallucinatory images. *Person-Centered Review, 3* (4), 426–41.

Rogers, C. R. (1957). The necessary and sufficient conditions of therapeutic personality change. *J. of Consulting Psychology, 21* (2), 95–103.

Rogers, C. R. (Ed., 1967). *The Therapeutic Relationship and its impact.* Madison: University of Wisconsin Press.

Ross, C. (1997). *Dissociative Identity Disorder.* New York: Wiley.

Souget, F. (1985). *De achterzijde van de menselijke geest* (The backside of the human mind). Lisse; Swets and Zeitlinger.

Stern, D. N. (1985). *The Interpersonal World of the Infant.* New York: Basic Books.

Sussman, M. (1995). *A perilous calling. The hazards of psychotherapy practice.* New York: Wiley and Sons.

Wilson, J. P. and Lindy, J. D. (Eds., 1994). *Countertransference and the treatment of PTSD.* New York: The Guilford Press.

Winnicot, D. W. (1965). *The maturational process and the facilitating environment: studies in the theory of emotional development.* New York: International University Press.

9 Prouty's Pre-Therapy and Contact-work with a Broad Range of Persons' Pre-expressive Functioning

Dion Van Werde

The work of Garry Prouty has put working with severely contact-impaired people on the (psycho) therapeutic map. What has continued to be underrepresented in person-centred literature so far, however, is the explicit and systematic description of how to work with clients who present themselves with rather extreme variations of contact-impaired functioning. By this I mean, on the one hand, very low-level and declining functioning — as a prelude to death (e.g. as in dementia) — and on the other hand, 'grey-zone functioning' (where 'normal' and 'contact-impaired' levels are present side-by-side, e.g. as in borderline psychotic states).

In this chapter, the author starts from Prouty's Pre-Therapy and looks at recent developments in its application. Both working with a broader range of levels of functioning than Pre-Therapy generally has been addressing, and working in home-situations seem to be promising expansions of 'classic' Pre-Therapy work. The notion 'grey-zone functioning' is defined and two case-illustrations are given to show how Pre-Therapy contact-reflections can be successfully integrated by (a) a professional in a hospital (grey-zone work) and by (b) a lay person in a home situation (dementia).

THE PROBLEMATIC OF 'CONTACT': CARL ROGERS AND GARRY PROUTY

In 1957, Carl Rogers describes 'psychological contact' as the first of the six necessary and sufficient conditions for constructive personality change to occur. Throughout his writings, this condition as such wasn't elaborated. Probably this was due to the clientele he worked with, whereby psychological contact was most of the time a 'given'. It is to Garry Prouty's merit that he brought the first condition back under the spotlight (Prouty, 1994). He not only defined contact and measured it, but also formulated a method of how this contact can be established or restored, when severely impaired or even absent.

Schematically, we could say that Rogers deals with the expressive elements of the client's behaviour. Prouty introduces the term 'pre-expressive functioning' to describe that level of functioning where a person's contact-functions are failing and thus contact with the surrounding reality, with one's own affective functioning, and with others, is lost. 'Pre-expressive' functioning means 'low-level functioning, by definition not yet meaningful but full of therapeutic potency' (Prouty, 1998; Prouty, Van Werde and Pörtner, 1998, 2001, in press). Figures 1 and 2 show how client functions correspond to the respective therapist activity.

Figure 1: *Client's level of functioning*

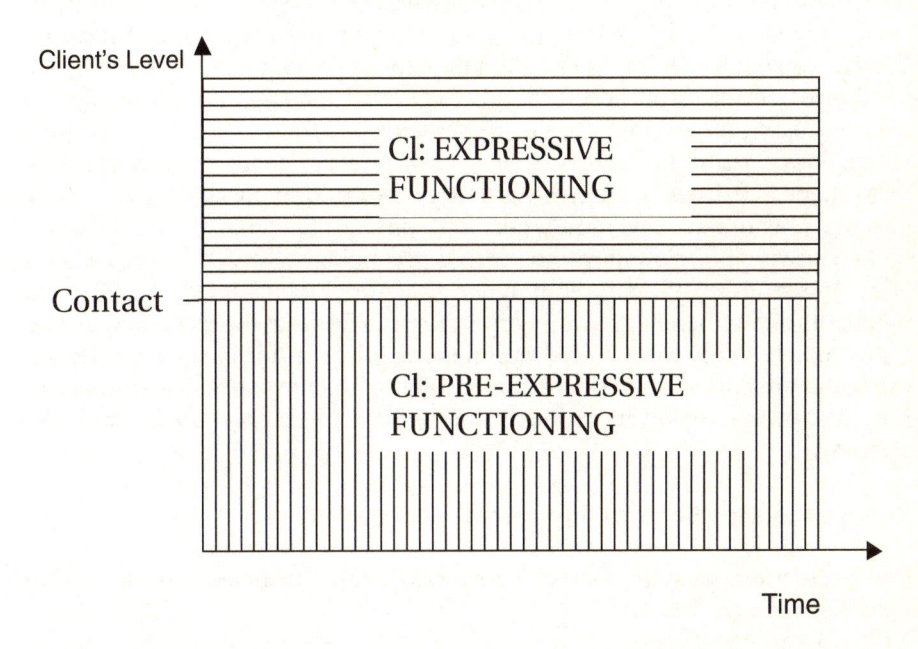

Figure 2: *Therapists' therapeutic interventions matched with clients' level of functioning*

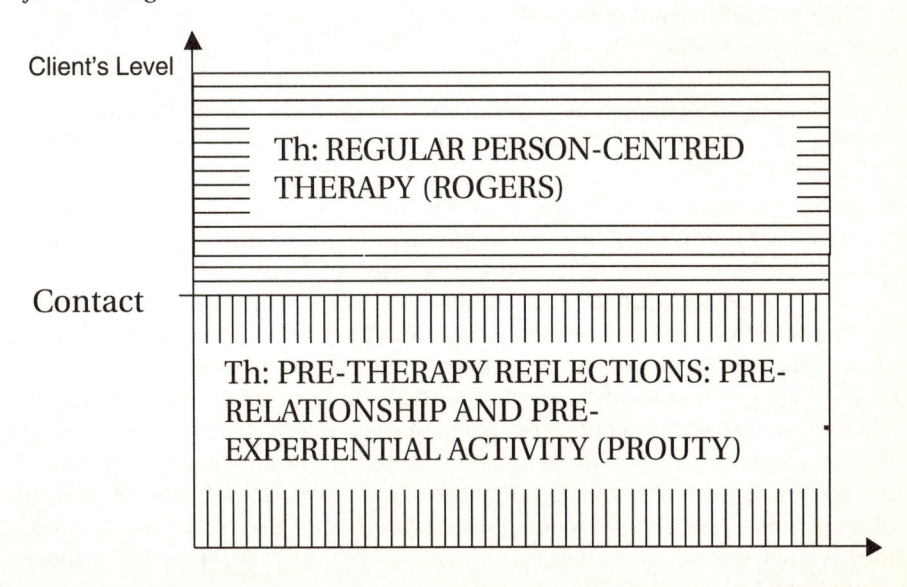

CONTACT AND PERCEPTION

PROUTY'S PRE-THERAPY

As Prouty's Pre-Therapy (Prouty, Van Werde and Pörtner, op.cit.) is increasingly being brought to the attention of practitioners, it is being applied in different fields of care for people who were usually considered as inaccessible for psychological/ psychotherapeutic treatment. Many caregivers are pleased to discover or to recognise in this way of working the basic values of humanity and compassion. They can read between the lines to find the utmost concern to the psychological freedom of the person or client. Prouty defines Pre-Therapy as a way of being with retarded, psychotic and geriatric clients *at their level of expression*. Pre-Therapy is an ideological commitment to the most basic levels of being in the world. This takes shape in existential relatedness to the client's world through a particularly concrete phenomenology (Prouty, personal communication).

Because the population worked with is psychologically withdrawn, isolated and presenting autistic features, the therapist does not have adequate access to the client's phenomenology. The therapist nevertheless tries to existentially attune to the totality of the client's lived experiences. It is pointing at the concrete, an extraordinarily literal and concrete form of empathic response. The practice of Pre-Therapy, i.e. applied empathic contact, is the actual therapeutic work in Pre-Therapy.

Prouty's contact reflections (Prouty, 1976, 1994)

Prouty describes what the therapist does, his therapeutic tools — as a set of five types of contact reflection:
  SR: situational reflection
  FR: facial reflection
  BR: body reflection
  WWR: word-for-word reflection
  RR: reiterative reflection

The reflections are concrete empathic descriptions to the client of what is or was present and observable. The therapist names people, places, events or things (SR) to offer anchorage in the shared reality. Facial expression is reflected to point at, or draw attention to, implicit affect, thus enabling the client or 'other' to contact his feelings (FR). Body posture or movement is reflected (by words or by actions) (BR) to build up a strengthened experience of here-and-now. Similarly, meaningful sounds and/or comprehensible words, fragments or sentences (WWR) are reflected literally to foster and strengthen the communicative process. The contact-reflections are used to restore contact with the World (reality contact), with others (communicative contact) and the Self (affective contact). In Pre-Therapy, we use the concept of 'bridging in', meaning that when we are allowed to enter the world of the other (when non-intrusive contact is made by the use of a certain reflection or series of reflections), this automatically means that the other is *coming out of his psychological isolation* (and gets more in contact with the therapist, the surroundings and himself). Reflections that enable contact to appear, can be repeated (RR).

Applications of Pre-Therapy

Each year since 1995, the Pre-Therapy Network International has held a kind of closed conference, where members of the Network from different countries, and who all work with Pre-Therapy, share and discuss their work and their specific field of application and practice. What became obvious was that Pre-Therapy, as used by others in caregiving to severely disturbed people (such as chronic hospitalised psychotic patients or intellectually challenged people with psychiatric comorbidity), closely resembles what Garry Prouty describes in most of his publications. In particular, the individual contact-facilitator or Pre-Therapist systematically works with an individual in a wide variety of settings: sometimes in a separate room (e.g. Dinacci, 1997; Peters, 1995, 2001; Krietemeyer, 1999; Van Werde, and Willemaers, 1992); sometimes in the context of a living room on the ward (e.g. Van Wyngene, Dumon and Coninckx, 2000) or maybe even in such places as the patio outside (Read Mental Hospital team, 2000). In addition, Pre-Therapy has been integrated in regular psychotherapy to process moments of pre-expressive functioning. For example, Coffeng reports on Pre-Therapy reflections used when dealing with surfacing trauma and dissociative functioning (1996, 1998), the work of Lucieer on dealing with psychotic moments during a psychiatrist consultation (1999). (For a detailed description of this work, see Chapter 9, this volume.)

Besides *official* caregiving situations, a whole new area that has opened up, is the application of the Pre-therapy reflections in home situations, e.g. Pre-Therapy used by a mother to relate better to her profoundly retarded daughter (McWilliams and Prouty, 1998); Pre-Therapy reflections applied to one's own son (Clarke, 2001); and Pre-Therapy reflections used by a woman to be with someone suffering a brain tumour (Zinschitz, 1999).

In most of these situations, due to the role of being, for example, a mother or a relative or a friend, no professional standards are set and certainly no systematically administered psychotherapeutic efforts are expected. It is about staying with 'the concrete' and seeing what the situation or the behaviour of the other brings. Reaching out for the other, offering him the 'shared' reality, eventually meeting him there or possibly meeting him in his private and idiosyncratic world are the only goals. Once contact is (re-)established, all options are open again, from making an invitation to do something (together) or simply just leaving it there and enjoying the contact-restoration as it is.

CONTACT-WORK WITH 'GREY-ZONE FUNCTIONING'

Clinical practice with less disturbed clients than those typically worked with by Garry, has shown that there is a conceptual category between 'healthy' and 'severely contact-impaired' functioning, and that clients in this category need to be handled in a specific way. People functioning at this level show in their behaviour a mixture of 'anchored' and 'problematic' functioning, e.g. when psychotic and realistic content are simultaneously present. For a detailed illustration of this see Van Werde and Prouty, 1992 and Prouty, Van Werde and Pörtner (in press). For example, a woman on our ward asks 'are they coming to get me?' After some therapeutic work, this question turns out to relate to not only the hour at which the parents would come to pick her up to go on a weekend leave, but also about a paranoid fear that 'things' would come and abduct her with death as a consequence. Sometimes, grey-zone functioning takes the format of psychotic and anchored behaviour quickly alternating: for example, on one occasion a client spoke to me in a very understandable way about all the things he had done on his weekend leave from the hospital. Almost every sentence, however contained words or expressions like 'Mr Devil' or 'Yes, Mr Devil', 'No, Mr Devil', that did not make sense to me at all. On top of this, the man did not even seem to have any awareness at all that he was talking in an odd way!

How should such a situation be handled? How can a therapist provide the relationship conditions in order to be therapeutic? Clearly, a bridge needs to be built between Rogers — who worked with rather high-level functioning clients — and Prouty, who worked with deeply disturbed patients. The problem is that, in the example mentioned, contact is partially present (e.g. when talking about the realities of the weekend leave) but needs to be strengthened to prohibit further contact-loss (e.g. by drifting off to full psychosis). The functioning that is psychotically charged (the client takes me for the Devil!) and sometimes reveals that the client has needs which deserve to be understood and dealt with without dehumanising and reducing him to simply his problem and without running the risk that the 'normal' functioning still operating (giving an overview of weekend activities in a comprehensible way) gets lost. This is not a point of simple technicality, rather it presents two challenges (a) to the Rogerian thinking that almost presupposes contact *as continuously present*, and (b) to the way Prouty has documented working with people whose contact-abilities are *totally absent* (as in a full psychotic crisis, for example).

Schematically we would present it as follows (Figure 3):

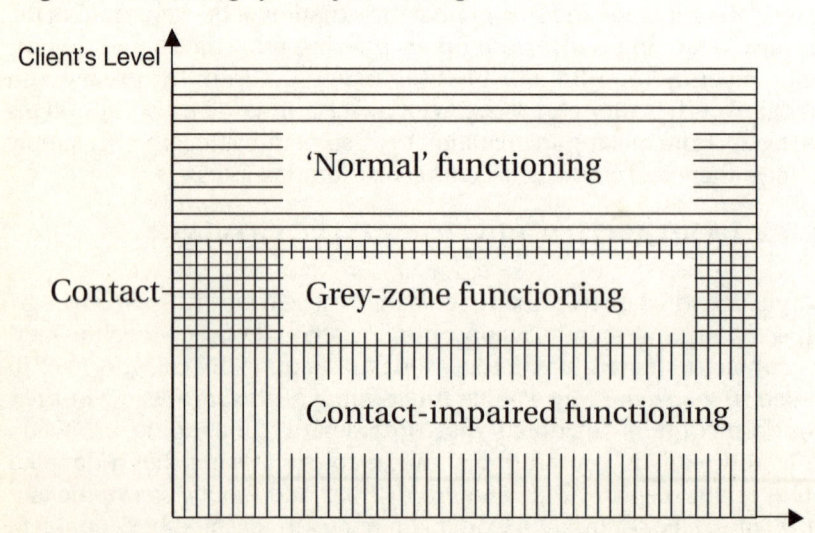

Figure 3: *Client X's grey zone functioning*

PRE-THERAPY AND CONTACT-WORK AND PRE-EXPRESSIVE FUNCTIONING

Grey-zone functioning is thus about an area that has some of the qualities of both ways of functioning. The way to handle this kind of mixed functioning involves the therapist staying tuned to the level present from moment-to-moment and by making a mixture of regular PC-therapy and Pre-Therapy reflections.

Figure 4: *Therapist's interventions matched with client's level of functioning*

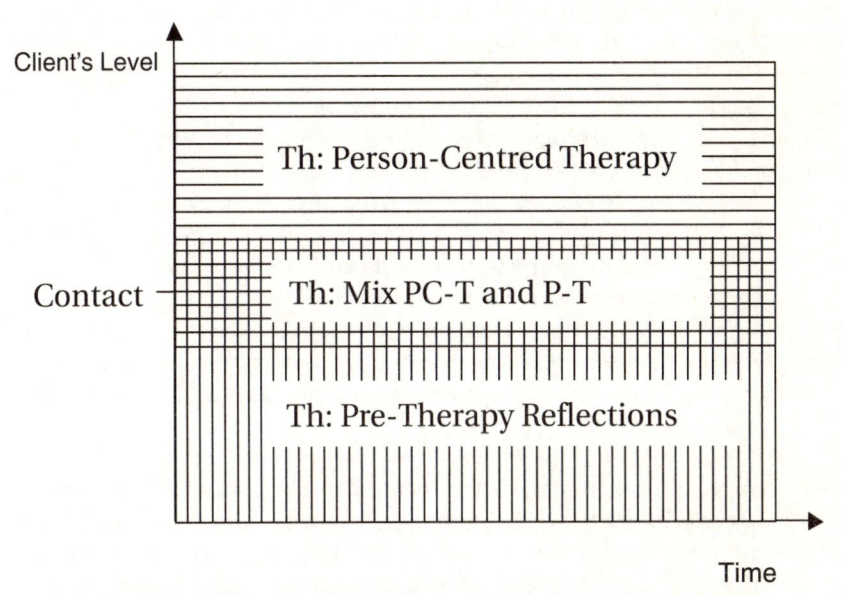

A case-illustration will highlight this way of working.

Illustration 1: grey-zone functioning in a ward situation
The first example takes place in the residential psychiatric hospital where I work (see Prouty, Van Werde and Pörtner op. cit.) and is an interaction between a professional caregiver and a patient who is functioning on the edge of contact. This means that the man is always close to psychotic functioning but nevertheless displays some 'anchored' functioning as well. The difficulty in dealing with this so-called 'grey-zone functioning' is to, on the one hand, have respect for the circumstantial givens (the ward setting, the house-rules, the history the patient and the nurse have together, and so on) whilst not closing down potentially meaningful pre-expressive communication on the other hand. In dealing with psychotic people, for example, it is very difficult to respect and safeguard the autonomy of the person worked with and to not reduce him psychologically and even ontologically to a dehumanised category of 'a patient'.

Simon is a young man, diagnosed as schizophrenic and who has already had several admissions on our ward (see also Van Werde, 2000). Jo, a nurse ('N') reports:

CONTACT AND PERCEPTION

'I'm sitting in the nurses' office when Simon ('S') enters, sits down on a chair by the door and asks the following question:
S1   Can you drive a race-bicycle, Jo?
(The question sounds as though it comes from a non-psychotic place and I respond on the same level)
N2   I think so, but I don't have one myself.
S3   Me neither, but I am learning it!
N4   So you do have one!?
S5   No, yes, I do have one.
(I presume psychotic content in his answer, want to make some space for that too, and thus use Pre-Therapy reflections to put the contradictory realities literally next to each other)
N6   WWR   First you say 'yes', than you say 'no'.
S7   I'm learning to ride a bicycle.
(surprised, I refer to a reality from the past)
N8   You do know how to ride a bicycle!? Do you remember yourself following that education programme during your previous admission? You did go from here to that programme by bicycle, didn't you?
S9   Yes, but that was an ordinary bicycle.
(I stay with the concrete and ask a question on that level)
N10   A race-bike and an ordinary bicycle don't differ that much, do they?
S11   No, but my bike does.
(S is getting a bit upset and agitated, obviously more is going on. I continue by literally reflecting his words, but put them as a question. This isn't 'real' Pre-Therapy, but has become my way of working with people going in and out of psychosis. Later on in our conversation you will see it happen again. It probably would be better if a question and a reflection were kept separate)
N12   Your bike does?
S13   Yes, I have a bicycle in my body.
(S is looking very attentive to me now. I could have reflected this by means of a FR. Also the previous intervention I could have used a FR to prevent S from just talking and not feeling, no real emotional processing)
N14   WWR   You have a race-bicycle in your body!?
S15   Yes, look, here are the spokes!
N16 BR, WWR   Here are the spokes.
S17   Yes, but I can't ride it because I can't get in the wheels.
(S now starts showing his psychotic system/functioning more and more. I word-for-word accept his pre-expressive messages, without wanting to go faster or further than he wants)
N18   WWR   (surprised) You can't get in the wheels.
S19   No, I still have a lot to practice.
(I again connect to the concreteness of his utterance and ask a question:)
N20   And how do you practise?
S21   By really trying to ride it.
(I continue by asking him what he means by 'really'. I carefully avoid to fill

PRE-THERAPY AND CONTACT-WORK AND PRE-EXPRESSIVE FUNCTIONING

in meanings or to introduce new themes, even when he sounds on a congruent level. I think that he can only stand a question as long as it matches where his attention is at and the given level of his functioning)

N22   What do you mean by 'really trying to ride it'?

S23   By doing it myself and not anybody else.

N24   WWR   When you used to ride the bicycle, it was not you but somebody else. Is that what you are saying?

S25   (obviously happy) Yeeesss, you got it! I want to try doing the things myself... just a while ago, I myself walked on the carpet in the living room for the first time!

N26   SR   You have been here on the ward for some time already, and you walk several times each day through the living room, on the carpet.

(I offer the shared reality in a very concrete way. I realise now that the way I did it was rather confronting, risking that S would feel criticised and not accepted. Our interacting does not stop here, however, probably since our relationship can stand it, since we have known each other for years)

S27   That isn't me, that was somebody else.

N28   WWR   That was somebody else.

(after a short moment of silence, he changes the subject. He evidently chooses to put the psychotic contents aside)

S29   The rear wheel of my bicycle squeaks.

(his remark seems to be on a congruent level. I continue on this level)

N30   How come?

S31   The brake shoes stay against the wheel after braking and that's why it squeaks.

(Seems a plausible and realistic explanation to me. I thus continue on this level and make a suggestion)

N32   Then you have to go to Luc at the day-care centre, he will be able to help you. They repair bicycles down there, you know.

S33   OK, I'll check the day-care centre.

(other patients come in, and S leaves the office)'

We see in this interaction how the nurse always tries to attune to the level of functioning of the client to establish and maintain contact. Sometimes his reactions take the form of a reflection (N16: BR, WWR: 'here are the spokes'), sometimes of a question (N20: 'and how do you practise?') or a comment (N26: 'you daily walk on the carpet'). The nurse stays with the concrete even when what has been said is contradictory (S5: yes and no the client has a bike) or even incomprehensible (S13: 'I have a bicycle in my body'). When the level of the client shifts up, the nurse follows (N32 and S33 about talking to each other about going to the day-care centre). We saw how shifting between Pre-Therapy reflections and interventions directed at the very concrete and present reality can be used to stay really person-centred, even in such an area of functioning where contact and contact-loss are so intertwined.

CONTACT-WORK WITH DECREASING LEVELS OF FUNCTIONING

What came to my attention recently, was the value of being acquainted with Pre-Therapy in order to be with someone's low level of functioning, even when their level of functioning is bound to decrease such as in cases of dementia or when a person is dying. This application is not so much therapeutically targeted (i.e. working towards an increase in functioning) but is more essentially and clearly a 'being with'. You can find the only published verbatim report of this kind of work so far (Van Werde and Morton, 1999) in Morton's pioneering and well-received book on Person-Centred Approaches to Dementia Care (Morton, 1999).

Figure 5: *Client's level of functioning (till death)*

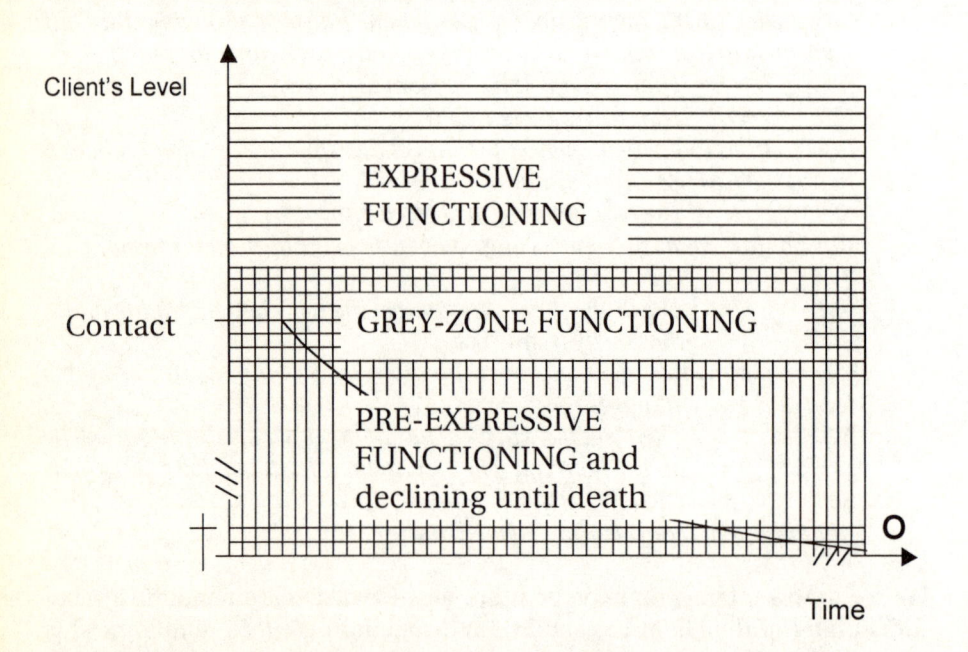

```
Client's Level
               ┌──────────────────────────┐
               │   EXPRESSIVE             │
               │   FUNCTIONING            │
               ├──────────────────────────┤
   Contact     │   GREY-ZONE FUNCTIONING  │
               ├──────────────────────────┤
               │   PRE-EXPRESSIVE         │
               │   FUNCTIONING and        │
               │   declining until death  │
               └──────────────────────────┘ O
                                        Time
```

Connected with this application of Pre-Therapy reflections, a third kind of outcome is to be expected. Besides the restoration of contact or moving the relationship into psychotherapy, the expectation is that the slope of the graph of inevitable contact-loss (figs. 5 and 6, line O) can become less steep (fig. 6, line PT).

This could be due to peaks of augmented functioning (fig. 7, line a), by successful crisis intervention (fig. 7, line c), by installing temporary plateaus of a non-decreasing level (fig. 7, line b), or by generally slowing down the rate at which the contact-level drops by effectively supporting the still-operative contact-functioning (fig. 6, line PT).

Figure 6: *Hypothetic outcome of therapist's P.T. interventions matched with with client's functioning till death*

PT ═ ═ ═ ═ level supported with P-T Reflecting

O ──────── normal declining level

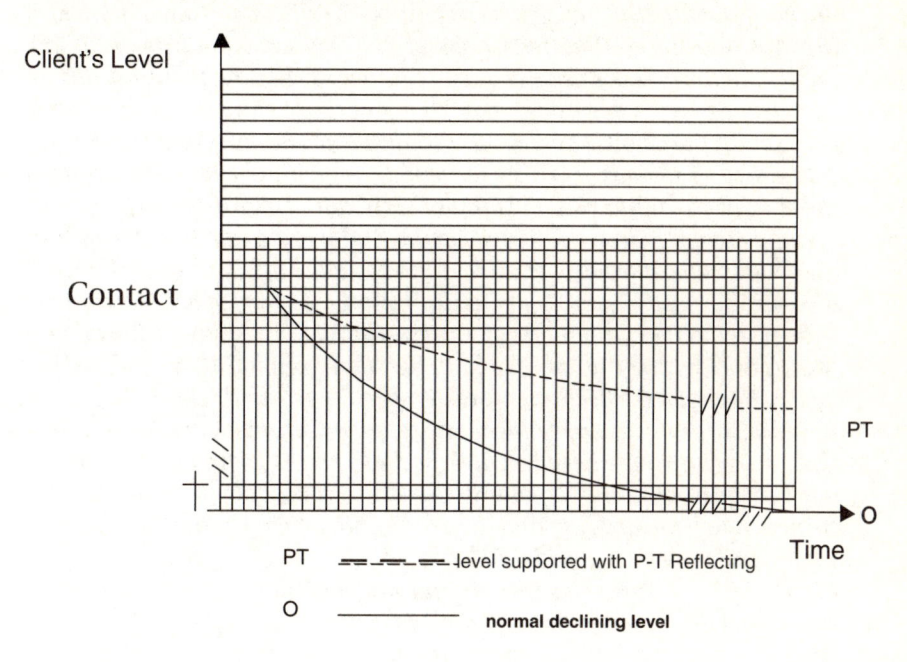

Figure 7: *Specific impact of therapist's P.T. contact work on declining functioning*

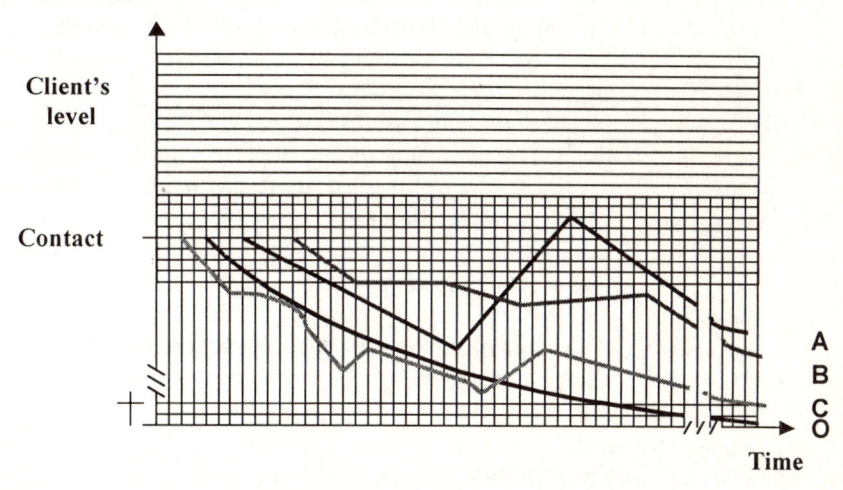

The following short case-illustration is given to show how the art of 'making contact' with these very low levels of functioning can be done. It is about someone in a home situation visiting a relative suffering Alzheimer's disease (and thus functioning on a lethally declining level).

177

CONTACT AND PERCEPTION

Illustration 2: being with a demented relative
Lisbeth Sommerbeck (2000) writes: 'To me, the decisive difference between the normal empathic reflections or empathic understanding responses of the PCA and the contact-reflections of Pre-Therapy is that the latter are applied with pre-expressive clients. This means that the therapist has no experience of an inner frame of reference of the client, no idea of what is going on in the client. The therapist understands nothing and feels "out of contact" with the client. This can be the case with clients suffering from many different ailments; for example, it is frequent with autistic, psychotic, mentally retarded and demented clients. And it is the case with the lady in the following example, a relative of mine, who suffers from Alzheimer's disease. She mostly just sits, staring expressionless ahead of her. After having learned about the contact-reflections, I realise how our (my own and others') attempts at getting into contact with her have been mostly way above her head. The contact-reflections are extremely concrete and I think that it was this quality that was enjoyable to my relative. I think it gave her a feeling that I was truly there with her, at least that's how it felt to me. The start of our conversation went something like this: I (L) sat down beside her (C), turned myself towards her and took her hand, which I know she likes:

L1	SR	I hold your hand.
C2		(Turns towards me and smiles at me)
L3	RR, SR	I hold your hand and you smile at me.
C4		(Smiles even more broadly)
L5	SR, FR	We are sitting next to each other and you look glad.
C6		I am. Do I look nice?

(She looks down on her dress and smooths out some creases in it. This is the first time in a very long while, I have seen her take such an initiative)

L7	WWR, SR	You ask: "Do I look nice?" and smooth the creases in your dress.
C8		Yes, I like it when I'm nicely dressed.
L9		Yes, you like it to look nice.

(I smile at her and squeeze her hand a little and we sit a while in silence...)

C10		(Looks out of the window)
L11	SR	You look out of the window - at the trees, and the bushes and the little pond.
C12		And the bird.
L13	WWR, SR	You look at the bird on the stone next to the pond.
C14		Yes, look, it's bathing.
L15		Yes.

(we watch it a while)

C16		Where are we?

(which I tell her, surprised and happy at her initiative and display of interest) And so on for about half an hour until she looked visibly sleepy and I just said nothing and she fell asleep. I am convinced this "contact-reflecting conversation" facilitated her potential to be in contact the most.'

What again is shown, is that Pre-Therapy reflections make contact possible by staying tuned in to the level of functioning present, even when it is so low as in the case of dementia. It involves listening and reacting in a way that specifically matches the client concretely. Instead of staring ahead or dozing off, this woman even reaches affective contact (by realising in C6 that she feels glad) and reality contact (she spots the bird outside in C12). The woman visiting is very surprised with the initiative taken by the relative (C16: 'where are we?'), when she starts looking for further anchorage herself! It is probable that, appealing to, and connecting with, the still-operative contact-possibilities might generally slow down the overall decline of functioning.

DISCUSSION

This approach has the appearance of being easy. It is certain that the technical aspects are less important than the human contact. The therapist or helper is not supposed to be a *contact machine* but rather, using Pre-Therapy can be seen as a sensitive act of existential empathy for ways of functioning that we normally neither take seriously nor pay attention to.

As Rogers did not explicitly comment on how to handle these levels of functioning, the work of Prouty has been well received by workers in the fields of psychiatry and care for the intellectually challenged. These are the obvious populations where Pre-Therapy can fill the simple need for knowing how to do your job in a thoroughly person-centred way.

We speak about '*facilitating* contact' and '*offering* contact' to stress that it is a very delicate act. In addition, the conditions as described by Rogers have to be met. It is thanks to (a) the attention paid to the concrete here and now, and (b) the capacity to stay with that (even in the expanded areas of clients' low-level functioning), that meaningful work can now be done. Psychological reductionism of the client or other is prevented. The other is more than simply and exclusively his experiencing, his biochemistry or his behaviour. He is listened to as a whole, as a person. An offer is made to him, if he wishes to and is ready for it. The helper/therapist starts from there and comes to a 'being with' and eventually to a 'letting go'.

As in regular person-centred psychotherapy (Rogers), this kind of work is meant to enable the other to master his own life, to become more and more empowered, to make his own decisions and to speak for himself as much as possible.

Many people have reported that they more easily came to 'be with' and even understood the other, by trying out some of the Pre-Therapy reflections in their concrete life situation. They no longer had to stay on the sideline when being confronted with someone suffering from psychosis, panic attacks, dementia and the like.

Prouty's Pre-Therapy reflections have a crucial place in the contact-work described here. The higher (in grey-zone functioning) and the lower (in lethally decreasing levels) these forms of pre-expressive functioning go, however, Pre-Therapy reflecting goes to the background. In higher functioning, 'regular' person-centred therapy takes over and everyday communication as asking questions, making comments and so on enters (see example 1). When death is approaching (see example 2), one tends to become more silent as a relative or caretaker and 'doing therapy' and 'facilitating contact' shifts to a deep 'being with', often in a non-verbal way.

REFERENCES

Clarke, C. (2001). *Pre-Therapy reflections applied to my son.* Personal communication and lecture at the Pre-Therapy International Network Meeting, N.P.K. St.-Camillus, St.-Denijs Westrem (België), October 26–7.

Coffeng, T. (1996). The delicate approach to early trauma. In Hutterer R., et al. (Eds.), *Client-centered and Experiential Psychotherapy, a paradigm in motion.* Frankfurt: Peter Lang, pp. 499–511.

Coffeng, T. (1998). Pre-experiencing: a way to contact trauma and dissociation. *The Folio*, 17(1), 43–53.

Dinacci, A. (1997). Ricerca sperimentale sul trattamento psicologico dei pazienti schizophrenici con la pre-therapia di Dr. G. Prouty. In *Psicologia della persona*, Vol II, nr 4.

Krietemeyer, B. (1999). *Practice experiences with Pre-Therapy.* Lecture at the Pre-Therapy International Network Meeting, N.P.K. St.-Camillus, St.-Denijs Westrem (België), October 22–3.

Lucieer, W. (1999). *Some reflections on Pre-Therapy.* Lecture at the Pre-Therapy International Network Meeting, N.P.K. St.-Camillus, St.-Denijs Westrem (België), October 22–3.

McWilliams, K. and Prouty, G. (1998). Life Enrichment of a Profoundly Retarded Woman: An application of Pre-Therapy. *The Person-Centered Journal*, 1, 29–35.

Morton, I. (1999). *Person-Centred Approaches to Dementia Care.* Bicester, Oxon: Winslow Press, pp. 139–66.

Peters, H. (1995). *Leny. Pre-Therapy met een ernstig zwakzinnige vrouw.* (demonstration video).

Peters, H. (2001). *Psychotherapeutische Zugänge zu Menschen mit geistiger Behinderung.* Stuttgart: Klett-Cotta.

Prouty, G. (1976). Pre-Therapy — a method of treating pre-expressive psychotic and retarded patients. *Psychotherapy: Theory, Research and Practice*, 13, 3, 290–5.

Prouty, G. (1994). *Theoretical evolutions in person-centered/experiential therapy. Applications to schizophrenic and retarded psychoses.* New York: Praeger.

Prouty, G. (1998). Pre-Therapy and the Pre-Expressive Self. *Person-Centered Practice.* 6, 2, 80–8.

Prouty, G. (2001a). A New Mode of Empathy: Empathic Contact. In Haugh, S. and Merry, T. (Eds.), *Rogers' Therapeutic Conditions: Evolution, theory and practice, Volume 2, Empathy.* Ross-on-Wye: PCCS Books.

Prouty, G. (2001b). Unconditional Positive Regard and Pre-Therapy: An Exploration. In Bozarth, J. and Wilkins, P. (Eds.), *Rogers' Therapeutic Conditions: Evolution, theory and practice, Volume 3, Unconditional Positive Regard.* Ross-on-Wye: PCCS Books.

Prouty, G., Van Werde, D. and Pörtner, M. (1998). *Prä-Therapie.* Stuttgart: Klett-Cotta.

Prouty, G., Van Werde, D. and Pörtner, M. (2001). *Pre-Therapie.* Maarssen: Elsevier gezondheidszorg.

Prouty, G., Van Werde, D. and Pörtner, M. (in press). *Pre-Therapy.* Ross-on-Wye, PCCS Books.

Read Mental Hospital team. (2000). Lecture at the Pre-Therapy International Network Meeting, N.P.K. St.-Camillus, St.-Denijs Westrem (België), October 20–1.

Rogers, C. (1957). The necessary and sufficient conditions of therapeutic personality change. *Journal of Consulting Psychology*, 21, 95–103.

Sommerbeck, L. (2000). Personal communication.

Van Werde, D. (2000). Persoonsgerichte psychosezorg: de tegenstelling 'maatschappij' en 'proces' overstegen? *Tijdschrift Cliëntgerichte Psychotherapie*, 38, 4, 274–9.

Van Werde, D. and Morton, I. (1999). The relevance of Prouty's Pre-Therapy to Dementia Care. In: Morton, I., *Person-Centred Approaches to Dementia Care.* Bicester, Oxon: Winslow Press, pp. 139–66.

Van Werde, D. and Prouty, G. (1992). Het herstellen van het psychologisch contact bij een schizofrene jonge vrouw: een toepassing van Pre-Therapie. *Tijdschrift Klinische Psychologie*, 22, 4, 269–80.

Van Werde, D. and Willemaers, R. (1992). *Werken aan contact: een illustratie van Pre-Therapie met een chronisch psychotische vrouw.* Gent, Seminarie en Laboratorium voor psychologische begeleiding, Rijksuniversiteit. Videoband met begeleidende brochure.

Van Wyngene, C., Dumon, L. and Coninckx, B. (2000). Werken aan contact: hoe contactreflecties een proces op gang kunnen brengen. *Tijdschrift voor hulpverleners in de geestelijke gezondheidszorg*, 2, 165–78.

Zinschitz, E. (1999). Personal communication.

10 Presence: Im-media-te co-experiencing and co-responding. Phenomenological, dialogical and ethical perspectives on contact and perception in person-centred therapy and beyond.

Peter F. Schmid

Abstract. *Although this volume appears as the last in the series, it deals with the precondition to the conditions described in volumes 1 to 3. Without relationship and its perception, the other conditions would make no sense. This chapter also links the description of the single conditions and brings them together under a common perspective. It first sheds light on what contact (or relationship) and perception mean from a dialogical stance[1]. Then it examines their significance for person-centred psychotherapy in particular — on both sides, the therapist's and the client's — how they develop in the therapeutic process and where they are aiming at. A phenomenological analysis deals with different kinds of relationships, their processual nature and the diverse forms of encounter: from the initial encounter of the therapist who meets the client, to a mutual encounter relationship. The quality of an encounter relationship in person-centred therapy leads from contact to presence in the encounter, from (self-)perception to (self-)realisation and (self-)acknowledgement.*

Person-centred therapy, be it in groups or in a dyad, describes 'a way of being with', which develops from relative one-sidedness to togetherness and from a relatively restricted perception of oneself and the others to a relatively open self-concept and view of the others. The therapist's task is to perceive the client as a person and respond to the client as a person, i.e. to establish and maintain a secure and yet challenging relationship. In doing so, his or her underlying 'way of being with' the client is 'presence' in the meaning of dialogical philosophy: the existential foundation for encounter, for this 'being together by being counter', is to be there, to be 'present'. From this point of view, presence can be understood as joint experiencing with the client in the given instant. Furthermore, from an epistemological perspective it is a moment-to-moment-process of joint responding to the given developments, experiences and challenges within the therapeutic relationship, which happens in the 'kairos', the fruitful moment. The core conditions of authenticity, acknowledgement and comprehension, carefully described by Carl Rogers and analysed in the three preceding volumes, explain the way in which the therapist opens up to the revelation of the client in the im-media-te presence. These attitudes also support and foster the client's striving for self-awareness and

---
1. See Schmid, 2001a, footnote 2.
Acknowledgement I am very grateful to Pete Sanders for his help in making the text understandable to the English reader.

encounter ability and, in addition, depict the changes clients undergo in such a relationship in dealing with themselves and others. Together, client(s) and therapist(s) aim for a person-to-person-relationship without preconceived means — co-experiencing and co-responding, thus co-creating a facilitative relationship.

'In the beginning there is relationship' (Martin Buber)[2]

KAIROS — THE FERTILE POTENTIAL OF THE PRESENT MOMENT

In ancient Greece there was the figure of the god *Kairós*. As the god of the fertile instant, of the favourable opportunity, he was thought to be a young man with wings at his heels, always walking on tiptoe, in the right hand holding a sharp knife, with a thick front mop of hair and close-cropped in the back.[3]

His wings symbolise that he is flying like the wind, always hurrying. The knife reminds that the favourable opportunity is sharper than any point. The front mop of hair enables anybody encountering him to seize him, when he is hurrying past — but only for one moment! From the back it's impossible to catch him; once he passed, it's over: there is no chance to grasp him at the close-cropped back.[4]

This means: if you don't use a fertile moment, it's over. Or conversely: the fertile moment is always *now*. The moment for the change is now and here. The moment to influence the future is now and here. The moment to profit from the past is now and here. There is only one time: the present. Future is the anticipation of what is coming in the present, past is the remembrance — in the present — of what happened. We only live in one time: in the present. We exist here and we exist now.

'*Kairós*' is the Greek word for the quality of time.[5] The applied meaning of 'kairos' denotes the existential time of the human being, the subjective meaning of time (while 'chrónos' means the objective time, which is counted by a watch). In the Bible 'kairós' is a central term[6] indicating that every moment is a moment for decision with the chance for encounter.

Kairology, an interdisciplinary science, is the knowledge and art of the right action in the right moment: how to read the signs of the time and how to act according to them. Kairological thinking tries to find out what 'living in the moment', grasping the kairos, means existentially. One of its founders was Søren Kierkegaard (1844, 1855), who stressed the fact that always the very 'moment' is the source of change. Thus it is necessary to perceive the moment and to seize it.

---

2. Buber, 1963, p. 604; intentionally and enthusiastically formulated according to the beginning of the Gospel of John (1:1): 'In the beginning was the Word'; also cf. compare the first words of the Bible: 'In the beginning God created the heaven and the earth' (Genesis 1:1). See Schmid, 1998c ('Im Anfang war Gemeinschaft').
3. The original statue of this god stood in Olympia, a copy of it still exists in a monastery in Trogir, Dalmatia.
4. In German there is the saying 'eine Gelegenheit beim Schopf packen [to seize an opportunity at the front mop of hair]'. More about a kairologic understanding of the person-centred relationship in Schmid, 1994, pp. 201–57.
5. As opposite to 'chrónos', which means the quantitative aspect of time — also derived from a god, Chrónos, who wolfed down his children.
6. Koh 3:1–8; Mt 25:1–13; 2 Cor 5:2.

CONTACT AND PERCEPTION

When we really take the moment seriously, we say goodbye to conventions and patterns and open ourselves up for new sights and developments. As a consequence, taking the moment seriously always demands a decision. Another kairologist, Karl Jaspers (1932), points out that the 'moment' is the very unity, the meeting point of history, present and future, of 'time and eternity', and therefore life can be understood as continuum of fertile moments. Hans Rotter (1993) emphasises the ethical and social moment of the kairos, which always asks the question: what's up for decision (for me, for our group, or for society) now?

Person-centred thinking is kairotic, person-centred therapy is a kairological therapy. It has its sources in this tradition of the kairotic benefit of the moment. This stance is opposite to a traditional psychodynamic understanding which comprehends the present only or mainly out of the past, and sees life as a series of reproductions of patterns gained early in life. The person-centred approach also stands opposite to an a-historical thinking which can be found for example in behaviour therapy methods. From a person-centred view the present moment is seen as the instant which encompasses past, present and future. The person-centred understanding of psychotherapy is rooted in the experience of the present moment as the fertile possibility to further actualise the person's capabilities. When we talk about personal presence[7] in psychotherapy we refer to the immediate experience of (two or more) persons encountering each other in a given moment, in a moment-by-moment process in the respective present.

Person-centred therapy understands therapy as 'relationship or encounter' (Rogers, 1962, p. 185), where the 'moment-to-moment encounter of psychotherapy' (Rogers, 1980, p. 2155) happens in the immediate present. This notion corresponds to the existential attitude of *'presence'*. What follows is an attempt to explore and explain the nature of this relationship, its preconditions and its development from a phenomenological, dialogical and ethical perspective. Both contact and perception, and their development during the therapeutic relationship, will be examined from epistemological and encounter philosophical points of view in parallel throughout this chapter.

FROM CONTACT AND PERCEPTION ...

Relationship was a central category of person-centred psychotherapy from the very beginning

Carl Rogers and the person-centred approach as such were quite often blamed for being individualistic, for promoting a one-sided, self-centred, even selfish

---

7. Throughout this chapter '(personal) presence' (in German: 'Gegenwärtigkeit') is used in the sense of encounter or dialogical philosophy which means to fully live in the present (in German: 'Gegenwart'). It is used to emphasize the intrinsic interrelation of the 'core conditions' and their encounter-philosophical import. Used within the frame of an encounter relationship, it points in the direction of Rogers' (1975, p. 4) 'way of living with'. It does not indicate rare moments or anything additional to the well-known conditions rather it indicates the underlying quality of the person-centred relationship as such. Rogers (e.g. 1986) himself used the term 'presence' differently, when he asked himself whether this might be an altered state of consciousness, talking about the mystical, transcendent, spiritual and additional quality of the relationship in special moments. (This is discussed in detail in Schmid, 1996, pp. 228–44, 283–6; see also 2001a, pp. 224–5.)

understanding of the human being. Together with other humanistic orientations in psychology and psychotherapy it was held responsible for supporting an egocentric society, as being 'typical US-American'.

To refute this reproach, advocates of Person-Centered Therapy often divide Rogers' work into two main periods: the individualistic one, with concentration on the self and single therapy, and the encounter-oriented one with the main focus on the relationship and on groups, large groups and political issues. Although it is obvious that Rogers put much more attention to the individual in the beginning, this argument ignores the fact that his basic statement, published in 1957, implies both essential dimensions of an image of the human being as a person, the individual and the relational one.[8] The first of his six well-known 'necessary and sufficient conditions for psychotherapeutic personality change' already deals with the interpersonal relation, stating that therapist and client must be in 'psychological contact'. Rogers himself said[9] that he originally wanted to use the term 'relationship' instead of 'psychological contact', but was afraid he might lose academic recognition and thus made use of the term only in the explanatory text and as a subtitle for the explanation of the condition, not in the formulation of the condition as such: 'The first condition specifies that a minimal relationship, a psychological contact, must exist. I am hypothesising that significant positive personality change does not occur except in a relationship' (Rogers, 1957, p. 96).

The five other conditions define the characteristics of such a relation. All of them include the belief that the human being has the possibility and tendency to develop in a constructive way on the basis of his or her resources, *if* a certain form of relationship is provided. In other words, the six conditions presuppose that a human being develops constructively on his or her own, if he or she finds him- or herself in a facilitative relationship. Without hypothesising an actualising tendency, which rests on both the individual resources *and* the ability of relating, the conditions two to six would make no sense.

In this statement we find these two dialectic dimensions of being human described, for which, in the occidental history of theology and philosophy, the term 'person' was coined, namely autonomy and interconnectedness (or relationality), independence and interdependence, self-reliance and commitment, sovereignty and solidarity.[10] In his precise description of person-centred psychotherapy, in the textbook by Koch, Rogers (1980, p. 2153) explicitly puts these two dimensions, autonomy and relationality, at the beginning of his article: 'Client-centered therapy is continually developing as a way of being with persons that facilitates healthy change and growth. Its central hypothesis is [1] that the person has within himself or herself *vast resources for self-understanding*

---

8. See the philosophical meaning of 'person' and its implication for the person-centred approach: Schmid, 1991, 1998a.
9. Personal communication, June 1984.
10. This is elaborated in detail in Schmid, 1991; see also 1998a. In the same way Swildens (1999) underlines the dependency on others in the perspective of the person-centred image of the human being: 'The other is part of one's self-actualising perspective'. He thinks of this as an implicit precondition to the person-centred approach to therapy and also points out that the unavoidable Other often is opponent first of all. Thus, according to Swildens, conflict, aggression and antagonism are part of our fate.

and for constructive changes in ways of being and behaving *and* [2] that *these resources can best be released and realized in a relationship* with certain definable qualities.' (Italics and numbering mine.) The fundamental hypothesis of the actualising tendency, which Rogers consistently asserts to be the only axiom, must be seen in the *dialectical* tension of these two dimensions (Schmid, 1999, 2001b). Whatever other motives might have been important to introduce the term 'person-centred' later on, it is obvious and clear that this was done consciously and purposely to denote an anthropology central to the 'person'-centred approach.[11]

So the relational dimension of the person-centred approach to the human being, and to psychotherapy, was formulated from the very beginning.[12] It was taken for granted in acting in a non-directive, client-centred way, even if its theoretical conceptualisation as encounter, and its practical differentiation in multiple forms of acting were elaborated only in later periods of the development of the paradigm. That the focal point was on the individual aspect at first, must be understood as necessary for historical reasons, particularly in rejecting the psychiatric, psychoanalytic and behaviouristic models.

The centrality of the relational conception is underlined by the fact that Rogers (1957, p. 96) speaks of 'contact' as a *precondition*. In other words: contact — relationship — is the underlying essence of a person-centred approach as being truly an '*approach*', a way of moving towards somebody.

This makes clear that person-centred psychotherapy is *the* relationship therapy (see Zurhorst, 2001), because it 'works' with the relationship only. All other forms of therapy have additional methods, skills, practices, etc. and only 'use' the relationship 'in order to . . .' (if indeed they acknowledge it at all). The person-centred way does not take the relationship as a precondition for special forms of treatment in addition to it, but as a precondition for the conditions who specify the kind of relationship as such. This is a fundamentally important difference and separates person-centred psychotherapy essentially from all other therapeutic orientations. It is also the core distinction between genuine person-centred therapy and other forms of therapy which claim to be in the Rogerian tradition.

Contact means touching and being touched

This raises the question, what do contact and relationship mean exactly in a person-centred context?

Rogers (1957, p. 96) specifies 'psychological contact' as 'a minimal relationship'. He defines that contact means that 'each makes some perceived difference in

---

11. For more references see Schmid, 1994, p. 107.
12. E.g. in a manuscript from 1955 (quoted in Schmid, 2001a, pp. 214f) Rogers gives a process definition of the person where relationality and individuality can be found as the two characteristics of the person. (More material on this can be found in Schmid, 1994, p. 107.) In 1940 at a lecture he later considered to be the 'birthday' of the person-centred approach Rogers (1942, p. 30) said: 'For the first time this approach lays stress upon the therapeutic relationship itself as a growth experience . . . In some respects this may be the most important aspect of the approach we shall describe'. (Details on the use of 'relationship' and 'encounter' by Rogers and others see Schmid, 1994, pp. 172–82.)

the experiential field of the other. Probably it is sufficient if each makes some "subceived" difference, even though the individual may not be consciously aware of this impact' (ibid.). This means that it requires at least some openness, some capability of awareness, of being able to be influenced by the Other.[13]

'Contact' means 'connection'; to have 'psychological contact' denotes to enter a relationship or to be in a relationship. Etymologically 'con-tact' (from Latin 'contactus') means 'to be in tact together', to be tuned, to be tuned in. It derives from Latin 'tangere' respectively 'contingere' which mean 'touch closely, border on, be contiguous to',[14] which shows the term's original bodily meaning. In addition, the substantive 'tactus' means 'feeling', 'sensibility' (hence 'tactful' and 'tactless'). To be tactful means to do the right thing at the right time. The musical meaning of 'tact' ('beat, time') comes from the meaning of 'tactus' as a measure for rhythmic movement — a feeling for tact is necessary when playing together (not only in music).[15]

So, in other words, and when formulated from an encounter philosophical perspective, to come into contact means to touch and to be touched. Physically touching somebody does not only make a difference to the one being touched but also to the one touching; the same applies to psychological or emotional or spiritual touching and being touched.

The direction of the movement in therapy always goes from the client to the therapist

In everyday life, contact may happen intentionally (think of an individual making a phone call) or unintentionally, i.e. by coincidence (think of two people colliding in a crowd). If at least one of the persons involved is interested in the other one, the contact which came about has a chance of lasting and developing into a continuing relationship.

Psychotherapy does not start out of unintentional collision. It can start with both: either the client addresses the therapist or the therapist 'makes contact' with the client. In most cases it is the client who takes the initiative, but there are also situations where the therapist is the initiator, e.g. in hospitals or prisons. Although the initiative might be different, the 'nature of the contact' has to be the same, if it is to become therapy.

Both client and therapist must be open and ready — the client at least to a minimal degree. If the therapist is open and ready for being touched, the client can touch him and vice versa. If one of them is not open to it and therefore not ready for it, contact will not happen.

When a relationship or contact does happen, both touching and being

---

13. To emphasise the encounter philosophical meaning, 'the Other' is written with a capital letter.
14. Compare the meaning of 'contact' in electrical engineering. All etymological specifications are taken from Duden, 1963; Hoad, 1986.
15. Duden, 1963, p. 356; Hoad, 1996, pp. 94, 481. It is also of interest that 'con-/com-/col-/cor-/co-' (from Latin 'con, com' = 'together') is related to 'contra' ('against'), which is built with the comparative suffix '-tero'. The Greek equivalent probably is 'katá', the German 'ge' (Duden, 1963, p. 352). The relation of 'con' and 'contra' and the shift of meaning from 'being together' to 'being opposite to, against' is relevant for the understanding of the meaning of 'en-counter' (see Schmid, 1994, 1998b, 2001a, and also below).

touched-are involved, but when we examine these processes more carefully, it becomes clear that it is always the client who 'comes first'.

If the contact is the outcome of the client's initiative, which is the usual procedure, e.g. in private practice, the client is the one who 'touches' first and the therapist is the one 'to be touched' first.

If contact happens on the therapist's initiative it is still the person-centred therapist who is touched first, when they first get sight of the client as a person. (If not, this will not become person-centred therapy, but some kind of directive treatment, or 'guidance' in the sense of the client being guided.) Addressing the client comes out of becoming aware of him or her as a person and thus from the very beginning is a response to the client's appearance. So, it is the client from whom the movement in the beginning relationship comes, even if the therapist is the initiator of the coming together.

A basic difference becomes obvious: on the side of the client, the only requirement is a minimal openness to sense or experience being addressed and thus to perceive or 'subceive' the difference in the phenomenological field by being contacted (as Rogers clearly states). On the side of the therapist the requirement is qualitatively different: he or she must perceive the client as a person and thus 'be present as a person' him- or herself. This is the underlying essence of the so-called core conditions and will be discussed at the end of this chapter.[16]

As shown in the etymological note above, contact is always the contact between *different* 'ones', whose 'tact' should go together. It therefore should be noted that it only makes sense to speak of contact if there is both difference *and* equality. The meaning of 'contact' in psychotherapy points to the fact that all understanding of therapy is based on the sameness *and* diversity of (at least) two human beings. What we have in common enables us to empathise and thus to do psychotherapy; what is different between us, stimulates us to increase the sensitivity of empathy and, therefore, self-exploration and the development of the client's identity.

Contact leads to communication

Contact is a precondition for communication (which might happen in a lot of ways, not only verbally). It is impossible to not communicate once there is contact. (In the 'worst' case the communication takes place in order to end the contact by purposely not continuing the contact, which itself is also a specific form of communication.)

Communication always aims at a common ground, even if there is no shared aim to have joint action or solidarity. Again it is etymology which helps to understand: 'com-munity' and 'com-mun-ication' come from Latin 'munus' meaning 'wall', and points to people who have a common wall, which means that they share a common ground: they live together. If one thinks of a medieval city, surrounded by a wall, the underlying meaning of commonality becomes immediately clear.

Communication always aims at commonality, at 'communion', which means

---

16. The quality of therapy as a response to the client is considered in Schmid, 2001c.

participating in the same. Thus the understanding of communication shows that it is *action aiming towards togetherness*.[17]

It follows that any attempt to separate communication from action does not make sense and the corresponding differentiation between action-oriented therapies and communication-oriented therapies is invalid and artificial. Even therapy by 'purely' verbal means is joint acting together, and indeed every form of action is intrinsically communication. Therefore, it is also nonsense to pursue the idea of *adding* action to communication in therapy. Only an understanding of therapeutic communication which aims at an understanding of it as *joint action*, and its symbolisation, corresponds to a *person*-centred comprehension of therapy. This also implies that therapists 'allowing' their clients to only *talk* and (often by merely not being open to anything else themselves) 'rule out' any other forms of communication, be it bodily or artistic (drawing, dancing, playing music, acting, writing and so on), are not at all person- or client-centred but most likely therapist-centred: they only let happen what they feel comfortable with, thus limiting the clients to the therapist's own limits. The same applies to any therapists who force their clients into certain ways of communicating. Therapists should not limit the client's symbolisation by limiting it to verbalisation or particular styles of verbalisation. Clients should have the freedom to choose their way of expressing themselves and communicating to the therapist (Schmid, 1994, pp. 402–4).

Contact also means to keep in touch

The task in psychotherapy is not only to get in contact but also to maintain contact: '... these six conditions exist, and continue over a period of time' (Rogers, 1957, p. 96). Random contacts often disappear as quickly as they appear. For psychotherapy it is necessary to stay in contact and to develop the growing relationship. This means that it is in some cases necessary to actively maintain the relationship as such, in order not to 'lose' the client.

To come into contact is the beginning but where does this lead those involved? It could lead in a lot of directions. One possibility might be to control or even dominate the other or the others, which in some cases might derive from being afraid to be controlled or dominated. Controlling the other might be an attempt to avoid this (by applying the same means, but in the other direction). Another possibility is to subordinate the other which is also most likely to be a way of avoiding conflict and anxiety and might be seen as a reverse power struggle. Sometimes the one seemingly controlled is the one doing the controlling as can

---

17. In my understanding, this is the foundation of why the theory of psychotherapy can adequately and truly be understood and conceptualised as Handlungswissenschaft ('action science') — a term introduced by Schelsky (1963) following the expressions 'behavioural science' and 'action research'. In respect to the essence of knowledge 'action science' — also as a theory, not only as a practice of action — derives from and relates to action and draws immediate consequences for further action. The theory of psychotherapy is gained from an inductive approach, based on experience, it uses empirical methods, is interdisciplinary in orientation, co-operating with other 'action sciences' and human sciences. It does not only analyse and interpret practice, but it imparts orientation for further action, aims at improving further action. Similarly person-centred research intrinsically is action research (Schmid, 1988c, pp. 164–5).

be seen in the various forms of sadomasochistic relationships. A third way is to negotiate on rules for the relationship, which in most cases is done anyway and without intention.

The way to go in person-centred psychotherapy is to open up for an encounter relationship that is as mutual as possible. It is only feasible to maintain a contact which took place, if at least one of the persons involved stays *present*. Therefore presence is the goal of contact and is what the core conditions are all about (see below).

Perception means to take what is offered

Rogers' (1957, p. 96) sixth condition states that the 'communication to the client of the therapist's empathic understanding and unconditional positive regard is to a minimal degree achieved'. Perception is what the client 'takes' (etymologically 'per-ceive' means 'to take thoroughly'[18]) from the therapist.

There is an eminent intrinsic connection between contact and perception[19] — they require and imply each other. More precisely there are three steps in maintaining a therapeutic relationship: (1) the clients 'enter the stage' explicitly, implicitly bring themselves into play as persons in need — the starting and 'moving' point, which always is on the client's side. This is where the 'motivation' comes from. (2) It is followed by the initial encounter (see below) of the therapist with the client and — as a response — the therapist's offer of his presence, i.e. the offer of a kind of relationship characterised by the core conditions. (3) The final step is 'the client's perception of the therapist' (Rogers, 1957, p. 99), which means that 'the client perceives, to a minimal degree, the acceptance and empathy which the therapist experiences for him' (ibid.) or, in other words, that the therapist's 'presence' makes a difference in his perception.

Like 'relationship', 'perception' also is a process which develops during psychotherapy on the client's as well as on the therapist's side. It will therefore be examined in the following considerations in its importance for both of them. In its full personal way it is 'personal realisation' (see below).

... TO PRESENCE AND PERSONAL REALISATION

The nature of a person-centred relationship is neither objectification nor identification but intersubjectivity

What happens after coming into contact? As already stated: relationship[20] is not relationship. Human beings have a lot of different possibilities to relate to things, to other humans and to themselves.

1. One way is *objectification*: to make something or somebody an object means

---

18. For details see Schmid, 2001b, p. 58; for the related 'ac-cept-ance' see Schmid, 2001c, p. 156.
19. If one of them is lacking therapy is impossible for the time being and pre-therapy (Prouty et al., 2001) might be necessary.
20. Relation derives from Latin 'relatio': 'latus' is the past participle of 'ferre' which means 'carry, bring' and 'move'. Here etymologically the processual quality of a relationship might be seen (Hoad, 1986, p. 396).

to put it, him or her opposite to oneself (Latin 'obicere') and to view it from the outside: look *on* it, think and talk *about* it, him or her. To talk *about* is not only possible if talking about things (e.g. talking about a house) or a third human (e.g. talking about a common friend); it is also possible to talk *with* someone *about* him or her. This is the case, e.g. when talking about diseases in form of a traditional medical diagnostic way or talking about somebody's work or performance, e.g. in school, or talking about somebody's thoughts and feelings from an outside perspective. The same applies to thinking and talking about oneself. The ability to 'put oneself outside of oneself' and look at oneself from an outside perspective, i.e. to objectify oneself, is a basic characteristic of the human being (and, e.g. in therapy, a central source of the freedom to change and deliberately develop in a certain direction). Other terms for this include the 'excentricity' of the human being (Plessner, 1928).

In most relationships in everyday life, the objectifying perspective and relationship is the usual one. It is a necessary way of relating and communicating and thus of living one's life. It is related to what Buber (1923) calls the 'I-It-relationship'. Here it might make sense to mention that it is a fundamental mistake to devalue this kind of relationship and exclusively estimate the value of I-Thou-relationships. Nobody could live in I-Thou-relationships only, since nobody could evaluate, judge, or make decisions without objectifying.

2. Another way is *identification*: in identifying I equate myself completely with the other, set myself in the place of the other, I feel like him or her, I think the same way they do, I completely lose distance, there is no moment of opposition or difference. Both merge into one.

3. Fundamentally different from both of these ways of relating is to relate to the other (be it a thing, be it a person) as a whole and in their essence without ignoring my own essence, i.e. keeping the difference. This is called a *personal relationship* (of which a person-centred relationship, e.g. in therapy, is a special case).[21] In the case of a relationship to another person, it is a subject-to-subject-relationship or a person-to-person relationship. This way of relating traditionally is named *encounter* (or 'meeting'[22]).

In this case the proper question for a personal relationship towards a concrete Other is not 'What is this?' (as with an object) and not 'Who is this?' (as about another individual), but it is 'Who are *you*?' — thus indicating the dialogical nature of encounter.

The differences between objectification and personal encounter become obvious when having a look at those characteristics of such a relationship, which for psychotherapy are held as 'core conditions'. Such a relationship does not aim to gain knowledge about the Other but rather is concerned to acknowledge him or her thus fostering self-acknowledgement. Encounter itself is furthered by acknowledgement (Schmid, 2001c) — its aim is not to know something about

---

21. Encounters can be friendly and loving, but also frightening and hostile. I can encounter something or somebody which or whom I experience as a threat, even a life threat. In this case there is no objectification either but rather a 'being impressed' and shaken or even shocked deeply in my existence.
22. To 'meet' means 'come face to face or into contact with' (from the thirteenth century on, Hoad, 1986, p. 288).

them but it is a way to connect, to establish contact. Its nature is holistic, it is belief and love instead of certainty and knowledge only. (I can believe that I love or that I am loved or not, but I cannot know this.) In terms of relating to feelings and attitudes of another person, empathy is the way of relating in the personal encounter, while 'cognitive social-perspective-taking' is the corresponding way of relating in objectifying forms of relationships (2001b). Such a relationship does not aim to be a directional relationship from an expert to somebody about whom an expertise is given, rather it aims to be a relationship between person and person; it is characterised by authenticity (2001a; see below).[23]

In an encounter relationship the usual active-passive-relation of subject and object is transcended into intersubjectivity: a We-relationship. This constitutes a situation of *'with'*, of *'co-'*, of togetherness.

Although there might be a striving for commonality in an intersubjective relationship, the Other is respected as a completely different individual, always having in mind that he or she is truly an Other in the sense of encounter philosophy, not to be possessed or destroyed or ignored (see 2001a, p. 217).

Therefore, encounter always has to do with *'counter'*, but in a completely different way than is the case in objectification. The human being as *'the* being counter' (Buber, 1986, p. 83) has the capability of having the relationship opposite to the other. To gain distance is a specific human quality — as a precondition for encounter. 'Being counter' is the foundation for meeting face to face, to acknowledge, to empathise with. Being counter appreciates the Other in his autonomy and as somebody of worth to be dealt with. Standing face to face avoids both, identification and objectification; it enables encounter (see Schmid, 2001c).

Whilst Moreno was the first (as early as in Freudian times) to think of aspects of therapy as encounter (1969; see Schmid, 1994), Rogers was the first to understand therapy as an encounter relationship in all its facets. In person-centred therapy the client is not only trusted and respected in terms of contents (the 'what'), but also in terms of the way to proceed (the 'how') and the therapist is 'simply' their facilitator (i.e. not an 'expert'). It is very different in for example gestalt therapy or classical psychodrama where the therapist is the one controlling the procedure and the specialist who takes the lead on the 'how', (e.g. regarding the methods).[24]

To encounter another person with acknowledgement instead of objectifying him or her by trying to get knowledge about the Other, is an essential paradigm

---

23. Generally, relationship can either be seen as preceding encounter, as a precondition to encounter, as the substratum of what can become fully through encounter, like Buber in 'I and Thou' (1923, p. 36) does, or can be seen as the fruit of encounter, when the actual encounter relationship emerges into a latent, lasting relationship (Buber, 1962/63, I; 1963; see van Balen, 1992, p. 170). Relationship can be first, but also spring from encounter. It can be both, disposition and consequence (see Böckenhoff, 1970, p. 434). It can be the space for encounter ('Begegnungsraum', Heindler, 1983, p. 299) and the outcome of encounter. Relationship, it follows, can be understood as facilitating encounter as well as resulting from encounter.

24. There is also an essential difference between (unintentional) openness to the experiencing (out of the attitude of encounter) and (intentional) focusing of the experiencing (out of the process expert's stance of furthering certain processes within the client) or even steering the client's process by process-oriented interventions. This view categorises person-centred, experiential and process-directive as different forms of therapy (Schmid, 2001d, 2002a).

shift in psychotherapy and helping relations of various kinds — it is the epistemological foundation of person-centredness.

Acknowledgement, the personal way of perception as realisation of the Other

The qualitative difference between objectifying and encountering is the way of perception: in an encounter we do not perceive the outside, the 'seeming', but the 'core': we perceive the essence of what we encounter. This means we do encounter the *reality*, be it a person or not. Hence the term 'realisation' properly describes what personal perception means. Real-ising means to become aware of what *really* is there (the Latin word 'res' means 'the things' themselves, as they 'really' are; compare the use of the term 'realness' by Rogers to describe the nature of congruence), thus pointing to the authentic being of a person. Personal realisation means to be open for the Other in his or her concrete, typical, unique way of being, in contrast with observing them as an object or on the surface only. In personal realising we touch the Other's reality; we do not only 'take' ('perceive') what we see and hear of them, we also 'take' what they might be and become. This means to accept them not only in their actual reality but, moreover, in their possibilities. It is a way of becoming aware of somebody in a process of opening towards the Other's actuality *and* possibilities. Buber (1984) coined the phrase of 'Realphantasie' *('phantasy of the real')*, which indicates that personal perception goes beyond a superficial view and encompasses the open future of the Other. Personal perception is more than getting to know, it is to acknowledge — the personal way of realising.[25]

It is obvious that such a way of perceiving provides an incredible power of support for the Other's development. And it also shows that self-realisation is only possible through being realised and acknowledged by somebody else. It marks an understanding of self-realisation as realisation both in and out of the relations in which the individual lives. Self-realisation is never possible without the realisation of the Other. In therapy this applies to both client and therapist.

If the personal perception of the Other is the basis of the relationship, an *ethical relation* is created. The epistemological paradigm change for psychotherapy achieved by Carl Rogers from knowledge to ac-knowledge-ment and from percept-ion to ac-cept-ance on part of the therapist, leads us to understand him or her as somebody who is called to respond due to his response-ability. This makes psychotherapy an ethical challenge (see Schmid, 2001a, 2001c). The Other is never an object to perceive or to know about, but, as Gabriel Marcel (see below) puts it, 'invocation' and thus 'demanding' a personal response. The Other cannot be understood by a refinement of the methods of perception, they must be understood by increasing the sensitivity of empathy and by increasing the openness of being touched by him or her through their revelation — by what they show and disclose. It is this reverse of the usual order of communication which makes the person-centred way of communicating unique among the therapeutic orientations and justifies the designation 'non-directive'.[26] In the

---

25. See Schmid, 1994, p. 259; 2001b, pp. 5–7; 2001c, p. 160.
26. See Schmid, 1994, pp. 116–55. More on the issue of non-directivity in 2001b, pp. 14–16.

process of therapy the client's response-ability grows and the therapist's 'responses' more and more become *co-responses* of the client and the therapist to the experiences in the relationship.

Taking a closer look at the core of person-centred theory, as expressed in Rogers' 1957 statement, we find that its ethical foundation is already included here: psychotherapy means responding to the client's incongruence (the second and often ignored necessary condition!), to a vulnerable or anxious person. Even more: if these six conditions are necessary and sufficient for a constructive development of the person by means of psychotherapy, then it is an obligation for the therapist to take them into account (contact, client's incongruence, communication of therapist's attitudes) or to offer them respectively (congruence, unconditional positive regard, empathy) (see Schmid, 2002a).

Approaches to understand an encounter relationship

The nature of an encounter relationship has been examined closely by personalistic or encounter philosophy.[27] Some examples of outstanding thinkers might give an impression of its meaning and lead to deeper understanding.

Romano Guardini (1885–1968) understands encounter as an amazing meeting with the reality of the Other. According to Guardini (1955), encounter means that one is touched by the essence of the opposite. To let this happen, a non-purpose-oriented openness, a distance which leads to amazement, and the initiative of man in freedom, are indispensable conditions. In interpersonal encounter, affinity and alienation can be experienced at the same time. Encounter is an adventure which contains a creative seed, a breakthrough to something new. The relationship 'centres in the Other'.

According to *Paul Tillich* (1886–1965), with whom Rogers entered into an open dialogue as he did with Buber (Rogers and Tillich, 1966), the person emerges from the resistance in the encounter of the Other: if the person

'were not to encounter the resistance of other selves, then every self would try to take itself as absolute . . . An individual can conquer the entire world of objects, but he cannot conquer another person without destroying him as a person. The individual discovers himself through this resistance. If he does not want to destroy the other person, then he has to enter into a community with him. It is through the resistance of the other person that the person is born' (Tillich, 1956, p. 208).

Bernhard Welte (1906–1983) sees the 'art of encounter' as a loving struggle between words and counter-words, as a creative act in which it matters to bring oneself into it in dialectic awakening 'in the flash of the contact', to open up and to expose oneself, but on the other hand to 'let yourself be you' (Welte, 1966).

Gabriel Marcel (1889–1973) emphasises that the Other has always been there in advance: it is only in (bodily) communication with the Other that I am. *He* (the object which I talk to you about) is not capable of responding, but *you* respond — to you I am responsible. What we talk about is the object. You are

---

27. For the central characteristics of an encounter relationship see Schmid, 1988b; 1994, pp. 273–8; see also 2001c.

never an object, but invocation and presence. I can *judge* objects, but in you I have to *believe*. You are only accessible through love. In particular, Marcel (1935, 1978) protests against the objectification of the body.

According to *Frederik J. H. Buytendijk* (1887–1974), encounter can be illustrated as a game: both are characterised by the oscillation between closeness and distance, opening up and closing up. Buytendijk (1951) emphasises that the loving encounter with the person opposite, in acting and in devotion, needs reciprocity and equality, even if this is hardly ever completely realised.

Martin Buber (1878–1965) is convinced that being a person is constituted by the event of encounter or dialogue, of communicating oneself. He defines encounter as the immediacy of the I-Thou-relationship, an event in which one becomes presence to the Other. The I is not constituted until such an encounter relationship: 'The I becomes through the Thou. Becoming an I, I say Thou' (Buber, 1923, p. 18). 'All real life is encounter' (ibid.). Therefore encounter is where dialogue happens.

Emmanuel Levinas (1905–1995) stresses in a much more radical way than Buber the 'absolute being-different' of the Other. He extends and understands encounter as a Thou-I-relationship, where the Thou must never be used for the I, denoting an ethical foundation of encounter and philosophy which is in contrast to the traditional occidental understanding which according to Levinas is mere 'egology'. Furthermore Levinas (1961, 1974, 1983) makes clear that such relationships are never isolated and must not be seen relatively contained but embedded in the reality of many relationships that each individual lives in, and in society as a whole. This is why 'the Third One' comes into play — a cipher for the necessary We-perspective of encounter: there is not only one Other, there are many Others (including the Others of the Others). Therefore how to act is no longer obvious, and the question of justice and the necessity of judgement arise. This provides space for freedom and makes it necessary for us to distinguish and to decide.

Initial and personal encounter — from experiencing to co-experiencing and co-responding

It might be helpful for the understanding of the nature of the therapeutic relationship that the very core of encounter is the same with persons as it is with other realities. We encounter for example nature (think of a sunset at the sea or in the mountains) or art (think of a painting, of music or of theatre). Böckenhoff (1970, p. 426) distinguishes between encountering the reality of things ('Wirklichkeitsbegegnung') and a Thou ('Du-Begegnung'). Both have in common that there is this moment of the principled otherness of the Other and of surprise by the unknown. This helps in understanding that for an encounter relationship it is not necessary to be mutual. The therapist can encounter the client although the client might not encounter the therapist (but may be busy with examining him- or herself or investigating the therapist's intentions. The mere fact that the therapist on his or her part encounters the client makes a difference to the relationship and thus to the client and his or her perception (if it does not, and until it is, according to Rogers' statement, therapy aiming at personality development will not be possible).

CONTACT AND PERCEPTION

Yet such 'initial encounter' has to be transcended into a personal encounter relationship, finally aiming at a reciprocal, mutual encounter relationship.

On further investigation of the phenomena of encounter, differences in encounter experiences and encounter relationships can be found: for the sake of the clarity of terms, we have to distinguish between the 'Thou-encounter in the beginning', as experienced by an unaffected child, and the 'personal encounter' which only becomes possible through reflection. At first there is the *initial encounter* which can transcend via an objectifying intermediate phase into *personal encounter*.

1. The *initial encounter* is often compared with lightning. It simply happens. The situation is 'given'. It seems to occur by coincidence. English 'co-incidence' (from Latin 'co' and 'cadere': 'to fall') like German 'Zu-fall'[28] indicates that the underlying experience is something coming from the outside which hits or strikes me. An example for this kind of encounter phenomenon is when you walk down the street and suddenly, one out of the hundreds of other people just 'catches' your eye. Similarly, lightning strikes when you fall in love — the stage of amorousness is an initial encounter relationship. A typical paradigm for an initial encounter relationship is the mother-child-relationship. In therapy this is the first 'im-pression' a therapist gets from his client, before reflection.

2. It is important to be aware that only after a 'step back' from the 'initial encounter' into an *objectifying position* is a mature encounter relationship — a 'personal encounter' — possible. After the 'naïve' beginning and, in the light of experience, we can look at somebody, analyse and critically reflect. This happens when being in love changes to loving — critical reflection takes place and changes the nature of the relationship.

This is particularly important for psychotherapy and counselling. After the first 'strike' there must be reflection about what happened. Just as it is necessary for the therapist to be impressed by the Other, to be astonished and questioned, so it is equally important to reflect on this. (In later states of therapy this might well happen together with the client, in earlier stages it is often the task for the therapist alone.) The necessary input for the client is when they can see that (self-)experiencing is followed by (self-)reflection. Since clients in most cases tend to view therapists as a model of treating oneself and others, the more the client can see this through the transparency of the therapist, the more facilitative it is for the client. Only after this does a mature encounter relationship become possible in a professional therapeutic relationship. The moment of reflection does not only take place in the therapist's supervision of his therapeutic relationships but also within the therapeutic relationship itself — most often in quick succession: being affected and reflecting cannot happen at the same time, but happen quickly after one another. What I just experienced makes me reflect and the outcome of that reflection leads to new affecting experiences, and so on.

In therapy and counselling, experiencing and reflecting alternate with each other and become *more and more co-experiencing and co-reflecting and in this they are co-creating the relationship and the persons*.

The closer reflecting follows experiencing, the more this is a holistic process

---

28. 'Etwas ist mir zuge-fallen.' (='It fell to me, was assigned to me.')

and feels as 'one whole step'. (In this light, merely cathartic therapies with the one-sided stress on action and experience, e.g. some body therapies, miss the importance of a personal process by avoiding or omitting the reflection, thus fostering 'actioning' or 'living without thinking'. On the other hand, therapies in which there only is reflection lack the experiential part, thus supporting 'rationalising' or 'thinking without living'.)

It is 'you' whom I encounter, and after that it is 'he' or 'she' whom I think about — not in order to overcome this experience but in order to integrate it and to facilitate the further relationship. (Therefore 'you' never become 'it' in the process of an encounter relationship which stays in the present moment.)

Whether an encounter is deliberately chosen (as in therapy to work with somebody) or whether it happens 'by coincidence', the initial encounter happens beyond freedom, decision and responsibility. After this, reflection provides room for freedom and responsibility.

Also, by this process correspondence, 'co-respond-ence' is sought for between my experience and the other person's experience, on the one hand tuning me into the experience of the Other, and on the other hand 'separating' my experience from his or hers and 'separating' my perception from the other's perception of his experience. As already stated this is a process of real-isation, of checking experience with reality. It is what congruence is about and what genuineness is about (Schmid, 2001a). As the term shows, this striving for *'co-respondence' is a way of responding together to a given experience.*

3. After this 'stage' of reflection a new way of encountering becomes possible. It is encounter out of responsibility due to the newly gained freedom by reflection. The Other becomes a Thou anew. This *personal encounter* opens up the possibility to deliberately form the relationship which is a way of *creating* it. This is what Carl Rogers was describing by the formulation 'therapy as relationship encounter' (Rogers, 1962, p. 185). A typical paradigm for a personal encounter is love between partners (Schmid, 1994, pp. 111–22). It is only after reflection that the therapeutic encounter enables both, client and therapist, to understand therapy as the co-creation of a unique encounter relationship which aims to strengthen the authorship of the client to enable him or her to 'create' their future.

Psychotherapy aims to become a mutual encounter — a social and political claim

Whilst person-centred therapy therefore is not simply a personal encounter at the outset, it aims for it. 'Therapeutic encounter', then, is reciprocal or at least open to reciprocity, even if it is asymmetric. It is a relationship which is equal in value, even if it is not equal in intensity. In the beginning it may be only the therapist who offers a personal encounter, in the sense that what is encounter for the therapist cannot yet be reciprocated by the client. The goal of the therapeutic process, however, is still the full — and thus mutual and symmetrical — personal encounter. In it, both persons face each other as persons freely and in full awareness of their responsibility and, thus, becoming one, on the one hand, and on the other acknowledging each as the Other in his or her essential difference, i.e. being *present* as persons *to each other*. Therefore the final goal of therapy is to be surpassed and done away with, to make space for mutual personal encounters. As soon as this is achieved, therapy has made itself superfluous — which is the emancipatory aim of psychotherapy anyway.

One of the most essential foundations of the person-centred approach is that it begins from a 'We'. In its basic statements it is rooted in the conviction that we are not merely a-contextual individuals. We can only exist within, and as part of this 'We'. If we don't pay any attention to that larger 'We' and if we are not aware that we are unescapably a part of it, we ignore our roots, our present and our future. This 'We' is not an undifferentiated mass of 'Us' nor is it a mere accumulation of 'Mes'; it is a 'We' which embraces sameness and otherness.

If we are not aware of this, as soon as we separate an 'Us' from a 'Them', we begin building a place where all the horrendous things we know, from the human race's history and present, can happen. An 'Us' is created with the possible over-identification of similarities with some people, and the narrow focusing on differences attributed to others who become 'Them'. Similarities are usually highly valued and differences are frequently seen as negative. 'Us' and 'Them' is not a contradictory dichotomy but rather an ever changing process within the 'We'. If we are not aware that each and every one of 'Us' is somebody else's Other we lose the feeling of and the knowledge about our principled interconnectedness. The social and political consequences are obvious.

Person-centred psychotherapy tries to bridge the differences among us by respecting and holding in high esteem otherness and diversity. Encounter is the proper kind of relationship for this.

By its nature especially the group tends to overcome one-sided forms of encounter, because the strict separation between therapist and client does not exist. Therefore the group can justly be called an 'experiential community' (Bebout, 1971/1972), where mutual co-experiencing takes place.[29]

'Psychological contact' already starts with at least a minimum of mutuality. It requires at least some openness, some capability of awareness of being able to be influenced by the other. Person-centred therapy is the kind of encounter relationship which, starting at some point of more or less (even almost complete) impaired mutuality and openness, strives towards full mutuality. Experiencing becomes co-experiencing; its symbolisation and communication become more and more congruent which is achieved by a joint process of checking; perceiving becomes realising and co-realising, encounter becomes a common experience; the person-centred relationship moves towards a mutual personal relationship. This is fostered by authenticity, acknowledgement and comprehension, which themselves are furthered by an openness to experience in a facilitative climate. The underlying way of being and developing the relationship towards mutual personal encounter is truly called presence in a kairological sense.

Presence: co-creating the therapeutic relationship

'Presence' is the proper term for the 'core conditions' in their interconnectedness

---

29. More on the importance of the group, on group encounter and the social and political dimension in the three volume handbook by Schmid (1994; 1996; 1998c); see also 2000; 2001a, pp. 228–30; 2001b, pp. 65–6; 2001c, pp. 166–8; 2002c.

as *the* way of being and acting of the therapist.[30] If one takes a closer look at the three 'core conditions', as described from a dialogical and encounter philosophical stance in the preceding volumes, and the light shed on them in the context of the 'We'-perspective, one can easily see that they are phenomenological descriptions of what 'presence' is all about. These 'core conditions' only can come into play if (1) there is a minimal *contact* between an (incongruent) client and a therapist, which is developed into an *encounter* relationship, and if (2) the client is *perceiving* the therapist's offer of this relationship, thus *realising* that he or she might develop out of so far unrealised resources.

The basic attitudes of authenticity, unconditional acknowledgement and comprehension can thus be understood as encounter conditions.

1. In its openness to the given moment, presence fosters *authenticity*. Authenticity (Schmid, 2001a) means that the person (the therapists as well as the clients) is regarded and trusted as his or her own, genuine author in the relationship to themselves and to the others. Being authentic is a precondition to enter dialogue — the way of communicating between persons where the Other is truly acknowledged as an Other, who is opening up, revealing him- or herself. Thus, in an epistemological perspective, authenticity is the foundation of personal and facilitative communication.

2. To expose oneself to the presence of the Other means to be open to being touched existentially by another person's reality and to touch his or her reality. Thus *comprehension* (Schmid, 2001b) points to psychotherapy as the art of not-knowing, i.e. the interesting and challenging part is the unknown and not-yet-understood. From a personal perspective to be empathic generally means to bridge the gap between differences, between persons — without removing the differences and without ignoring them. In expecting the unexpected, empathy is the epistemological foundation of person-centred therapy.

3. In its careful respect of the other persons as truly being Others and at one and the same time being aware of the commonality of the basic and unescapable 'We', presence furthers *acknowledgement*. Acknowledgement (Schmid, 2001c) without conditions, is a pro-active way of deliberately saying yes to the Other as a unique person. It means the person as such is 'ap-preciat-ed' in his or her worth and dignity — esteemed as a 'precious' being. It aims towards a mutual *acknowledgement* as persons instead of *knowledge about* another. The presence of the Other which always 'comes first' is a call for a response (compare Schmid, 2001a) from which I cannot escape, because nobody can respond in my place. We have response-ability and we are obliged and responsible to the Other and owe him or her an answer — making a 'priority' of the Other. And from the response follows respons-ability which is grounded in the fact that nobody else can respond instead of me in a given situation. Thus, the ethical dimension of encounter is denoted.

To sum it up: presence means to confidently take part in the present moment of life. In a relationship it means to jointly learn from, and to respond to, what just happened, to jointly experience the presence and to jointly create the future.

---

30. For a phenomenological analysis of presence and encounter see Schmid, 1994, pp. 245–78; see also 2001a, pp. 224–5; 2002b. 'Gegenwärtigsein' ('being present') is discussed in 1994, pp. 263–6.

CONTACT AND PERCEPTION

Presence is *the* kairotic quality.

Immediacy takes advantage of the potential of the kairos

As mentioned above, one of the essential characteristics of an encounter relationship — and thus for person-centred psychotherapy — is the renunciation of preconceived means and methods. Im-media-cy is born through the fact that all 'media', that separate us, 'decay' (Buber, 1923, p. 19), become unnecessary, surplus (which also expresses that this always is a process, not simply a state). For this it is important first of all to dispense with all techniques and methods, all means that serve as a protection to defend against what comes across or what is encountered, because encounter lies beyond all methods. It is involvement in the immediacy of the experience of relationship. Only when this is achieved does presence become possible.

The person-centred approach not only rules out, on part of the therapist, any conception of oneself as an expert on the problems, or on the person, of the 'partner' in counselling and therapy; it also rules out that the therapist considers him- or herself to be an expert in the correct usage of methods and means, and even excludes any preconceived use of methods and techniques[31], which is not rooted in the immediate experience of the relationship.

A person using preconceived methods is relating to the past not to the present, a person using techniques 'in order to' achieve something is relating to the future not to the present. Such a person is not in relation to the person he or she is encountering right here and right now. Presence is im-media-te. It is the encounter person to person, co-experiencing without anything in between. It is because of this that it seems to be so challenging: both frightening and fruitful. The only 'means' or 'instrument' employed is the person him- or herself.

Therefore the person-centred approach differs radically from those other approaches both in therapy, education and in many other fields of life, which in the meantime have all more or less found their way to the core conditions of authenticity, unconditional positive regard and empathy described by Rogers. However, these approaches consider Rogers' conditions only as a preparatory scheme or design meant to establish a certain climate or rapport, as obviously-human preconditions, so to speak, upon which the actual therapeutic work still has to be constructed. For the person working in the person-centred field the realisation of these basic attitudes means that no further supplementation by specific methods and techniques reserved for the expert is necessary. 'Expertism', if such a thing can be described, lies exactly in the ability to *resist* the temptation of behaving like a traditional expert (even against the client's wishes). Or to put it in Rogers' words: 'The client is the expert' — or even more radical — 'Dammit, we have the best resource for knowledge right there in the other chair'[32] (meaning the client). The task of the therapist is to take the risk: not to 'make' experiences but to *co-experience* with the client.

---

31. The notion of the terms changed drastically. The original Greek meaning of the term 'method' ('méta hodós'), meant: 'to be on the way with somebody, to follow somebody', the original meaning of 'technique' ('techné') was 'art'.
32. E-mail by John Shlien, Oct 27, 2001.

To encounter a human being means to give them space and freedom to develop themselves according to their own possibilities, to become, and to be fully the person he or she is able to become. On the one hand this is opposed to any use as a means to a particular end or any 'intention' and on the other hand it is also opposed to interaction based on a role or a function.

In the 'way of being with' called 'presence' the relationship becomes realisation, and realisation becomes relational: in a certain sense 'contact' and 'perception' unite.

Encounter means risk and daring. But it also provides the chance to receive the gift of the revelation of another person and the possibility of full personhood. The existential and im-media-te presence as understood by encounter philosophy, the personal being-with which leads to a togetherness, means that in his or her psychophysical presence, the person who offers a person-centred relationship opens up to his or her partner(s) the possibility to concentrate on the fertile instant and thus on oneself and his or her relations. In the kairos, out of a basic attitude of wonder, astonishment and amazement, it is important to take advantage of unrealised potential and to seize the opportunity of personalisation, of becoming a person.

REFERENCES

Bebout, J. (1971/72). The use of encounter groups for interpersonal growth. *Interpersonal Development* 2, 91–104.
Böckenhoff, J. (1970). *Die Begegnungsphilosophie*. Freiburg i. Br.: Alber.
Buber, M. (1923). *Ich und Du*. Heidelberg: Lambert Schneider, 8th ed. 1974; orig. 1923.
Buber, M. (1962/63). *Werke*, 3 volumes. Munich: Kösel.
Buber, M. (1963). Antwort. In Schilpp, P. A. and Friedman, M., *Martin Buber. Philosophen des 20. Jahrhunderts*. Stuttgart: Kohlhammer, pp. 589–640.
Buber, M. (1984). *Das dialogische Prinzip*. Heidelberg: Lambert Schneider, 5th ed. 1984.
Buber, M. (1986). *Begegnung: Autobiographische Fragmente*. Heidelberg: Lambert Schneider, 4th ed. 1986.
Buytendijk, F. J. H. (1951). Zur Phänomenologie der Begegnung. *Eranos Jahrbuch* XIX Zurich, 429–86.
Duden, K. (1963). (Ed.) *Etymologie: Herkunftswörterbuch der deutschen Sprache*. Mannheim: Dudenverlag, 7th ed.
Guardini, R. (1955). Die Begegnung: Ein Beitrag zur Struktur des Daseins. *Hochland* 47,3, 224–34.
Heindler, E. (1983). *Begegnung und Gesprächspsychotherapie*. Zurich & Graz: Koralpendruckerei.
Hoad, T. F. (Ed.) (1986). *The Concise Oxford Dictionary of English Etymology*. Oxford: Clarendon Press.
Jaspers, Karl (1932). *Philosophie, Bd. II: Existenzerhellung*. Berlin: Springer.
Kierkegaard, S. (1844). *Begrebet Angest*. Kopenhagen.
Kierkegaard, S. (1855). *Øieblikket*. Kopenhagen.
Levinas, E. (1961). *Totalité et infini: Essai sur l'extériorité*. Den Haag: Nijhoff.
Levinas, E. (1974). *Autrement qu'être ou au delà de l'essence*. Den Haag: Nijhoff, 2nd ed. 1978.
Levinas, E. (1983). *Die Spur des Anderen: Untersuchungen zur Phänomenologie und Sozialphilosophie*. Freiburg i. Br.: Alber, 3rd ed. 1992.
Marcel, G. (1935). *Être et avoir*. Paris: Aubier.
Marcel, G. (1978). Leibliche Begegnung. In Kraus, A. (Ed.), *Leib, Geist, Geschichte*. Heidelberg: Hütig, pp. 47–73.
Moreno, J. L. (1969). The Viennese origins of the encounter movement. Paving the way for

existentialism, group psychotherapy and psychodrama. *Group Psychotherapy* XXII, 1/2, pp.7–16.

Plessner, H. (1928). *Die Stufen des Organischen und der Mensch. Einleitung in die philosophische Anthropologie.* Berlin & Leipzig; new ed.: Frankfurt/M.: Suhrkamp, 1981.

Prouty, G., van Werde, D. and Pörtner, M. (2002). *Pre-therapy.* Ross-on-Wye: PCCS Books.

Rogers, C. R. (1940). *Some newer concepts of psychotherapy.* Manuscript.

Rogers, C. R. (1942). *Counseling and Psychotherapy: Newer Concepts in Practice.* Boston: Houghton Mifflin.

Rogers, C. R. (1955). *Some personal formulations.* Manuscript.

Rogers, C. R. (1957). The necessary and sufficient conditions of therapeutic personality change. *Journal of Consulting Psychology* 21,2, 95–103.

Rogers, C. R. (1959). A theory of therapy, personality, and interpersonal relationships, as developed in the client-centered framework. In Koch, S. (Ed.), *Psychology: A Study of Science. Volume III: Formulations of the Person and the Social Context.* New York: McGraw Hill, pp. 184–256.

Rogers, C. R. (1962). Some learnings from a study of psychotherapy with schizophrenics. In (quoted from) Rogers, C. R. and Stevens, B., *Person to Person. The problem of being human.* Moab: Real People Press, 1967, pp. 181–92.

Rogers, C. R. (1975). Empathic — an unappreciated way of being. *The Counseling Psychologist* 5,2, 2–10.

Rogers, C. R. (1980). Client-centered psychotherapy. In Kaplan, H. I., Freedman, A.M. and Sadock, B. J. (Eds.), *Comprehensive Textbook of Psychiatry, III.* Volume 2. Baltimore, MD: Williams and Wilkins, 3rd ed., pp. 2153–68.

Rogers, C. R. (1986). A client-centered/person-centered approach to therapy. In Kutash, I. L. and Wolf, A. (Eds.), *Psychotherapist's Casebook: Theory and Technique in the Practice of Modern Times.* San Francisco: Jossey-Bass, pp. 197–208.

Rogers, C. R. and Tillich, P. (1966). *Dialogue Between Paul Tillich and Carl Rogers, Parts I and II.* San Diego: San Diego State College.

Rotter, Hans (1993). *Person und Ethik: Grundlegung der Moraltheologie,* Innsbruck: Tyrolia.

Schelsky, H. (1963). *Einsamkeit und Freiheit: Idee und Gestalt der deutschen Universität und ihrer Reformen.* Reinbek: Rowohlt.

Schmid, P. F. (1991). Souveränität und Engagement: Zu einem personzentrierten Verständnis von 'Person'. In Rogers, C. R. and Schmid, P. F. (1991), *Person-zentriert: Grundlagen von Theorie und Praxis.* Mainz: Grünewald, pp.15–164; 4th ed.

Schmid, P. F. (1994). *Personzentrierte Gruppenpsychotherapie: Ein Handbuch. Volume I: Solidarität und Autonomie.* Cologne: Edition Humanistische Psychologie.

Schmid, P. F. (1996). *Personzentrierte Gruppenpsychotherapie in der Praxis: Ein Handbuch. Vol. II: Die Kunst der Begegnung.* Paderborn: Junfermann.

Schmid, P. F. (1998a). 'On becoming a person-centered approach': A person-centred understanding of the person. In Thorne, B. and Lambers, E. (Eds.), *Person-Centred Therapy: A European Perspective.* London: Sage, pp. 38–52.

Schmid, P. F. (1998b). 'Face to face': The art of encounter. In Thorne, B. and Lambers, E. (Eds.), *Person-Centred Therapy: A European Perspective.* London: Sage, pp. 74–90.

Schmid, P. F. (1998c). *Im Anfang ist Gemeinschaft: Personzentrierte Gruppenarbeit in Seelsorge und Praktischer Theologie, Vol. III: Beitrag zu einer Theologie der Gruppe.* Stuttgart: Kohlhammer.

Schmid, P. F. (1999). Personzentrierte Psychotherapie. In Sonneck, G. and Slunecko, T. (Ed.), *Einführung in die Psychotherapie.* Stuttgart: UTB für Wissenschaft — Facultas, pp. 168–211.

Schmid, P. F. (2000). 'Encountering a human being means being kept alive by an enigma' (E. Levinas). Prospects on further developments in the Person-Centered Approach. In Marques-Teixeira, J. and Antunes, S. (Eds.), *Client-Centered and Experiential Psychotherapy.* Linda a Velha: Vale & Vale, pp. 11–33.

Schmid, P. F. (2001a). Authenticity: the person as his or her own author: Dialogical and ethical perspectives on therapy as an encounter relationship. And beyond. In Wyatt, G. (Ed.), *Rogers' Therapeutic Conditions: Evolution, Theory and Practice. Volume 1: Congruence.* Ross-on-Wye: PCCS Books, pp. 217–32.

Schmid, Peter F. (2001b). Comprehension: the art of not-knowing. Dialogical and ethical perspectives on empathy as dialogue in personal and person-centred relationships. In Haugh, S. and Merry, T. (Eds.), *Rogers' Therapeutic Conditions: Evolution, theory and practice. Volume 2: Empathy*. Ross-on-Wye: PCCS Books, pp. 53–71.

Schmid, P. F. (2001c). Acknowledgement: the art of responding. Dialogical and ethical perspectives on the challenge of unconditional personal relationships in therapy and beyond. In Bozarth, J. and Wilkins, P. (Eds.), *Rogers' Therapeutic Conditions: Evolution, Theory and Practice. Volume 3: Unconditional Positive Regard*. Ross-on-Wye: PCCS Books, pp. 155–71.

Schmid, P. F. (2001d). Interpellation et réponse. La psychothérapie centrée sur la personne: une rencontre de personne à personne. *Mouvance Rogerienne* 24, 2–18.

Schmid, P. F. (2002a). 'The necessary and sufficient conditions of being person-centered': On identity, integrity, integration and differentiation of the paradigm. In Watson, J. et al. (Eds.), *Client-Centered and Experiential Psychotherapy in the 21st Century: Advances in Theory, Research and Practice*. Ross-on-Wye: PCCS Books, in press.

Schmid, P. F. (2002b). Défis pour l'approche centrée sur la personne au commencement du 21ème siècle d'un point de vue dialogique et éthique. *Carriérologie*, UQÀM, Montréal, Canada, in press.

Schmid, P. F. (2002c). *The ongoing challenge of becoming person-centered. Infochange* (American Counseling Association), special winter 2002 issue, 100th anniversary of Carl Rogers: our emerging vision, in press.

Swildens, H. (1999). Woher wir kommen und wohin wir gehen: über den Werdegang der personzentrierten Psychotherapie. Paper, given at the congress of the ÄGG, November 1999, unpublished.

Tillich, P. (1956). *Systematische Theologie*. Vol. 1. Berlin: de Gruyter, 3rd ed.

van Balen, R. (1992). Die therapeutische Beziehung bei C. Rogers: Nur ein Klima, ein Dialog oder beides? In Behr, M. et al. (Eds.), *Jahrbuch 1992 für personzentrierte Psychologie und Psychotherapie, Bd. III*. Cologne: GwG, pp. 162–83.

Welte, B. (1966). Zum Begriff der Person. In Rombach, H. (Ed.), *Die Frage nach dem Menschen: Aufriss einer philosophischen Anthropologie*. Freiburg i. Br.: Herder, pp. 11–22.

Zurhorst, G. (2001). Die Erneuerung der philosophisch-anthropologischen Grundlagen des personzentrierten Ansatzes. In Gesellschaft für wissenschaftliche Gesprächspsychotherapie (Ed.), *Visionen für ein gesellschaftliches Miteinander: Der Personzentrierte Ansatz im Zeitalter von Digitalisierung und globalem Wertewandel*, Cologne: GwG, pp. 112–31.

11 Psychological Contact Through Person-Centered Expressive Arts

Shellee Davis

Creativity happens in the realm where life and imagination overlap. It engages a larger sense of self, taps our wholeness, our inner resources, the conscious mind and the unconscious, imagination and intuition. As children it is our natural way of engaging the world. As Carl Rogers (1961, pp. 350–1) said, creativity springs from the innate impulse to manifest our human potential, and that is the curative force in psychotherapy.

In stark contrast to this holistic view, society marginalizes art as frivolous and superfluous or defines it as an elite endeavor reserved for only the special few. As a result, most of us are steered away from our own creativity. The power it has to awaken our spirit, revitalize us and transform our lives seems lost to us.

As a child I loved art, so it was a major blow when I was told that I couldn't pursue it because art was not a practical way to make a living. I studied other disciplines, but for years I was only going through motions, feeling increasingly rudderless. Creativity felt charged and out of reach like forbidden fruit. In despair I decided to do the only thing I hadn't tried: go against conventional wisdom and follow my heart.

In 1973 I enrolled in the School of Expressive Arts at Sonoma State University and discovered person-centered expressive arts, which became the central healing force in my life. In this nurturing, non-judgmental environment I at last felt safe enough to contact my creative spirit and express my authentic self. My experience felt rich, full, scary, challenging, and most important, self-empowering. Eureka! This was my life path.

In 1986 I entered the Person-Centered Expressive Therapy Institute (PCETI), a training program founded by Natalie Rogers and Frances Fuchs, the daughter and granddaughter of Carl Rogers. Participants came from a variety of fields — the arts, psychotherapy, education, health care, and business — to learn to use expressive arts in their professional work and for personal growth and healing. I have now been a PCETI faculty member for 15 years. In that time I have observed the profound effect that the person-centered approach and the power of the arts have had on those who embrace them. Within a year of starting the program virtually all participants change their lives in some significant way to more faithfully reflect and embody their values, dreams and desires.

In this chapter I will show:
- the power of expressive arts to facilitate psychological contact, increasing

self-awareness and accessing healing resources within each person.
- why a psychologically safe, person-centered environment is most effective for this therapeutic process and how we create it.
- how deeper psychological contact with oneself through expressive arts facilitates communication with others more authentically and effectively.
- how creative expression develops a more empowered, resilient and imaginative response to everyday life in both personal and societal arenas.

WHAT IS EXPRESSIVE ARTS AND HOW DOES IT FACILITATE PSYCHOLOGICAL CONTACT?

Expressive arts refers to a multi-arts approach to creativity and learning that encourages free expression through drawing, painting, dancing, sculpting, play-acting, sound and writing. At PCETI we use the arts in combination with each other to stimulate the imagination and deepen and amplify feelings and awareness. This propels the creative process and psychological contact through personal exploration.

For instance, we may do movement in response to how we feel and then continue to express our thoughts, feelings, gestures and sensory awareness through clay or color and then writing. Each shift to another art medium wakes up emotional energy, insights, possibilities, and new perspectives. Natalie Rogers calls this process the Creative Connection®.

This creative process increases awareness by giving the psyche many ways to show various aspects of ourselves and explore them. Sharing our inner worlds and the feelings we have contacted through our expressive arts creations also helps make deeper and more authentic psychological contact with other people. By practicing the person-centered approach to expressive arts we develop a respectful, nurturing way of supporting our creative adventures and deepening psychological contact as soul work.

HOW DOES EXPRESSIVE ART DIFFER FROM FINE ART?

In fine art the focus is on art as a product, techniques to create it, and the art is judged good or bad. In contrast, we use expressive art to promote psychological contact with ourselves and others through spontaneous, creative expression for enjoyment, therapeutic emotional release, and self-revelation. We focus on what we can learn about ourselves from the creative process and from reflecting on our art as messages from our inner worlds.

YOU DON'T HAVE TO BE AN ARTIST TO BENEFIT FROM THIS PROCESS

Marcia hates clay because she feels inept in that medium. Her flat clay figure of a woman lies on a paper plate. Initially she dismisses it as poorly done and ugly. However, in a person-centered environment we practice being non-judgmental toward ourselves and others, so she acknowledges her judgments and then goes a step further. She writes a description of the clay piece and her process, puts an

CONTACT AND PERCEPTION

'I am' in front of each sentence and reads it out loud to see how it feels to her. She reads: 'I am flat on my back. I can't stand up for myself. I want myself to be different, because I don't accept myself the way I am. I'm critical of what I do when I feel I don't know how to do it' (Marcia, 1999a).

Writing helps Marcia articulate feelings in response to what she has expressed in clay. She then realizes that her clay sculpture is an expression of how she's feeling and a metaphor for her current situation in life. She really is feeling 'flat on her back', i.e. physically and emotionally exhausted. She says her job used to be very satisfying, but a change in management increased her workload dramatically and eliminated what she most valued about her profession. Now she is miserable, demoralized and doesn't know how to 'stand up for herself' in this new situation.

Marcia's claywork and writing promote psychological contact with herself which enables her to consciously acknowledge the depth and reality of her inner experience. These reflections make her aware that her job is now eroding her life force more than it supports her, and she notices this is a recurring message in her subsequent artwork. As a result Marcia decides she can no longer ignore or endure this and uses art to explore making a transition to a more satisfying job. When she returns home she actively seeks a new position and with happy relief later calls to say that she has found a much better job (Marcia, 1999b).

WHY ARE THE ARTS SO EFFECTIVE FOR MAKING PSYCHOLOGICAL CONTACT WITH OURSELVES AND OTHERS?

The arts are non-verbal languages for expressing thoughts, feelings, and the inner life. In both individual counseling and in group work, the arts offer avenues of expression that invite people to move into their inner process more deeply. Non-verbal expression is ideal when people don't know where to begin saying what they think and feel. It also helps when verbal expression is keeping people stuck in their rational mind and away from their feelings.

Creative expression can bypass the limits of the linear, logical approach to thinking and addressing problems. You need not be stymied by confusion and not-knowing. Through spontaneous expression, whether playful or serious, something will emerge. Instead of thoughts circling in your mind, you express them outwardly and have something visible and tangible to relate to as a point of departure.

For example, Wendy (1998) refers to the emotional paralysis caused by her childhood of violent physical and sexual abuse and her awakening from it, saying,

> I was raised in hell . . . I was shut down, unable to communicate and trust others. I couldn't touch the deepest wounds I received during my childhood. Therefore years of therapy were fraudulent. I sank into depression and addictions and became increasingly distrustful of people around me. Eventually I became free of drug and alcohol addiction and was productive in my community, but depression lingered. I was contending with immobilizing factors of sadness, paranoia, shame and depression.
>
> Person-centered expressive arts therapy has enabled me to slowly pull back the layers of my psyche using art, movement, group work and journaling. I've

broken barriers of personal distrust within the safe supportive environment PCETI offers. I brought out the darkest memories of my past using art forms to express what I couldn't speak. I touched the innermost core of my being and discovered music which resonates with my soul.

Now instead of going through the mechanics of life in self-exile, I found myself engaging with dis-engagement. Curling up, reaching out, giving expression to wounds too deep for words, sounding, drawing awful, wonderful images. On a subtle yet profound level, I felt the messages revealed in these therapeutic forms were allowing strength, self-understanding and self-acceptance to slowly take root in me. I realized that I was just scraping the surface of an inner iceberg, but my hard shield had finally cracked (p. 1–7).

Wendy's account demonstrates the power of the expressive arts to effect direct and deep psychological contact with herself, bypassing her conscious and unconscious defenses. She also makes it clear that the safety of the person-centered environment was necessary for her to trust that she could reveal and face her pain and that her psyche could heal her through her creative process.

HOW DO WE CREATE A PSYCHOLOGICALLY SAFE ENVIRONMENT THAT FACILITATES PSYCHOLOGICAL CONTACT THROUGH THE EXPRESSIVE ARTS?

The psychological safety of a person-centered environment is most optimal for people to open to new experiences of themselves and integrate them in a healing and self-empowering way. There is much misunderstanding about how to facilitate expressive arts processes in a person-centered way. Most therapy using the arts is not person-centered, and most people, including therapists, don't understand or fully appreciate the person-centered environment until they have experienced it personally.

There is also misunderstanding within the Person-Centered Approach community, because typically they think that using the arts is not person-centered because it is not verbal therapy as Carl Rogers modeled it. Their other concern and criticism is that offering the arts is directive and, therefore, not person-centered.

When Rogers wrote about fostering creativity in order to foster wholeness and healthy personal growth, he said that this would most likely occur when three internal elements were present in the person:

1) Openness to experience. A nondefensive receptivity to all stimuli whether originating within the organism or in the environment . . .

2) An internal locus of evaluation. A trust in one's own judgment of one's products . . .

3) The ability to toy with ideas, concepts, materials — the ability to be playful with the elements which go into the creative product. A willingness to experiment . . . (Rogers, 1961, pp. 347–59).

He then described four nurturing external factors as essential for psychological safety:

1. Acceptance of the individual as a person of worth. Accepting the individual

as she/he is...
2. An absence of external evaluation. An environment that is free of critical judgment...
3. A climate of sensitive empathetic understanding...
4. Complete freedom to express all feelings in symbolic form... (Rogers 1961, pp. 357–9).

To create an environment where people feel safe enough to open up and make genuine psychological contact with themselves and each other, first the PCETI faculty explains the person-centered philosophy. Then we continually model the core conditions of empathy, congruence and unconditional positive regard and encourage participants to practice them. People learn to value this nurturing, non-judgmental support by experiencing it in mind, body and emotions. Then they are able to embody it and pass it on to others, co-creating a supportive atmosphere.

Our faculty also developed guidelines to support this process based on the necessary internal and external conditions that Carl Rogers described. These help in three important ways. They:
- alert people to the inner challenges they may encounter through the creative process, so when personal challenges arise, they are more readily accepted and supported as learning experiences
- orient people to the inner resources and choices they have to meet these challenges
- act as reminders to help people consciously co-create a mutually supportive environment that empowers each person in their unique process.

The guidelines are useful for those wanting to use person-centered expressive arts therapeutically with groups or in one-to-one sessions with clients. Whether working with adults or children, we explain these guidelines to create a mutually supportive environment. They reflect values we agree to practice with each other. We use them as reminders to see if the way we are working and playing with each other is consistent with our intention to create a safe, non-judgmental, person-centered climate. These guidelines provide a way to talk about what is happening in the group in order to raise everyone's conscious awareness about it.

Person-centered expressive arts guidelines

1. Be aware of your feelings as a source for creative expression that can be channeled into art
Whether you are feeling happy or sad, emotions are energy that can be expressed. If you are angry, you may lash out at the paper with color or pummel clay into a shape. Feeling tired, bored or blocked often feels like having no energy, but energy is still there to be found. You might express your ennui by moving your hand listlessly across the page or by moving your body vacantly or grumpily around the room. As you express your feelings, rather than holding them in or disregarding them, notice what you experience. Are you going deeper into them or are they changing? What thoughts and images arise? Perhaps your feelings

will shift and change, or they may be validated by insights that arise during this process.

When you release feelings creatively, your own internal, balancing mechanisms can work the way they are supposed to. Spontaneous emotional release through creative expression facilitates deeper, more extended psychological contact within yourself so you can learn from your mind, emotions, body and spirit and have safe and healthy ways to acknowledge and work with your feelings.

2. Be aware of your body and take care of yourself
Only you know what your body can do, so when a facilitator suggests any movement, please modify suggestions to safely accommodate your own ability.

3. Our suggestions are only suggestions. You have the option to not follow them
Our culture trains us to obey and follow the rules 'for our own good', whether we want to or not. Instead, each of us can cultivate the habit of listening to the wisdom of our own needs, desires and limits. The goal of the person-centered approach to expressive arts is to create an environment where you are the authority on your own experience and determine what is appropriate for you.

When I was a participant in PCETI, a movement exercise was suggested that scared me. I felt too self-conscious and embarrassed to try it. 'No matter what they say, I'm not going to do it,' I resolved to myself, 'and no one can make me!' Then I noticed the PCETI guidelines on the wall and realized, 'Oh, that's right! They aren't going to make me do anything!' I relaxed a little and wondered what the movement would feel like. If I didn't try, I wouldn't know. So I did try it, but my own interest and curiosity motivated me to participate, rather than any feeling of having to comply. The psychological freedom engendered through a person-centered environment encouraged and allowed me to go beyond my defenses, trust my own judgment, be open to a new experience and experiment creatively.

4. Doing any of the arts can stir up emotions. That is okay
The goal is to make psychological contact with yourself and tap your inner resources. You can do this by including your feelings as information, doors to increased awareness and understanding. Expressing feelings, such as crying, laughing or making loud sounds, is a natural way for your body to release that energy. Emotional expression is a path into your inner knowing, vitality and spontaneity that facilitates psychological contact with yourself. Blocking or withholding feelings can also block inner information from conscious awareness.

5. If you choose not to participate, be a participant observer
Each person is a part of the group, whether you actively participate or not. You can observe and learn from watching other people's experience. While you observe others, you can also observe yourself. What are you noticing, feeling, thinking, learning? Be aware of any judgments that come up.

Although we will always make judgments, if we practice suspending them, they won't limit what we can learn about ourselves and each other. The quality of psychological contact you make with yourself and others is enhanced if you are not reflexively critical, because it is safer to be open in a non-judgmental environment. This does not mean you no longer have powers of discrimination; you are just opening to more possibilities so you can practice treating yourself and others with more compassion.

6. *There is no right or wrong way to create movement, art, sound or writing. The purpose is to involve yourself in the process of creativity for self-learning*
These guidelines are based on the person-centered belief in the innate capacity in each person to be creative, self-balancing and to realize their full potential. Given a supportive, encouraging, stimulating environment, each person has the capacity for self-understanding, insight and the ability to find their own direction. The safety to explore and express freely encourages psychological contact with ourselves and others. For some, these guidelines may seem like common sense. For others, they may seem new and unfamiliar. The challenge for everyone is to be mindful of them in the face of habitual patterns.

Guidelines for responding to art

We also have person-centered guidelines for talking about our art with each other because when we express our feelings and inner world through art, we can feel vulnerable and exposed. In person-centered expressive arts we do not interpret or analyze each other's work. In order to exercise the capacity for self-understanding and insight, it is important for each person to discover their own personal meaning in their art and movement experiences.

To create a respectful, psychologically safe environment in which to share art with each other, we first invite the artist (participant or client) to share what the process was like and the meaning the art has for that person. Before we offer our response to the artwork, we ask if the artist would like to hear it. If yes, we acknowledge our responses to their art as our own feelings and reactions. For instance, 'When I look at your art, I feel . . .' Or, 'If this were mine, this is what it might mean to me.' This helps to remain person-centered instead of acting as an authority who can interpret and diagnose others as in the medical model of counseling.

PSYCHOLOGICAL CONTACT THROUGH THE POWER OF SYMBOLIC EXPRESSION

Following are examples of how various arts have helped people make psychological contact with themselves and others, bringing unconscious feelings, desires, issues and potentials to light in transformative ways:

Visualization and movement

A facilitator puts on music and says, 'Imagine leaving the tribal campfire to journey into the wild. You will meet an animal that is your twin soul. When you find it, come back embodying the gift of its power.'

The music begins. In my mind I run through the jungle searching, wondering what I will find. Finally I see a black panther. As the music ends I rejoin the tribal circle, open my eyes and 'wake up' as a panther. I move catlike, slowly, deliberately and fluidly through the animals our group has become: big cats hissing and snarling, birds swooping, smaller animals scurrying, and two titans engaged in a roaring mock battle. I realize that my strength, the gift of the panther, is fearlessness. I look calmly and directly into everyone's eyes. I neither intimidate nor am I able to be intimidated. It is as if I have created an invisible shield around me. No one, not the fiercest predator, challenges my centered presence.

I am amazed that inner strength can be communicated without words, simply through unwavering eye contact and confident body language. What am I usually communicating with my attitude and body language? I want to adopt this panther way of being.

Years later I experience a thought-provoking variation: visualize meeting a power animal that we dislike. I'm surprised to see a rhinoceros. They are ugly. I don't want to identify with one, but here it is. This time our group chooses costumes to express the attributes of our animals. We form a circle, an arena where each person can go into the center acting like their animal. Then anyone else can go in, interact and see what happens.

As soon as I, a short, 100-pound weakling, enter the circle, another rhino, a tall woman who outweighs me considerably, enters, snorts and stomps. We charge. There we are on all fours, head to head, pushing mightily. My legs make rapid forward motions, but I slide backwards as this larger rhino steadily advances.

While this is going on, I realize that I don't usually 'butt heads' like this. I am diplomatic rather than confrontational. But now, though it appears that I am losing ground, my rhino spirit perseveres and keeps thrusting forward. This reminds me of when I was ten years old, when I passionately butted heads, arguing with my parents or friends, certain that I was right about everything. Now in play, the energy and exhilaration of this come back to me.

Suddenly the other rhino gives up and backs off. I have no idea why, since she is winning. I rear up on my knees and flex my biceps as if I am the victor, making us all laugh because I have certainly not won in rhino terms. When we talk about our experiences, I learn that she retreated because I am the teacher of this course. She was afraid that I might retaliate, if she won on our play battleground.

This has brought up a painful issue for her. As a child she was seen as pushy and impudent and was punished for it. She became quiet and compliant. She still feels fearful and cautious in response to teachers and authority but now considers how it might benefit her to stand her ground openly like a rhino. Rather than feeling overwhelmed by fear of teachers, she might use her uneasiness as a signal to evaluate her present situation with the possibility of responding differently as a self-empowered adult.

Imagination, movement and reflection on our experiences have led us into psychological contact with our inner selves and each other, expanding our sense of identity in a helpful way. Sharing our experiences gives us an opportunity to become aware of old emotional issues and patterns that we bring into our relationship and explore new possibilities.

CONTACT AND PERCEPTION

Clay and writing

Thea has expressed her inner experience through clay and has written an imaginal dialogue with her sculpture. Later, in retrospect she writes again:

> When I picked up clay, it was a completely sensuous experience . . . the smell, the touch, the body of clay had its own voice that I loved and it loved me back and gave me an incredible gift. One of the figures was a complete surprise. It felt like a goddess, the embodiment of integration . . . A few days later at home, my cat knocked over this sculpture and the head broke off. My first inclination was to be angry and feel that the artwork was ruined. Something deep and quiet inside of me asked me to listen. The clay was still speaking. I lifted up the broken head and let it be cradled in the arms of the clay goddess. As I took this in, the clay spoke again. 'You have lived your life with your head always ruling. Your head is very tired and wants to share this responsibility with the rest of your body. Will you let your head rest cradled in these loving arms? Making your head do all the work and neglecting the wisdom of your body will always be your weakness. Take this gift as a remembrance of this knowledge' (Thea, 1998).

Learning to view her sculpture and her creative process metaphorically engenders new and better psychological contact with herself that continues to bring Thea helpful insights in her subsequent reflections.

Drawing, writing and movement

In a Body Wisdom session to heighten awareness of the 'different sides of ourselves' and what they represent, we move one side of the body to music, then the other side, and then draw the feeling of each. We spontaneously write our associations and feelings about the picture of each side, and later we explore this further by using that drawing as inspiration for more movement and more insights.

Lake gets up to move in response to the body image she has drawn. When she begins moving in front of her body picture, she talks about her 'big butt' in a disdainful tone. She goes on to complain about everything she dislikes about her body while she moves. Gradually, as I witness her move I sense a shift, as if something is grabbing her attention from the inside. She seems to have an Aha! experience that transforms her movements and her perception of herself which changes how she treats herself. Her movements become more exploratory. Her tone changes to wondering. She describes the physical sensations of her movements with pleasure and speaks appreciatively of the parts of her body she has been criticizing. She ends up dancing jubilantly, freely, exulting in this new experience of herself as if she has shaken off a spell. Successive stages of drawing, writing and movement have helped Lake make psychological contact with her inner spirit, freed her from her negative self-image and transformed her physical and emotional sense of self in a positive way.

The power of sound

What does it mean to find your own voice or to put your voice out into the world? How about having a voice in your own fate? I was often told to be quiet as a child. 'Don't make a ruckus! Be nice! Don't talk back!' I became shy at the thought of speaking out, of speaking up for myself, of speaking in public, or of 'sounding off,' i.e. expressing strong emotions or opinions. So how do I reclaim my voice? Or for those who never lost it, how do we explore it further for fun and personal growth? Playing with voice and sound are ways to explore these questions.

Instead of worrying about what we sound like, I suggest we play like kids and get goofy. I have my partner stand with her back to me. As I make sounds, she uses them as inspiration for movement. I sing a sweet, little tune, and my partner skips as if along a flower path. Without warning I change to sound like a fire engine siren, and her body melts into long waves of intensity with her arms and fingers splayed wide. Then I cough repeatedly, and she looks like a car chugging and lurching along about to stall.

Many watch skeptically. However, once they begin, they are entirely caught up in the process. They must concentrate to hear their partner's sounds in the midst of a sudden cacophony. The variety of movement and sound is jumping, alive and versatile. Their comments reflect the surprising freedom that spontaneity brings: 'I made sounds I didn't know I could make!' 'I moved in ways that I never usually do!' Being out of control in a playful way has been releasing for most. Whether it feels hard, easy, fun, or challenging, each person can reflect on the experience for increased self-awareness.

Making sounds to express thoughts, emotions and physical feelings helps people make new or more profound psychological contact with themselves. When this occurs they are more able to share their authentic experiences with each other. For example, Sandy has all her pictures from ten days of work up on the wall. She wants to write in response to them, but she cannot bring herself to put her feelings into words that others might see. That feels too personal, too exposed. So she sings in an operatic style without words to vocalize her feelings about each picture. Later she decides that she will talk about her art and her inner experience, because this process has freed whatever was blocking her.

Theater improvisation

In play-acting, our focus is not on performance but rather on acting out stories with each other the way we did as children. On one level this is fun, and on another it is deep play. Whether we choose a fictional story or one from real life to act out, the psyche is selecting according to its own logic and imperatives. It engages emotions, memories and feelings stored in the body because we symbolically embody the drama as if it were true. This is invariably surprising and touching.

For example, Lisa tells us her favorite story from childhood: Suzy Squirrel likes to keep everything pretty and clean and the chipmunks like to scare her and ruin everything. Someone comes, scares the chipmunks away and helps Suzy put things back into order. When we start to act this, Lisa can't because she suddenly feels overwhelmed. With tears rolling down her cheeks, she chooses to watch her story played out. Afterwards, she tells us this fictional scenario of invasion and turmoil was too reminiscent of the abuse she endured as a child. We ask if she wants to act the story out in a different way that might feel better. She says yes. Playing Suzy Squirrel, she confronts the chipmunk vandals, shouts angrily, chases them away, and puts her house back in order. At the end of this play she feels much better.

Play-acting helps Lisa make psychological contact with childhood trauma, *and* it catalyzes the transformational power of her psyche. By consciously changing the outcome of the story and her part in it, she moves from being emotionally paralyzed to acting successfully on her own behalf. This role-playing gives her the emotionally real experience of facing a frightening challenge and overcoming it. She can continue to build on this strength. The support of the group is a powerful catalyst that breaks her old pattern of believing she is isolated and helpless, which helps her make better contact with others here and now.

Insight can come from re-imagining a real life scenario as well. Struggling with negative inner voices, I make a list that reads like the 'Shoulds and Shouldn'ts' I heard throughout childhood. With two partners playing my parents, I hear 'my parents' say these things again. I feel upset and angry, resentful and defensive. My body feels physically braced and armored.

Then we re-create the scenario. This time my partners say loving, encouraging statements. I discover that my childhood yearning to hear that from my parents is still in me. This takes me by surprise, and I cry, which melts away my armor. Then I feel sensitive, open and vulnerable. I say what I would like to have said to my parents about my pain and my love for them. My role-played parents' responses are kind and loving. My heart eases even though I know that they are not really my parents and that this is 'just an exercise'.

I'm amazed by how deeply opened and touched I am by loving messages in contrast to corrective, punitive ones. I already know this intellectually, but experiencing it emotionally has powerful impact. This feels like healing magic I can consciously use to counter my negative inner voices. Through physically acting out my family relationships, I catalyze psychological contact with myself and bring up emotions and insights that feel helpful and transformative.

THE NECESSITY OF FREEDOM TO EXPRESS ALL FEELINGS IN SYMBOLIC FORM

In clinical findings from psychotherapy, Carl Rogers (1961) discovered that the more an individuals are open to and aware of all their experiences, then their behavior will be creative and their creativity may be trusted to be essentially constructive, leading to constructive social living.

When a society or its individuals fear certain emotions and aspects of ourselves and label them negative and unacceptable, such as anger, hostility or shame, we may attempt to hide them from others and deny they exist. If we can't even admit to ourselves that they exist, they can become an unconscious source of destructive action and expression. Fearing and withholding emotions is a way to develop fear and distrust in yourself. The arts are the safest way to express feelings, to cathart emotions and become consciously aware of our experience so we can learn from it and transform 'negative' emotional energy in positive ways.

Hearing me say this, a participant asks me, 'What if I feel angry? What if I want to throw and break things?' These are good questions asked in exactly the right place. Imagination is the middle ground between the psyche and the physical world. Asking a 'What if?' question invites the imagination to portray a possibility that we can consider without having to act it out first. Through creative expression we can imaginally act out real feelings in symbolic ways for emotional catharsis and psychological healing. The arts let us explore what we call our 'negative', or forbidden feelings and express them in a safe way that is emotionally true for us.

Rogers wrote,

> While there may be restrictions on acting one's feelings, any feeling can be freely expressed in words, pictures, sound or other symbolic form (p. 359).

In sessions where anger is being released, you may violently hit a pillow or fight a willing partner with padded bats. You may fling paint at paper screaming, or pound clay on the floor shouting, or tear up a picture that represents whatever or whoever enrages you. This is a safe way to express real feelings with all the force they have. The facilitator is with you as a witness and supporter.

For instance, B (1996) says:

> I made pots of clay depicting objects which I had desired that had been denied me in my marriage. I later went outside with my supporters and ritually shouted my anger and threw the objects against the wall, smashing them into tiny pieces. The tremendous relief at getting rid of that anger! I have never felt the need for those things again, even though I could now easily buy them. The process had enabled me to move on so very far, (p. 4).

Sometimes crying or yelling is enough of a catharsis to get some relief, or the relief may be temporary because there is a deeper issue agitating. Tracking yourself through this wild, inner territory as you express your feelings, thoughts, images and memories through art, clay, movement, and writing is like following a trail to the source of the anger, pain or dilemma. It may be a current issue or may date back to a childhood wound that continues to fester. Trying to get to the source can sometimes feel like answering the question, 'How did the universe begin?' We can speculate, but we may never know for sure. What we *can* do is notice recurrent patterns and create different patterns of response that work better for us.

Other repressed feelings we may contact through creative expression are grief, floating anxiety, embarrassment or shame. As we invite our inner world to speak to us through the arts, hints of these feelings and aspects of ourselves may arise unexpectedly, as they did for Wendy (1998):

> My intention was to create a collage expressing the strength I had found . . . instead images such as an amputated body, a savage tiger, a blurred man jumped out at me. In order for me to release the painful poison of my childhood, it had to first be leached from my blood, guts and marrow so it could dissolve and heal. [In PCETI] I felt supported. There was room for the good, the bad and the ugly (p. 9).

'Negative' emotions may not be welcome in our families or social circles and can

CONTACT AND PERCEPTION

be a source of lonely struggle. Hopes, dreams and aspirations may also be repressed in our psyche, rejected, deferred or unexplored because they are judged unrealistic. In a supportive group or with a counselor these feelings can move and change.

Lynda was initially intimidated by the idea of doing movement in response to her imagery. She thought of movement only in terms of dance and felt she couldn't or shouldn't do it. However, she reports:

> I came to see that movement continued the colors and shapes of my pictures. My pictures were from within me, and my body had a natural need to shift to stay in connection with them. I liked the feeling of being able to move to what I'd drawn which represented how I felt. A girlhood dream of being a dancer surfaced. I thought of this desire with wonder because dance is an awkward thought to me now. It leaves me feeling open and exposed. Connecting it with my art gave me permission to let that desire take flight — limited flight, but flight.

Doing movement in response to her art put Lynda into psychological contact with a long-forgotten part of herself in a way that eased her fears and freed her from limitations that she had unconsciously accepted or imposed on herself.

COMMUNICATION AND RELATIONSHIPS WITH OTHERS

> *It is doubtful whether a human being can create without wishing to share his creation.* (Carl Rogers, *On Becoming a Person*)

At PCETI, first we show people how to use the arts to make psychological contact with their inner worlds and issues, and then we use interactive arts to help them get acquainted with each other and communicate about their issues. Sharing the creative, inner journeys expressed in their art helps each person articulate and expand their own awareness, discoveries and feelings. As we inspire and support each other, we broaden our awareness and respect for diversity and for what is universally human, which improves the quality of our relationships.

Personal experiences of expressive arts therapy become a strong and useful foundation for learning to incorporate the arts into individual counseling or group sessions. When we directly experience the way expressive arts bring up emotions and insights, we understand the powerful dynamics we are offering to clients. This helps us facilitate their process in a respectful, supportive way.

In her book, *The Creative Connection*, Natalie Rogers writes:

> I find I can rapidly understand the world of the client when she expresses herself through images. Color, form and symbols are languages that speak from the unconscious. As I listen to a client's explanation of her imagery, I poignantly see the world as she views it. Or she may use movement and gesture to show how she feels. As I witness her movement, I can understand her world by empathizing kinesthetically . . . (p. 3).
>
> [T]he therapist can offer the visual arts process any time the client is using imagery and color to describe herself (such as feeling heavy hearted, or feeling blue). The flow of the therapy is thus enhanced rather than interrupted . . . (p. 112).

Patricia Waters, an expressive arts therapist, worked in a locked ward at Napa State Hospital and said patients responded well to doing art. One schizophrenic young man spoke only in an unintelligible babble, but he always did art and then wrote about it. One day he made a picture of someone floating in air and wrote a title: Man disconnected from thoughts. After that he had a real conversation with her about his life and the drugs he'd taken. He had never talked about it before. Through his artwork there was a meeting of his world and Patricia's world. Art was a bridge that they both could view and discuss for the first time.

Speaking of her group work with seniors with Alzheimer's and dementia, Patricia (Waters, 2001) says,

> this is not traditional therapy, talking therapy, because many of the seniors have little or no memory, but it *is* therapeutic. Making art is a self-nurturing process that is enjoyable and gives comfort and satisfaction. These patients feel chronically disoriented and mentally scattered. Doing art helps them focus, because it is absorbing. Coloring is especially like a form of meditation. It eases people who are troubled, anxious, or angry, helping them to become quiet and engrossed.

Patricia invites them to paint and color with total permission. Their art-making is not a crafts project but an activity to make psychological contact with themselves and each other. It is important that they do it of their own free will and that they can appreciate whatever they are able to do. Patricia stopped a helper who started to paint for a woman because she wasn't doing it 'right'. She advised him to let the woman paint in whatever way she could because the activity is more important than the product. Patricia says, 'Once the woman gets started, she becomes engaged and calm and by the end she is beaming. She will forget what she did, but when reminded she is very pleased.'

Lack of memory and dementia can limit communication, but Patricia feels she knows more about these people through their art. One woman always colors very carefully. That is a way her personality reveals itself, so through art Patricia can affirm her in positive ways. She acknowledges and honors this woman's carefulness and gets smiles. Although this woman is very self-critical in general, she is proud of her work. Art enables Patricia to say, 'Look at what you've done so carefully, or so colorfully, or so freely', depending on the individual artist. She makes a connection to each person that is unique to how they express themselves.

Because there are many different levels of ability and disability, it is difficult to find an activity that everyone can do. Those who don't want to do art are free to go, but they stay and watch. Whether they are making art or kibitzing, a focused art activity sitting around a table brings people together as a group and helps them develop relationships and communicate with each other. Their individual and collective art is put up and becomes their environment (Waters, 2001).

PSYCHOLOGICAL CONTACT THROUGH SHARED ART PROJECTS

Shared art experiences can be used in couples therapy and in family counseling to heighten awareness of relationship issues and help people communicate about them. These are especially effective for children in family counseling who may not have the verbal skills of their parents. It equalizes the power in the relationship by allowing children to express a variety of emotions — anger, closeness, distance — non-verbally, scribbling near, far away from or even on their parents' images.

The process of doing a shared project often brings up boundary issues, and the way people work together with shared paper, colors, clay, movement or drama often reflects real issues or conflicts they have in their relationship. Spontaneous creative expression can help people move through deadlocked arguments or misunderstandings, because they can each release tensions, reveal feelings, and then talk about their differing perceptions in a non-combative way. They can explore their conflicts or boundary issues with each other by discussing the ways they are reflected in their art.

Drama improvisation engages mind, body and emotions and helps people learn more about their parts in the conflict. When they role-play each other's position in their conflict, they gain insight into each other's perspective which heightens empathy and compassion. People also can sculpt each other into a tableau, or a still scene, that represents the conflict. This ensures a pause for reflection and discussion. Each person in the tableau can contribute questions and insights from their part of this group sculpture. They can act out possible solutions, which is a cooperative way of exploring alternatives to conflict.

Because these 'shared art conversations' help people attune to each other, the resulting creation can be bonding. When I worked with children with special educational needs, drawing together helped us develop a rapport in a playful, informal way. Over time the drawings we created became visual representations of shared experiences that we valued, a tangible record that affirmed our relationship.

A co-created group art project can also be bonding and facilitate communication. Families and support groups can do it for fun and personal growth. This can be used with children in the classroom for cooperative learning and social cohesiveness. In a community or business it aids team-building and the development of a shared vision or project as well as being used to explore and resolve conflicts. Cooperative problem-solving can help a group of any age feel a sense of kinship and camaraderie.

THE ARTS AND SOCIAL CHANGE

Carl Rogers (1961) wrote that there 'is a desperate social need for the creative behavior of creative individuals'. He continued:

> Many of the serious criticisms of our culture and its trends may best be formulated in terms of a dearth of creativity... In the clothes we wear, the food we eat, the books we read, and the ideas we hold, there is a strong tendency toward conformity... To be original or different is felt to be dangerous.
>
> In a time when knowledge, constructive and destructive, is advancing by the most incredible leaps and bounds... genuinely creative adaptation seems to represent the only possibility that man can keep abreast of the kaleidoscopic changes in his world... Consequently it would seem to me that investigations of the process of creativity, the conditions under which this process occurs and the

ways in which it may be facilitated are of the utmost importance (pp. 348–9).

Through this investigation of creativity, Natalie Rogers has brought person-centered expressive arts to many other cultures as a bridge for cross-cultural understanding. She found that '[t]he nonverbal, symbolic, and mythic expressions that arise from our deeper selves when we express creatively are understood across cultures' and goes on to say that

> [b]uilding bridges across cultures is citizen diplomacy at its best. Using the expressive arts can help us discover that we are all humans with hopes and aspirations, with suffering, anger and love, and that we each have our own uniqueness and worth. Although I am emphasizing the person-centered approach to expressive arts as a form of social activism, I know that using these methods to foster awareness and changes in behavior in personal relationships is the hub from which all other changes are made.

In his book *Through Our Own Eyes: Popular Art and Modern History*, Guy Brett (Brett, 1987) describes the power of art to effect social change. One of his most compelling examples demonstrates Natalie's point that the arts can increase personal awareness, change personal relationships and become the hub of larger changes.

During the Chilean dictatorship, mass unemployment and the risk of starvation motivated groups of women to create arpilleras (patchwork pictures made by sewing cloth scraps onto burlap bags) to support their families. Under martial law, people were forbidden to gather publicly in groups of even two or three. Only in church were these women allowed to come together to do their craft. There, they discovered that their images reflected what they saw in their lives: they expressed the pain and horror they felt about their loved ones being kidnapped, tortured and killed by the dictatorship. Realizing that they shared a common experience of terror and loss, of helplessness and grief, they began to act as a support group for each other. Art was their language, when it was forbidden to speak.

As international interest grew in this folk craft, the women sewed messages and explanations into the hems of the arpilleras. Along with their pictures, word of their plight slipped out of Chile right under the nose of the military. Once the rest of the world became aware of this oppression, international attention and scrutiny grew. The world became a conscious witness to the death and destruction, and the Chilean government was no longer able to operate with impunity. It had to answer for the human rights violations and atrocities it had committed (Brett, 1987).

This Chilean arpillera movement illustrates the same transformative dynamics occurring in the same progression as I have described above in therapeutic situations. Through their creative work, the women gained an avenue of personal expression, a release for their feelings, and a means of communication with each other. Together they found the courage to risk reaching out to the world through their art and catalyzed important political changes. No longer feeling isolated as individuals, and no longer isolated from the world by enforced secrecy, the women found that art had changed their lives.

CONTACT AND PERCEPTION

The person-centered approach to expressive arts is one way of educating people to embrace creativity as a life-enhancing survival skill. Once people learn to encourage and respect their authentic selves, they can extend this respect to their relationships, community and environment. Once they have experienced making creative, constructive changes in their own lives, they see the real possibility of making a positive difference in the world.

REFERENCES

B. (1996). Unpublished Final Internship Paper for PCETI.
Lynda, (1999). Course Response Paper for PCETI.
Marcia, (1999a). PCETI intensive participant (July).
Marcia, (1999b). Telephone conversation with the author (August).
Rogers, C. R. (1961). *On Becoming a Person*. Boston: Houghton Mifflin, pp. 347–59.
Rogers, N. (1993). *The Creative Connection: Expressive Arts as Healing*. Palo Alto, CA: Science and Behavior Books. (Published in the UK in 2000 by PCCS Books Ltd.)
Thea, (1998). Unpublished Final Internship Paper for PCETI.
Waters, P. (2001). Interview with the author (December).
Wendy, (1998). Unpublished Final Internship Paper for PCETI.
Brett, G. (1987). *Through Our Own Eyes: Popular Art and Modern History*. Philadelphia: New Society Publishers.

12 Sexual Orientation and Psychological Contact

Dominic Davies and Maggie Aykroyd

INTRODUCTION

The chapter is intended to address some of the professional development needs of therapists working in the Person-Centred Approach, irrespective of sexual identity. We feel the issue of *psychological contact* matters as much in same-sexual orientation dyads as it does where sexual orientation of client and therapist are not matched.

Whilst we have been asked to explore the implications of sexual orientation on psychological contact, our findings and recommendations could probably be extended to other groups where difference exists between therapist and client (i.e. race, ethnicity, class, age, gender, etc.). There are some issues that are unique to sexual minority clients, but one would say that about any of the other groups too. There are probably more similarities than differences though, and the reader is encouraged to try extrapolating from our subject matter to other groups with whom they work. For simplicity we make use of the term 'sexual minority' to include lesbian, gay, bisexual and transgender clients, as well as those people who may not identify with these labels but who may nonetheless experience prejudice as a result of having relationships with people of the same gender.

This chapter has been co-written by a lesbian and a gay man. Both of us have been practising in the Person-Centred Approach for a number of years, and one of us (Aykroyd) came out as a lesbian, quite late in life, and brings a unique perspective to this chapter, which is shared with the reader later. The other author (Davies), 'came out' in his early twenties and has written extensively on the subject of working with sexual minorities. This is our first writing collaboration together, and we find our views and experiences to be surprisingly similar.

HOW DO I KNOW IF WE'RE IN PSYCHOLOGICAL CONTACT?

When there is psychological contact between therapist and client the flow of experiencing between the two is unhindered. The quality of contact at these times is known by both and is almost taken as a given. Certainly, we accept as a *sine qua non* that psychological contact is essential for a successful therapeutic relationship. When there is sufficient contact it informs our felt sense of the quality of our meeting with each other. We also find that psychological contact can be progressive and deepen over time or even at specific moments within a particular session. We understand this to be akin to the *'relational depth'* proposed by Mearns (1996).

It is probably much easier to be aware of the times when we are *not* in contact with our clients. The times when the flow of experiencing is blocked in some way are the times when either party may feel bored, uncomfortable or judgemental. Perhaps as therapists, we are aware of feeling inhibited — of not feeling free to be most fully ourselves in relation to our client. We may become aware of holding back, of feeling and being guarded.

These are the times in any therapeutic relationship when the source of this loss of contact needs to be explored. Is it my block? Is it the client's? Is it something that is happening within our relationship? Therapists may want to ask themselves: What stops me being in contact with *all* of my lesbian, gay, bisexual or transgender client? Am I willing to explore myself openly in supervision to discover the source of my discomfort, boredom or judgement? Am I willing to explore my own prejudice in relation to sexual minorities? Am I willing to seek out a supervisor who has required this degree of self-awareness of herself and who can therefore fully accompany and facilitate my exploration? It is the therapist's responsibility to the client to ensure that they do everything they can to establish high quality psychological contact early on in the relationship. Later this may become a shared responsibility.

If the block is my client's, can I offer acceptance and understanding to him in his fear of contact with me or with aspects of himself in order that this, too, is available for therapeutic exploration? Have I educated myself about the culture of lesbian, gay, bisexual and transgender people in order that I can hear more accurately my client's unique experience? What do I understand about the nature and effects of institutionalised homophobia? What can I do to examine my attitudes for any trace of heterosexism? Do I have an historical understanding of the experience of sexual minorities? How can I be most fully in psychological contact with my lesbian, gay, bisexual and transgender client?

HOW CAN I DEMONSTRATE MY AVAILABILITY TO BE IN CONTACT?

It is thought that clients begin to form a relationship with the therapist even before meeting them. Burgess (2000) describes it thus: 'as the first call is made and the first intake of breath is heard before any words are uttered by the counsellor, the surge of psychological energy is ignited, activated. It is truly a cataclysmic moment.' The decision to seek help indicates a readiness at some level, to enter into 'contact' with a therapist. However, the client is likely to be wary and watchful for signs that the therapist is trustworthy and able to understand them. Rogers (1951, p. 72) recalls his own experience of reaching out for help: 'I still remember the warm, acceptant voice of the counsellor and my feeling that it was just a little more acceptant than I could be of the fears I was expressing but not enough different to be reassuring in a threatening way.'

The therapist will want to demonstrate their availability to be in contact with clients. We consider there are four key areas to manifesting this availability. The four parts are *pre-contact,* or how you present yourself to the world in publicity and image; the *initial contact* between you and the client; your *working environment* which encompasses the physical space you work within and your *manner* or *way of being*. In working with sexual minority clients we suggest therapists will need to pay close attention to all four elements as it is highly likely, due to the history of persecution and (mal) 'treatment' by 'helping professionals' that they will have a hypervigilance to being pathologised as sick or deviant.

Pre-contact

Clients very often arrive in our consulting rooms having checked us out. A current or former client may have referred them, they may have learned about us from a referral directory or register or another counsellor may have referred them. However it is that they find us, clients have often made enquiries of others about our training, our sexuality, and our reputation as a way of ensuring their safety, and in preparation for them to be in psychological contact with us (Davies, 1998). This may account for some colleagues feeling that they rarely see sexual minority clients, and others seeing many people from sexual minorities.

The reader might like to consider the following questions:
- What are your links with lesbian, gay, and bisexual community and voluntary organisations?
- Where do you publicise your practice — do you or your organisation pay for advertising, and if so do you advertise in the gay press?
- If you work for an organisation, does the publicity mention either explicitly or implicitly that you welcome sexual minority clients? Do you, for example, state that you work with 'couples' or offer counselling for 'marital difficulties'? This may lead to some sexual minority clients feeling unable to present if they are in an 'open' relationship (i.e. a non-monogamous relationship). It could imply that the therapist holds a belief that extra-dyadic relationships are not healthy or fully functional. The use of the term *relationship counselling* may be less heterocentric.
- Do you mention your interest in 'sexual minorities' or advertise yourself as 'gay affirmative' in your referral directory entries and other publicity?
- If you are an experienced gay affirmative therapist have you considered offering consultation and training to sexual minority support groups and organisations? (See Davies and Neal, 1996, 2000, and Neal and Davies 2000 for further reading about gay affirmative therapy.)
- Do your colleagues know that you have an interest in working with this client group and would welcome referrals? If the therapist is also from a sexual minority group, they may have a specific interest in offering their services to other sexual minority clients. However, as we demonstrate in this chapter, they too will have considerable work to do in terms of their personal and professional development before they are ready to work at *relational depth* (Mearns, 1996) with lesbian, gay, bisexual and transgender clients, as *a shared sexual identity is not sufficient preparation for working with sexual minority clients*.

CONTACT AND PERCEPTION

Working environment

In discussing the six necessary and sufficient conditions, Rogers states it is important that '. . . each person makes some perceived difference in the experiential field of the other. Probably it is sufficient if each makes some "subceived" difference . . . ' (Rogers, 1957, 1990, p. 221). The reader may care to reflect on how their physical presentation and that of their working environment may impact a sexual minority client. What are the different perceptions and *subceptions* clients might have of them? (Subception is the subliminal perception or *edge of awareness* experiencing which is not in our conscious awareness.)

A more defensive therapist may be thinking, 'What difference does my sexuality make to how I make contact and to how my client makes contact?' However, we think it is valuable to reflect on 'how is my (hetero) sexuality in their face?' To many lesbian, gay, and bisexual clients, my close-cropped hair, and the ring worn on my little finger (or 'pinkie ring') gives a clear message of my 'out' gay identity. Others may not notice these, or not recognise them as gay symbols. Many lesbian, gay, and bisexual people have a highly developed sixth sense or *'gaydar'* and will scan for visible and intuitive references to the therapist's sexuality and attitudes.

We invite the reader to look again at their working environment and try to see what, at a subceived level, does the environment say about them. They may even want to ask a non-therapist friend to give them feedback. How might another person perceive the therapist? As heterosexual? Gay? Married with or without children? Reflecting on the sort of pictures they have on their walls? Do they work in a book-lined study? If so, what might this say about them? Are there books that are positively connoted to homosexuality visible on their shelves? (This might be subceived as accepting of homosexuality.) Or do they perhaps, in an attempt to demonstrate their valuing of other therapeutic models, have books, which come from, for example, a traditional psychoanalytic model, and which may describe lesbian, gay, and bisexual people pathologically? Have they, for example, popular psychodynamic bestsellers like Laufer and Laufer (1984) and Malan (1979), or gay-affirmative analytic texts, such as Isay (1989, 1996), and O'Connor and Ryan (1993)? What sort of magazines are in the waiting area and what might these say about them or the agency they work?

The therapist's orientation

Clients report that it is often important to know their therapist's sexual orientation. This is rarely as simple as whether the therapist can identify with the issues the client is presenting. Some therapists might experience this desire to know as an intrusive invasion of their personal life. Therapists may assume that if they say they are heterosexual that the client will not want to work with them. Aside from this being the client's right to choose, it might be that the client is also attempting to establish psychological contact with the therapist, by 'being in personal . . . contact with each other' (Rogers, 1957, 1990, p. 222). Davies (1996, pp. 38–9) has discussed elsewhere some of the implications for therapists being open to a discussion about their sexual identity. There are clear clinical and ethical obligations in doing so, and therapists should always be willing to enter into such dialogue with clients.

Sexuality and sexual orientation is often seen as a private matter and irrelevant to one's professional practice. Lesbian, gay, and bisexual therapists might sometimes be heard to say, 'What I do in bed is my own affair,' whilst heterosexuals may say a variation of 'I don't mind homosexuals as long as they don't flaunt it, or force it down my throat.' The professional therapist is encouraged to treat everyone the same. Fear of action arising from a breach of equal opportunities policies or our Codes of Ethics can cause therapists to put on their most politically correct bib and tucker and to mind their P's and Q's (policies and quotients?). However, this avoidance of difference and denial of cultural variables can be very damaging for the therapeutic relationship (Brauner, 2000). Clients may spend a lot of time trying to work out the therapist's real frame of reference, and look for subtler signals of genuineness or of incongruence.

CLIENT BLOCKS TO PSYCHOLOGICAL CONTACT

There are common themes which affect sexual minority clients and may help our understanding of a client's reluctance or inability to stay in psychological contact within the therapeutic relationship. These are the client's degree of comfort with their sexuality and how comfortable they are about being open about this; their internalised homophobia and levels of shame; the impact of heterosexism and fear of heterosexuals; fearing the therapist's voyeurism and curiosity about their sexuality; and wondering about the therapist attitudes and beliefs.

Client's degree of comfort with sexuality and being 'out'

For some sexual minority clients being 'out', i.e. openly owning their sexuality to themselves and others, is a source of great discomfort and fear. The powerful messages of hatred and disgust that we experience every day inform our conditions of worth and self-concept. Sexual minority clients have grown up with the reality of society's oppression. This inevitably has an effect on their degree of comfort with their sexuality and their willingness to be open about who they are.

In my case (Aykroyd), the result of this fear was that I was out of contact with so much of myself for most of my life. When I first recognised my difference as a child and felt open and joyful, the messages I had in response to my openness about my same-sex attractions were that I would 'grow out of it'. If I didn't, I would no longer be acceptable or accepted, no longer be lovable or loved. That was too fearful for me to contemplate. I knew as an adolescent the reality that gay men were imprisoned for simply being openly themselves. I knew the disgust with which lesbians were reviled. I knew that homosexuality was classed as a mental illness and that gay men were subjected to the most horrific abuses in the name of aversion therapy and 'cure'.

I took the only way possible as an isolated youngster for whom there were no positive images to hold on to. I hid myself away. I built a box for myself and willingly crawled into it. I began to stick labels on the outside of the box, all of which spoke of my 'normality'. See! I have a boyfriend! See! I'm married! Even my beloved children were to some degree a comforting seal to my heterosexual exterior. And in the deep, dark corners of the box, I was dying. All that was fundamental to my existence, my sexuality, my spirituality, my creativity, was locked away, inaccessible, out of contact. It was only when the last question, life or death, was posed that I dared to choose life and slowly and with enormous fear began to push open my box and crawl into the light. It was a terrifying journey out of my box. Would my children, who were now young women themselves, reject me? Would my women friends no longer welcome my embrace? I risked losing everyone I loved, but if I didn't risk, I would surely die.

My story is not uncommon, particularly amongst older lesbian, gay, bisexual and transgender clients. Even today where more gays, lesbians and bisexuals are 'out and proud', the degree of comfort or discomfort with one's sexuality and the extent to which one feels safe to declare it openly remains an idiosyncratic choice for each client. This may well affect the extent to which a client is able to be openly in psychological contact within the therapeutic relationship.

Internalised homophobia and shame

Sexual minority clients will, at some point in their therapeutic journey, give expression to and become more aware of their internalised homophobia. It is impossible to live every day of our lives in receipt of the hatred and contempt for our difference expressed by this society and by many of the individuals we meet without internalising some of this loathing. Davies (1996, p. 55) suggests that an important part of the therapeutic work with a lesbian, gay or bisexual client is to help them to acknowledge these beliefs and ways of behaving for what they are — a response to 'societal pathologizing of their natural and healthy sexuality'.

Case Example One

James (24) was speaking of a recent visit to his parents where his brother, his wife and their eight-year-old son Ben were also visiting. At one point in the visit, James found himself alone in the lounge with his nephew sitting on his lap watching a video. The other adults were all out in the garden. James spoke of his discomfort when his sister-in-law returned to the lounge and saw her son cuddled up on James' lap. He felt guilty about being 'caught' holding Ben. He had been enjoying the contact, although he had also been anxious about being found with Ben in what could be viewed as a 'compromising' position. Whilst he felt clear about his own intentions, and felt his behaviour to be innocent, he also harboured some shame due to the erroneous linking of homosexuality with paedophilia. His heterosexual female therapist responded: 'I can imagine why you would be worried, I guess it's right to be cautious as I imagine his mother may be anxious seeing you both like that.' This reinforced one of James' configurations of self (Mearns and Thorne, 2000) as 'unsafe' and 'untrustworthy'. A more appropriate response may have been to empathise with each of James' configurations, as another part of him felt angry that he had to censor his behaviour which could have prevented his nephew getting the affection he sought from his uncle. This barrier to psychological contact, erected by the therapist, took much work to repair.

A client experiencing the force of her internalised homophobia may find it difficult to stay in psychological contact. If she is working with a heterosexual therapist it may be that she feels protective of her lesbian and gay community. When her feelings of shame about her difference begin to surface, it may be safer to withdraw from contact with a therapist whose heterosexuality embodies the source of her community's oppression. Therapists working with such clients need to be aware and willing to explore openly their understanding of internalised homophobia and to have a high degree of awareness of their own homophobia.

If she is working with a lesbian therapist it might feel too painful or too dangerous to subject her companion on her therapeutic journey to her own homophobic hatred. This again may be a time when withdrawal of psychological contact feels like a safer option to the fear of rejection. Again, it is vital that lesbian, gay and bisexual therapists have explored their own internalised homophobia in order that they are free to be fully with their client in their own unique experience.

Heterosexism

Therapists from sexual minority groups may also find that clients are unwilling or unable to enter psychological contact because of their own rigid beliefs that heterosexuality and traditional gender norms are the only acceptable way of being in the world.

Case Example Two

The therapist, Jean, has offered a potential new client, Mary, an exploratory session in order that Mary might make an informed choice about working in a therapeutic relationship with her. Jean asks Mary where she would like to start with the exploration. Mary says that it is important to her that her therapist shares her views, particularly relating to her spiritual beliefs. She goes on to explain that as an evangelical Christian she has very firm opinions, backed by biblical teaching, about human sexuality and the evil of homosexuality and sex before marriage. It is important to her that she can trust her therapist and this means that she needs to ask what Jean's beliefs on these issues are. As an out lesbian person-centred therapist, Jean's desire to respond honestly to Mary's questions means that she owns a different belief, but she lets Mary know that it would be her intention to be with her in her exploration of her own reality and that she feels able to offer that. To Mary's surprise, Jean continues with the exploratory session as though satisfied with the answer she has received and works at some depth. At the end of the session Jean checks out Mary's experience of this therapeutic contact and Mary says that she has felt more fully met in this session than by other therapists she has checked out before, but she will not be returning because of Jean's sexual difference.

CONTACT AND PERCEPTION

This was a particularly painful experience for Jean as the cost of being willing to enter another's reality, which is essentially dismissive and denying of her own, is always felt keenly. In this case her pain was increased by her recognition of Mary's denial to herself of what she had experienced as good psychological contact and a therapeutic relationship in which she felt truly met. Jean realised just how threatened Mary's rigid heterosexist concepts must have been by her willingness to enter Mary's reality and accompany her there.

CLIENT'S FEARS ABOUT HETEROSEXUAL THERAPISTS

Heterophobia

For some sexual minorities there may exist an equal rigidity of belief that all heterosexuals are to be rejected and dismissed. Heterosexual therapists are unlikely to meet such clients. One manifestation of this defence against the experience of homophobia is to avoid all heterosexuals and thus actively discriminate against the hated or feared group. Inter-orientation psychological contact will not be contemplated. For some clients there may exist a less rigid position in which they are willing to work with a heterosexual therapist but in all aspects of the work, because sexuality is such a fundamental of who we are, their belief is 'you can't understand me'. This presents great challenges to the relationship and needs to be openly addressed by the therapist to try to ensure psychological contact is achieved.

For any therapist working with a client who manifests this symptom, it will be vital to recognise the malignancy of internalised homophobia at work. It is a responsibility of therapists working with any gay, lesbian or bisexual client to be alert to and to recognise the manifestations of internalised homophobia and to be willing to work to counter its effect. Understanding these effects will help to conceptualise the client's process when his withdrawal from psychological contact is experienced and will support the therapist in maintaining his 'being' in the therapeutic relationship with real understanding and acceptance.

Fearing voyeurism and curiosity of the therapist

Some sexual minority clients may be wary of the therapist's interest in their lives. This may be a fear of being judged, or misunderstood. They may feel that, for example, discussing their committed, but sexually 'open' relationship will be viewed by the therapist as avoiding intimacy. The client may be reluctant to discuss their sexual practices for fear that the therapist is repulsed or, on the contrary, even aroused by such discussions. Any hindrance to the client being able to discuss any aspect of their lives is an unacceptable barrier to psychological contact and something that needs attention. Therapists should make every effort to have rigorously examined their feelings and attitudes to sexual minority experiences prior to establishing working relationships with this group.

Some clients might be reluctant to express dissatisfaction with either their sexual identity or aspects of the way that the lesbian, gay, bisexual and transgender communities operate. This can be a way of protecting themselves (and the therapist) from their own internalised homophobia or feelings of shame due to heterosexism. It is our experience that a fruitful discussion can often be had from not only exploring 'what do you like about being gay' as well as 'what do you dislike about it?'

What work has the therapist done on attitudes and beliefs?

The historical legacy of therapy's relationship to homosexuality is clearly not a secret! Hundreds if not thousands of gay men endured 'treatment' by having electro-shock therapy whereby electrodes were attached to their genitals and they received a painful shock if they responded to homoerotic images. Others underwent long-term psychoanalytic psychotherapy with detached and often emotionally punitive therapists. Sexual minority clients have, to borrow a concept from the Jungians, a *collective unconscious* memory of being labelled 'bad, mad and dangerous to know'; this is similar to African-Caribbean people's experience of having been subjected to centuries of slavery. The memories reside in both the unconscious and conscious memory of the community. It is likely therefore that clients will be wondering what we 'really' think about them and their lives. Whether we still believe that homosexuality is a mental illness, and since homosexuality was only declassified by the World Health Organisation in 1992 (ICD, 1992) there will be many of us practising today who were trained to see it as a mental illness, a sexual deviation, a perversion or a sin.

Clients are justified in asking their therapist what work they have done on their attitudes and beliefs about sexual minority sexualities and what training they have undertaken to be able to work effectively with them. It is our responsibility to ensure that we are able to offer clients the best therapeutic experience we can.

THERAPIST BLOCKS TO PSYCHOLOGICAL CONTACT

Unresolved sexuality issues in the therapist

It is an insufficient defence to claim that simply because the Person-Centred Approach eschews diagnosis and labels that therapists do not hold the belief that lesbian, gay, bisexual and transgender people are in some way damaged or disturbed. *A belief in the actualising tendency and organismic self does not immunise the person-centred therapist from endemic societal and cultural homophobia and heterosexism.*

Too often, the authors have heard of person-centred therapists stating words to the effect that: 'I'm not prejudiced, I accept everyone, we're all the same underneath.' This denying of personal prejudice and claiming that sexual minority clients are just the same as them is as offensive as claiming black people are the same as white. It shows a naïve complacency about the insidious and endemic effects of culturally sanctioned discrimination and prejudice. It indicates, just how little awareness the person has of anti-oppressive practice issues and how much they are in need of training.

The absence of implicit prejudice within the approach does not mean that the person-centred therapist will necessarily be free from unresolved issues around homosexuality or gender issues. It could be that the therapist is envious of some of the freedom from culturally constructed norms in terms of gender behaviour that the lesbian or gay person enjoys. For example, the freedom to openly express affection and the capacity for emotional intimacy with other men that many gay men are able to enjoy and with which it is often much harder for heterosexual men to feel comfortable.

We know that many people have same-sex experiences or erotic feelings during their adult life. It could also be that earlier same-sex sexual experience or crushes perhaps in adolescence or early adulthood have left the therapist with unresolved issues. The different choices they made may impede their availability to work at relational depth with the lesbian, gay or bisexual client for fear of being seduced off the 'straight and narrow' path.

Heterosexism

'We're all the same underneath' usually also implies a complete lack of awareness that there is a predominant culture in this society that is *different* from the cultures of sexual minority groups.

When a heterosexual definition of human sexuality is the first assumption of the therapist, there will inevitably be a block to psychological contact with the sexual minority client. This can be particularly damaging to trust in the therapist and therefore in the therapeutic relationship for a client in the early stages of owning their difference — the very time when a trustworthy companion is so vital for the client to work through their fear of rejection.

This attitude can be overtly expressed or it can seep out because it is the unchallenged belief of the therapist. As such it will inform every thought about the client, every response made to the client. When a client refers to their partner and the therapist's immediate assumption is that this is someone of the opposite gender, the client will know they are working with a therapist who is unaware and is ignorant of the possibility of difference. When a woman talks of her children and the therapist assumes a heterosexual union to be the only possibility for the conception of children, she demonstrates her ignorance. When a gay man talks of his desire for children and the therapist harbours the attitude that children should have a mother and a father, that discriminatory belief will block psychological contact. The list of examples is endless. Do you hear your client only in the context of your own culture? Are you willing to explore your heterosexism?

Homophobia

In their book *Pink Therapy*, Davies and Neal (1996) give a clear and thorough description of the ways that the homophobia that is endemic in the institutions of western society is internalised and acted out by individuals. Therapists are not immune from this. Homophobia is always a block to psychological contact with sexual minority clients regardless of the sexual orientation of the therapist.

The client's response to an experience of homophobic attitudes in their therapist may vary according to the stage they have reached in their process of self-acceptance. The client who has found a degree of self-love may well be able to experience a homophobic therapist and survive the encounter with their self intact. Such a client is likely to leave this relationship. Clients with self-respect do not expect to be attacked by, or have to educate, their therapist. *The oppressed does not have a responsibility to enlighten the oppressor.*

Far more damaging is the homophobic therapist working with the client who is just beginning the fearful journey towards self-acceptance. A homophobic response to a client whose internalised homophobia attacks them from within will simply affirm all they believe to be true about themselves: that they are disgusting, shameful and perverted. Such affirmation from the very relationship you have entered to seek psychological health is, at best, a block to the therapeutic process and, at worst, can lead to the abandonment that means that to continue to live feels more painful than to end their life for some sexual minority clients.

It is naïve for lesbian, gay and bisexual therapists to assume that because they belong to the sexual minority they have no homophobia. It is worth repeating here that the effect of living every day with the experience of institutionalised homophobia means that inevitably we too, take in some of these powerful messages of hatred and rejection. Our status as gay *and* therapist does not mean we are unaffected. For a gay client to meet with distaste or disapproval for his personal lifestyle, which is not shared by his gay therapist, might be an even greater blow than to meet with it from a member of the oppressing majority. For example, an older gay therapist who is mostly closeted may find himself reacting with distaste and disapproval when confronted by the openness of an effeminate young queen who he feels 'flaunts' his gay identity.

Making generalised assumptions

Even the modern lesbian or gay therapist may be forgiven for believing the myths created by the media that to be lesbian or gay you need to be in your 20s or 30s, white, middle class and physically able. The visible exclusion of disabled people, people of different social classes, older people, transgender people from the photographs and reports of community events in the gay and straight media, does a major disservice to the diversity of the lesbian, gay, bisexual and transgender communities. If one has little contact with sexual minority communities, we imagine it is even harder to hold the frame that lesbian, gay, bisexual and transgender peoples are everywhere, in every community. Making the assumption of heterosexuality about your client is likely to irreparably alienate you. Assume Nothing!

It should not be assumed that psychological contact between same-sex therapist-client dyads is any easier. Two people are meeting together and both are, to some extent, revealing their vulnerabilities. At a psychospiritual or existential level they are encountering each other. It is likely that the client is more comfortable with some aspects of their sexual minority identity than their therapist is. For example, the client may have come out to their parents, where the therapist has not. The client may be more openly gay, and the therapist may carry greater levels of shame due to heterosexism and internalised homophobia than the client may. This may lead the therapist to be more guarded in their ability to be in psychological contact with their client. This can also happen, where there is a concordance with experiencing similar problems, i.e. working with someone on relationship problems or loneliness, when the therapist herself has similar issues.

WAYS TO ACHIEVE AND DEVELOP PSYCHOLOGICAL CONTACT

Supervision by an experienced lesbian, gay and bisexual therapist

One way to ensure that you have support in your journey to increase psychological contact with your sexual minority clients is to seek supervision with someone who has experience and understanding of the issues raised in this chapter. Whatever your sexual orientation, when working with sexual minority clients a supervisory relationship in which you feel free to bring the worst of yourself in your practice, where your inexperience and lack of awareness can be revealed without fear of criticism, is essential in order to ensure best practice. A supervisor who is alert to the subtleties as well as the blatancies of homophobia and heterosexism will be an essential support to you and to your work with your clients.

Such a supervisor will be able to suggest training courses which address the gaps in your knowledge and awareness, and may point you in the direction of relevant films or reading, both fact and fiction, which will increase your understanding of the diversity within the cultures of the sexual minorities in order that you might hear your client's unique experience more clearly.

Such a supervisor will be willing to share his or her own experience to increase your understanding of the effects of homophobia and heterosexism.

We maintain that addressing the issues and facilitating increased awareness and personal development is necessary to work with professional responsibility with clients from all oppressed groups and should be a core element in all counsellor and therapist training. Until it is, it is the responsibility of therapists to seek out training that helps them to address their prejudice, assumptions, beliefs and knowledge about such groups. When this happens, more gay, lesbian, bisexual and transgender clients will be met more fully and openly in their therapeutic relationships.

REFERENCES

Brauner, R. (2000). Embracing Difference: Exploring Race, Culture and Sexuality. In C. Neal and D. Davies (Eds.) *Issues in Therapy with Lesbian, Gay, Bisexual and Transgender Clients.* Buckingham: Open University Press.

Burgess, N. (2000). Personal Communication.

Davies, D. (1996). Towards a Model of Gay Affirmative Therapy. In D. Davies and C. Neal (Eds.) *Pink Therapy: A Guide for Counsellors and Therapists Working with Lesbian, Gay and Bisexual Clients.* Buckingham: Open University Press.

Davies, D. (1998). The six necessary and sufficient conditions applied to working with lesbian, gay and bisexual clients. *The Person-Centered Journal.* 5 (2), pp. 111–20.

Davies, D. and Neal, C. (Eds.) (1996). *Pink Therapy: A Guide for Counsellors and Therapists Working with Lesbian, Gay and Bisexual Clients.* Buckingham: Open University Press.

Davies, D. and Neal, C. (Eds.) (2000). *Therapeutic Perspectives on Working with Lesbian, Gay and Bisexual Clients.* Buckingham: Open University Press.

International Statistical Classification of Diseases and Related Health Problems (ICD) (1992) Tenth Revision. Geneva: World Health Organisation.

Isay, R. A. (1989). *Being homosexual: Gay men and their development.* New York: Avon Books.

Isay, R. A. (1996). *Becoming Homosexual: The journey to self-acceptance.* New York: Pantheon Books.

Laufer, M. and Laufer, E. (1984). *Adolescence and developmental breakdown.* New Haven: Yale University Press.

Malan, D. (1979). *Individual psychotherapy and the science of psychodynamics.* London: Butterworth.

Mearns, D. (1996). Working at relational depth with clients in person-centred therapy. *Counselling,* 7 (4), pp. 306–11.

Mearns, D. (2000). The Nature of Configurations within Self. In D. Mearns and B. Thorne *Person-Centred Therapy Today: New Frontiers in Theory and Practice.* London: Sage Publications.

Neal, C. and Davies, D. (Eds.) (2000). *Issues in Therapy with Lesbian, Gay, Bisexual and Transgender Clients.* Buckingham: Open University Press.

O'Connor, N. and Ryan J. (1993). *Wild desires and mistaken identities: Lesbianism and psychoanalysis.* London: Virago Press.

Rogers, C. R. (1951). *Client-centered therapy: Its current practice, implications and theory.* Boston: Houghton Mifflin.

Rogers, C. R. (1957). The necessary and sufficient conditions of therapeutic personality change. *Journal of Consulting Psychology,* 21(2), pp. 95–103.

Rogers, C. R. (1990). The necessary and sufficient conditions of therapeutic personality change. In H. Kirschenbaum and V. L. Henderson (Eds.), *The Carl Rogers Reader.* London: Constable. Original work published in 1957. See full ref. *op. cit.*

13 Madness and Mysticism in Perceiving the Other: Towards a radical organismic, person-centred interpretation

Ivan Ellingham

Blessed are the pure in heart for they shall see God.   Jesus

The mystic, endowed with natural talent for this sort of thing and following stage by stage the instruction of the master enters the waters and finds he [sic] can swim; whereas the schizophrenic [sic], unprepared, unguided, and ungifted, has fallen or has intentionally plunged, and is drowning.   Joseph Campbell

Mostly formulated by Carl Rogers, person-centred theory is at heart an outgrowth of an emerging paradigm of scientific understanding, an ideational world-view to which the names *general systems*, *holism*, *organismic*, and *process* have been attached (see Bozarth, 2001; Seeman, 2001 — my preferred term is organismic). To lay claim to scientific pedigree, person-centred theory needs to be a coherent expression of such an organismic paradigm. Person-centred theory exhibits crucial flaws, I have argued, to the extent that its base concepts are not congruent representatives of this emerging paradigm but of the Cartesian-Newtonian paradigm that it supersedes (see Ellingham, 2001). To remedy such flaws I have proposed a strategy of 'organismic assimilation', a strategy involving assimilating into person-centred theory ideas drawn from organismic thinkers outside the person-centred fold: ideas developed by such thinkers as John Bowlby, Ernst Cassirer, Robert Kegan, Arthur Koestler, Susanne Langer, Kurt Lewin, Fritz Perls, Jean Piaget, Michael Polanyi, Rupert Sheldrake, Daniel Stern, Alfred North Whitehead and Lancelot Whyte (see Ellingham, 2000).

Employing this strategy in the present paper, my aim is to extend and deepen understanding of the meaning and relevance of the first and last of the six conditions that Rogers hypothesized to be 'the necessary and sufficient conditions of therapeutic personality change' (1957).

Of these conditions, it has always been the therapist-related 'core conditions' that have commanded most attention: namely, Rogers' proposal that for therapeutic change to take place in the client the therapist must (a) be 'congruent', personally whole and genuine in the relationship, (b) enjoy an empathic understanding of the client's experiential inner world, and (c) possess toward the client an attitude of acceptance and non-judgemental caring, an attitude Rogers technically terms 'unconditional positive regard'.

Aside from the condition that the client 'is in a state of incongruence, being vulnerable or anxious', the other two conditions that have been relatively neglected are Condition One, that there exists at least 'a minimal relationship' between therapist and client: that the two persons are in 'psychological contact' (1957, p. 221); and Condition Six, 'that the client *perceives*, at least to a minimal degree, the *unconditional positive regard* of the therapist for him, and the *empathic understanding* of the therapist' (1959, p. 227). Later, in emphasizing the 'logically intertwined' character of all three core conditions, Rogers hypothesized that 'therapeutic movement' for the client depends not just on the client perceiving 'to some degree the presence' of the therapist's 'unconditional positive regard' and 'sensitively accurate empathetic understanding', but also on perceiving the presence of 'the therapist's congruence or genuineness' (1966, p. 11). A further point is that there is an alternative version of Rogers' original statement of Condition Six, i.e. that 'the communication to the client of the therapist's empathic understanding and unconditional positive regard is to a minimal degree achieved' (1957, p. 221).

In what follows, focusing in the main on the character and role of perception, I respectively explore and critique certain of Rogers' theoretical ideas relating to Conditions One and Six.

In my critique, my aim on the one hand is to identify problematic aspects of Rogers' views associated with Cartesian-Newtonian thought. Key features of such thought are: taking the fundamental constituents of reality to be unchanging bits of 'stuff'; considering reality to be ultimately made up of two kinds of such stuff, 'mind' and 'matter'; regarding activity in the material world to be akin to that found in machines, of unchanging material bits being moved around by external forces; in contrast to unconscious matter, assuming consciousness to be a defining attribute of mind; deeming mind/consciousness to operate according to the principles of thought and to be of a different order to those that govern material activity. Note, though, that a materialist offshoot of Cartesian-Newtonian thought assumes the same mechanistic principles to govern mind as govern matter (much of Freud's thinking fits into this category as does that of the modern 'cognitive scientists' who treat the mind as an information processing computer).

In tandem with identifying Cartesian-Newtonian aspects of Rogers' theorizing, the other purpose to my critique is the double-sided one of (a) noting where Rogers' ideas are at odds with a radical organismic point of view, and (b) proposing the remedial introduction of ideas formulated by other organismic theorists, i.e. deploying the strategy of organismic assimilation. Spawned by evolutionary theory in biology and quantum theory and relativity theory in modern physics, a radical organismic perspective is characterised by the following assumptions: that all aspects of reality can be construed in process terms, i.e. as units of patterned activity or events; that like a wave in the sea an event has a pulse-like character; that, as with waves within the sea within the ocean, events interlock to form more complex events termed a field or an organism; that events take the form they do due both to their own impulse to self-actualize and to the space allowed them by other events similarly seeking to self-actualize; that the unchangingness of 'things' is due to a sequence of events exhibiting the same pattern, as the rhythmical repetition of the same vibratory pattern in a violin string is perceived as an unchanging musical note; that a fundamental creative principle is the ground of all activity, whether expressed in terms of unchanging or changing patterns; that the workings of this creative principle has given rise to evolution in the guise of the emergence of ever more complex patterns of activity; that, as a complex pattern of activity, the *stage-like* emergence of ever more complex processes in the life of the living organism serves to epitomise evolution and development at both a micro- and macro-level; that the continued existence of earlier, less complex forms of process alongside more complex forms, both within individual organisms and within the universe as a whole, means that all enduring 'things' exhibit a hierarchical, multi-level structure; that associated with the emergence of ever more complex forms of process are ever more complex and differentiated forms of consciousness.

These, then, in a highly condensed and abstract form are key tenets of the emerging organismic paradigm and of its Cartesian-Newtonian forebear. As I explore in turn Rogers' views relating to Conditions One and Six, I shall endeavour to clarify in concrete terms the meaning and relevance of these abstract notions.

ROGERS' VIEWS RELATING TO CONDITION ONE

A basic premise of Rogers' formulation of person-centred theory is that we each live in a 'continually changing world of experience', an experiential or perceptual field that we react to as reality (Rogers, 1951, p. 483). To have a relationship with another, for two people to be in psychological contact and thus for Condition One of Rogers' six necessary and sufficient conditions to be satisfied, a situation must exist in which 'each makes some perceived difference in the experiential field of the other' (Rogers, 1957, p. 221). Thus, what Rogers is saying, as I understand him, is that psychological contact, the necessary requisite of an interpersonal relationship, is defined on the basis of each person perceiving the other in some fashion. Psychological contact, that is to say, is a function of perception. Of interest here is that, in his writings as a whole, Rogers makes reference to different modes of perceiving another, and thus to different forms of relationship. I examine these different modes below.

Subception, perception without perception

Subception, relates Rogers, is a way of 'knowing without knowing' identified by McCleary and Lazarus (1949) whereby the human organism is able to pre-perceive the 'positive or negative value' of a stimulus, to discriminate 'its meaning for the organism without utilizing the higher nerve centers involved in awareness' (1951, p. 506; 1959, p. 200).

Rogers' main reference to subception is as a mode of 'perception' that 'permits the individual to discriminate an experience as threatening, without symbolization to awareness' and thereby 'deny experiences to awareness without ever having been conscious of them' (1959, p. 200; 1951, p. 507). In the case of individuals whose conscious picture of themselves is at odds or incongruent with their actual experience — say, in the case cited by Rogers, of the boy who has no awareness of sexual desire yet finds himself lifting up little girls' skirts (Rogers, 1951, p. 509) — an individual may subceive an experience as threatening, threatening to their existing sense of self; but while they may experience anxiety, they do not have an accurate and conscious perception of the other, for instance, as a sexually attractive person.

Individuals who deploy subception in this fashion, whose perception of others is distorted to avoid becoming aware of their own inaccurate and inadequate self-picture (their self-concept), are individuals popularly known as neurotics, or even psychotics. Whether a person might be termed a neurotic or psychotic depends on the degree of such inaccuracy and inadequacy, i.e. of their incongruence. Under such circumstances, for a relationship to exist between two people, opines Rogers, it 'probably . . . is sufficient that each makes some "subceived" difference' in the experiential field of the other 'even though the individual may not be aware of this impact' (1957, p. 221). 'Thus', he elaborates, 'it might be difficult to know whether a catatonic patient perceives a therapist's presence as making a difference to him [sic] — a difference of any kind — but it is almost certain that at some organic level he does sense [or subceive] the difference' (1957, p. 221; [interpolation from Rogers, 1967, p. 99]).

In these instances, then, as a mode of perceiving another, Rogers associates the deployment of subception with personal incongruence, a lack of psychological well-being.

This, though, is not an exclusive usage since he does at one point refer to the therapist's behaviour communicating the attitudinal conditions of congruence, unconditional positive regard and accurate empathic understanding 'so that to some degree they are perceived or *subceived* by the client' (Rogers and Truax, 1967, p. 107, author's emphasis). Elsewhere, too, without using the term 'subception', Rogers (1977) once more cites the example of the boy who lifted the little girls' skirts and denied it was him. Here, rather than 'subception', Rogers prefers to speak of 'the nonconscious aspects of our living', of the organism's 'wisdom' that is 'wiser than our intellects', of trusting 'the unconscious' (pp. 245 and 248).

Perception synonymous with awareness, symbolization, consciousness

For Rogers, 'consciousness (or awareness) is the symbolization of some of our experience', its 'symbolic representation (not necessarily in verbal symbols)' — the three terms 'awareness, symbolization, and consciousness' therefore being 'defined as synonymous' (1959, p. 198; 1951, p. 483). In this regard also, while 'we might say that perception and awareness are synonymous', perception has the narrower meaning being 'usually used when we wish to emphasize the importance of a stimulus in the process, and awareness the broader term, covering symbolizations and meanings which arise from such purely internal stimuli as memory traces, visceral changes, and the like, as well as external stimuli' (1959, p. 199).

What Rogers says of awareness and symbolization thus applies to perception, as when he speaks of symbolizing experience 'in some accurate form at the conscious level' and of there being 'varying degrees of completeness in symbolization' (1959, pp. 197–8). This means that 'when an experience can be symbolized freely, without defensive distortion and denial, then it is available to awareness' (p. 198). When, that is to say, my experience of another is freely symbolized in awareness, then I have an accurate perception in relation to that person. Further, the more open I am to my organism, as Rogers puts it, the more nearly I come to being *fully functioning*. As the idealized 'end-point of optimal psychotherapy', the fully functioning person is the person who displays 'optimal psychological maturity, complete congruence', someone who 'has the capacity and tendency to *symbolize* experiences accurately in *awareness*' (1959, pp. 234 and 235). In such a person, Rogers further elaborates,

> every stimulus, whether originating within the organism or in the environment, would be freely relayed through the nervous system without being distorted by a defensive mechanism. There would be no need of the mechanism of 'subception' whereby the organism is forewarned of any experience threatening to the self (1983, p. 286).

By way of an illustration of what it means to enjoy an accurate perception in relation to another, Rogers describes a man who due to denial and distortion is at one time unable to 'feel tenderness and love for his child' (p. 287). Subsequently, however, the man became 'genuinely open to the experience of his organism' and able to enjoy 'the full experiencing of whatever was organismically present'. He is now a person, relates Rogers, who can 'freely feel the love he feels for his daughter'.

Mystical perception

A further mode of interpersonal perception described by Rogers is also one he associates with the person who is fully functioning. It is a mode that he mainly portrays in relation to his own experience as a therapist, one that he eventually came to characterize as partaking of 'the mystical . . . the transcendent, the indescribable, the spiritual' (1980, p. 130). The following are prominent features of this mode:

- It is highly intuitive involving the operation of an individual's 'nonconscious intellect [or] mind or [sensing]', a 'wisdom of the organism' that is beyond consciousness (Rogers, 1986, pp. 206 and 208).
- It provides knowledge much more than the conscious mind is aware of (Rogers, 1986, p. 206).
- It involves a 'total organismic sensitivity' to the other person, a 'resonating' to the other person 'at all levels' (Rogers, 1961, p. 202; 1980, p. 8).
- At the same time as allowing the apprehension of 'the words, the thoughts, the feelings, the personal meanings' of the other, it also enables detection of meanings that are 'below the conscious intent of the speaker', meanings that can make their presence felt in the perceiver's mind as an aural and visual image (Rogers, 1980, pp. 8 and 15).
- It tends to be momentary and associated with an altered state of consciousness (1986, pp. 198 and 206).
- It is experienced both as the 'the height of personal subjectivity', and yet as a deep, empathic indwelling in the other's world, of being completely in tune

with that world and feeling a sense of communion and mutuality of oneself with the other. At such 'I-Thou' moments, says Rogers, speaking of his own experience, 'it seems that my inner spirit has reached out and touched the inner spirit of the other', psychological contact wherein 'our relationship transcends itself and becomes a part of something larger' (1986, p. 199).
- It not only transcends the everyday experience of a sense of personal separateness from another, but it also seems to transcend the sense of time associated with the everyday world. 'It is', attests Rogers, 'a timeless living in the experience which is *between*' the one and the other (1961, p. 202).
- It is associated with the release of 'power and energy . . . which transcends what we thought was involved', and with the presence of 'profound growth and healing' (Rogers quoted in Baldwin, 1987, p. 50; Rogers, 1986, p. 199).
- Beyond the personal communications of another, it enables the individual to sense 'orderly psychological laws' and 'what is universally true' (Rogers, 1980, p. 8). In other words, to not only be 'in touch with, but grasp the meaning of . . . [the] evolutionary flow', to comprehend the working of 'a strong formative tendency in our universe, which is evident at all levels' (Rogers, 1980, pp. 124 and 128).

CRITIQUE FROM AN ORGANISMIC PERSPECTIVE OF ROGERS' VIEWS RELATING TO CONDITION ONE

From an organismic perspective, at least one fundamental criticism can be levelled at Rogers' characterization of the preceding modes of perception, a criticism that thereby has an important bearing on what it means to say that one person enjoys a relationship, is in psychological contact, with another (i.e. on Condition One). It is a criticism that has to do with Rogers' definition of the nature of human consciousness, and *ipso facto* his definition of perception as a conscious experience. For intrinsic to Rogers' definition of consciousness in general and, more specifically, to his differentiation between unconscious subception/ organismic experience and conscious perception is a formulation redolent of the quasi-Cartesian formulations of Sigmund Freud.

To Descartes, consciousness was the mark of 'mind', of mental functioning, whereas unconsciousness by contrast represented a defining attribute of 'matter', the other basic constituent of reality in Descartes' dualistic world-scheme. Freud (1915) thus saw himself as contravening Cartesian thought when he employed the term 'the unconscious' to denote certain mental processes that affected the perceptions and behaviours of his 'neurotic' patients, processes that these adult individuals were not conscious of. Thanks to 'once-in-a-lifetime insight', Freud came to identify a logic to the workings of these 'unconscious' mental processes, a logic by which similar 'things' were taken to be identical (as in the 'transference' relationship), symbolic images were not differentiated from the real thing, and time had no place insofar as what was taken to exist existed only in the present, episodic moment. It was Freud's claim that this logic was representative of a mode of mental functioning dubbed by him 'the primary process', a mode that operated in an exclusive and dominant fashion in generating the experiences and perceptions of the dreaming adult, the human infant and those who are mad.

CONTACT AND PERCEPTION

Despite the fact that he had distanced himself from Descartes in claiming that mental processes could operate in an unconscious fashion, Freud, unbeknownst to himself, remained in Descartes' thrall in his further claim that unconsciousness was a defining characteristic of such processes, i.e. that on a par with Descartes' definition of material processes such mental processes could *never* in themselves be consciously experienced.

For to say that the experiences and perceptions of the dreamer, the infant, and the mad are expressive of a primitive or primary mode of sense-making, a mode that in the human adult generally operates in an unconscious fashion, is not to say that the dreamer, the infant and the mad do not, as such, enjoy these experiences and perceptions in some conscious form — albeit that it is not the everyday form of consciousness of the human adult.

The general thrust of organismic theorizing has been to claim that both in terms of the evolution of the race and the development of the individual, human consciousness advances from a global and undifferentiated condition to a form that is more precisely focused and differentiated. So, for instance, even though the human infant may employ 'primary processes' to perceive the world in a fashion that we may regard as diffuse and indefinite, this does not mean that such perceptions are not consciously experienced.

From an organismic perspective, therefore, Rogers simply gets things wrong when he formally defines 'awareness, symbolization, consciousness . . . as synonymous' (1959, p. 198).

Because, given that the modes of experiencing/perceiving of the infant is clearly a *pre-symbolic* form of sense-making, i.e. do not involve symbolization, it is apparently Rogers' view that it does not involve awareness or consciousness, even as he claims that the infant exhibits complete congruence and is fully functioning.

Such an interpretation is borne out by the way in which Rogers defines the undistorted perception of the fully functioning person vis-à-vis not only the human infant, but also the non-human animal. Rogers speaks, for example, of the accurate symbolization of the fully functioning person being a matter of adding 'the gift of a free and undistorted awareness of which only the human animal seems capable . . . to the sensory and visceral experiencing which is characteristic of the whole animal kingdom' (1961, p. 105). And in like fashion, he describes 'the functioning of the psychologically mature [fully functioning] individual as being similar in many ways to that of the infant, except that the fluid process of experiencing has more scope, and that the more mature individual, like the child, "trusts and uses the wisdom of his [sic] organism, with the difference that he is able to do so knowingly"' (1963, p. 20). Akin to Freud's characterization of the primary process operating in an unconscious fashion, Rogers thus envisages the infant's behaviour to be governed by 'an organismic, not a conscious symbolic function' in which 'operative, not conceived values' are at work (1983, p. 258). To illustrate which, he reminds us of the experiment 'in which young infants had spread in front of them a score or more dishes of natural (that is, unflavored) foods'. 'Over a period of time', Rogers recounts, 'they clearly tended to value the foods which enhanced their survival, growth and development'. For, on Rogers' interpretation, each child 'was utilizing the wisdom of the body in her value choices, or perhaps more accurately, the physiological wisdom of her body guided her behavioral movements, resulting in what we might think of as objectively sound value choices'.

Now, while infants obviously do not possess the post-symbolic, self-reflexive form of consciousness of the human adult; and while consciousness may not have been involved in the infants' choice of foods in the described experiments — albeit that rats have been shown to sense the 'taste' of distilled water, so conceivably the infants could actually consciously taste differences in the bland food; nevertheless the idea that infants do not possess a (pre-symbolic) form of awareness is highly questionable. And indeed in a description of the complete congruence of the infant, Rogers speaks of 'a matching of experience, awareness and communication' (1961, p. 339). In which case, if awareness is indeed synonymous with symbolization, the implication is that the infant from birth must enjoy a form of awareness mediated by symbols — which clearly she does not.

In relation to the notion of a pre-symbolic form of awareness, Susanne Langer (1972) has written a detailed and plausible account of the nature of animal mentality based on the notion of an animal's behaviour actually being governed by 'feeling', a pre-symbolic mode of awareness. She posits that 'animal perception might be normally a matter of locating situations for action, in which a center of highest value draws the agent's interest; that center — for us "the object" — presumably has sensory properties which the animal recognizes without conceiving them descriptively, i.e. without distinguishing them as shapes, colours, surface feelings or even characteristic smells' (1972, p. 116). Langer relates how such an interpretation fits with William James' assertion 'that to a broody hen an egg is not a smooth, pale object of characteristic form, but "just a beautiful, never-too-much-to-be-sat-upon-object"' (p. 54). John Bowlby (1969), for his part, has made much of the similarity between 'attachment' and distressed behaviour in animals and in human infants, so in the case of the human infant we might easily see her as governed by an intense feeling of desire to cling onto her mother, or consumed by a rageful feeling of seeking to distance herself from a stranger.

Of particular interest with respect to Langer's account of animal mentality is her supposition that in non-human animals 'subception' constitutes a dominant form of value apprehension, or sense-making. That is to say, what to the adult human is a mode of perception that is non-conscious or at the edge of awareness, to the animal is the primary mode of perception and conscious experience operating in the fashion described above, where what is perceived is 'felt in other than cognitive ways, either as an uneasiness . . . or an eager expectation' (1972, p. 116).

So described, such a mode of perception would appear to be essentially equivalent to Eugene Gendlin's (1984) conception of a bodily felt sense at the edge of awareness. Gendlin, for instance, refers to a perception of this form constituting 'the holistic, unclear sense of the whole thing', of it being the felt sense '*of* a whole situation', of its being 'indefinable, global, puzzling, odd, uneasy' (1981, p. 55; 1984, p. 79; 1986, p. 3). And not only that but he describes such a 'from the gut' mode of experiencing/perceiving as that principally employed by non-human animals (1974, p. 234; 1986, p. 143); while one of his leading followers acknowledges that such a mode of perceiving is 'paramount to the child' (Leijssen, 1998, p. 135).

CONTACT AND PERCEPTION

If this is indeed the case, then *subception* as practised by the catatonic patient is an equivalent mode of perceiving to Rogers' *sensory and visceral functioning* in the animal and *the wisdom of the organism* or *non-conscious intellect* in the infant — overall each being equivalent to Gendlin's *bodily felt sense*. But not only does Gendlin (1984) consider such a mode of sense-making to be a mode whereby the human adult can tune in to the depths of the universe beyond themselves, but, as we have seen, Rogers describes such a mode of sense-making as being employed by the fully functioning adult or mystic — albeit, compared to infant, 'knowingly', and in relation to the animal by adding 'the gift of a free and undistorted awareness of which only the human animal seems capable' (Rogers, 1961, p. 105).

Rogers' idea that the mode of awareness enjoyed by the fully functioning adult consists of accurate perceptual awareness *plus* unconscious organismic experience/subception would, though, seem to be in conflict with his statement elsewhere that the perceptual awareness of the fully functioning person involves accurate perceptual awareness *minus* subception — where, that is, he describes the fully functioning person as someone not needing to employ 'the mechanism of "subception"' to perceive an experience as 'threatening' (1983, p. 286). In this regard, therefore, Rogers seems to be employing the term 'subception' in two different ways: (a) to denote the unconscious organismic capacity of perceiving whether the object of perception is positive and non-threatening or negative and threatening; (b) to denote a 'defensive mechanism' operating to forewarn and prevent the 'free relaying' of the perception into awareness. To illustrate these different usages, consider the role of a night-club bouncer. Rogers, on the one hand, appears to be saying that subception is comparable to the activity of a bouncer who labels individuals at the door as good or bad dancers before letting them into the club where everybody can see their label and know them as good or bad dancers; on the other, that subception is comparable to the bouncer labelling would-be entrants as before but not allowing the bad dancers in — in which case only if subception did not take place would all the dancers be freely admitted.

So viewed, complementing Rogers' questionable characterization of consciousness and conscious perception is a lack of clarity in the manner in which he portrays non-consciousness and non-conscious perception.

Both these weaknesses in Rogers' theorizing have to do, in my view, with his tendency, originally pointed up by Gendlin (1962), to treat psychological events, especially 'feelings', and 'experiences', in a quasi-Cartesian manner, i.e. as 'thing-like'. It is a tendency bound up with the further criticism that Rogers depicts the process of symbolization as the 'passive' naming of these previously existing psychological 'things'. Symbolization, for Rogers, thus consists in attaching a symbol to an already existing feeling, experience or perception, comparable to the way in which labels are attached to products in a supermarket (see Rogers, 1951, pp. 144–5). Summarizing the views of her husband, Mary Hendricks-Gendlin relates how Gendlin has highlighted that 'Rogers' formulations imply that experience sits there first outside awareness waiting to be accurately perceived, as though it were something already separately formed apart from the perceiving', and the act of symbolization (1999, p. 1). Rogers' depiction for Gendlin, she continues, 'is like the "flashlight" model that Freud used with unconscious id impulses sitting there in the person and the work of therapy is to bring the light of awareness or consciousness upon them'. And like Freud's model, too, Rogers' passive labelling view of symbolization conjures such ridiculous notions as the existence of a pain of which one has no awareness due to its not having been symbolized, i.e. a pain in which there is no feeling of pain; and an unfelt feeling, i.e. a feeling that is not felt — although see the argument put forward by person-centred author Per-Anders Tengland (2001) in favour of such nonsensical notions, an argument whose logic escapes me.

Rather than being the passive affair that Rogers portrays, symbolization is an active, constructive process by which meaning is enshrined in our perceptions; by which, that is, previously diffuse and affectively charged pre-symbolic perceptions become differentially transformed into the everyday, common-sense perceptions of the human adult. It is a creative process by which qualitatively different modes of perception and consciousness are brought into being, a process that in person-centred terms is representative of the workings of what Rogers (1963) calls the 'formative actualizing tendency' (p. 21).

Neither, also, is symbolization in itself unitary — certainly not as explicated by Langer (1967, 1972, 1982) and Cassirer (1955a, 1955b, 1957). The two of them identify both a non-discursive mode of symbolizing as well as a discursive, language-laden mode — in evolutionary terms non-discursive symbolizing emerging from animal sense-making and preceding the discursive mode. Thus, in comparison to the pre-symbolic sense-making of the animal — and we can presume the early infant — non-discursive symbolizing has 'the primary function . . . of conceptualising the flux of sensations, and giving us concrete *things* in place of kaleidoscopic colors or noises' (Langer, 1957, p. 93). Alternatively termed an iconic, presentational or expressive symbol, the non-discursive symbol mainly employs visual images — although images of sound and bodily movement can also be employed — to encapsulate the subceived feeling pervading a particular situation or object. A whole sequence of sensorimotor bodily action, bodily 'knowing' of another or of a situation, can thus be represented in a single moment by means of a single image. The feeling that the iconic image presents may be difficult to distinguish from the original subceived felt sense, but it is different nevertheless, being an idea of a feeling rather then the raw feeling itself. Iconic imagery provided the building-blocks for the subsequent emergence of discursive symbolization in terms of the development of language. Whereas the iconic symbol can be compared to a ball of wool in which its import is contained in the single image, 'language has a form which requires us to string out our ideas even though their objects rest one within the other; as pieces of clothing that are actually worn one over the other have to be strung out side by side on the clothesline' (Langer, 1957, p. 81).

The relevance of such considerations for our present discussion is at least twofold. The first point concerns the notion of our dwelling in qualitatively different perceptual fields depending upon the dominant mode of perceptual sense-making/symbolization within the field, albeit that particular areas within the field may operate in a different mode. For instance, although in general I may dwell in the common-sense world of everyday discursive symbolization, I may perceive those that love me in terms of the diffuse amorphous feelings that are focal in the infant. The second is the idea that our first and most basic mode of sense-making and perception is couched in terms of the diffuse feelings of bodily sensing. If this can be relied upon as a source of wisdom, as Rogers and Gendlin suggest, it is in terms of this mode that we first sense new learnings about ourselves and others. It is the first mode by which we process information. Later this information may be further processed and expressed in terms of either discursive or more immediately iconic symbolization. For, as Whitehead describes matters, 'mysticism is direct insight into depths as yet unspoken', where the subsequent challenge is 'to rationalize mysticism; not by explaining it away but by the introduction of novel verbal characterizations' (1938, p. 174) — or, we might add, through iconic symbolizations. If we regard Rogers' mystical perception of the other as indeed an example of true insight into the nature of things, then I would suggest that the vision he presents is an organismic one, of both ourselves and the other being organisms, fields of activity, that are part and parcel of a larger field. It is a perspective in which perceptions, experiences, feelings are not considered things, but felt aspects of the field of activity, the patterns of process, of which both I and the other are part — in the manner, that is, of two whirlpools immersed in a larger stream.

I discuss such an organismic conception in relation to Rogers' views regarding Condition Six. For the moment, suffice it to say that from an organismic perspective the conception of a relationship existing between two individuals when each makes a subceived/perceived difference on the perceptual field of the other is markedly more complex than Rogers describes.

ROGERS' VIEWS RELATING TO CONDITION SIX

To fully make sense of Rogers' account of the process by which the client's perception of attitudinal conditions in the therapist facilitates positive personality change in the client, we first need to appreciate how it is, according to Rogers, that the client came to be in a condition of incongruence and therefore in need of such facilitation. For, as related above, it is Rogers' view that infants start life in a condition of complete congruence, of being fully functioning. What Rogers presents, therefore, is a saga of *paradise lost* and *paradise regained*, a saga, as such a description suggests, that closely corresponds to religious and spiritual teachings down the ages — a fact highlighted by Brian Thorne (1996, 2002). In such teachings, 'the pure soul' — the equivalent of Rogers' fully functioning adult — is said to be 'like a lens from which all irrelevances and excrescences, all the beams and motes of egotisms and prejudice, have been removed; so that it may reflect a clear image of the one Transcendent Fact within which all other facts are held' (Underhill, 1915, p. 36). 'If the doors of perception were cleansed', as William Blake famously put it, 'everything would be seen as it is, infinite' (quoted in Huxley, 1958, p. 197).

Losing paradise

Rogers, as we have seen, describes the fully functioning adult as someone capable of perceiving the other without distortion and denial, someone who in so doing apprehends the fundamental truth of the workings of the formative actualizing tendency. 'The crucial point', he says, 'is that when a person is functioning fully, there are no barriers, no inhibitions, which prevent the full experiencing of whatever is organismically present' (1980, p. 128). In other words, to genuinely perceive, we need to be genuine. Apropos the congruent organismic functioning of the infant and non-human animals, this means that 'if man's [sic] magnificent symbolizing capacity can develop as a part of and guided by the tendency toward fulfilment which exists in him as in every creature, then the "animal harmony" is never lost' (Rogers, 1963, p. 21). What we are talking about, therefore, is 'the incredibly difficult but not impossible task of permitting the human individual to grow and develop in a continuing and confident relationship to the formative actualizing tendency and process in himself [sic]'. Mirroring such congruent development, it is thus Rogers' view that incongruence — the 'dissociation' that is 'the basis of all psychological pathology in man [sic], and the basis of all his social pathology as well' — comes about due to inaccurate and inadequate symbolization, symbolization that is not in accord with the formative actualizing tendency. As to the origin of such deficient and discordant symbolization, symbolization that constitutes the barriers and inhibitions to 'whatever is organismically present', Rogers identifies two basic causes.

Under the influence of Lancelot Whyte, Rogers deems one of these two causes to be cultural. To blame, in this respect, he says, is 'the peculiarly western development of static concepts — in the formation of our language, our thought, and in our philosophy' (1963, p. 19). 'Though nature is clearly process', Rogers enlarges, 'man [sic] has been caught in his own fixed forms of thought'. Thanks to Whyte's influence, concedes Rogers, 'now I believe that individuals are culturally conditioned, rewarded, reinforced, for behaviors — ["behaviors guided by rigid concepts and constructs"] — which are in fact perversions of the natural directions of the unitary actualizing tendency' (p. 20).

The other basic cause of an incongruent person's inaccurate symbolizations, according to Rogers, is interpersonal in nature. As we have seen, Rogers' view is that an individual starts out in life in a fully functioning condition of unknowing congruence. What she encounters during her development to defile such innocent integrity, says Rogers, are interpersonal relationships conspicuous in their lack of a vital ingredient, an ingredient that Rogers formally defines as 'unconditional positive regard', and informally as 'love'. What we are talking about are formative relationships, with significant others especially, in which the giving of love to the child is conditional upon the child's activity being seen as worthy of such a gift.

In his theoretical explication of the impact on the child of conditional regard, Rogers does not 'divide the development of the child into hard-and-fast stages' (Rogers quoted in Evans, 1975, p. 11) — as Freud did with his oral, anal, phallic and genital stages. Judging such an approach to be 'somewhat artificial', Rogers adopts instead a field theory perspective 'in the sense of analyzing all the influences on the individual in the present situation'; and, while he certainly does not dispute that 'early experience is a powerful force', he prefers to conceive the child's personal growth as 'a gradual development of the picture that he [the child] carries of himself', i.e. in terms of their self-concept.

In the theory that Rogers puts forward, therefore, love/positive regard is pronounced a universal human need that is 'pervasive and persistent' (1959, p. 223). 'The infant learns to need love', Rogers declares, 'Love is very satisfying' (1959, p. 225). And so wanting it, 'the infant . . . tends to behave in ways which bring a repetition of this wanted experience' (Rogers, 1983, p. 259). Thus the need for love develops 'as the awareness of self emerges', emergence whereby 'a portion of the individual's experience becomes differentiated and symbolized in an awareness of being, awareness of functioning' (1959, p. 223). With the tendency toward differentiation and symbolization being 'part of the actualizing tendency', the awareness so generated is 'self-experience', and it is through elaboration of such awareness, 'through interaction with the environment, particularly the environment composed of significant others' that 'a concept of self' is formed, 'a perceptual object in . . . [the individual's] perceptual field'.

The self having so emerged and the need for love/regard experienced, the infant seeks to satisfy this need, such satisfaction being 'necessarily based upon inferences regarding the experiential field of another' (1959, p. 223). For example, when interacting with his mother should the infant need 'to know whether he is receiving it [love/positive regard] or not he must observe his mother's face, gestures and other ambiguous signs' (p. 225). Since it is rewarding to satisfy his own and his mother's need for positive regard, the infant 'develops a total gestalt of the way he is regarded by his mother', where a key feature of such a developmental process is that 'each new experience of love or rejection tends to alter the whole gestalt'. 'Consequently', explains Rogers, 'each behavior on his mother's part such as specific approval of a specific behavior tends to be experienced as disapproval in general'. 'So important is this to the infant', affirms Rogers, 'that he comes to be guided in his behavior not by the degree to which an experience maintains or enhances the organism, but by the likelihood of receiving maternal love'.

Therefore, while it may be organismically satisfying to pull his sister's hair, when he does so he 'hears [from mother] that he is "a naughty bad boy"' (Rogers, 1983, p. 259). He may stop doing this in order to be the 'total configuration' of the 'good boy' as viewed by his mother (Rogers, 1959, p. 225). When, though, he reaches the point of perceiving himself as a good boy if he does not pull his sister's hair and as a bad boy if he does, he has, says Rogers, introjected 'the value judgement of another, taking it in as his own' (1983, p. 259). The child has now become 'in a sense his own significant other', whereby he perceives himself positively and as having worth on the basis of 'self-regard', not on the basis of receiving love or rejection from a 'social other' (1959, p. 224). To the extent that the individual now lives in terms of alien 'introjected values . . . or conditions of worth . . . [or] self-regard' (1959, p. 225), says Rogers,

> to that degree he loses touch with his own organismic valuing process. He has deserted the wisdom of his own organism, giving up the locus of evaluation, and is trying to behave in terms of values set by others, in order to hold love (1983, p. 259).

Which is to say, he has in this respect developed an incongruent self-concept, a perception of himself that is not true to his organismic experiencing. 'Because of the distorted perceptions arising from conditions of worth', the individual thus has departed 'from the integration which characterizes his infant state' (1959, p. 226). Paradise has been lost.

In specifying how incongruence and distorted self-perceptions result in distorted perceptions of the other, or a perception of the other that is denied to awareness, Rogers once more cites the case of the boy who indulged in sexual behaviour towards young girls by lifting up their skirts. The boy, says Rogers, had had an upbringing 'that created a self-concept of purity and freedom from "base" sexual impulses' (1951, p. 509). On being arrested, the boy 'insisted that he could not have performed this behavior, and when presented with witnesses, was positive that I was not myself' (pp. 509–10). What we see here, declares Rogers, is a situation in which the boy's sexual impulses are not symbolized to awareness and integrated into his picture of himself, a situation in which 'the organism behaved in such a way as to gain satisfaction', although the boy himself did not feel the behaviour to be part of the self or under his conscious control (p. 510). In line with Rogers' theorizing, we might imagine the boy indulging in (so-called 'neurotic') 'defensive behaviors' that lead him to perceive the girls in a distorted fashion so that he can continue to deny his sexual nature (1959, p. 227). 'Fantasy', 'projection', and 'rationalization' might be involved as he maintains his self-concept of being sexually 'pure' through perceiving the young girls as sexual seductresses or little demons that exercise a power over him that is not in his control (1959, p. 228).

Incongruent individuals like the boy, avers Rogers, hold on to rigid and distorted perceptions of themselves in the way they do because of the need for self-regard, for 'if the experience were accurately symbolized in awareness, the self-concept would no longer be a consistent gestalt, the conditions of worth would be violated, and the need for self-regard would be frustrated (1959, p. 227). Rather than the experience being accurately symbolized in awareness, what the incongruent individual may become aware of is anxiety, anxiety brought about by *subceiving* that the experience is a threat to the existing self-gestalt. Should, though, the processes of defensive distortion and denial break down and the previously denied experience break through and be 'accurately symbolized in awareness', then a situation arises in which 'the gestalt of the self-structure is broken by the incongruence in awareness' (p. 229). Under such circumstances of 'disorganization' we are talking of a condition of psychosis rather than neurosis, a condition in which the individual is both subject to, and aware that he is subject to, forces beyond his control. For Rogers, therefore, both 'neurosis' and 'psychosis' are rooted in incongruence and may be labels that others have used to describe the incongruent and vulnerable individual whom the person-centred therapist seeks to help in recapturing their childhood authenticity and innocence.

Paradise regained

With distortion, denial and disorganization construed as developing from the original integrated condition of the infant, the problem non-integrated clients face, says Rogers, is that of 'assimilating denied experience into a reorganized self' (1951, p. 104). Rogers' hypothesis of the conditions required for such 'reintegration or restoration of personality' to occur is, of course, his hypothesis of the six necessary and sufficient conditions of therapeutic personality change (p. 231). What is necessary, says Rogers, is for 'the process of defense to be reversed' such that 'the congruence between self and experience' increases. Where originally positive regard was given on a conditional basis, now in order to decrease the conditions of worth, unconditional positive regard must be communicated to the non-integrated person (stereotypically, the client) by a significant other (stereotypically, the therapist). However, in order for such positive regard to be communicated, says Rogers, the client must perceive that the therapist is not only experiencing such regard for him or her, but that he or she empathically understands the client's inner world. For, to perceive the therapist as fully accepting, the client must also perceive the therapist as fully knowing 'a wide variety of . . . [their] feelings and behaviors' (p. 231). Such comprehensive unconditionality is a matter of the client perceiving that they are always accepted and prized, despite the fact that the therapist might not permit the client to commit certain acts in the counselling room. It is an unconditionality that frees the client to evaluate their experiences in terms of their own organismic valuing process. Now, not experiencing any threat, and with conditions of worth 'weakened or dissolved', the actualizing tendency functions freely as the individual comes to integrate previously denied experiences into the self-concept. The person becomes more 'nearly fully functioning'; 'the organismic valuing process becomes increasingly the basis for behavior'; and allied to 'increase in his own unconditional self-regard', the person's 'positive regard for others is increased' (p. 231). That is to say, as the person perceives themselves as lovable, so they see others as lovable too.

In the case of a client he terms Miss Cam, Rogers presents a graphic illustration of a client perceiving their therapist in a negative or positive manner according to their own sense of personal well-being. The client having come to see herself 'as having reached an insoluble dead end of a pointless existence, the counselor's face blackens, and takes on a disapproving look' (Rogers, 1951, p. 117). With an improvement in the client's mood during an interview, relates Rogers, 'the counselor's face, which had appeared dark is suddenly seen as clean, fresh, and individual' (pp. 116–17). 'It appears to be very significantly true', concludes Rogers, 'that the client perceives others in much the same terms that he [sic] perceives himself, and alteration in self-perception brings about changes in the way others are perceived' (p. 117). Rogers' point here is that even though the therapist may be consistently attempting to communicate the core conditions the client may perceive the therapist differently at different times dependent upon the character of the client's momentary self-perception. Certainly, avows Rogers from his own experience, 'I have learned, especially in working with more disturbed persons, that empathy can be perceived as lack of involvement; that an unconditional regard on my part can be perceived as indifference; that warmth can be perceived as threatening closeness, that real feelings of mine can be perceived as false' (1962, p. 96).

However, according to Rogers, what happens as the end-point of successful psychotherapy is approached and the client becomes more fully-functioning is that the relationship between therapist and client becomes increasingly one of 'communion' and 'mutuality' (Rogers, 1951, p. 114). With the client trusting the 'wisdom of her organism' ('her non-conscious mind') to guide her path, there are those moments when the oneness between client and therapist is such that not only does the therapist get in touch with parts of the client that the client has lost touch with, but both therapist and client 'are perhaps in a mutual and reciprocal altered state of consciousness' (1986, pp. 207 and 208). If we recall Rogers' words that at those mystical moments 'our relationship transcends itself and becomes part of something larger' (p. 199), it would appear that his words apply not only to the therapist's perception of the client, but also to the client's perception of the therapist.

CRITIQUE FROM AN ORGANISMIC PERSPECTIVE OF ROGERS' VIEWS RELATING TO CONDITION SIX

In detailing Rogers' views on the causes of incongruence I briefly mentioned that Rogers saw one such cause to be the attempt in western society to make sense of nature in terms of fixed and rigid concepts when nature is process. To speak in terms of process is to speak in terms of patterned activity, where 'the reality is the process' (Whitehead, 1967, p. 72), and such organisms as ourselves are complex patterns/fields of such activity enmeshed in greater fields. In the present context, a significant question to be asked of Rogers himself, therefore, is how adequate in organismic/process terms is his account of both the development and resolution of incongruence as it pertains to interpersonal perception and to Condition Six.

An organismic/process thinker

That Rogers is very much an organismic/process thinker with respect to his conception of the person is vouched for by Harry Van Belle (1980) in a summation of Rogers' views that Rogers himself endorsed. For Rogers, the person, as Van Belle concludes,

> is an actualization process . . . a tendency, an activity or a functioning rather than an entity which then *does* the actualizing . . . This actualization process, this actualizing that . . . [the person] is . . . is an organized whole. It functions as a whole with all its part-functionings contributing inescapably to this total activity . . . [The person], as an actualizing process, has this total quality *originally* and every step of its development. Originally . . . [the person] is an organism, and remains this however he might change and however complex his activity may become . . . [the person] is . . . always and everywhere a total, active actualizing gestalt (1980, pp. 70–1).

Van Belle goes on to highlight how Rogers' conception of personal growth/actualization implies the differentiation and further development of 'parts' or 'aspects' of the person out of an original 'dynamic unity . . . an originally undifferentiated organism becomes differentiated' (p. 71). A two-movement, dialectical process takes place: 'in a normal growth process', first differentiation occurs, followed spontaneously by 'assimilation' (p. 72). In this process 'the organism integrates *earlier* differentiations at the newly differentiated level of complexity'. 'Under adverse conditions', though, the differentiation process can become 'arrested' or 'blocked' and 'the latest differentiation fails to assimilate the earlier differentiations'. 'Two or more actualizing principles' now operate with the earlier, less complex differentiation seeking actualization in a manner that is independent of and at odds with the more complex one. What Van Belle is here expressing in abstract terms is the condition of personal incongruence where less complex organismic experiencing is blocked from being assimilated into the self-concept and so functions outside its bounds, as with the boy whose sexual impulses were blocked from being assimilated into the 'pure' picture of himself and so took on a life of their own.

A hierarchical developmental pattern

Made explicit by Van Belle in such a summation is the fact when differentiation and development are organismically conceived, then the pattern to the growth of any organism, including ourselves, is that of hierarchical stages. Further, that this pattern will be reflected in the organism's contemporary structure insofar as the more complex patterns emerge from and incorporate their less complex forebears. A simple illustration of such a state of affairs is that entailed in drawing diagrams of cubes in the following stages: at stage one, a number of same length straight lines are drawn; at stage two, sets of four straight lines are joined to form squares, and at stage three, sets of six square are joined to form cubes. Employing the terminology of Michael Polanyi (1968), what we see in such an example is the way in which as new 'focal' forms emerge (those of the square and the cube), the form of the straight lines continues to exist as a 'subsidiary' constituent of the more complex form, albeit that as part of a greater whole it becomes 'the side of a square' or 'the edge of a cube'. In terms of such a scheme, incongruence or developmental arrest would be the situation where, cubes having been drawn, some squares remain 'unassimilated' and retain their focal form or, more fundamentally, straight lines are unassimilated in squares and are similarly focal. What Rogers terms 'disorganization' is then equivalent to the situation where a straight line, and a more complex form, a square, alternate in terms of being focal, without the straight line being assimilated into the focal form of the square. The straight line exists, that is to say, in a raw, 'unprocessed' form.

Given the hierarchical, multi-level nature of development from an organismic point of view, a significant criticism of Rogers' portrayal of the child's personal development is his aversion to describing such development in hierarchically organized developmental stages. Apropos which, John McLeod comments that 'in the area of the understanding of the development in childhood' and by comparison to 'the density of psychodynamic theory', 'the person-centred approach, in its use of the concept of "conditions of worth", is little more than silent' (1993, pp. 43 and 44).

The hierarchical structure that organismic thinkers see as pervading the world and all organisms within it is perhaps most obvious to us in the realm of biology: in the bulb becoming the shoot becoming the tulip; in the frogspawn becoming the tadpole becoming the frog; in the fertilized egg becoming the embryo becoming the baby; and far less so in the development of the child's sense-making capacities, a stratification made explicit by Piaget. But however obvious the stratification, the organismic theorist's claim for the omnipresence of such hierarchical structuring leads to the further claim that responsibility for it lies with a universal organizational/ordering principle or tendency.

There is thus a certain irony in Rogers' positing of his *formative tendency* as just such a universal principle. Since not only does the general way in which he defines it imply a universe-wide hierarchical structure, but he actually refers to it as a tendency that 'exhibits itself as the individual moves from a single cell origin to complex organic functioning, to knowing and sensing below the level of consciousness, to a conscious awareness of the organism and the external world, to a transcendent awareness of the harmony and unity of the cosmic system, including humankind' (1980, p. 133). In other words, Rogers appears to be conceiving such personal growth (allied as it is to qualitatively different modes of perceiving) in terms of developmental stages. And not only this, but he conceptualises therapeutic growth in the client (again allied to qualitatively different modes of perceiving) in terms of a hierarchical seven-stage scale (Rogers, 1961, Chapter 7). There seems a marked inconsistency, therefore, in Rogers' failure to generate or propose a hierarchical child development theory linked with qualitatively different modes of perceiving and concomitant perceptual fields.

Elsewhere (Ellingham, 2002), I have explored Lancelot Whyte's conception of a 'formative' or 'morphic tendency' from which Rogers' own 'formative tendency' derives. On Whyte's testimony, 'the universal morphic process generates a coordinating tendency of organisms and order-seeking tendency in the human mind and in all these the morphic tendency operates on levels forming a hierarchy' (1974, p. 61). In consequence, he contends, 'the known universe as a whole, and every organism, including man [sic] contains a graded sequence of units in each of which a formative tendency, has been, or still is, present' (p. 58). What this means with respect to the person, maintains Whyte, is that we should think in terms of 'a hierarchy of mental processes' (p. 106); and, so far as the universe as a whole is concerned, conceive it as 'arranged in a sequence of discrete "levels", which for precision we call a hierarchy of wholes and parts' (p. 43). For, 'the first fact about the universe is its organization as a system of systems from larger to smaller, and so also is every organism'.

When, therefore, Rogers describes his formative tendency as 'an evolutionary tendency toward greater order, greater complexity, greater interrelatedness', 'which can be equally well observed at every level of the universe' (1980, pp. 125 and 133); and when he sees its existence evidenced in the fact that 'every form we see or know emerged from a simpler, less complex form' (p. 125), one can only wonder why he did not follow Whyte's lead in making explicit the implied hierarchical blueprint to the workings of such a tendency. Perhaps if he had, he would have seen the need to rework his characterization of both the child's personal development and of the nature of incongruence, allied as they both are to the manner in which self and other are perceived. For if there are more than the two stages of *organismic experiencing* and *symbolization to awareness* in the development of our perception of self, and thereby our perception of others, then the concomitant incongruence in our perceptions would no longer be seen as a two-level, but as a multi-level affair — a position I have argued in an article on Rogers' definition of congruence (Ellingham, 2001).

CONTACT AND PERCEPTION

Psychodynamic assistance

In seeking to account for such matters in a multi-level, authentic person-centred fashion, there are a number of theorists within the psychodynamic tradition whose ideas might be drawn upon, theorists whose formulations or individual concepts are in tune with person-centred theory in that they are expressive of an organismic world-view. Here I have in mind, for instance, John Bowlby, Robert Kegan, Heinz Kohut, Daniel Stern, the object relations' theorists, and to some extent Carl Jung. In order to be seen as part of the tradition begun by Freud, the fact that such organismic psychodynamic theorizing is alien to, and incompatible with, certain of Freud's fundamental concepts — viz., the unconscious — is customarily glossed over, or perhaps not even recognized. It might cause consternation amongst the ranks of psychodynamic devotees, therefore, were they to realize that Rogers' concept of the formative actualizing tendency, or its equivalent, is exactly the 'foundation block' that their organismic theorizing requires. When suggesting that the flaws in Rogers' conception of child development referred to above can be remedied by making use of ideas drawn from organismic psychodynamic theorists, I thus see myself as giving their ideas a person-centred identity, not giving person-centred ideas a psychodynamic identity.

Self-object love

This said, in looking to psychodynamic theorists to so aid the development of person-centred theory, one pressing matter is the need to amend Rogers' account of the part that the giving and receiving of love plays in the development and remedying of incongruence. Rogers, it will be recalled, describes the infant as having to 'observe his mother's face, [and] gestures' in order to 'know whether he is receiving' love/positive regard, the satisfaction of receiving it 'necessarily based upon inferences regarding the experiential field of another' (1959, pp. 223 and 225). Expressing the matter in this way invites the interpretation that such 'knowing' is based upon quasi-adult reasoning by inference: 'Oh, I see my mother is smiling, I must be on the receiving end of positive regard!'; rather than the immediate apprehension of the features of the mother's face as centring and being infused by an all-encompassing and intensely vivid, bodily experiencing of joy. The term 'inference' may merely be loose terminology. But it does point to possible 'adulto-morphism' on Rogers part — of his reading into the infant's way of being, the way of being of an adult. It is a danger more likely to arise if one has a thing-like notion of feelings, since once having labelled a feeling as 'love' or 'unconditional positive regard', it gets easily seen as the same 'thing' whether in the 'envelope' of the child's perceptual field or that of the adult. To conceive feelings in this way, as akin to billiard-balls located in different chambers of the mind, is intrinsic to Freud's thinking and has very much a Newtonian rather than an organismic character.

Be that as it may, set against contemporary psychodynamic ideas regarding the development of self from infancy (see Bowlby, 1969 and Stern, 1985), Rogers' notion that it is not from birth but only after developing an awareness of self that the infant becomes aware of the need for love, represents a clear-cut case of putting the cart before the horse, as David Brazier (1993) points out. For it is not through the development of self that love is experienced, but through the experiencing of love that the self develops. As Brazier puts it, 'it is the altruistic orientation which is fundamental and . . . "self"-development . . . is derivative of this' (1993, p. 77). 'The moment the mother-child dyad is formed, Eros is constellated', declares Jungian Anthony Stevens, 'and it is out of love that ego-consciousness, selfhood and personal identity grow' (1982, p. 13). 'We are', as the African saying has it, 'therefore I am'.

Such a dyadic-field interpretation corresponds with Len Holdstock's claim, as reported by Dave Mearns and Brian Thorne of 'a conceptual confusion at the heart of the [person-centred] approach' (2000, p. 81), one that arises from Rogers' conception 'of the self as an independent unit of the social system' (Holdstock, 1996, p. 399); whereas 'the therapeutic relationship, as conceptualised by Rogers, is based on the *interdependent* nature of the self' (Mearns and Thorne, 2000, p. 81). Certainly, the self so construed fits with Rogers' mystical perception of himself and his client as both one at their core, yet part and parcel of something larger than themselves, a condition in which such in-depth knowing/loving/perceiving of the other involves the mutual perception of each as they truly are. From an organismic field perspective, it accords, too, with the notion of the two-in-one being concentrations of patterned activity within a larger field of activity, 'process immersed in process beyond ourselves' (Whitehead, 1968, p. 8); 'a complex micro-system within and connected to a complex macro-system' (Sanders and Tudor, 2001, p. 149).

And, if indeed the feeling of mystical oneness that client and therapist so share is akin to the awesome feeling of 'love' that the infant feels for the mother (aside from the 'unknowing' character) then without doubt we are talking of a type of perceiving that arises from a deep empathic attunement and resonance of one organism with another (Stern, 1985), an interactional mode of perceiving that Stern pictures as the mother sending out 'curved lines of force flowing into space' by which her baby 'can move along her rays of attraction' (1998, p. 92). It would seem to be the case, therefore, that the inversion from 'self-to-loving relationship' to 'loving relationship-to-self' helps make better sense of how it is that unconditional positive regard when 'perceived' by the client facilitates self-growth in the client, on the grounds that it is love of the kind that the infant genuinely and empathically shares with the mother that constitutes the germinal source of our personhood.

Attachment and relational schemas

In looking to organismically enhance person-centred understanding of the powerful impact of interpersonal perceptions at the deepest interpersonal level, much is to be gained too, in my view, through examining the ideas of John Bowlby regarding 'attachment' and the formation of 'internal working models' — and, beyond Bowlby, 'relational schemas', the more general term for such models (see Baldwin, 1992). Such schemas or models are seen as developing in infancy and constituting 'engraved' patterns in the infant/significant other relational field, rather as skiers skiing down a mountain 'engrave' grooves in the snow. The more the interactional patterns are repeated, the more they become a template for subsequent interactions.

That such relational schemas take the form they do is based on the one hand on the infant being drawn to concordant and resonant interactions that give rise to intensely positive feelings of love and attachment; on the other, to her being repulsed by discordant and disharmonious interactions that rise to intensely negative distressful feelings. Thereby emotionally charged 'me-you' relational schemas emerge, from which through the process of symbolization we subsequently differentiate out our perceptions of self and perceptions of the other. Given that the original formation of the relational schema begins in infancy, the original affectively charged sensing of the other can be described as a form of subception. Perhaps, too, this is the same mode of 'perceiving' the other that is involved when Rogers talks of his mere presence having a therapeutic effect on a client (1980, p. 129).

Disorganization and psychosis

The essential requirement of a symbol is that it should be congruent with, have the same pattern as, that which it seeks to represent. In line with Rogers' theorizing regarding inaccurate symbolization, we can thus envisage situations in which the symbolically expressed representations of self and other do not accord with those expressed in terms of subceived relational schemas. The result, as Van Belle indicated, is that the patterns of certain relational schema regarding self and other are not assimilated into subsequent symbolization — there may also be the pattern of fundamental impulses that are excluded from a relational schema in the first place. Activation of unassimilated lower-level processes can lead to the kind of behaviour exhibited by Rogers' sexually 'pure' boy. They may actually become activated to the point that they give rise to strange, intense and often fearsome perceptions and forms of experience — the equivalent we might surmise to knowing 'from the inside' what it is like to be an animal governed by its instinctual feelings, as with the frozen-in-fear response of the catatonic individual. Hallucinations may occur, where such feelings are enshrined in an iconic image. The relational schema or iconic image of a feared father may, for example, become activated and in governing the client's perception of a male therapist lead to that therapist being seen as the feared father, the 'transference' image being taken for the reality. Indeed the powerful nature of such iconic perceptions and their accompanying motivational force can be such as to completely take over the person — for controlling such perceptual experiences of 'archetypal' or 'numinous' intensity, to use Jung's terms, is no easy matter and can well lead to psychosis.

Mystical and spiritual traditions, with their religious rituals and monastic practices, have developed the means and, in their own symbolisms, charted the path whereby safe passage may be reached from such powerful forces, and 'salvation', i.e. adequate symbolization, achieved. The path is that of the hero who survives the descent into the underworld to return with a new truth; the story of the self that partially dismantles itself to become transformed; the psychoanalytic narrative of regression in the service of the ego. Above all, though, it is the universal creative logic of *reculer pour mieux sauter* (regress to progress) epitomizing the workings of the formative actualizing tendency (see Ellingham, 2002), of amplifying and focusing upon inaccurate and distorted symbolizations in order to cleanse 'the doors of perception'.

Powerful forces may be unleashed, but as Rogers personally attests, for the individual who is not alone on such a tempestuous journey but accompanied by a faithful and trustworthy soul-mate, someone who is perceived as genuinely loving and empathically understanding their inner trials and tribulations, for such an individual 'profound growth and healing and energy are present' (1980, p. 129). It is as though the perception of the therapist constitutes an area of calm in the individual's perceptual field, so allowing turbulent experiences to be activated, tolerated and assimilated through symbolization, without capsizing the vessel of the self. The secure 'attachment figure', as Bowlby expresses it, thus provides firm anchorage for exploring and taming the deep.

In *Trials of the Visionary Mind* (1999), John Weir Perry buttresses such an interpretation in summing up his own life's work of ministering to and establishing a safe haven for individuals undergoing the tempests of acute psychotic episodes. 'Turmoil and disorder', narrates Perry,

> are anything but disastrous if we can actually look into the process giving rise to them. If we listen to the individuals in the episode in an empathetic and caring manner, without the need to manipulate, control, or make them be quieter or different in some way, we find, much to our surprise, that they may change spontaneously in a quite short period of time. We have only to sit and relate openly with persons in the episode to find that what had once been a fragmented state of scattered associations, may now begin to assume a coherent form with clarity of thought. Setting up a bi-personal field of relationship, that is, one in which two psyches are in a process of opening up to each other, may stimulate an organizing effect that stimulates an integrative process (p. 4).

Initially, fragments of unassimilated, inadequately symbolized experiential data become amplified to generate a confusing potpourri of multi-modal perceptions of 'self/other/world' mixed with existing symbolized perceptions of 'self', 'other' and 'world'. Thereafter, from the fused self/other/world perceptions discretely symbolized perceptions of self, world and other become differentiated out, and over time coherently integrated into the person's pre-existing symbolizations of 'self', 'other' and 'world'. In the acute psychotic episode, therefore, what we are encountering, according to Perry, is 'a disintegrative phase of what may be regarded as a developmental process' (p. 3): the working of the formative actualizing tendency.

CONCLUSION

In exploring and critiquing Rogers' views to do with the defining of an interpersonal relationship (Condition One) and the therapeutic perception of the other (Condition Six), I have argued that persons be characterized in a multi-level manner: namely, as symbolizing organisms that are fields of patterned activity set within an overarching field or fields. So viewed, perception of self and other is nothing but the felt sense of harmony and/or discord of the activity of the *organismic* field that we are and/or of the field(s) of which we are a part. It is a characterization that I have further explicated elsewhere (see Ellingham, 1984 and 2002) and one that I believe represents an authentic development of Rogers' theoretical formulations and insights.

For Carl Rogers left us with the profound vision that not only the mystical heights, but also the psychotic depths of our perception of self, other, and world are a function of the nature of the love shared with another at the core of ourselves. In the name of love, it behoves us to articulate that vision in the clearest possible form, to expunge inaccurate symbolizations and excrescences, both in relation to our personal perceptions of ourselves and others, and to our abstract perceptions (our theoretical formulations) of reality as a whole.

REFERENCES

Baldwin, M. (1987). Interview with Carl Rogers on the use of self in therapy. In M. Baldwin and V. Satir (Eds.), *The Use of Self in Therapy*. New York: Haworth Press, pp. 45–52.

Baldwin, M. W. (1992). Relational schemas and the processing of social information. *Psychological Bulletin*, 112 (3), 461–84.

Bowlby, J. (1969). *Attachment*. London: Hogarth Press.

Bowlby, J. (1979). *The Making and Breaking of Affectional Bonds*. London: Tavistock.

Bozarth, J. (2001). Client-centered unconditional positive regard: a historical perspective. In J. Bozarth and P. Wilkins (Eds.), *Rogers' Therapeutic Conditions: Evolution, Theory and Practice, Volume 3: Unconditional Positive Regard*. Ross-on Wye: PCCS Books, pp. 5–18.

Bozarth, J. and Wilkins, P. (2001). Unconditional positive regard: towards unravelling the puzzle. In J. Bozarth and P. Wilkins (Eds.), *Rogers' Therapeutic Conditions: Evolution, Theory and Practice, Volume 3: Unconditional Positive Regard*. Ross-on Wye: PCCS Books, pp. 220–30.

Brazier, D. (1993). The necessary condition is love. In D. Brazier (Ed.), *Beyond Carl Rogers*. London: Constable, pp. 72–91.

Cassirer, E. (1955a, 1955b, 1957). *The Philosophy of Symbolic Forms, Vols., 1, 2 and 3*. Yale University Press: New Haven.

Ellingham, I. H. (1984). Towards a science of mind: Schizophrenia, mysticism, artistic creativity, scientific discovery, psychedelic experience and extrasensory perception as functions of a symbo-organismic scheme of human mental functioning. *Ann Arbor: University Microfilms International*, No. DE084-09767.

Ellingham, I. H. (2000). Key strategy for the development of a person-centred paradigm of counselling/psychotherapy. In T. Merry (Ed.), *The BAPCA Reader*. Ross-on-Wye: PCCS Books, pp. 38–44.

Ellingham, I. H. (2001). Carl Rogers' 'congruence' as an organismic not a Freudian concept. In G. Wyatt (Ed.), *Rogers' Therapeutic Conditions: Evolution, Theory and Practice, Volume 1: Congruence*. Ross-on-Wye: PCCS Books, pp. 96–115.

Ellingham, I. H. (2002). Foundation for a person-centred, humanistic psychology, and beyond: The nature and logic of Carl Rogers' 'formative tendency'. In J. C. Watson, R. N. Goldman and M. S. Warner (Eds.), *Client-Centered and Experiential Psychotherapy in the 21st Century*. Ross-on-Wye: PCCS Books.

Evans, R. (1975). *Carl Rogers: The Man and his Ideas*. New York: Dutton.

Freud, S. (1915). The unconscious. In A. Freud (Ed.), *The Essentials of Psychoanalysis*. Harmondsworth: Penguin, 1986, pp. 142–83.

Gendlin, E. T. (1962). *Experiencing and the Creation of Meaning*. New York: Free Press.

Gendlin, E. T. (1974). Client-centered and experiential psychotherapy. In D. A. Wexler and L. N. Rice (Eds.), *Innovations in Client-Centered Therapy*. New York: Wiley, pp. 211–46.

Gendlin, E. T. (1981). *Focusing*. New York: Bantam Press.
Gendlin, E. T. (1984). The client's client. In J. Shlien and R. Levant (Eds.), *Client-Centered and Experiential Psychotherapy*. New York: Praeger.
Gendlin, E. T. (1986). *Let Your Body Interpret Your Dreams*. New York: Delta.
Hendricks-Gendlin, M. (1999). Rogers' congruence and Gendlin's carrying forward. *CCT/PCA Network*, e-mail communication.
Holdstock, L. (1996). Discrepancy between person-centred theories of self and therapy. In R. Hutterer, G. Pawlowsky, P. F. Schmid and R. Stipsits (Eds.), *Client-Centered and Experiential Psychotherapy: A Paradigm in Motion*. Frankfurt am Main: Peter Lang, pp. 395–403.
Huxley, A. (1958). *The Perennial Philosophy*. London: Fontana.
Langer, S. K. (1957). *Philosophy in a New Key*. Cambridge, Mass.: Harvard University Press.
Langer, S. K. (1967, 1972, 1982). *Mind: An Essay on Human Feeling, Vols. 1, 2 and 3*. Baltimore: Johns Hopkins University Press.
Leijssen, M. (1998). Focusing: interpersonal and intrapersonal conditions of growth. In B. Thorne and E. Lambers (Eds.), *Person-Centred Therapy: A European Perspective*. London: Sage, pp. 131–58.
McCleary, R. A. and Lazarus, R. S. (1949). Autonomic discrimination without awareness. *Journal of Personality*, 18, 171–9.
McLeod, J. (1993). *An Introduction to Counselling*. Buckingham: Open University Press.
Mearns, D. and Thorne, B. (2000). *Person-centred Therapy Today*. London: Sage.
Perry, J. W. (1999). *Trials of the Visionary Mind: Spiritual Emergency and the Renewal Process*. Albany: State University of New York Press.
Polanyi, M. (1968). The body-mind relation. In W. R. Coulson and C. R. Rogers (Eds.), *Man and the Science of Man*. Columbus, Ohio: Merrill, pp. 85–111.
Rogers, C. R. (1951). *Client-Centered Therapy*. Boston: Houghton Mifflin.
Rogers, C. R. (1957). The necessary and sufficient conditions of therapeutic personality change. In Kirschenbaum, H. and Henderson, V. L. (Eds.), *The Carl Rogers Reader*. London: Constable, 1990, pp. 219–35.
Rogers, C. R. (1959). A theory of therapy, personality and interpersonal relationships, as developed in the client-centered framework. In S. Koch (Ed.), *A Study of a Science: Vol. 3. Formulations of the Person and the Social Context*. New York: McGraw-Hill, pp. 184–256.
Rogers, C. R. (1961). *On Becoming a Person*. Boston: Houghton Mifflin.
Rogers, C. R. (1962). The interpersonal relationship: the core of guidance. In C. R. Rogers and B. Stevens (Eds.), *Person to Person*. Moab: Real People Press, pp. 89–103.
Rogers, C. R. (1963). The actualizing tendency in relation to 'motives' and to consciousness. In M. R. Jones (Ed.), *Nebraska Symposium on Motivation, Vol. 11*. Lincoln: University of Nebraska Press, pp. 1–24.
Rogers, C. R. (1966). Client-centered therapy. In H. Kirschenbaum and V. L. Henderson (Eds.), *The Carl Rogers Dialogues*. London: Constable, 1990, pp. 9–38.
Rogers, C. R. (1977). *On Personal Power*. New York: Dell.
Rogers, C. R. (1980). *A Way of Being*. Boston: Houghton Mifflin.
Rogers, C. R. (1983). *Freedom to Learn for the '80s*. Columbus: Charles E. Merrill.
Rogers, C. R. (1986). Client-Centered Therapy. In I. Kutash and A. Wolfe (Eds.), *Psychotherapist's Casebook*. San Fransisco: Jossey-Bass, pp. 197–208.
Rogers, C. R., Gendlin, E. T., Kiesler, D. J. and Truax, C. B. (1967). *The Therapeutic Relationship and its Impact: A study of psychotherapy with schizophrenics*. Madison: University of Wisconsin Press.
Sanders, P. and Tudor, K. (2001). This is therapy. In C. Newnes, G. Holmes and C. Dunn (Eds.), *This Is Madness Too*. Ross-on-Wye: PCCS Books, pp. 147–60.
Seeman, J. (2001). On congruence: a human system paradigm. In G. Wyatt (Ed.), *Rogers' Therapeutic Conditions: Evolution, Theory and Practice, Volume 1: Congruence*. Ross-on-Wye: PCCS Books, pp. 200–13.
Stern, D. (1985). *The Interpersonal World of the Infant*. New York: Basic Books.
Stern, D. (1998). *Diary of a Baby*. New York: Basic Books.
Stevens, A. (1982). *Archetype: A Natural History of the Self*. London: Routledge and Kegan Paul.
Tengland, P-A. (2001). A conceptual exploration of incongruence and mental health. In G.

Wyatt (Ed.) *Rogers' Therapeutic Conditions: Evolution, Theory and Practice, Volume 1: Congruence.* Ross-on-Wye: PCCS Books, pp. 159–73.

Thorne, B. (1996). Person-centred therapy: The path to holiness. In R. Hutterer, G. Pawlowsky, P. F. Schmid and R. Stipsits (Eds.), *Client-centered and Experiential Psychotherapy: A paradigm in motion.* Frankfurt-am-Main: Peter Lang.

Thorne, B. (2002). *The Mystical Power of Person-Centred Therapy.* London: Whurr.

Underhill, E. (1915). *Practical Mysticism.* New York: E. P. Dutton.

Van Belle, H. (1980). *Basic Intent and Therapeutic Approach of Carl R. Rogers.* Toronto: Wedge Publishing Foundation.

Whitehead, A. N. (1967). *Science and the Modern World.* New York: Free Press. (Original work published 1925.)

Whitehead, A. N. (1968). *Modes of Thought.* New York: Free Press (Original work published 1938.)

Whyte, L. L. (1974). *The Universe of Experience.* New York: Harper and Row.

14

In the Space Between

Rose Cameron

INTRODUCTION

This chapter will explore what happens in the psychological and *physical* space between therapist and client. I will focus on the first of Rogers' six conditions for therapeutic change — that two people are in psychological contact, and the last condition — that the client perceives the unconditional positive regard[1] and empathic understanding extended by the therapist (Rogers 1957 p. 221). Unlike the other conditions, which are concerned with what is happening inside either the therapist or client, the first and last conditions are concerned with what happens between them, with relationship. The existence, or otherwise, of both conditions is dependant on perception. Psychological contact is dependent on mutual perception — each must perceive the other to be psychologically available — whereas the last condition is wholly dependent upon the client's perception of the therapist. Given that the client's perception is half of the first condition, and all of the last, this chapter will concentrate upon the client's perception, although much of what is said would also apply to the way in which the therapist perceives the client.

I will begin by discussing psychological contact and unconditional positive regard, and I will discuss empathy towards the end of the chapter. I intend to suggest a hierarchy by this structure. Although it is often the case that the therapist is able to accept the client without judgement because they understand the client empathically, and can therefore understand events from the client's point of view, the interdependence of these conditions is reversed for the client. The client will not perceive the therapist as empathic unless they continue to feel accepted. The therapist's understanding may be accurate, but, if the client no longer feels accepted, they will, by definition, feel judged, rather than empathically understood.

---

1. Unconditional positive regard consists of various different qualities, such as respect, warmth, non-judgement and acceptance, and I will use these words as synonyms for unconditional positive regard when I want to emphasise that particular quality.

Readers are welcome to contact the author at *mail@energyawareness.co.uk* or to visit *www.energyawareness.co.uk*

CONTACT AND PERCEPTION

RELATIONAL EXPERIENCE

Psychological contact

Rogers says that all he means by psychological contact is that '... two people are to some degree in contact, that each makes some perceived difference to the experiential field of the other' (1957, p. 221). He defines psychological contact in very minimal terms and suggests that it is so basic it should be considered a precondition. He even suggests that it may be sufficient if a client, who does not appear to notice the therapist, is impacted by them 'at some organic level'. However, he is not suggesting that contact *should* be minimal. I have, elsewhere (Cameron, in press), identified four levels or degrees of psychological contact: basic contact (acknowledgement), cognitive contact (understanding), emotional contact (having an emotional response) and subtle contact. Subtle contact happens in the space between therapist and client, and between the body and psyche. It can be said to happen 'at some organic level', and is simply 'some perceived difference to the experiential field of the other'. Two people can sit together in silence, without looking at each other, and feel either utterly alone or connected in the most profound way, depending on whether they are in subtle contact or not. There is nothing minimal about this kind of contact in terms of importance. It is my contention that it is this level of contact that determines the depth of relationship. This chapter will explore this subtle contact between therapist and client, and how it impacts on conditions one and six of the therapeutic relationship.

When exploring, in workshops, the subtle contact that happens in the space between therapist and client, I suggest to participants that each person either withdraws or extends towards a partner, and does so without speaking or moving. Participants then ask their partner for feedback. I use this exercise to illustrate three points. The first is that therapists can, and do, extend towards, and withdraw from, their client without moving or speaking; the second, important, point is that the client will notice this; and the third is that it will mean something to them.

The partners usually find, even with their eyes shut, that they know whether the other person withdrew or extended towards them. It is rare for anyone to perceive no difference at all. Interactions of this subtle nature are an everyday experience, an aspect of every interaction we have. They are almost tangible. They determine whether we feel in psychological contact at an unspoken level, and determine the flavour of the relationship. The client senses the therapist move towards them or withdraw away from them at a very subtle level, and draws conclusions about the therapist's availability for psychological contact (which are usually correct), and also about how the therapist feels towards them (which may be incorrect). The client is likely to moderate their own availability for psychological contact on the basis of these conclusions. Psychological contact is thus negotiated, and the degree of intimacy or distance agreed.

Unconditional positive regard

The third point of this exercise — that the therapist's subtle expansion, or withdrawal, will mean something to the client — is the most important. I am going to consider psychological contact and unconditional positive regard together because the experience of feeling unconditionally accepted is dependent on the quality of the subtle contact described above. Some workshop participants just seem to sense whether their partner has withdrawn or extended; others draw conclusions from their own emotional response. Most people feel warmly received when their partner is extended towards them, and rejected when the partner withdraws. It is unfortunate that the contrived nature of a workshop exercise seems to inhibit an emotional response in many, but the subtle expansion or withdrawal clearly still means something. Those who have no particular emotional response, but accurately perceive whether their partner has extended or withdrawn, tend to describe the extension in terms of 'giving to me', and the withdrawal in terms of closing down or coldness.

I initially believed, on the evidence of the first few workshops (and my own preference), that everyone is likely to feel warmly received when they sense another person extending towards them, and to perceive them as cold when withdrawn. I now know this to be a gross generalisation. Nevertheless, being a generalisation, it is generally true, and it is useful to know. As a generalisation, it is also a simplification, and it is essential to remember this. The exceptions are as important as the general case. Some people feel invaded, or threatened in some other way, when they sense another person extending towards them. It is not a case of extension being good, and withdrawal bad, but of it being important to be aware of this level of relationship, and the unique meanings within each relationship.

Whether a client's preference is for intimacy or distance, what happens between themselves and the therapist at this level determines not only the quality of the psychological contact they make, but also whether the client is likely to perceive the therapist as warmly accepting, as cold and judgmental or as respectfully reserved. It informs the client's intuitive sense of the therapist, which, for many clients will be their gauge of the therapist's authenticity. In short, this level of contact determines whether the client perceives the therapist as holding them with genuinely unconditional positive regard, or not. Unless contact at this subtle level is made successfully, i.e. felt to be appropriate by both parties, the client will not perceive the therapist as respectful, warm or accepting. And if the client does not feel accepted, they will not perceive the therapist as empathic. It is the client's perception that determines whether the relationship is helpful or not. If the client does not perceive the therapist as unconditionally accepting and empathic, no therapeutic change is likely to happen.

THE SUBTLE ENERGY PARADIGM

These subtle, unspoken interactions are clearly of considerable importance. Although many therapists (and all clients!) are aware of such interactions, it is difficult to bring this level of relationship into full awareness because it is difficult to talk about something for which there is no concept or word. There is no commonly accepted word in English for a part of the person that can extend beyond the skin, and then be drawn back in. It is difficult, without words, to develop sufficient awareness of interactions at this subtle level to be able to reflect upon them in supervision, or to discuss them with clients. This section offers some words and a theoretical model with which to understand this very subtle layer of relationship.

Due to the lack of a commonly accepted vocabulary, I generally introduce this work experientially. Prior to asking participants in workshops to expand towards, or contract away from a partner, I ask everyone to imagine something or someone for whom they experience unreserved liking or love. Many people choose a child or a pet. I then ask them to imagine this person or pet in another part of the room, and to just focus on them for a few moments. Then I ask them to draw themselves back in. If everyone understands what I mean when I say, 'draw yourself back in', I consider the exercise to have served its function. If not, I suggest a further exercise. I am seeking to remind participants that they are familiar with a sense of being able to somehow extend beyond their skin and then pull themselves back in.

There is no psychological term for an aspect of the person that can extend beyond the skin and then be pulled back into the body. Sensations of somehow opening out or expanding, or of retreating inside oneself are common, as is feeling disembodied or un-grounded (especially when elated, shocked, or ill). However, the idea that moving in and out of one's body in such a way is really possible, is not congruent with the contemporary Western world-view, which considers individuals to be discrete entities, contained by the boundary of skin. This has not always been the case.

The subtle body

Philosophical investigations
The notion of discrete entities, contained by an absolute boundary of skin, is not only a particularly Western view, but also, in terms of Western beliefs, rather recent. The idea that we can extend beyond the skin has been persistent in European culture, but has become increasingly marginalised over the centuries. Figures such Pythagoras and Newton, to whom we attribute some of the foundations of rational thought, believed that human beings are not wholly contained by the physical body, but also by a more subtle body. Pythagoras had a theory of vital energy within a luminous body (Pierrakos, 1990). Newton, who was an alchemist (Westfall, 1980), also subscribed to the idea of a semi-material or 'subtle' body. As the centuries have passed, the distinction in the West between the material and immaterial, between body and psyche has become more distinct, and we currently view individuals as distinct entities, separated from each other by an absolute boundary of the skin.

Such an absolute distinction does not exist in a great many other parts of the world. Cultures that have no concept of Satan, mainly understand the world, and life itself, to be balanced between two polarities, which, although they are often described in terms of positive and negative, are different from the concept of good and evil. They are not opposites struggling in opposition to each other, but interdependent polarities giving way to each other. Yin is not good and yang bad: they complement, rather than oppose, each other. Life manifests between the polarities like an electrical force emerging between positively and negatively charged terminals. The creative force, the being-ness that emerges, is variously known as mana to the Polynesians, axe to the Yoruba, (Leal, 1988), qi to the Chinese, ki to the Japanese, tane to the Hawaiians, shakti to Hindus and Sikhs, ntoro to the Ashanti and sila to the Inuit. Obviously some of these cultures are very different from each other, but the basic concept of a fundamental creative force is very similar indeed, although it may be expressed differently (Cameron, 2002). This creative force is central both to medical understanding and esoteric practice in, for instance, China and India (see Shaykh Hakim Moninuddin Chisti, (1985) for evidence that this is as true of Muslim esoteric practice as it is of yoga).

These words are usually translated in English as 'energy' or 'life force'. There is no exact translation. 'Energy' seems too general a word to contain the profundity and complexity of the idea (although it is the word I usually use), and 'life-force' is misleading because everything, animate and inanimate is understood to be imbued with it, or even made of it. It connects all that is. It is both sacred and earthly. It unites body and psyche indivisibly. Chinese medicine, for instance, treats both body and psyche by re-balancing the patient's vital energy. If the patient's energy is in balance, the symptoms of imbalance, whether manifested physically or psychologically, will be relieved. Chinese culture has a particularly sophisticated map of how vital energy, qi, travels through the body (e.g. Hill, 1997; MacRitchie, 1993).

European culture also has a concept of an energy body, though this is not as well known. The focus of the European idea of the energy body is different, being concerned with energy radiating from the body, rather than flowing within the body. The idea that we have a semi-material 'body' made of a subtle energy, is a constant thread running throughout the history of European thought from shamanism to Pythagoras, to the alchemists of the Middle Ages, and through mystery schools such as the Rosicrucians before appearing in more recent schools of European mysticism such as The Golden Dawn, Theosophy and Anthroposophy. Various Christian mystics have spoken of a 'radiant body' or 'sidereal body' (Mead, 1920, 1991) and Jewish mystics have a similar concept called Yesod (Knight, 1986).

Alchemists had a particularly well developed concept of the subtle body, or pneuma, as it was also called. *The Complete Oxford English Dictionary* defines pneuma (and 'psyche') as meaning, in Greek, that which is blown or breathed and spirit. (It further defines 'psyche' as 'the animating principle in man'). The European alchemists were influenced by the alchemical theory of China, India and Afghanistan in particular, and their concept of pneuma is remarkably similar to the contemporary Chinese concept of qi and the yogic concept of prana, both of which mean 'spirit' and 'that which can be breathed'. Neither the Chinese, the yogis, nor the European alchemists are referring to oxygen, but to all pervasive, vital energy — spirit. This concept of vital energy is central to the generally accepted worldview of these cultures. The concept of an all-pervasive, vital energy and the subtle body, the domain between the material and immaterial, faded from European consciousness along with the rest of alchemical theory at the end of the seventeenth century. It is currently given little credibility.

Scientific investigations

Like philosophers and mystics, scientists who have investigated the possible existence of subtle body or energy field, as it is more commonly called in contemporary scientific investigation, have been marginalised (see Pierrakos, 1990 and Brennan, 1993 for summaries of scientific investigators). Valentina and Semyon Kirlian are perhaps the best known scientific investigators of subtle energy fields since alchemy was discredited as a science. Many people are familiar with the images of a milky luminescence surrounding the subjects of Kirlian photographs. There has always been controversy regarding what is actually shown by Kirlian photographs. They are taken by putting the subject and photographic film or screen in a high frequency electrical field. A vibrant and colourful radiance of flares and flashes becomes visible. This effect was already known to scientists, and attributed to a well-known electrical phenomenon known as corona discharge, or the cold emission of electrons. It was understood to be an effect of the high voltage field, and dismissed as unimportant. (Chesterman, et al., 1974). This is still the general view of the scientific orthodoxy today.

Although most researchers currently accept that it is corona discharge that actually produces the image, the corona discharge theory on its own does not explain why the radiance or aura can be seen to change as the subject's physical and psychological state changes (see Chesterman et al., 1974 for a fuller discussion of this). The other main theory was put forward by a team of scientists in the USSR, led by Vladimir Inyushin (White and Krippner, 1970). They proposed that, as well as having a physical body made up of atoms and molecules, all living organisms also have a counterpart body, a biological plasma body. This body is not made of atoms and molecules, but bio-plasma, an additional kind of matter to the solids, liquids, gasses and plasma recognised by physics. Inyushin conceived of the biological plasma body as 'very similar, if not identical to the "aura" or "astral body" as defined by Yogic literature' (Krippner and Rubin, 1973 p. 29). Although the bio-plasma and corona discharge theory are not mutually exclusive (Chesterman, et al., 1974), and although the bioplasma theory may explain what corona emission cannot, the scientific orthodoxy has rejected it.

The energetic relationship

Despite the skepticism of the scientific orthodoxy, The Kirlians' work attracted much scientific interest in America and Europe, as well as the USSR. It took a couple of decades for their work to pass through the iron curtain to Europe and America. When it arrived in the 1960s it was corroborated and developed by American and European researchers. One development is of particular relevance to this chapter. It was accidentally discovered that the aura around a subject became much bigger and brighter when he was in the presence of someone he felt warmly towards, and became much smaller in the presence of someone he disliked or felt intimidated by (Chesterman, et al. 1974).

Many therapists, and clients, have had, in moments of great therapeutic intensity, the sensation that there is some kind of force field between themselves and the other person. The idea that there is more than thin air between therapist and client is useful in understanding more about clients' perception. The client will experience a change in the inter-personal field if the therapist suddenly withdraws their energy body. They are likely to experience themselves as being in psychological contact one moment, and out of contact the next. There is an almost tangible change when someone withdraws their energy: there is an almost palpable change when they extend it. Participants in workshops report sensations of warmth and heat when their partner expands, and coolness or coldness when they withdraw. Although they are not speaking metaphorically, but literally, it is striking that we use 'warm' and 'cold' metaphorically to describe the quality of relationships.

Both the observations of researchers into Kirlian phenomena, and my workshop exercise in which participants draw back in after focusing on someone or something they feel warmly towards, suggest that people tend to extend energetically when they want to make contact, when they feel warm, friendly, loving, etc. A client will experience a change in the interpersonal field if the therapist extends towards them, or withdraws. The therapist may, or may not, be aware of having done anything. But the client will be aware of the change on some level, and generally, their perception that the therapist has either extended or withdrawn will be right.

However, not all people respond positively to energetic expansion in all circumstances; everyone has their own energetic boundaries, and it is important to be sensitive to them. The client's preferences with regard to energetic proximity will play a part in determining whether they find the therapist unconditionally accepting, warm and respectful or as invasive and overpowering. Some time ago, a supervisee of mine was puzzling over a client who was becoming increasingly emotionally distant despite the fact that she had been making strenuous efforts to be as warm as she possibly could. We looked, in supervision, at what might be happening in the space between them, and she decided to 'pull herself in' energetically. Her client seemed to notice the difference immediately; she noticed him visibly relax. They discussed what had happened, and the therapist realised that the client had found her well-intentioned extension towards him so invasive that he had been withdrawing as steadily as she had been extending. They began to explore what was comfortable, or not, for both of them. Once this aspect of their relationship had been acknowledged, the client began to let her know how he was experiencing her at this level. He later began to ask her to challenge him by allowing herself to be bigger, coming a little closer. He seems to be finding, so far, that he feels more able to 'stand his ground', and seems gradually to be becoming less fearful of energetic and emotional intimacy.

Generally (but not always), the client is unlikely to feel unconditionally accepted if they sense the therapist holding back energetically. The therapist may be respectful, but if they are energetically withdrawn, they will not be experienced as warm. Neither therapist nor client will feel themselves properly to be in relationship. The client is likely, at best, to understand the therapist's respect as a quality they possess as impersonal, distant, rather than something that is being extended towards them. Or the therapist may seem false. Most people are quick to notice energetic incongruence, even if the only way they can describe it is as something just not feeling 'right'. Following the principle that, because it is largely outside awareness, non-verbal rather than verbal communication, is more revealing, I believe that many people use what they perceive at an energetic level as a gauge of authenticity.

'Perception' is often used when what is really meant is interpretation. I use 'perception' to mean the ability to work out what has changed in the field e.g. whether the other person has extended or contracted. I will use 'interpretation' for the process of giving this perception meaning.

Interpretation

The client is likely to interpret what they perceive because, in Europe, there is no concept of the space between two physical bodies being anything other than empty space. There is no commonly accepted concept of something non-physical (or semi-physical) that may enter into, or be withdrawn from, this space. This makes it difficult to pause between perception and interpretation. A change in the inter-personal field, a sudden coolness or feeling of being distant will alert the client to the fact that the therapist has withdrawn energetically, but they are unlikely to conceptualise it as such, and pause before attributing meaning. The likelihood is that they will instantly interpret it as meaning that the counsellor's acceptance has become conditional; they may feel rejected, judged.

The client's interpretation may or may not be correct. The therapist may be contracted for all sorts of reasons — they may indeed be making a judgement, or they may be in a bad mood, or they have been concentrating hard, are premenstrual or because they are permanently contracted. The therapist's contraction may, of course, have nothing whatsoever to do with the client, but the client will nevertheless sense it, and almost certainly interpret it in terms of the therapist's attitude towards them.

It is important that person-centred therapists validate the accuracy of the client's perception, even whilst challenging a misinterpretation. A client may perceive the therapist as unconditionally accepting, or not, depending on how they interpret changes in the energetic field. I once stopped going to a therapist because I misinterpreted his energetic withdrawal, and might have ended with a second had he not immediately acknowledged his withdrawal and accounted for it. I assumed that the first therapist was judging me when I became aware that he had suddenly become distant. At the time I had no concepts with which to become aware that all I had really experienced was a change in the energetic field, and that all my perception could tell me was that he had withdrawn, but I did not actually know why. Energetic withdrawal meant judgement to me, and I knew I had sensed him withdraw. He denied that he had judged me, although he did say that he had felt frightened on my behalf. I did not believe him. I left because I did not want to work with someone who was unable to be congruent, and because I felt my experience had been invalidated.

The second therapist was able to validate my actual experience whilst helping me understand that my interpretation was only interpretation. I was relating something of some importance to him when I experienced a sudden distance between us. Again I assumed he was judging me. Before explaining that he had felt afraid, he acknowledged that he had withdrawn from me. My experience of his withdrawal had been validated, I felt secure in the trustworthiness of my perception, and was, this time, able to hear that what I had interpreted as judgement was in fact, fear on my behalf.

Summary of psychological contact and unconditional positive regard in an energetic framework

It is not possible to pretend psychological availability, or unconditional positive regard, and be convincing. Despite what the therapist may try to portray, the client will be aware of any incongruence between overt and subtle communication. My own workshop research, and observations of Kirlian researchers, lead me to believe that most people tend to expand in the presence of someone for whom they have positive feelings, and with whom they want to have contact, and to contract away from people towards whom they feel negatively, and from with whom they want to keep a distance. (This is only generally the case — some people, for example, become energetically stuck and move very little). The client uses their perception of whether the therapist energetically opens out to receive them, or withdraws away from them, as a measure of the therapist's availability, and consistent unconditional positive regard. This does not necessarily mean that the client is correct in their assessment — they may misinterpret. Nevertheless, that interpretation will be part of their experience of being in relationship with the therapist.

Working with awareness

As with most other aspects of the therapeutic relationship, self-awareness on the part of the therapist is always helpful. If the therapist is aware of changes in their energy field, they can be acknowledged. Any misinterpretation can be explored, without invalidating the client's perception. Sudden changes are relatively easy to bring into awareness. It is more difficult to bring habitual energetic states into awareness because there is no change to experience, and because what is habitual feels so utterly normal. Feedback from others is useful for those who do not have the opportunity directly to explore their own energetic state. It is useful to know if one tends towards being relatively expanded or relatively contracted. I know, for example, that I am usually fairly expanded, that some people feel comfortable with this, others can find it invasive or overpowering, and some people lose sense of me altogether if I expand even more than usual. I also know that my energy field can become contracted if I have been concentrating hard, and that this can make me seem distant. Energetic self-awareness enables me to alter my field if appropriate (usually by breathing and relaxing, or grounding myself in some way) and it enables me to own, more fully, my part in what happens between myself and my clients.

I try to be sensitive to my clients' verbal, bodily and energetic communication to gauge how comfortable they are with my energetic state, and sometimes I am able to check it out directly. I may work with the discomfort if we are in an established relationship. However if we are trying to establish a relationship, I aim to find an energetic distance or closeness that is comfortable for both of us. Unless the energetic contact is comfortable for both of us, we are unlikely to feel as if psychological contact has been properly established. I personally dislike being energetically contracted, and also believe that it can be harmful (it is equivalent to holding one's breath). If it seems I am too extended or too big for my client's comfort, I usually try moving my awareness back into my physical body (this feels like 'stepping back' or 'sitting back'). If the problem seems to be not that my attention has been focused too much on my client (because I have extended towards them too far), but that they just find my presence too much (because my energy field is normally, and, for me, comfortably expanded), I may try to 'gentle down' my energy field. I generally avoid simply contracting by tightening my energy body.

In summary, whether the therapist is energetically extended or contracted has a great bearing on whether the client experiences them as psychologically available, as psychologically distant or as psychologically invasive. The therapist's (and client's) energetic state will determine not only the quality of psychological contact made, but also the degree to which our client experiences the therapist as unconditionally accepting, respectful and warm. The therapist's energetic state will also affect their ability to empathise, and contribute to the client's sense of being understood empathically.

The perception of empathy

Just as the client's perception of unconditional positive regard is dependant on appropriate subtle contact, so their perception of empathy is dependant on feeling themselves to be accepted unconditionally. As indicated in the introduction, I have, for this reason, chosen to chosen to discuss empathy after discussing unconditional positive regard. Although the therapeutic attitudes are discussed, theorised and written about as if they are separate and distinct qualities, my own experience as a client is that I perceive them as indistinct and all dependent on the energetic contact I have with my therapist. I do not feel warmly received if the person I am working with is contracted away from me. I do not feel in contact with them, or as if we are in any sense on the same wavelength, even though they may technically convey empathic understanding.

Non-cognitive empathy

Greenberg and Elliott (1997) and Stern (1985) all elaborate on cognitive processes involved in empathic understanding. Tudor and Merry, however, with the deft use of parentheses, suggest that empathic understanding is more than a purely cognitive process. The phrase empathic understanding, they say, '. . . carries the connotation that empathy is (only) a cognitive process' (2002, p. 46). Rogers, in his 1957 formulation of the six conditions, emphasises the non-cognitive function of sensing. He describes empathy as the ability to,

> . . . *sense* the client's private world as if it were your own, but without ever losing the 'as if' quality — this is empathy, and this seems essential to therapy. To *sense* the client's anger, fear, or confusion as if it were your own yet without your own anger, fear, or confusion getting bound up in it, is the condition we

are endeavoring to describe (1957, p. 226, my italics).

The theoretical development of the cognitive, rather than the sensing aspect of empathy, is due, perhaps, to the fact that it is more congruent with the prevailing world view in the West. Although it may be in a process of fundamental change, the prevailing consensus reality in the West is that emotions are physiologically experienced events that are necessarily contained within the body and boundaried by skin. Logically, feelings cannot be 'sensed' by another — they are either heard or seen, or rather indications of feeling are heard or seen. Person-centred training tends, mostly, to focus on developing trainees' listening skills rather than their ability to sense what is happening in another person.

It is possible to argue that anything additional to careful listening results in the therapist being ahead of (and hence 'leading') the client, and is therefore undesirable. Careful listening and accurate understanding of what is said is, of course, essential, and adequate. However, Rogers, in the above definition does use the word 'sense' rather than 'listen and understand'. He describes something additional to listening to what is said i.e. sensing what is felt. I recently sensed what felt like a current of energy travelling towards me, through space, from someone I was working with. It seemed to be coming from just below his navel. It had a very distinct emotional tone, which I could identify although I did not experience it within my own body. I named the emotion, and the person I was with, claimed it, with some surprise, as a feeling that was very familiar to him, but outside his awareness at the time. I did not know him, or his inner world well, and until he made links between the feeling and situations in his past, I had no cognitive understanding whatsoever of why he might feel this particular way in relation to the issue he had been talking about.

Sometimes I sense what my client is feeling, and it seems as if the feeling is literally in the space between us. Sometimes I feel it within my own body. Comparatively little has been written from a person-centred perspective about these kinds of empathy, although Neville (1996) discusses them. However, a great deal has been written about the Kleinian concept of projective identification. Projective identification is a process in which the client projects parts of their unconscious into the therapist, who then feels the client's denied feelings as if they were their own. It is a specifically psychodynamic concept in that it concerns counter-transference. However, it does seem to be a different way of understanding, and working with, the phenomenon, familiar in person-centred practice, of apparently experiencing someone else's emotion within one's self. It is not uncommon to hear person-centred therapists talk of having picked up unexpressed feelings or other material on the client's edge of awareness by experiencing it themselves — of having felt, for example inexplicably anxious in the presence of a client who was also feeling anxious, but had not mentioned it, or having 'picked up' a client's headache etc.

Non-cognitive empathy and the energetic relationship
Although there is a wealth of literature on projective identification, few seem to ask, much less answer, the rather obvious question of how it happens. Nathan Field (1991), an exception to this trend, asks how the client's unexpressed feeling

gets across the space between themselves and the therapist, and, once it has done so, how it manages to lodge itself in the therapist's psyche. He concludes by suggesting the necessity, and difficulty, of a paradigm shift,

> [Projective identification] ... provides the basis of all human empathy ... it is a factor of the profoundest psychological significance. The massively pervasive effect of unconscious interaction in everyday relationship appears to have gone largely unrecognised, in much the same way as the law of gravity remained unrecognised until Newton thought to wonder why an apple fell to the ground. If we look at the problem of unconscious communication from the standpoint of consciousness we must logically infer some invisible psychic agency that carries the message from one individual to another. Until now, no such agency has been identified. But if we make the radically different assumption that we are not only separate, but also unconsciously connected, projective identification can be seen as the restoration of a vital, pre-existing condition. Since the laws which characterise this condition are paradoxical and appear to defy common sense, we have great difficulty in recognising its existence (Field, 1991, p. 107).

The concept of an energetic relationship serves well as the 'invisible psychic agency' that Field believes is inferred, and provides a model of how the therapist senses, rather than thinks, their way to empathy. I have looked, so far, only at a simple energetic interaction — at whether the therapist is relatively extended or contracted, and how the client may interpret this. The client will have an energetic response to the therapist. Depending on what the therapist's relative extension or contraction means to them, and how they feel about it, the client will either contract away from the therapist, or extend closer towards them.

The energetic relationship that transpires from such subtle interactions is as rich and complex as any other layer of relationship. There are degrees of energetic intimacy, just as there are degrees of physical intimacy. The subtle bodies of therapist and client may be standing a respectful distance away from each other. They may be touching, or they may, to varying degrees, merge. There is no absolute boundary around the subtle body. It does not fully exist as a separate, boundaried thing because it is only semi-material. Through it, we can merge to varying degrees with the universe around us, and with other people. I suggest, in workshops, that having experienced what it is like to be with someone extending out to meet them, participants experiment with extending towards a partner who is also extending towards them. Although many dyads stop short of merging, it is not uncommon for virtual strangers to have very intense experiences of intimacy.

One participant described her experience as,

> ... just amazing, totally amazing. We were together and as we met there was just this incredible joy ... we just couldn't stop smiling. And really wanting to touch her — I just wanted to grab hold of her hands, and later I wanted to touch her face but I found that my eyes kept going from her face to here [indicates chest], I kept looking at this part of her and I felt real warmth coming back to my chest and I really wanted to hold her, and then her face almost went really out of focus and I felt I was wrapping myself round her. And at this

point (and this is the first time this has ever happened to me), I could see this outline around her, it was shimmering. And I wanted to look at all her body, not just her face and upper chest and it felt like, to me, that we were really, like, one thing at the end, like we just didn't want to separate and it was wonderful. And I felt like I was connecting to a different person to the one I had been looking at all weekend. That I didn't just meet this presentation . . . that I really met her. And we both cried.'

The ability to merge is, in itself, neither a good nor a bad thing. Its appropriateness is dependent on circumstances. The intense intimacy of merging is not always possible or appropriate in a therapeutic relationship. However, Neville suggests that the ability to experience oneness with the universe is 'the ground of our empathic experience of other people' (Neville, 1996, p. 443). The therapist's ability to transcend separateness enables them to sense what is happening inside another person, to '. . . sense the client's private world as if it were your own' (Rogers, 1957, p. 226). It also impacts on the client's perception of the therapist as empathic, or not.

The client's experience of non-cognitive empathy
Bozarth (1996) points out that in the 1959 theoretical formulation of the six conditions, Rogers, instead of saying that the therapist must strive to communicate their empathic understanding and unconditional positive regard, says only that the client must perceive the therapist as experiencing these conditions. Words are not always essential. Sensing, rather than hearing what is happening for the client, enables the therapist to be empathic even when little or nothing is said. A client taught me the extent to which I could empathise without having to be told what was going on. Knowing that he was clever with words, he decided to spend a session in complete silence. We both sat still and silently contemplated each other. At the end of the session, I checked out, for my own interest, whether I had accurately perceived his flow of feeling. I had. What is more striking, is that he was in no doubt that I had been fully 'with' him. Although he'd experienced himself as more distinctly himself than usual during the session, he had also felt merged with me. I did not need his words in order to sense his inner world, and he did not need mine in order to experience me as being there with him.

Experiences of this kind of wordless empathy are not unusual. Mearns (1996) cites several. When watching the video, a client recounts that Mearns:
> . . . seems to be very quiet and there are a lot of silences. But 'silences' isn't a word that I would use. It felt like — at points it was unbearable, the amount of emotion and the intensity of the interaction between the two of us. Another client talks of feeling as if the therapist was 'right inside me — feeling me in the same moment that I was feeling myself' (Mearns, 1996, p. 307).

A subtle energy model enables us to take phenomenological experiences of unity literally. The subtle body is only semi-material, and so does not comply with the laws of material reality. Energetically, one person really can be right inside another, their subtle bodies merging like one mist into another, or the auras around two candles becoming one.

The intense intimacy of energetic merging is not appropriate in all therapeutic relationships, and not essential to non-cognitive empathy. Much non-cognitive empathy is facilitated not by energetic merging, but by energetic resonance. The subtle body pulsates just as the physical body pulsates with the heartbeat and the rhythm of the breath. Our energetic vibration, or the rate at which our subtle body is pulsating, may change in response to another person. Like a drum, which resonates when another is played nearby, one energy field may energetically resonate with another. This enables one person to be 'in sync', 'in tune', on 'the same wavelength' as another. This is, I believe, the mechanism for bodily empathy, feeling the client's feelings within one's own being, and intuitive sensing. Energetic resonance allows the therapist to sense as well as hear the client. The client, in sensing the similarity, or otherwise, of the therapist's pulsation, will know whether the therapist is truly on the same wavelength or not.

CONCLUSION

Whether the client senses the therapist as energetically withdrawn or extended has great bearing on whether the client perceives them to be available for psychological contact, as respectful, warm, accepting and empathic. It is important to be sensitive to an individual client's energetic boundaries. It is also important for the therapist to be aware of their own energetic process as this will have an impact on how they are perceived by the client. However, it is difficult fully to be aware of either without a vocabulary and some model with which to think about the level of relationship I have called the 'energetic relationship'. The energetic relationship is a model for understanding the mysterious 'chemistry' between therapist and client, and as such can do much to help us understand the client's experience of the therapist.

REFERENCES

Brennan, B. (1993). *Light Emerging*. New York: Bantam.
Bozarth, J. (1996). The integrative statement of Carl R. Rogers. In R. Hutterer, G. Pawlowsky, P. F. Schmid, R. and Stipsits (eds.) *Client Centered and Experiential Therapy : A paradigm in motion*. Frankfurt am Main: Peter Lang pp. 25–33. Reprinted in J. Bozarth (1998) *Person-centered Therapy: A revolutionary paradigm*, (pp. 103–110). Ross-on-Wye: PCCS Books.
Cameron, R. (2002). Subtle bodywork. In Staunton *Body Psychotherapy*. Hove: Brunner Routledge.
Cameron, R. (in press). Basic and cognitive contact: Emotional and subtle contact. In J. Tolan, *Skills for Person-Centred Counselling and Psychotherapy*. London: Sage.
Capra, F. (1992, 1976). *The Tao of Physics*. London: Flamingo.
Chesterman, J., Marten, M., May, J., Murphy-Ferris, M., Moggs Seton, N., Torrey, L., Trux, J. and Watt, J. (1974) *An Index of Possibilities: Energy and power*. New York: Pantheon
Chisti, Shaykh Hakim Moninuddin (1985). *The Book of Sufi Healing*. New York: Inner Traditions International.
Diamond, N. (2001). Towards an interpersonal understanding of bodily experience. *Psychodynamic Therapy*, 7(1)41–61.
Field, N. (1991). Projective identification: Mechanism or mystery? *Journal of Analytical Psychology*, 36, 93–109
Greenberg, L. S. and Elliott, R. (1997). Varieties of empathic responding. In A. C. Bohart and L.

S. Greenberg (Eds.) *Empathy Reconsidered: New directions in psychotherapy.* Washington DC: American Psychological Association. Pp. 169–86.
Hill, S. (1997). *Reclaiming the Wisdom of the Body : A personal guide to Chinese medicine.* London: Constable.
Kirschenbaum, H. and Henderson, V. L, (1990). *Carl Rogers: Dialogues.* London. Constable.
Knight, G. (1986). *A Practical Guide to Qabalistic Symbolism.* Kent: Kahn and Averill.
Krippner, S. and Rubin, D. (1973). *Galaxies of Life: The human aura in acupuncture and Kirlian photography.* New York: Gordon and Beach.
Leal, E. (1988) *The Orishas in Brazil.* Rio de Janeiro: Spala.
MacRitchie, J. (1993) *Chi Kung: Cultivating personal energy.* Shaftsbury: Element.
Mead, G. R. S. (1920; 1991). *The Doctrine of The Subtle Body in Western Tradition.* Largs: The Banton Press.
Mearns, D. (1996). Working at relational depth with clients in person-centered therapy. *Counselling, 7* (4) pp. 306–11.
Neville, B. (1996) Five kinds of empathy. In R. Hutterer, G. Pawlowsky, P. F. Schmid, and R. Stipsits (eds.) *Client-Centered and Experiential Therapy: A paradigm in motion.* Frankfurt am Main: Peter Lang, pp. 439–53.
Pierrakos, J. C. (1990). *Core Energetics.* Mendocino: LifeRhythm.
Rogers, C. R. (1957) .The necessary and sufficient conditions of therapeutic personality change. In H. Kirschenbaum and V. Henderson (Eds.) *The Carl Rogers Reader.* London: Constable, pp. 219–36.
Rogers, C. R. (1959). A theory of therapy, personality and interpersonal relationships, as developed in the client-centered framework. In S. Koch (ed.) *Psychology: A study of science: Vol. 3 Formulation of the Person and the Social Context.* New York: McGraw-Hill, pp. 184–256.
Rogers, C. R. (1980). *A Way of Being.* New York: Houghton Mifflin.
Schwartz-Salant, N. (Ed.) (1995). *C. G. Jung on Alchemy.* London: Routledge.
Stern, D. N. (1985). *The Interpersonal World of the Infant.* New York: Basic Books.
Tudor, K. and Merry, T. (2002). *Dictionary of Person-centred Psychology.* London: Whurr.
Westfall, R. S. (1980). *Never at Rest: A biography of Isaac Newton.* Cambridge: Cambridge University Press.
White, J. and Krippner, S. (1979). *Future Science.* New York: Doubleday.

15 Sharing Life Therapy: A personal and extended way of being with clients

Regina Stamatiadis

Abstract. *The author describes a personal way of being in relationship with two severely troubled clients. In the desire to offer the person-centered core conditions a way of working develops in which client and therapist stay together for longer periods of time than hourly sessions. In addition, client and therapist choose to share daily life activities and other ways of being. A series of therapeutic tools is presented and the part they play in the evolution of the clients' lives. Evidence of their change is given. The author concludes by exploring the reasons for the impact of this therapeutic style she calls 'sharing life therapy'.*

> There is one best *school of therapy. It is the school of therapy you develop for yourself based on a continuing critical examination of the effects of being in the relationship.* Carl R. Rogers, 1986a, p. 135.

The purpose of this article is twofold. First, I will present an intense way of working with individual clients that I have come to call 'sharing life therapy'. Second, I will offer my thinking, as it has crystallized, about my work. I will define sharing life therapy, outline how it has developed, and illustrate how clients and therapist work. I will also sketch the relevant personal background that influenced my actions and identify the changes observed in my clients. Further, I will explore the possible implications of sharing life therapy and its rationale.

Sharing life therapy is an intense form of working in which client and therapist, instead of meeting for hour-long sessions — meet, work, and share activities of daily life for a longer period of time, from several hours to several days, while residing in the same surroundings. For the latter, I initially used the term *residential therapy* when I spoke about this area of my work. Sharing life therapy is a person-centered therapy. It is based on Rogers' essential writings about personality change and growth. Bozarth (1988) notes that the essence of this therapy is 'the therapist's dedication to going with the client's direction, at the client's pace, and with the client's unique way of being' (p. 2).

First Published in the *Person-Centered Review*, 5 (3),(1990), pp. 287–307. Newbury Park: Sage. Reprinted with kind permission of the editor.

BACKGROUND

Sharing life therapy evolved out of special circumstances. During an international meeting on the person-centered approach, a man, Leonard (pseudonym), asked me whether I would undertake therapy with him. There was something special in the way he spoke, in the whole situation, as if 'it was meant to be'. Hence, I accepted. But how would we manage to work together? Leonard lived in a country different from mine, and for one of us to reach the other's residence required seven hours of traveling. Weekends became the only viable possibility. The second client, Annamaria (pseudonym), happened to live in the same town as I. We met at a focusing workshop, where I was asked to take her home because she was in a bad state and it was doubtful whether she would make it home on her own. We traveled together, and Annamaria felt willing to come to see me for therapy.

In the first brief contacts I had with Leonard (about 50 years old) and with Annamaria (about 30), both told me that they had received a variety of psychological and medical treatment over more than a decade without being helped. They were afraid of being abnormal, and both lived with the constant idea of committing suicide. They told me that I was their 'last go'. How did the situation look to me? In both instances, I continued to believe in the effectiveness of the attitudes that are part of the person-centered approach. I hoped that these attitudes could be perceived to the degree necessary for these individuals, that these attitudes would make a difference to them and have meaning for them. On the other hand, the pressure for success was enormous. I realized that unless I became free to fail, I would not be able to choose my behavior freely.

WAYS AND MEANS OF WORKING

Only a few principles were involved. These principles were to go with the client's direction at the client's pace and with the client's unique way of being, to bear in mind that 'the only learning which significantly influences behavior is self-discovered' (Rogers, 1961), and that 'significant learning involves experiencing things as well as intellectual learning about them' (Rogers, 1987, p. 39).

The personal ways and means of working emerged from the therapy process. I will talk about these in some detail later. Some methods and tools can be categorized; others stand on their own. The following examples illustrate these methods and tools.

Verbal tools

Interviews made up by far the largest part of my client-therapist interactions. They were kept in what might be called a 'classical' style with mainly 'testing understandings' and 'checking perception[s]' responses (Rogers, 1986b, p. 376) in a flowing-with-the-client process. There were occasional self-disclosures and therapist initiatives.

Annamaria expressed her experience to me as follows: 'I hardly know who you are, and I cannot yet care to know who you are. But I know that you understand me, almost always, and that here is a place where I can be.'

CONTACT AND PERCEPTION

Understanding Annamaria did not mean to be empathic only to her but also to her vivid image of a big, imaginative worm living in her company. I made room for it in my office and stroked it or covered it with blankets when the worm felt cold. One day Annamaria realized that the worm had stopped existing. With Annamaria I experienced, to an previously unknown degree, that 'understanding makes for healing and growth, misunderstanding makes for injury and destruction' (Shlien, 1987, p. 44).

Leonard expressed his hunger and need for understanding in different ways. He took my understanding for granted until the moment I misunderstood a message. Then he could shout, 'You are not empathic!' which amounted to saying, 'Your job is to be empathic — if you're not, you can go . . .'

Leonard made *tape recordings* of the interviews to compensate for his weak memory (he suffered from amnesia) and to profit additionally between sessions. Annamaria was afraid of tape recordings but once asked for a single session to be recorded to save an extraordinary moment of her becoming.

There were *telephone calls* from both clients in emergency situations. These often turned into phone interviews. Spontaneous calls from me to say hello to the clients conveyed to them mutuality of relationship. I also wrote *letters* in response to theirs or for special events like birthdays and read *books and articles* at their invitation.

Body tools

Touching, smelling, focusing, breathing, wrestling, walking — what I call 'body tools' — were important. For Leonard, my capability of expressing *physical tenderness* and joy toward him and my willingness to accept his tentative expressions of tenderness and joy were the conditions for serious work. They counterbalanced the rejection he had experienced early from his mother and later from his wife. For Annamaria *touching* was a basic means of communication. For months she hardly ever looked at me. When Annamaria was in a state of great inner chaos, holding her or touching her in ways she indicated as being good for her was therapeutic. Physical contact with me made her relax and feel secure and sometimes happy, whereas the mere thought of the physical experiences she had had with her father and her mother made her shudder. One therapy event deserves special mention. As a result of a long, cautious process, Annamaria sensed a growing urge to become a baby again, to be reborn. Rogers' words sounded in my mind: 'I would do better to rely upon the client for the direction of movement in the process' (in Kirschenbaum, 1979).

Step-by-step, Annamaria and I came to trust each other to live that experience. We settled down on a mattress. I held Annamaria tenderly on my lap. Annamaria felt herself to be inside my womb, where she enjoyed being totally safe and whole. Then she felt herself growing into a very small baby 'lying in Mummy's arms'. I allowed Annamaria's hands and lips to find their way to my breasts and agreed to 'feed' her like another child. Annamaria continued to grow. She became a little child, a bit more independent but still needing to *smell* Mummy. I gave Annamaria my scarf to take home and later my cushion (unwashed at her request), so that she could smell me when she was on her own. Annamaria also entreated me to always put on the same perfume so that I would always smell the same. After two years or so, Annamaria recalled the event and named it 'a great, great giving' on my part.

Focusing was offered as a way to engage in an I-Thou relationship with one's own body, to be in dialogue with it. As therapist I accompanied these dialogues without giving instructions (teaching 'steps') or looking for 'shifts'. Annamaria used this 'free-style' focusing regularly to determine the accuracy of her verbal communications and to become conscious of the location of her self, whether outside or inside her body.

When Leonard first witnessed my consulting my body before making a decision, he thought I was crazy (as he confessed later). Leonard was a person living predominantly in his head. Nevertheless he became sufficiently intrigued to try it out for himself and discovered that his body did give messages. For example, he discovered that his body had the desire for showers and that it wished to live in a cleaner home.

Breathing was used when appropriate. When experiencing psychological threat Annamaria would — in a split second — become like the dead, remaining motionless while holding her breath. In her separate reality she thus made herself 'nonexistent' or 'invisible' (her words). In contact with my breathing she learned to dare to breathe again. Through physically *wrestling* with me (on my initiative), Annamaria came into contact with a deep inner will that refused change. At the same time she discovered a will that could choose change. For the most part, however, she felt ruled by forces beyond any sort of will.

Walking with a client after an interview frequently seemed to deepen its impact. In addition it helped both client and therapist to restore physical balance after the strain of intense concentration. It also allowed for just being and for taking in the beauty of nature.

Art tools

Leonard had two wonderful musical instruments, though they didn't look as though they were being used any more. On one occasion, I sat down at the piano and started improvising. Something stirred in Leonard that made him want to find out whether his fingers remembered some long-forgotten favorite pieces. After listening to him for a while, I joined in by singing. Deep communion was experienced. Leonard gained the energy he needed to begin practicing again. During breaks between interviews Leonard played records or cassettes of excellent music of varying styles. Often I just danced spontaneously for myself. Leonard seemed to enjoy it, and I ventured to invite him to be my partner for a folk dance. He did well. We were both surprised and happy. For a moment Leonard felt that he was partaking of life.

Annamaria once brought a record of modern music to the therapy session and asked me to listen to one piece. I recognized in it the two distinct and sharply alternating parts of her worlds: her rational world where she functioned and the separate reality where she felt alienated. Annamaria was pleased that I noticed the abrupt passage between the two worlds as exemplified in the music.

Drawing and *painting* were sometimes chosen by Annamaria as a means to express her inner experiencing and by myself to explain thoughts. Leonard would send me art cards symbolizing his present state or where he was in his relationship with me. I sent art *pictures* to both clients to convey empathy and to summarize symbolically my understanding of their situation at that moment. The pictures had the advantage that the clients could hold on to them as long as they found meaning in them. We all profited from the exchange of art, in the immediacy of its language and in its beauty.

At the beginning of therapy Annamaria struggled with murderous impulses toward a former therapist, a man, who seemed to have failed her when she felt love for him. She had bought a knife to kill him. She viewed this as the only way to resolve her emotional deadlock — other than to 'murder herself' (her words). During a four-hour interview she became able to express some of her despair, and the following night she had a dream: she was engaged in battle, in the Middle Ages, and killed her personal enemy with an arrow from her bow. Annamaria had gained inner distance, was my guess, the distance of a bowshot. For the next session I suggested to Annamaria that we go to the forest together, to cut a tree for a bow, make arrows, and shoot. 'And I will use the knife!' Annamaria added spontaneously. We did as we had planned. From there on, Annamaria's compulsions were slowly transformed, and she moved in the direction of greater harmony. 'I have certainly dealt with plenty of people . . . who are doing things that are socially destructive. But if you can get behind that shell, if you can get to know the person inside, you will find that the person would like to live in harmony and is constructive by nature' (Rogers, 1987, p. 41).

Leonard's dreams seemed to reveal forthcoming events. We used them to gain wisdom for the strategies we needed to devise to protect Leonard at work, where he was threatened by his boss and certain colleagues. For example, his boss had made him a seemingly friendly offer. Leonard then dreamed that he had a swollen leg, which had an opening out of which a wasp came. We decided not to accept the offer, which apparently contained something nasty, and made a counterproposition.

Gift-giving

At the beginning of therapy, Leonard lived in a state of total apathy. After many hours of work he identified a faint wish for a video camera, yet the amount of money necessary for its purchase seemed out of reach. At the following meeting I brought him a little bag with lots of chocolate money. A couple of months later he did buy a camera and start filming. He had found ways to gather the money, to fulfill his wish, and to move a step away from apathy. On another occasion, Leonard proposed to buy me a pullover. I hesitated. Then I understood that Leonard was struggling to gain esteem for himself as a man in relation to women. So I accepted. He took me to various shops and was radiant when I found a pullover that suited me perfectly.

Annamaria was delighted by a gift of earrings from me for Christmas. She explained that she had never received a gift from her parents with which she was addressed as a female human being.

Intuition

I tapped spontaneous knowledge or recognition of knowledge in many situations. I don't consider intuition something mysterious. In a therapy context I mainly see it as the result of the therapist's 'immersion' in the client's inner and outer world 'involving all the capacities of the organism' (Rogers, in Cain, 1987, p. 453). The instances described in the paragraphs on dream work and gift giving may serve as examples. I might add that I check my intuitive knowledge with my clients.

Activities

Leonard lived by himself. When I first went to work at his home, where we had agreed to start therapy, I found his flat in a desolate state. In his depression and lack of interest in life he had totally neglected his household. After completion of the first series of interviews, I went about cleaning the kitchen and dining-room table with Leonard's mute consent. He remained a bystander. When I wanted to start cooking (we had agreed to eat at home), I found only canned food. In my understanding of Leonard's situation this food had the connotation of 'dead food'. I invited him to join me and buy 'living food' at the colorful open market a hundred yards from his house. I prepared a fresh, tasty meal, the like of which Leonard seemed not to have eaten at his home for a very long time. At a later meeting I found healthy food at Leonard's home, and still later, he began to participate in housekeeping and cooking himself. There was a memorable event: I arrived to find fish on the stove ready to be served. I took out the first two fish and put them whole on the plate. Leonard took out the other two fish, and they broke apart. Overtaken by the image, Leonard acknowledged, 'I do not invest myself fully when I do things!' and concluded that this was the reason he was not more successful in his undertakings. He began to remember the moments of his life when he did do things well.

Annamaria felt honored and stimulated when I accepted her invitation for a meal at her home. She prepared food she imagined I would like and was all the more satisfied when she hit the nail on the head, as we say.

Organizing time

Organizing or giving structure to a longer period of time than an hour-long session (consecutive hours, days, weekends) involved a number of processes, some taking place before the event, some within. Consensus had to be reached on where we met, our working hours, our time for rest, shopping, meals (whether at home or at a restaurant), and on time for pleasure; train and hotel arrangements had to be made and special needs assessed. All these processes required that we find inner positions, maintain or yield them, and live with their rewarding or unpleasant consequences. These formed, in their turn, the basis for self-regulation in the next phase of therapy. For example, Leonard and I discussed 'going out' in his town. On the phone I had expressed my wish to go to the theater; Leonard chose the play and booked the seats. When the evening came, I went to the hotel to change. I was very much looking forward to going to the theater in that town and dressed beautifully. Downstairs I met Leonard waiting for me, but — what a shock — he was wearing the very same boots and clothes as on our afternoon walk in the forest, with his raincoat buttoned lopsidedly. We stared at each other. 'Why did you dress?' Leonard asked in amazement. 'To enjoy myself!' I replied shortly. The whole evening I stood my ground bravely at the side of my unequal cavalier, not making a single remark. In his vulnerability he would have inevitably experienced it as a rejection. The impact of the evening on Leonard was enormous. Clothing began to appeal to him, and he started dressing in ways appropriate to particular situations.

Health care

As a child, Annamaria had been sent to school even when she was ill. The experience must have been so painful that she managed to avoid becoming physically ill, until, in the course of therapy, she developed a high fever. It was an exhausting yet good state for her to be in, as she felt 'one' in herself, 'not separated' (her words). I went to look after her in her tiny room, where she had not let any adult enter before (she had allowed children to come in). She found the courage to report her absence from work, and from there on physical illness became acceptable to her and was something she later handled on her own.

Leonard was careless with regard to health. He began to change in the course of his contact with me. He improved his diet and became interested in holistic medicine in order to be better able to look after himself.

Fees

Annamaria thought that the amount of money I deserved as a therapist was much higher than she could afford to pay a person she had adopted as her 'mummy'. With Leonard, fees varied: mostly they were mutually agreed upon. Once I invited him to pay me according to his perception of my effectiveness. Prior to this Leonard had noticed contradictions in the way he spent his money. He took advantage of this opportunity to think about money and the many issues involved in its use. On one occasion, I imposed a fee. Previously, Leonard had boasted about breaking laws like circulation rules or work regulations while showing contempt for people who conformed. But when he was caught by the police and got into serious trouble, he assumed that I would support him before the authorities. For doing so I decided to require an extra fee. On a later occasion Leonard sent money to me unexpectedly, after a conversation on the phone he had experienced as particularly helpful.

When he felt the need, Leonard would choose a recorded interview, play it to me, and tell me where he felt misunderstood or judged. I would make a new attempt to understand and to offer unconditional positive regard. At the conclusion of therapy Leonard asked me to bring him several therapy rating scales. I brought published and personal ones I had constructed. He made a selection and answered the questions in a loud voice.

Annamaria and I proceeded differently. We would interrupt the therapy process as soon as either of us became aware that we had drifted apart. We would analyze what beliefs, emotions, or thoughts were behind each sentence or gesture we had expressed until we came to the origin of our misunderstanding. Annamaria was especially proud of our capacity to do that because her close relationships so far had mostly ended up in chaos. She discovered that a relationship could survive misunderstandings and even be strengthened. Leonard, who had trouble accepting any kind of authority, appreciated being an authority himself as my supervisor. Both clients felt truly empowered by my accepting them as my supervisors.

Other therapeutic approaches

Telepathy
From time to time while doing my daily housework, I would consciously open myself to receive whatever sensations would come to me from the clients. My perceptions frequently turned out to be accurate. At other times I would concentrate on my clients, hoping to strengthen them. When they became aware of it, they were moved.

Prayer
I often prayed — for myself, asking for assistance and the spirit to truly embody therapeutic attitudes, and then for the strength to carry through the task of therapy. Praying helped me to find a degree of closeness to and distance from the clients that was, I believe, facilitative. It also helped me to find where I did have responsibility for their lives and where I did not. Bearing in mind that traditional forms of psychological help (including the person-centered approach) had not worked for these two clients, I felt that I had to take considerable risks and invest much of myself. Laying everything open before God gave me courage and a deep sense of peace. I also prayed for strength and protection for the clients in their efforts to move forward. And I gave thanks.

STRUCTURE IN THERAPY

Crucial structures necessary for therapy to take place reside in the therapist. They are known as the facilitative attitudes or the necessary and sufficient conditions. I call them structures because they model, when internalized, the therapist's behavior, which does not occur by chance but flows along an inner pattern.

Facilitative time structures

Leonard and Annamaria seemed to have profited from a variety of time structures.

Nonlimited sessions
Both clients were allowed to go exactly at their own pace, as long as they needed or wanted to, with responsibility and power for termination of the interview being totally their own. Through this approach Leonard and Annamaria strongly experienced that the locus of control was theirs. Interviews frequently lasted from two to four hours.

CONTACT AND PERCEPTION

For Annamaria the open-ended sessions were vital. In her separate world, time did not exist (as she later communicated). Early in our work, I made a single attempt to terminate an interview that had already lasted three hours. Annamaria experienced this as total rejection, and it cost me another hour to help her recover from her deathlike crisis (in a split second she had become almost lifeless, hardly breathing). After approximately two years of work, Annamaria brought a watch and started to limit the sessions on her own accord. As for Leonard, the nonlimited sessions gave him an intense experience of not being overpowered.

Sessions limited by agreement
An emphasis on shared responsibility and shared power resulted from sessions limited by agreement. This confronted Leonard and Annamaria with the difficulty of keeping an agreement once reached and challenged their capacity for self-discipline and adaption.

Sessions limited by external forces
Train schedules, work obligations, or family commitments to which either party was subjected helped clients to concentrate on the essential during interviews and to keep in touch with reality outside therapy.

Varying rhythms
Interviews took place at regular hours or at any time. This flexibility offered clients double security: they could count on a particular time to be attended to and also knew that they were accepted when they had spontaneous needs. This possibility seemed to diminish their fear of forthcoming events and to encourage them to take new risks. It also had a secondary effect: they handled things as much as possible on their own and did not make undue use of my availability. The frequency of my contact with Leonard came to be a three-day weekend approximately every three months (with one interval of six months), with intense letter and telephone contact in between. With Annamaria one evening per week served as a basis. She had weeks of daily contact during the day and whole days of meeting as well as letter and telephone contact ranging from frequent to rare.

Our meetings took place anywhere client and therapist chose to be together. Any place that made sense to them worked out to be facilitative. Places of shared life included the following:
- the therapist's office and her home (including time with her family)
- the client's home
- public places such as restaurants, hotels, shops, the market, the street, trains, the theater, church, lectures
- places in nature — forest, countryside, river, garden

Each place provided the background for unique experiences and opportunities to think and allowed clients to 'gain an understanding of [themselves] to a degree which enabled them to take positive steps in the light of [their] new direction' (Raskin, 1985, p. 178).

The enhancing effect of particular surroundings was demonstrated by two events — one that took place at the therapist's home with her family, and one on a train. In a moment of great anxiety Annamaria fled to my home. I received her surrounded by my children, who sensed the bad state Annamaria was in. My eight-year-old son went to fetch a bear he loved and gave it to Annamaria for comfort. The bear became so meaningful to her that I decided to buy her a similar one of her own. She was delighted beyond words — the bear became the symbol of her new self. She put it next to the bear of her childhood, a sad and miserable-looking animal, a picture of her wounded self. Later Annamaria bought a very small bear herself, which she gave to me. It symbolized her baby self, and to know it was with me made her feel secure. A number of interactions still took place between Annamaria, the bears, and the therapist until they lost their importance as a result of her therapeutic progress.

In the meantime Leonard had moved toward family themes. I invited him to my home. When he arrived, my husband and children gave him a hearty welcome. Leonard felt quickly at home, too much at home. Without asking he emptied a bottle of whisky and opened another. Later he dared to stroke my cheek in front of my husband. This was the limit for my husband! He did not say one more word to Leonard; nor did he look at him. Leonard began to worry seriously. After his return he called me to inquire how all this had affected me and admitted that he had, for the first time, recognized some nonadaptiveness in his behavior. I told him that I had been able to explain things to my husband, but if he wanted to be of help he could write a letter of apology to him. He did so and even made the effort to write in a foreign language. In addition to this learning, Leonard profited from my family surroundings. He saw two parents, and especially a man, relating warmly and effectively to their children.

On another occasion, Leonard and I had been working at his home, and he accompanied me back to the train. The seat I had booked for the journey happened to be occupied. I carefully checked my reservation ticket and then asked the person to be so kind as to find another seat. Leonard followed the scene attentively and concluded in surprise, 'When I am in the right, I withdraw; when I am wrong, I insist!' The clarity of his discovery further paved the way toward greater flexibility of behavior and brought strength to him in situations where he was treated unjustly.

THERAPEUTIC LIMITS

Thus far, ways and means of working have been described that were governed by my intention to offer facilitative conditions for learning. This endeavor, however, has had limits. The limits have not been limits of understanding but limits of commitment beyond which I was not willing to go.

Leonard had promised, on his own accord, to repair and renovate his home and to create a slide show of his work. Happy to sense him move out of his passivity and turn toward action, I looked forward to the next meeting. But . . . Leonard had done nothing! Tears filled my eyes; I cried out loud and paced back and forth in despair. Eventually I said something like this: 'Leonard, you have been complaining that people do not respect you. I have trusted you, but if all my warmth and efforts lead to nothing, I can give up doing therapy with you!' Leonard did not make promises again. He did deeds.

CONTACT AND PERCEPTION

With Annamaria, time after time I had entered with her the special world of her separate reality. I had supported her in every difficult situation in her outside life. Finally, I had become a person permanently existing for her, and Annamaria had reached greater integration. Then one day I announced to her that I intended to make a trip and would therefore be absent for some time. 'If you go, you stop existing for me!' Annamaria reacted. 'Then everything has been for nothing.' I held my breath, held my words, but inwardly I howled, 'Well, if this is the end (of our relationship) and all has been for nothing, so be it!' I needed to go and do something just for myself. And moreover, if I didn't, I could not go on functioning reliably as a therapist.

Annamaria sensed that she had said something terrible for me but repeated that this was the way she felt. I could acknowledge this fact. Slowly we found the reasons for her feelings. Annamaria had quite accepted my going away with my family, with my husband and children, whom she knew, but letting me go alone into the unknown was too much for her. To help her, I gave her all possible details of where I was going and what I would do. I called her from the airport just before leaving. As I returned from my trip, Annamaria returned to continue therapy. In hindsight my limits, which were about to produce disaster, produced growth. What seemed at that moment to be nonfacilitative conditions turned out eventually to be facilitative.

PERSONAL BACKGROUND

Sharing life therapy developed out of special circumstances briefly described earlier (see Background). When I met Leonard, and later Annamaria, I had the feeling each time that I was called forth as the person I was; that is, as the person I had become through the particular circumstances of my life. Several of these circumstances are relevant to sharing life therapy.

When I was a girl I used to take home persons in need of help, or visit them at their own homes. I would meet them and their problems with the whole of myself (with my heart, my mind, and my body) and give them attention — as much in dialogue as in practical ways. As best I can remember, it seemed to help. These were happy moments for me.

Through my upbringing and other circumstances I became, little by little, overresponsible and overcontrolling of many stirrings in me. Viewed from the outside, I had received a very fine education. Experienced from within, I lived the 'Drama of the Gifted Child', as I found it later described by Alice Miller (1987). On becoming a therapist, I realized I needed to let go of my self-consciousness but was unable to do so for a long time. Then I met a therapist whom I felt was free to let me overrun time (the time normally set for interview sessions), and I managed to loosen my control. This experience induced in me many reflections upon the use of time in psychotherapy. My reflections were further fostered by my observation of nature, which gave me examples of almost any rhythm's being the right one for a particular organism.

For my inner healing as well as for my professional development, groups played an enormous part. They were, for the most part, intensive groups, also known as residential groups. I especially recall one group session in which my 50 co-participants paid attention to me, and an overwhelming number of them gave her or his response to the difficulty I had brought forward. I took in each person's viewpoint. What a richness of truths for me to go on with! When research seemed to confirm the therapeutic effectiveness of groups, I began to ask myself, How can I as a therapist be more of a 'group' to an individual client? In my mind the various 'mes' or my various roles, entered the room and started building a circle. There was the psychotherapist, the educator, the dancer, the musician, the scientist, the farmer, the 'big-city lady', the psychomotor therapist for the handicapped, the secretary, the craftswoman, the mountaineer, the woman-mother-housewife, the person immersed in several cultures, and the person engaged in peace work. These rather active 'mes' were followed by the 'mes' representing my manifold ways of being, of being myself, of being human. There were the ones I valued more and the ones I valued less. These different aspects of myself formed a large group. If it was clear that I could not possibly embody them at one and the same moment as a real group can, I might embody them naturally over a period of time in suitable surroundings and thus offer to a client both something of the richness of a group and the privacy and security advantages of individual consultation.

A number of changes have been hinted at in the sections on ways and means of working. The objective of this section is to give a general and systematic view of the results of sharing life therapy as achieved in each client.

Leonard
After 18 months Leonard had evolved from
- a person without any expressed motivation who slept with lethal pills beside his bed to a person who wanted to live and to achieve;
- taking heavy medication to combat his amnesia to succeeding in being present with very little medication;
- being very critical of others, at odds with authority and law, and indulgent toward himself to looking critically at his own behavior, seeking lawful ways to defend his rights, and showing more respect toward others;
- the extremes of either surrendering to somebody's will or transgressing an agreement to looking for a middle ground, for alternative solutions;
- being tortured by feelings of guilt over masturbation to being able to seek contact with women;
- a person rationalizing and talking incessantly, despising his body and neglecting his outlook, to a person more and more interested in doing, sensing, paying attention to the needs of his body and dressing appropriately;
- having abandoned the practice of music to committing himself to regularly play for a local community;
- enduring frustrating relationships with his sons to being recognized as an acceptable parent;
- living gloomily in a dirty house to remodeling it inside and out and transforming it into an attractive home.

Annamaria
Within two years and three months Annamaria, who was on the brink of

'murdering' another person or 'murdering herself', evolved from
- hesitating whether to 'kill' herself, to wanting to 'die', to 'waiting for death', to 'enduring to go on living' to 'wanting to live and learn';
- acting as if she were dead when a person, thought, or event seemed to become dangerous to recognizing the mechanism on occurrence and bearing her terror while remaining as alive as possible;
- feeling alienated when overwhelmed to being able to accept physical illness;
- viewing the therapist as nonexistent as soon as she was out of contact with her to experiencing her and others as permanently existing;
- physically and morally splitting up her body into a right, good, strong, and functioning side and a left, evil, weak, and withdrawn side to being able to sit and stand in a centered parallel way and to perceive good and bad aspects in either side;
- not knowing who she was and where she was (inside or outside her body) to being able to point to the inside of her chest while saying, 'Here is the true me';
- believing that any feeling she had could only be imaginary while, on the other hand, living day and night with an imagined monster, to asking to be recorded on tape and stating, 'I am I!' and 'To keep on my way [toward health] means to let reality be reality!' (not to transform, avoid, or negate it).

Annamaria and Leonard have continued to see me both for therapy and as friends. Their lives have changed but continue to be difficult for them in a number of aspects. They have given their consent to my presenting our way of working and its results to the professional public. My life has been enriched by them, their difficulties, their talents, and their profound intelligence. At this point I want to inform the reader that I have offered sharing life therapy to a few more persons, to a similar or a lesser extent. With the majority of my clients, I work in traditional person-centered ways.

A RATIONALE FOR THE IMPACT OF SHARING LIFE THERAPY

Sharing life therapy operates on the same principles as client-centered therapy and in this respect is no different from it. On the other hand, it considerably extends the ways and means by which the underlying theory is implemented. Therapy as a way of being becomes a way of sharing life.

To both clients it was clear that therapy did not take place in an artificial world, under artificial conditions, or according to routine. They were convinced that the basis was a person-to-person relationship in which the professionalism consisted in making all events and circumstances relevant to the clients' ultimate goal of leading a more satisfactory life. The sharing of long hours and whole days with the many tiny and unforeseeable events in places known and unknown, at moments when the therapist was in good health and poorer health, gave the clients many opportunities to observe and test her consistency of being, action, and expression. They could experience that they were exposed to no hidden power and no tricks. Great personal risks taken by the therapist and her wide range of behavior seemed to reach the clients beyond their defenses. Such risk-taking was palpable enough to mobilize a force stronger than the immobility created by their deep insecurity, by their fear of change, and by the paradoxical comfort they had found in their tragic but well-known suffering. The relatively long periods of time spent together and the protection offered by the therapist allowed clients to try out new behaviors and to put insights into practice, alone or with the therapist's help. The facilitative conditions of time and space, together with a selection of tools relating to a variety of aspects of the person and of life, intensified the facilitative conditions of genuineness, caring, and sensitive understanding. The author believes that sharing life therapy derives its impact from the intensity it offers. The intensity is created by

- the 'real life' quality of therapist attitudes and work situations;
- the multiple stimuli that deepen, broaden, and change perceptions;
- the multiple use of time and place;
- the multiple opportunities to venture and practice new behavior.

CONCLUSION

Sharing life therapy is an extended way of being with clients. Sharing life therapy is a joint and continuous process of creation between client and therapist. It offers opportunities for learning through experiencing, thinking, and action in an intense relationship that includes many areas of real life. The effect of the facilitative attitudes embodied by the therapist is heightened by time and place conditions. Sharing life therapy, in all its aspects, is an expression of the willingness 'to go with the client's direction, at the client's pace, and with the client's unique way of being' (Bozarth, 1988, p. 2).

REFERENCES

Bozarth, J. D. (1988). *The essence of the client-centered approach*. Paper presented at the Client-Centered and Experiential Therapy Conference, Leuven, Belgium.
Cain, D. J. (1987). Carl Rogers the scientist. *Person-Centered Review,* 2, 451–4.
Kirschenbaum, H. (1979). *On becoming Carl Rogers*. New York: Dell.
Miller, A. (1987). *Drama of the gifted child*. Virago. (Original work published 1979.)
Raskin, N. J. (1985). Client-centered therapy. In S. I. Lynn and J. P. Garske (Eds.). *Contemporary psychotherapies: Models and methods* (pp. 155–86). Toronto: Charles E. Merrill.
Rogers, C. R. (1961). *On becoming a person*. Boston: Houghton Mifflin.
Rogers, C. R. (1986a). Rogers, Kohut, and Erickson: A personal perspective on some similarities and differences. *Person-Centered Review,* 1, 125–40.
Rogers, C. R. (1986b). Reflections of feelings. *Person-Centered Review,* 1, 375–7.
Rogers, C. R. (1987). The underlying theory: Drawn from experience with individuals and groups. *Counseling and Values, 32(1),* 38–46.
Shlien, J. M. (1987). A countertheory of transference. *Person-Centered Review,* 2, 15–49.

16 Contact and Perception: A beginning
Pete Sanders and Gill Wyatt

A BEGINNING

We have chosen not to summarise or draw conclusions from the chapters presented in this book, since we believe it is too soon to arrive at a verdict or even interim report about Rogers' Condition One (psychological contact) and Condition Six (client's perception of the therapist's empathy, UPR and congruence). This book is a beginning, a belated beginning for person-centred theory to really examine the significance of these marginalised and ignored conditions. We suggest that within these conditions lie complex elements which will enrich and carry person-centred theory and practice forward in the years to come.

The previously existing work by Goff Barrett-Lennard and Garry Prouty stands alongside more recent developments exploring the meaning of these conditions. The new work in this book speaks for itself and we trust the reader to draw their own conclusions or generate their own new questions. It is a pity that it is an over-worked cliché to assert that the work in this book is exciting, except that on this occasion, in our view, it really is the most exciting work we have read for years.

AN INVITATION

We invite you to consider the following scenarios and questions — hoping to leave you, and ourselves, with more questions than answers concerning psychological contact and the client's perception of the counsellor. It is your ideas and questions that will fuel the necessary future development of person-centred theory and practice.

> **One**
> *Harold was a first-year undergraduate. He had been referred to the student counselling service by the student health service because he had attempted suicide. It was the early seventies and it was policy to make such referrals 'routinely' in such cases.*
> 	*Harold sat uneasily in one of the threadbare chairs in the counselling room. I introduced myself, 'Hello, I'm Pete, you must be Harold. Do sit down.*

CONTACT AND PERCEPTION: A BEGINNING

I know that Dr X asked you to come and see me because you took an overdose last week. I don't know if I can help but . . .' I told Harold that I was in the final stages of my training as a counsellor and asked if he would mind if I tape-recorded the session to play to my tutor and supervisor. He agreed.

We sat in silence for maybe 30 seconds. (That's a long time at the start of a session — time it.) I said something like 'I am happy to listen to anything you would like to talk about.' We sat in silence for a minute or so, after which I remember saying something like, 'It can sometimes be difficult to know where to start. I am happy to wait until you are ready'. Harold and I sat in silence for a few more minutes and I soon exhausted my repertoire of possible responses to silence. We sat for the remainder of the session in silence until I said, 'It is time to finish now. I will be here next week at the same time if you want to come.'

Harold did indeed come the following week, during which session he said nothing. This pattern was repeated for a further six sessions. My practice supervisor would listen sagely to my introductions and endings, and a portion of the silence in-between and advise me to, 'Hang on in there'. I hung on in there and hung on every breath, every flicker of the eyes (Harold would look at the wall), every slight movement of his hand, arm, foot, chest. Every moment was pregnant with the possibility of his first utterance. He was at the centre of my attention and I concentrated on his every move. This continued for weeks. Then, mid-way through session eight Harold spoke. He said, 'Please don't stare at me'.

Two
Recovering from a general anaesthetic having had some dental work done, I drifted into semi-consciousness. I felt terrible. Nauseous, swollen mouth, sore throat, very uncomfortable, disoriented and frightened. I groaned and half-opened my eyes to see my friend, Keith who had accompanied me that day (it was the rule that all day-patients having general anaesthesia must take an adult to escort them safely home.) I couldn't remember where I was, nor could I work out what Keith was doing there. I couldn't think straight. 'Hold my hand,' I croaked. Keith reached out and held my hand. Suddenly everything improved. I wasn't frightened any more, my discomfort greatly reduced, I didn't feel so sick.

Three
In 2001 Tony Merry wrote:
> In the late 1960s, I took a fairly menial job in what was then one of the largest 'mental hospitals' in the South-East of England . . .
>
> One wing of the hospital housed a number of children. Much time has passed since those days, and I can't remember if they were resident at the hospital or merely stayed during the day, but the children's wards were slightly more pleasant surroundings than the drab and depressing 'decor' of the adult wards. Consequently, I spent as much time there as I could get away with.
>
> There were two main groups of children. One group were Down's Syndrome children, and the other went under various labels, but included

'autistic' children. The contrast between the two groups was remarkable. The Down's Syndrome children were noisy, active, interested and affectionate. The 'autistic' children, as I remember them, were exactly opposite. In the main they were deeply withdrawn, showed very little interest in their surroundings, communicated very little if anything, and displayed almost no emotion. I remember one small boy particularly vividly. He would have been about six or seven years of age and he was, quite simply, a beautiful child, but he was completely withdrawn and appeared to make absolutely no contact whatsoever with anything or anyone. No amount of time spent trying to attract his attention, or get him to focus on you even for an instant, was ever rewarded with any sense that contact had been made, and no expression of any emotion ever appeared on his face. Until, that is, just for a fleeting moment or two, on one particularly memorable day.

It was the habit of the hospital staff to reward 'good' behaviour with a boiled sweet, and one little Down's Syndrome girl had been given a sweet (I think for finishing all her lunch), which she sucked noisily and somewhat messily with great delight and satisfaction. Suddenly, she noticed, sitting on the floor in his usual place, silent and almost motionless, the beautiful autistic boy. She was clearly fascinated by him, and hesitantly approached him, eventually squatting on the floor directly in front of him. She took his face into her hands and brought her own face close to his so that they were only inches apart. As I watched she stared into his eyes, and seemed for a short while to be lost in deep thought.

After a moment or two in this position (it seemed to me like an age), the little girl reached into her mouth and took out the much sucked and much loved boiled sweet, now (to my eyes at least) a rather sticky and unattractive looking mess. Without warning, she opened the little boy's mouth and popped the sweet inside.

. . . just for the briefest moment, the little boy smiled. For the tiniest moment in time, maybe no more than a second, maybe even less, the little boy's face was transformed from being blank and expressionless, to displaying the uncomplicated, straightforward emotion of pleasure.

It was both the unexpectedness of the moment, and its profound simplicity that made it so moving. Somehow, from somewhere, the little girl found a way to make contact with this deeply isolated child, and he had reciprocated in the simplest of ways. I can't tell if his intention was to communicate anything to the little girl, or if his reaction was a reflex one devoid of meaning and empty of intent. But he did smile, and, it seemed to us adults, he smiled at the little girl, in response to the little girl, and not just to himself, locked away as he seemed to be, in some mysterious private world in which others played no part. (pp. 1–3)

Four
Recent years have seen an increase in the use of computer-mediated counselling, largely in the form of e-mail counselling. Sometimes used as an adjunct to regular face-to-face therapy, sometimes an entire therapeutic relationship in its own right, e-mail shares many features with regular written

correspondence (see Murphy and Mitchell, 1998) with the advantage of speed.

Colin Lago asked a key question in 1996, 'Do the existing theories of psychotherapy continue to apply, or do we need a new theory of e-mail therapy?' (p. 289). Starting with Rogers' (1957) therapeutic conditions he looked at a list of therapist competencies necessary in computer mediated therapy, including: the ability to establish contact; the ability to establish a relationship; the ability to communicate accurately with minimal loss or distortion, and the ability to demonstrate understanding.

In 1995 Lea and Spears wrote 'Love at first byte?' exploring the possibility of falling in love via computer-mediated communication, and now, in 2002, stories of 'e-mail affairs' and 'cyber-sex' can be read in the daily papers. Are other intimate relationships possible at distance, mediated by computer? Can Rogers' therapeutic Conditions One and Six (and of course Three, Four and Five) be successfully transmitted and received via e-mail? Those working in the field of computer-supported cooperative work (CSCW) have been using the concepts of 'social presence' and 'psychological distance' in computer group-work for decades. Can psychological contact be understood in the same way?

SOME QUESTIONS

Is there a connection between Rogers' Conditions One and Six?
Many authors in this book suggest that perception is a fundamental part of contact but the corresponding argument that contact is a part of how the client perceives the therapist's conditions is not made to the same degree. Are these two conditions two sides of the same coin, and is the coin in question, as asserted by many, *the relationship*?

What part does the therapist play in the quality of psychological contact and how they are perceived?
Whether we are talking about Rogers' congruent self-structure, Seeman's personality integration, Prouty's intrapsychic contact, or Whelton and Greenberg's dialectical constructivist process, is it simply that the therapist's self, their degree of congruence or integration that determines the quality of their contact and how they are perceived?

What is the relational nature of these two conditions? What happens in the 'in between' that might then reflexively influence the quality of contact and how client and therapist perceive each other?
What is the nature of the feedback loop that explains the fluid, ever changing nature of the quality of the contact between two people and the way they perceive each other?

Does psychological contact have to be reciprocal?
Does psychological contact have to be reciprocally experienced in order to be therapeutic? Or can one person be experiencing contact and the other person be out of contact? If it must be reciprocally experienced, in practice, how do

therapists check this, or do they just assume it?

Is psychological contact a curative factor in its own right or is it only a precursor or, conduit or carrier of therapeutic agents?
Is psychological contact no more than a vector for therapeutic agents? Is it an otherwise empty conduit for messages, the carrier of interpersonal communications whether they be messages of aggression, overt or covert influence, love or healing?

Or is psychological contact itself healing, curative, growthful, facilitative or therapeutic as Rogers suggested when he talked about his presence alone being therapeutic?
Can psychological contact be 'content free', or does it always have a flavour, a note, a colour. Does it always carry the essence of the person who is extending this offer of contact?

What are the dimensions or domains of contact?
Is it meaningful for our understanding to separate out physical, psychological, energetic and spiritual contact? Are only some of our senses necessarily involved in the process or must we use all — looking, hearing, tasting, smelling and touching? What *is* the process by which we 'receive' another person and 'offer' ourselves so that contact is made and we have a particular perception of the other person or of the contact between us?

Psychological research has traditionally been conservative when it comes to exploring modes of communication and the relative importance and/or meaning of sensory stimuli. Emphasis on the visual and auditory has meant it is difficult to ascertain the relative importance of sensory information in the processes of contact and perception.

What is the process when the client doesn't perceive the therapist's empathy, UPR and congruence?
On some occasions we may suggest that the client's incongruence is responsible. Perhaps on other occasions we might look at incongruence in the therapist. Is this simply literal miscommunication between two people — a 'mistake'? Or is this explanation naïve — must we invoke a hypothesised inbuilt tendency of humans to misperceive, such as transference and countertransference?

What is the nature of reality? Is there something 'there', or only that which is socially constructed?
Is this a key philosophical question for the person-centred therapist puzzling over the nature of psychological contact and the perception of each by the other, or is it marginal and of no significance?

REFERENCES

Lago, C. (1996). Computer therapeutics. *Counselling, 7,* 287–9.
Lea, M. and Spears, R. (1995). Love at first byte? Building personal relationships over computer

networks. In J. T. Wood and S. Duck (Eds.) *Under-studied relationships: Off the beaten track.* Thousand Oaks, CA: Sage.

Merry, T. (2001). Editorial. *Person-Centred Practice, 9* (1), 1–3.

Murphy, L. J. and Mitchell, D. L. (1998). When writing helps to heal: e-mail as therapy. *British Journal of Guidance and Counselling, 26* (1), 21–32.

Index of Authors

Arieti, S. 51, 74
Arizmendi iv, v
Asay, T. P. 117, 129
Atwood, G. E. 77, 95
Aykroyd, M. ix, 15
Bachelor, A. 118, 129
Badelt, I. 147, 151
Baldwin, M. 253, 256
Bandler, R. xi, xiii
Barach, P. M. 164
Barends, A. W. 119, 130
Barkow, J. 82, 95
Barrett-Lennard, G.T. ii, iii, v, viii, ix, 9, 10, 11, 12, 15, 17, 23, 27, 28, 29, 30, 32, 34, 39, 43, 45, 47, 116, 117, 118, 129, 159, 164
Bebout, J. 198, 201
Bergman, A. 160, 166
Beutler, L. iv, v, 118, 129, 130
Bieri, J. 123, 132
Biermann-Ratjen, E. 90, 93
Binder, J. 138, 151
Binder, U. 91, 92, 138, 151
Binswanger, L. 74
Blake, W. 244
Böckenhoff, J. 192, 195, 201
Bohart, A. C. 44, 47, 90, 92
Bohun, E. 161, 164
Bowlby, J. 153, 160, 165, 234, 241, 252, 255, 256
Bozarth, J. D. i, iv, v, 14, 17, 23, 45, 46, 47, 117, 118, 129, 131, 234, 256, 271, 272, 274, 287
Braun, B. G. 154, 165
Brauner, R. 225, 232
Brazier, D. 253, 256
Brennan, B. 264, 272
Brett, G. 219, 220
Brown, D. P. 161, 165
Brykczynska, C. 123, 129
Buber, M. 51, 57, 74, 183, 191, 192, 193, 194, 195, 200, 201
Burgess, N. 222, 232
Burton, A. 56, 74
Butler, J. M. 13, 22
Buytendijk, F. J. H. 195, 201
Byrne, B. 41, 47
Cahoon, R. A. 47
Cain, D. J. 279, 287
Cameron, R. ix, xi, 260, 263, 272
Capra, F. 272
Carkhuff, R. R. iv, v, vi, 9, 10, 24
Cartwright, D. S. 35, 48
Cassirer, E. 234, 243, 256
Chalmers, D. 82, 93
Chesterman, J. 264, 272

Chisti, Shaykh Hakim Moninuddin 263, 272
Christensen, L. B. 61, 74
Chu, J. A. 157, 165
Clark, A. 82, 93
Clark, J. V. 37, 48
Clarke, C. 171, 180
Cline, E. W. 40, 48
Cloerkes, G. 144, 145, 152
Cluckers, G. 160, 161, 165
Coble, H. M. 123, 131
Coffeng, T. ix, 20, 22, 90, 93, 153, 156, 157, 160, 162, 163, 164, 165, 180
Cogar, M. C. 119, 130
Cohen, J. 62, 74, 88
Coletti, I. 161, 163, 166
Coninckx, B. 171, 181
Cooper, C. L. 38, 48
Corbett, M. H. 119, 130
Cosmides, L. 81, 95
Crago, M. iv, v, 118, 130
Cramer, D. iv, v, 21, 23, 41, 42, 48, 117, 129
Crockett, J. 123, 129
Cronwall, M. 57, 69, 75
Culbert, S. A. 37, 48
Dahlquist, Z. M. 123, 129
Davies, D. ix, 15, 223, 224, 226, 230, 232
Davis, S. ix
Day, S. M. 123, 128, 129
de Haas, O. 134, 135, 141, 148, 150, 152
De Vre, R. 62, 74
DeJulio, S. J. iv, vi
DeJulio, S. S. 117, 130
Deleu, C. 62, 91, 93
Descartes, R. 239, 240
Diamond, N. 272
Dinacci, A. 171, 180
Dixon, N. F. 7, 23
Dosen, A. 53, 55, 74
Duan, C. 117, 118, 129
Duden, K. 187, 201
Dumon, L. 171, 181
Duncan, B. L. iv, v
Durana, C. 161, 165
Dymond, R. S. ii, 27, 34, 48, 49
Eckert, J. 93, 93
Elkin, I. 36, 48, 118, 129
Ellingham, I. H. ix, x, xi, 7, 36, 48, 118, 129, 234, 251, 255, 256
Elliott, R. 117, 118, 130, 132, 268, 272
Emmerling, F. C. 40, 48
Evans, R. 245, 256
Everall, R. D. 119, 131
Farber, M. 51, 74
Fay, A. S. 123, 129
Field, N. 269, 270, 272
Fiske, D. W. 35, 48

INDEX OF AUTHORS

Freud, S. 7, 239, 240, 245, 252, 256
Fromm, E. 161, 165
Gantt, D. L. 123, 131
Gaylin, N. 2, 10, 23
Gendlin, E. T. iv, x, xiii, 3, 15, 16, 18, 20, 23, 49, 64, 76, 77, 81, 82, 85, 86, 88, 93, 153, 154, 155, 156, 163, 165, 166, 241, 242, 256, 257
Gilmour-Barrett, K. C. 41, 48
Giovacchini, P. L. 156, 161, 166
Gladstein, G. A. 117, 130
Goleman, D. 140, 152
Gomes, W. B. 39, 48
Goodman, P. 56
Gordon, K. 126, 128, 130
Gormally, J. 118, 130
Gray, L. 161, 166
Greenberg, L. S. v, viii, x, xi, xiii, 44, 47, 76, 82, 88, 93, 117, 121, 130, 268, 272
Grinder, J. xi, xiii
Grindler, D. 156, 166
Gross, W. F. 41, 48
Grummon, D. L. 35, 48
Guardini, R. 194, 201
Guidano, V. F. 122, 130
Gurman, A. S. iv, v, 32, 33, 48, 117, 130
Gurswitch, A. 51, 74
Haigh, G. V. 13, 22
Halkides, G. 27, 48
Hart, J. T. ii, vi, 6, 12, 13, 18, 23
Hatcher, R. L. 119, 130
Haugh, S. 117, 130
Havens, L. 64, 74
Heindler, E. 192, 201
Henderson, V. L 77, 93, 273
Hendricks-Gendlin, M. 242, 257
Herman, J. J. 157, 161, 164, 166
Hill, C. 117–19, 123, 129, 130, 132
Hill, S. 263, 273
Hoad, T. F. 187, 190, 191, 201
Holdstock, L. 253, 257
Holland, D. A. 42, 48
Howard, K. I. 117, 131
Hunter, M. 161, 166
Hurley, A. 69, 75
Husserl, E. 53, 75, 136
Huxley, A. 244, 257
Iberg, J. R. 155, 166
Inyushin, V. 264
Isay, R. A. 224, 233
Jackson, S. 123, 132
Jacob, T. 33, 49
Jaeger, T. K. 40, 48
Jaspers, K 184, 201
Jennings, J. L. 52, 52
Jesus 234
Karon, B. 56, 74
Kegan, R. 146, 152, 234, 252
Keilson, H. 157, 166
Kelly, G. 122, 130
Kernberg, O. 161, 166
Kierkegaard, S. 183, 201

Kiesler iv, 15
Kirlian, S. 264
Kirschenbaum, H. 77, 93, 273, 276, 287
Kirtner, W. L. 35, 48
Knight, G. 263, 273
Koch, S. ii, 17, 185
Koestler, A. 234
Kokotovic, A. M. 123, 130
Krauft, C. C. iv, vi, 117, 131
Krietemeyer, B. 171, 180
Krippner, S. 264, 273
Kubiak, M. 64, 67, 75
Kurtz, R. R. 35, 48
Lafferty, P. 118, 130
Laing, R. D. 53, 74
Lambers, E. 90, 93
Lambert, M. J. iv, vi, 117, 118, 129, 130
Langer, S. K. 234, 241, 243, 257
Laufer, E. 224, 233
Lazarus, R. S. 6, 7, 236, 257
Leal, E. 263, 273
Leijssen, M. 55, 74, 90, 93, 241, 257
Levant, R. 19
Leventhal, H. 123, 130
Levinas, E. 195, 201
Lewin, K. 234
Lietaer, G. v, 36, 39, 45, 46, 48, 49, 117, 118, 121, 130
Lindy, J. D. 163, 164, 167
Linville, P. 123, 130, 131
Loewenstein, R. J. 161, 163, 166
Luchterhand, Ch. 147, 152
Lucieer, W. 171, 180
Lyddon, W. J. 123, 132
Machado, P. 118, 129
MacRitchie, J. 263, 273
Mahalik, J. R. 125, 131
Mahler, M. A. 160, 166
Mahoney, M. J. 115, 121, 122, 131
Malan, D. 224, 233
Mallin, S. B. 53, 74
Mallinckrodt, B. 123, 131
Marcel, G. 193, 195, 201
Marmar, C. R. 153, 166
Marques-Teixeira, J. 38, 49
Maurer-Groeli, Y. A. 57, 74
May, R. 115, 131
McCann, I. L. 161, 163, 166
McCleary, R. A. 6, 7, 236, 257
McGuire, M. 156, 166
McLeod, J. v, 250, 257,
McWilliams, K. 171, 180
Mead, G. R. S. 263, 273
Mearns, D. v, 17, 23, 45, 49, 80, 88, 93, 223, 233, 253, 257, 271, 273
Meek, V. C. 41, 50
Merleau-Ponty, M. 53, 75, 135
Merry, T. 268, 273
Metzler, T. 153, 166
Miller, A. 284, 287
Miller, H. E. 4, 23
Miller, J. B. 77, 93

295

Minkowski, E. 55, 75
Minton, K. 161, 166
Missirlian, T. 123, 131
Mitchell, K. M. iv, vi, 117, 131
Mitchell, S. A. 77, 93
Mithen, S. 82, 94
Montada, L. 137, 139, 152
Moore, T. E. 7, 23
Moreno, J. L. 192, 201
Morton, I. 176, 180
Mowrer, O. H. 26, 49
Moynihan, D. iv, v
Murphy, D. M. 88, 94
Murphy, N. 147, 152
Nakayama, E. Y. 117, 130
Neal, C. 223, 230, 233
Neimeyer, R. A. 121, 131
Neisser, U. 115, 122, 131
Neufeldt, S. 118, 129
Neville, B. 269, 271, 273
O'Connor, N. 224, 233
Oerter, R. 139, 152
Ogden, P. 161, 166
O'Grady, K. E. 123, 130
Okishi, J. C. 118, 130
Olsen, L. 156, 161, 166
Orlinsky, D. E. 117, 131
Osborne, W. L. 36, 49
Parloff, M. B. iv, vi
Pascual-Leone, J. viii, xiii, 76, 88, 93
Patterson, C. H. iv, vi, 117, 131
Paulson, B. L. 119, 131
Pearlman, L. A. 161, 166
Perls, F. S. 55, 56, 75, 115, 131, 234
Perry, J. W. 255, 257
Pesso, A. 153, 160, 161, 166
Peters, H. 75, 55, 171, 180
Petrullo, L. 123, 132
Piaget, J. 234, 250
Pierrakos, J. C. 262, 264, 273
Pietrzak, S. 154, 167
Pine, F. 160, 166
Plessner, H. 191, 202
Polanyi, M. 234, 250, 257
Polster, E. 56
Polster, M. 56
Pörtner, M. 19, 20, 21, 91, 94, 146, 147, 148, 151, 152, 169, 170, 171, 180, 202
Powell, G. S. 33, 50
Pritz, A. 146, 152
Prouty, G. F. v, viii, ix, 3, 10, 16, 20, 21, 23, 55, 57, 61, 64, 67, 69, 75, 76, 78, 79, 80, 85, 88, 90, 91, 92, 94, 134, 135, 136, 141, 142, 148, 151, 152, 153, 154, 155, 156, 157, 158, 159, 166, 168, 170, 171, 172, 179, 180, 202
Purton, C. 45, 49
Pythagoras 262
Quick, E. 33, 49
Raskin, N. J. iii, vi, 1, 23, 64, 91, 94, 282, 287
Read Mental Hospital team. 180
Rennie, D. L. 118, 125, 131

Rice, L. N. v, 16, 24, 82, 88, 94
Riepe, D. 51, 75
Robert Kegan 234, 252
Robertson, R. J. 35, 48
Roelens, L. 55, 74
Rogers, C.R. cited on almost every page
Rogers, N. 64, 204, 205, 216, 220
Rosen, H. H. 39, 49
Ross, C. 154, 157, 167
Rotter, H 184, 202
Roy, B. 90, 92, 94
Rubin, D. 264, 273
Rumelhart, D. E. 115, 131
Rupert Sheldrake 234
Ryan J. 224, 233
Sachse, R. 117, 118, 126, 131, 132
Samuels, R. 82, 85, 94
Sanders, P. vii, 182, 254, 257
Sanford, R. iv, 17
Sarbin, T. R. 77, 95
Sartre, J. P. 52, 75
Satterfield, W. A. 123, 132
Scheler, M. 52, 75
Schmid, P. F. i, vi, 135, 151, 182–6, 188–94, 197–9, 202
Schmutzler, H.-J. 144, 152
Schneider, W. 122, 132
Seeman, J. x, xiii, 1, 3, 24, 234, 257
Sheldrake, R. 234
Shiffrin, R. M. 122, 132
Shlien, J. M. xi, xiii, 7, 13, 16, 18, 19, 24, 200, 276, 287
Sinclair, L. M. 123, 132
Singer, D. L. 123, 130
Sommerbeck, L. 180
Sorrentino, A. M. 145, 152
Souget, F. 161, 167
Sovner, R. 69, 75
Spence, D. P. 77, 95
Spiegelberg, H. 75
Sprenkle, D. H. 39, 50
Stamatiadis, R. ix
Standal, S. W. iii, vi, 1, 24, 35, 49
Stein, D. M. iv, vi, 117, 123, 130
Stern, D. N. 81, 95, 139, 140, 149, 152, 160, 167, 234, 252, 254, 257, 268, 273
Stephenson, W. 13, 24
Stevens, A. 253, 257
Stevens, B. 18
Stich, S. 88, 94
Stolorow, R. D. 77, 95
Struwe, J. 161, 166
Stuart, J. 119, 131
Stubbs, J. P. iv, vi
Stumm, G. 146, 152
Sue, D. W. 123, 132
Sue, S. 123, 132
Sundaram, D. K. 42, 49
Sussman, M. 164, 167
Swildens, H. 185, 203
Swildens, J. C. 95
Taft, J. 1, 2, 24

INDEX OF AUTHORS

Taguiri, R. 123, 132
Takens, R. J. 117, 129
Tausch, B. iv, v
Tengland, P-A. 243, 257
Thompson, B. J. 119, 130, 132
Thorne, B. 45, 49, 88, 257, 257, 258
Thornton, B. M. 31, 39, 49
Tillich, P. 194, 203
Tomlinson, T. M. vi, 6, 12, 13, 18, 23
Tooby, J. 81, 82, 95
Tosi, D. J. 37, 49
Toukmanian, S. G. ix, x, 121, 122, 123, 127, 128, 132
Townsend, M. E. 42, 49
Tracy, T. J. 123, 130
Tripodi, D. 123, 132
Truax, C. B. iv, v, vi, 9, 10, 15, 24, 237
Tudor, K. 22, 24, 254, 257, 268, 273
Valsi, A. 36, 50
van Balen, R. 192, 203
Van Belle, H. 249, 258
van der Kolk 154, 157, 166
Van der Veen, F. 10, 13, 14, 15, 24, 35, 49
Van Werde, D. ix, 19, 20, 22, 23, 57, 62, 75, 91, 93, 95, 152, 169, 170, 171, 176, 180, 202
Van Wyngene, C. 171, 181
Vansteenwegen, A. 39, 40, 50
Wampler, K. S. 33, 39, 50
Wargo, D. G. 41, 50
Warner, M. S. v, viii, ix, xi, 17, 24, 82, 83, 87, 88, 89, 90, 91, 92, 95
Waskow, I. E. iv, vi
Waters, P. 217, 220
Watson, J. 121, 130
Watson, N. iv, vi, 14, 19, 20, 24
Weber, G. 144, 147, 149, 152
Weimer, W. B. 115, 132
Weiss, D. S 153, 166
Welte, B. 194, 203
Westfall, R. S. 262, 273
Wexler, D. A. v, 82, 88, 95
Whelton, W. viii, x, xi
White, J. 264, 273
Whitehead, A. N. 234, 244, 249, 258
Whyte, L. L. 234, 245, 251, 258
Wilkins, P. 45, 50, 117, 118, 132, 256
Willemaers, R. 171, 180
Wilson, J. P. 163, 164, 167
Winnicot, D. W. 153, 160, 167
Wolfe, B. E. iv, vi
World Health Organisation 229
Wuchner, M. 90, 93
Wyatt, G. i, vi, 5, 46, 50, 127, 132
Zimring, F. M. iv, 13, 16, 24
Zink, D. A. 123, 128, 132
Zinschitz, E. ix, 3, 22, 146, 147, 148, 151, 152, 171, 181
Zurhorst, G. 186, 203

Contributors to this Volume

THE EDITORS

Gill Wyatt writes: I am the Director of Person-Centred Connections, an organisation committed to extending the understanding and application of the Person-Centred Approach. I have both managed, designed and tutored on BACP accredited Diplomas in Person-Centred Counselling at postgraduate and undergraduate levels for the last 15 years. My private practice is in Nottingham where I offer counselling (BACP accredited), psychotherapy (UKCP registered), supervision, facilitation and consultancy. My current interests include — congruence and authenticity, groups and group-centred facilitation, aspects of spirituality and energy work, and the nature of power. It is becoming increasingly important for me to find ways of living more authentically in all areas of my life — work, relationships and within the larger contexts of my community, the society within which I live and the environment.

Pete Sanders was a person-centred counsellor, trainer and supervisor for more than 25 years. Eventually he got fed up with the drive to professionalise and regulate everything and found that the values of the 'professional' bodies in the UK no longer fitted with his own. Rather than stay and work for a better alternative he chickened out. He believed he could be of more use as a publisher of person-centred books and other books that challenge othodoxy in psychotherapy. However, he still has a keen interest in tracking the developing theory and practice of client-centred and experiential psychotherapy and occasionally writes, exploiting his privileged position as a publisher to make sure it gets published.

CONTRIBUTORS

Maggie Aykroyd lives with her partner on the West Coast of Scotland and works in private practice in Argyll and in Glasgow. She was trained by Dave Mearns, Brian Thorne and Elke Lambers (PCT Britain). Her commitment to the Person-Centred Approach and to gay affirmative therapy informs her work as a trainer on Diploma in Person-Centred Therapy courses at the University of Strathclyde and on Person-Centred Supervision training with PCT Professional Development.

Godfrey (Goff) Barrett-Lennard is Honorary Fellow in Psychology at Murdoch University in Perth, Australia, and in part-time practice. He left Perth in the mid-fifties, to study with Carl Rogers, graduating (PhD, 1959) from the University of Chicago. His career continued in the United States, New South Wales, and Canada — until the mid-1980s, when he settled again in Perth. Besides his saga of work with the Relationship Inventory, he has published in the areas of empathy and listening, small group theory and research, the helping relationship and course of therapy, family process, and community. Author of *Carl Rogers' Helping System: Journey and substance* (Sage, 1998), he is nearing completion of a further book *The Healing of Relationship*. Although 'retired', he feels himself 'older and growing' (in Rogers' phrase), and the current book centres on his contributions and unfolding thought to the present.

Rose Cameron writes: my primary interest as a trainer is in helping counsellors become aware of the energetic dimension of the therapeutic relationship. My work as a supervisor and therapist is also concerned with facilitating energetic self-awareness, and developing a vocabulary with which to discuss it. I am in private practice in Manchester.

Ton Coffeng, MD, client-centered/experiential therapist in the Netherlands (Leeuwarden), coordinates a network of Trauma/Dissociation. He published and produced videos about focusing, phasing and timing in therapy, group therapy, grief, trauma and burnout. He is trainer/supervisor of the Neth. Ass. of Client-c. Therapy, coordinator-trainer of the Focusing Institute and member of the

Int. Pre-Therapy Network. He has a post-graduate program of focusing and experiential psychotherapy.

Dominic Davies works in private practice in London. He has written extensively about therapy issues with sexual minority clients, including co-editing (with Charles Neal) three volumes of the Pink Therapy Series (Open University Press, 1996-2000). He is a BACP Senior Registered Practitioner and was trained in the Person-Centred Approach by Mearns, Thorne and Lambers in the FDI programme (1985-88). He hosts the National Directory of *Pink Therapists* on his website: www.pinktherapy.com which welcomes applications from therapists of all sexualities.

Shellee Davis is an artist, expressive arts therapist and international educator whose focus is the transformative power of creativity for personal and social change. On the faculty of the Person-Centered Expressive Therapy Institute (PCETI), she co-founded both the Expressive Arts Program at World College West in California and the PCETI program in England. She also teaches dreamwork and chi-gung in northern California in an expressive arts community, where she lives with her husband, a musician, woodworker and smallscale organic farmer. She is writing two books: *Imagination and Power* and *Love in the Time of Menopause*.

Ivan Ellingham. After meeting Professor C. H. Patterson when completing a diploma in counselling at the University of Aston in the 70s, I went to study with him at the University of Illinois gaining a PhD in counselling psychology in 1984. Two highlights of my time in the US were attending the La Jolla Program and being introduced to the writings of Susanne Langer by another of my teachers, Michael Piechowski. The further development of person-centred theory remains an abiding interest, alongside my work as counselling psychologist in the NHS and tutor on two person-centred counselling diploma programmes. I live in rural Hertfordshire with my partner, Derryn Thomas, our two dogs and seven cats.

Leslie Greenberg, PhD is Professor of Psychology at York University in Toronto, Ontario. He is the Director of the York University Psychotherapy Research Clinic. He has co-authored: *Emotion in Psychotherapy* (1986); *Emotionally Focused Therapy for Couples* (1988); *Facilitating Emotional Change* (1993) and *Working with Emotions in Psychotherapy* (1997). He recently co-edited *Empathy Reconsidered* (1997) and *The Handbook of Experiential Psychotherapy* (1998). Dr. Greenberg is a founding member of the Society of the Exploration of Psychotherapy Integration (SEPI), a past President of the Society for Psychotherapy Research (SPR) and is on the editorial board of a number of psychotherapy journals. He conducts a private practice for individuals and couples and trains people in experiential and emotion focused approaches.

Dr. Garry Prouty PhD is a fellow of the Chicago Counseling Center and an Honorary Member of the Chicago Psychological Association. He is author of *Theoretical Evolutions in Person-Centered/ Experiential Therapy: Applications to schizophrenic and retarded psychoses* (Praeger). He is also co-author of *Pre-Therapie* (Klett-Cotta, Stuttgart). He is currently serving as an editorial consultant to several international client-centered journals. Also, he has served as a consultant to *Psychotherapy: Theory, Research and Practice* and *The International Journal of Mental Imagery.* As the founder of the Pre-Therapy approach, he has toured Europe over the past 16 years, lecturing and providing workshops at universities, clinics and training programs. Currently he is a member of the Pre-Therapy International Network and consults for the *International Pre-Therapy Review.* Dr. Prouty has delivered the Frieda Fromm-Reichman Memorial Lecture at the Washington School of Psychiatry, and is preparing several articles for the International Society for the Psychological Study of Schizophrenia.

Peter F. Schmid, Univ. Doz. HSProf. Mag. Dr. born in 1950; Associate Professor at the University of Graz, Styria and teaches at European universities. He is a person–centred psychotherapist, practical theologian and pastoral psychologist, founder of person-centred training and further training in Austria, and co-director of the Academy for Counselling and Psychotherapy of the Austrian 'Institute for Person–Centred Studies (IPS of APG)'. He is a Board Member of both the World Association (WAPCEPC) and the European Network (NEAPCEPC), and has published many books and articles about anthropology and further developments of the Person–Centered Approach.

Regina Stamatiadis works in private practice with individuals and groups in Berne, Switzerland, were she lives. She is also a state expert in music and movement education and its application to therapy. She has searched from childhood for a profession whose core activity would be promoting understanding between human beings. She studied languages, expressive arts, therapies for handicapped people and psychology, until her interdisciplinary career and cross-cultural life found their integration in the philosophy and practice of the person-centred approach. She received her training at the Person-Centered Approach Institute International, founded by Charles Devonshire, Alberto Zucconi and Carl Rogers.

Shaké G. Toukmanian, Ph.D, is Associate Professor of Psychology and the current Director of Graduate Training in Clinical Psychology at York University in Toronto, Canada. She has extensive experience in teaching, supervision, and research in person-centred and experiential approaches to psychotherapy. A member of the York University Psychotherapy Research Group, her focus is on the application of relevant concepts in cognitive sciences to the study of change processes in psychotherapy. She has authored and co-authored several book chapters and research articles and is the co-editor of *Psychotherapy Process Research: Paradigmatic and Narrative Approaches* (Sage, 1992).

Dion Van Werde was born in 1957 and studied psychology, specialising in Person-Centred/ Experiential Psychotherapy, at the Louvain Katholic University (Belgium). He is very involved in the study, teaching and spreading of Pre-Therapy and coordinates the Pre-Therapy International Network, based at the hospital where he works. He is employed in St.-Camillus neuro-psychiatric hospital, at St.-Denijs Westrem (near Gent), Belgium, were he organises a person-centred ward along Pre-Therapy lines for treating people suffering psychosis. He co-authors with Garry Prouty and Marlis Pörtner the most recent book on Pre-Therapy.

Margaret S. Warner, Ph.D is a client-centered teacher and theorist who has written extensively about the value of client-centered therapy in working with clients who face more serious psychological disorders, and on client-centered theory as it relates to other disciplines in clinical psychology and the behavioral sciences. She trained in client-centered therapy at the Chicago Counseling Center, an offshoot of Carl Rogers' original center at the University of Chicago. She has a doctorate in Behavioral Sciences from the University of Chicago, and is currently a Professor at the Illinois School of Professional Psychology — Chicago Campus.

Bill Whelton recently completed a doctorate in clinical psychology at York University in Toronto. Les Greenberg supervised his dissertation on 'Emotion in Self-Criticism' and trained him in the art and science of experiential psychotherapy. Bill now works as an assistant professor of counselling psychology in the Department of Educational Psychology of the University of Alberta in Edmonton, Alberta, Canada. His research focuses on self-criticism, vulnerability and resilience to depression and Emotion-Focused psychotherapy.

Elisabeth Zinschitz, born 1959, is a client-centred psychotherapist and offers psychotherapy for clients with (mental) disabilities, counselling for parents of disabled children, supervision for assistants in the disability sector. Her previous professional experience includes: early care and guidance of families with disabled babies and toddlers, training of assistants in the disability sector, translation of articles and books on psychotherapy. She has published in several languages on psychotherapy with mentally disabled clients, and lectures on Pre-Therapy internationally and has worked with Garry Prouty on workshops in Austria and Slovakia.